# NOBILITY REIMAGINED

# NOBILITY REIMAGINED

*The Patriotic Nation in Eighteenth-Century France*

## JAY M. SMITH

CORNELL UNIVERSITY PRESS
*Ithaca and London*

First published 2005 by Cornell University Press
First printing, Cornell Paperbacks, 2005

Printed in the United States of America

*Library of Congress Cataloging-in-Publication Data*

Smith, Jay M., 1961–
   Nobility reimagined : the patriotic nation in eighteenth-century France / Jay M. Smith.
       p. cm.
   Includes bibliographical references and index.
   ISBN 0-8014-4332-6 (cloth : alk. paper) — ISBN 0-8014-8949-0 (pbk. : alk. paper)
   1. France—Civilization—18th century.   2. Nobility—France—History—18th century.   3. Patriotism—France—History—18th century.   I. Title.
   DC33.4.S553 2005
   305.5′22′094409033—dc22

                                    2004030941

Cornell University Press strives to use environmentally responsible suppliers and materials to the fullest extent possible in the publishing of its books. Such materials include vegetable-based, low-VOC inks and acid-free papers that are recycled, totally chlorine-free, or partly composed of nonwood fibers. For further information, visit our website at www.cornellpress.cornell.edu.

Cloth printing          10 9 8 7 6 5 4 3 2 1
Paperback printing      10 9 8 7 6 5 4 3 2 1

*For Debbie*

# Contents

# Illustrations

*Acknowledgments*

The acknowledgments page is a strange artifact, conveying in its own unique way a message of simultaneous humility and grandiosity. Although the product that provides the occasion for this particular statement of acknowledgments warrants no grandiose posturing on the part of the author, an acute sense of humility nonetheless compels me to credit many friends and allies for assisting in its composition. I have been struggling with the subject of eighteenth-century French patriotism for many years now, and I take real pleasure in finally being able to thank the many individuals and institutions who helped make my struggle possible; they certainly made it much less maddening (though in some cases, longer) than it otherwise would have been.

At the University of North Carolina, the College of Arts and Sciences awarded me two consecutive Spray-Randleigh fellowships; those uncommonly generous awards funded two summers in Paris and enabled me to finish research I had begun several years earlier thanks to a grant from the American Philosophical Society. UNC's Department of History, and my endlessly supportive chair, Peter Coclanis, also provided an essential sabbatical year in 2001–2, during which I discovered my argument and wrote the first draft of the manuscript (not in that order). During the course of my research, librarians at UNC, Duke University, the Library of Congress, Cornell University, the University of Michigan, and—in Paris—the Bibliothèque Nationale de France, the Bibliothèque de l'Arsenal, and the Bibliothèque Historique de la Ville de Paris offered helpful assistance. My project took a decisive turn in 1997–98, during a year at the National Humanities Center, and I thank the Center, the Research Triangle Foundation that funded my fellowship, and the cheerful and tireless staff at the Center for providing me the most rewarding and enjoyable year in all my experience as a *prétendu* intellectual. I especially want to thank the former director of the Center, Bob Connor, and two fellow fellows—Michèle Longino and Claude Reichler—for a long series of instructive conversations about honor, eighteenth-century literature, Periclean Athens, and the Center's ever fascinating lunch menu.

The conversations I have found useful over the years really are too numerous even to try to recall, but try I must, especially since it will be abundantly clear to several of my interlocutors that some of those conversations had a direct impact on the content of the book. Stubborn to a fault, I have not always followed the advice offered me, and I'm sure that some will be less than satisfied by the ways I implemented the ideas I *did* accept, but the book is better for my having talked to and learned from all of the individuals noted here. For sharing their ideas or tipping me off to valuable references, sometimes over e-mail, but more often over meals, coffee, or wine, I gratefully thank Gail Bossenga, Rafe Blaufarb, Orest Ranum, Doina Harsanyi, Patrice Gueniffey, François-Joseph Ruggiu, Mi Gyung (Mimi) Kim, John Headley, Lloyd Kramer, Anne Schroder, Don Reid, Dan Sherman, Raymonde Monnier, Annegret Fauser, Matt Adkins, Philip Stewart, and Michael Kwass. David Bell, Rafe Blaufarb, John Shovlin, and Tom Kaiser were also kind enough to share unpublished manuscripts when I asked for them; they should know that I will happily reciprocate in the future, assuming I can muster the energy to put pen to paper again in the years ahead.

The Triangle French Studies Seminar discussed two of my chapters at an especially critical time during my final revision, and I thank the members of the group for their suggestions, some of which I acted on, some of which I did not (probably to my lasting regret). I also presented early versions of my ideas to audiences at the University of Georgia, Cornell University's Modern European History Colloquium, and the annual meeting of the American Historical Association in Boston in 2001. At Georgia and Cornell, the tough questions and informed criticisms of Michael Kwass, Laura Mason, Josh Cole, Steven Kaplan, and Peter Holquist forced me to rethink critical assumptions. At the AHA, Sarah Maza provided a customarily thought-provoking comment.

Friends and colleagues who took time from their own busy schedules to read and react to chapters of the manuscript deserve special thanks.

Michael Kwass (again), Kent Wright, Lloyd Kramer, Steven Vincent, Michael Lienesch, and Mimi Kim, who treated me to a particularly close and incisive critique, all read various chapters of the work at one time or another, and I benefited from all of their criticisms and encouragement. In 2002, the students in one of my graduate colloquia—Max Owre, Christina Hansen, Jacob Miller, Miriam Aronin, Sarah Shurts, and Bethany Keenan—read rough versions of two chapters, and not only did they refrain from complaining to the department chair, but they even offered useful suggestions for improving and cutting—OK, especially cutting—the manuscript-in-progress. Tom Kaiser and John Headley read the entire manuscript in one or more of its incarnations, and they offered characteristically smart and sympathetic advice. The two anonymous readers for Cornell University Press also made many useful suggestions, the results of which they will find without difficulty. The book has been enriched by the ideas and guidance of all these friends and critics.

My greatest debts are to my children, Alyssa and Connor, and to my wife, Debbie. Alyssa and Connor have tolerated my intermittent physical absences and my alarmingly frequent (and frequently alarming) mental absences with good cheer and a rejuvenating sense of humor, always in evidence when we reconnected over family meals. Debbie has supported this project and the frazzled author in more ways than I can list, never with much to expect in return except for the occasional junket to Paris. Although this book—any book—represents a poor return on her heavy investments of time, energy, and angst, I dedicate it to her with love and gratitude, a token of an appreciation beyond the power of words to convey.

Chapter 3 first appeared, in a very different form, in an article published by the *Journal of Modern History* 72 (2000): 339–374. Some of the material from chapter 4 was previously published in *Tocqueville and Beyond: Essays on the Old Regime in Honor of David D. Bien,* ed. Robert A. Schneider and Robert M. Schwartz (Newark, 2003). The *JMH* and the University of Delaware Press have kindly permitted republication of that material.

# Abbreviations

AESC    *Annales: Economie, Société, Civilisation*
AHR     *American Historical Review*
AHSS    *Annales: Histoire, Sciences Sociales*
AL      *Année Littéraire*
AN      Archives Nationales
BNF     Bibliothèque Nationale de France
FHS     *French Historical Studies*
H&T     *History and Theory*
JE      *Journal Encyclopédique*
JMH     *Journal of Modern History*
JT      *Journal de Trévoux*
MF      *Mercure de France*
P&P     *Past and Present*
RH      *Rethinking History*
RHMC    *Revue d'Histoire Moderne et Contemporaine*
SHAT    Service Historique de l'Armée de Terre
SVEC    *Studies on Voltaire and the Eighteenth Century*

# NOBILITY REIMAGINED

## HONOR, VIRTUE, AND PATRIOTISM
## IN EIGHTEENTH-CENTURY FRANCE

Like many books, this one scarcely resembles the study first conceived by its author. Some years ago, I embarked on an investigation of honor disputes that had played out in the courtrooms of eighteenth-century France. I collected evidence for the different conceptions of honor expressed by individuals from different social and cultural milieus, thinking to use legal contests over the meaning of honor to throw new light on the structure and evolution of social relations in pre-Revolutionary France. To fill out the context for that work, after a first fruitful trip to several departmental archives, I began to explore prescriptive literature on honor written over the course of the eighteenth century. I expected to encounter socially grounded representations of honor's meaning and import, representations that would be complicated and enriched by the language of the widely varying depositions I had read in the judicial archives.

What I actually found in the prescriptive literature ultimately changed the design and purpose of my project. The corpus of literature I confronted proved to be much more rich and extensive than anticipated. Moreover, the discussion contained within this literature followed unexpected paths. I encountered varying definitions of honor, as I had suspected, but the variations did not reflect, at least not in any direct sense, the social status of the author or the status of those in behalf of whom the author happened to be writing. Variations in the understanding of honor correlated more directly with the manner in which the author made use of another key word in the social and political lexicon of the eighteenth century: virtue. To put it in the simplest terms, at some risk of misrepresenting complex realities, the more closely honor approximated virtue in the mind of the author, the more likely it was that the author would associate honor with many social classes, and not only the nobility. Significantly, the frame of reference for these discussions was not the scale of dignities traditionally thought to differentiate all the vocations that made up the social hierarchy. In the eighteenth century as in earlier times, the truism that each calling had its own distinctive form of honor entitled all inhabitants of the realm—with the exception of beggars, criminals, servants and day laborers—to claim a kind of honor as productive, self-respecting, and well-regarded members of the community.[1] Public ceremonies and the adjudication of private disputes reinforced the official hierarchy in which each of the crown's subjects found his or her place in the wide social spectrum of honor.[2]

When writers discussed the subject of honor in the published literature of the eighteenth century, however, in general they referred not to the gradation of honors associated with this organic conception of society. Instead, they fixated on the great divide that separated the noble from the *roturier* (commoner). The published commentary focused on the moral character of the nobility, the nature of moral claims to public distinction in French society, and the moral threshold that separated truly noble from merely ordinary thought and behavior. Because of its fixation on moral boundaries, the eighteenth century's long meditation on the relationship between honor and virtue carried as a subtext the proper relationship between those who enjoyed noble status and those who did not.

1. The older view certainly persisted in the eighteenth century. In 1766, for example, the moralist Denesle observed that, although very few possessed honor "in all its purity," people of all conditions had the capacity to behave honorably, and each profession had an "honor that is proper to it." See Denesle, *Les Préjugés du Public sur l'Honneur, avec des Observations Critiques, Morales, & Historiques*, 3 vols. (Paris, 1766), 1: 89. For an example of the application of the idea in a specific socio-professional setting, see James R. Farr, *Hands of Honor: Artisans and Their World in Dijon, 1550–1650* (Ithaca, N.Y., 1988).

2. For the various forms of adjudication, see, for example, Henri Carré, "Querelles entre gentilshommes campagnards, petits bourgeois et paysans du Poitou, au XVIIIe siècle," *Revue du Dix-Huitième Siècle* 2 (1914): 24–39; Thomas Brennan, *Public Drinking and Popular Culture in Eighteenth-Century Paris* (Princeton, 1988); Yves Castan, *Honnêteté et relations sociales en Languedoc, 1715–1780* (Paris, 1974); and Julius Ruff, *Crime, Justice, and Public Order in Old Regime France: The Sénéchaussées of Libourne and Bazas, 1696–1789* (London, 1984). On ceremonial expressions of honor hierarchies, see the discussion of Robert Darnton, "A Bourgeois Puts His World in Order: The City as a Text," in *The Great Cat Massacre and Other Episodes in French Cultural History* (New York, 1984), 107–43. For a broader perspective, consult Edward Muir, *Civic Ritual in Renaissance Venice* (Princeton, 1981), and James Amelang, *Honored Citizens of Barcelona: Patrician Culture and Class Relations, 1490–1714* (Princeton, 1986).

The contours of this published discussion about honor intrigued me for two reasons. First, the willingness—indeed, the compulsion—of a wide range of writers to talk about "the nobility" as a meaningful category seemed to contradict the findings of revisionist historians of the old regime and Revolution who had tended to emphasize the cultural fragmentation and professional and social diversity that marked the second estate. In reaction to an unsatisfying Marxist interpretation of the French Revolution, which had seen a declining, defensive, and largely feudal aristocracy eclipsed by a dynamic and newly self-conscious bourgeoisie at the end of the eighteenth century, revisionists had set out to show the great variations in the cultural, social, and intellectual life of the aristocracy, and they stressed the divisions within the nobility—robe versus sword, court versus country, rich versus poor—that precluded united thought and action by the order as a whole.[3]

Divisions indeed existed within the nobility. Military families (the *noblesse d'épée*) often continued to look with scorn upon nobles in the law courts (the *noblesse de robe*). In comparison to their counterparts in the military, noble magistrates in the parlements were less apt to view nobility as a synonym for courage on the battlefield, and, as Marisa Linton has shown, they had a special affinity for the rhetoric of virtue in their various clashes with the crown over fiscal and religious policy.[4] Nobles from established families regularly expressed disdain for *anoblis,* and nobles at court seem to have earned the contempt of everyone—including *other* courtiers.[5] Still, despite these real divisions, many social commentators, both inside and

---

3.  The key texts are Elizabeth Eisenstein, "Who Intervened in 1788? A Commentary on The Coming of the French Revolution," *AHR* 70 (1965): 77–103; Colin Lucas, "Nobles, Bourgeois, and the Origins of the French Revolution," *P&P* 60 (1973): 84–126; and David Bien, "La réaction aristocratique avant 1789: L'exemple de l'armée," *AESC* 29 (1974): 23–48, 505–34. Among the first French historians to emphasize the theme was François Bluche, *La vie quotidienne de la noblesse française* (Paris, 1973), though the definitive statements were François Furet, *Interpreting the French Revolution,* trans. Elborg Forster (Cambridge, 1981), 1–79, 100–108, and Guy Chaussinand-Nogaret, *The French Nobility in the Eighteenth Century: From Feudalism to Enlightenment,* trans. William Doyle (Cambridge, 1985). The theme is further developed in Pierre Serna, "Le noble," in *L'homme des lumières,* ed. Michel Vovelle (Paris, 1996), 39–93; and Ran Halévi, "The Illusion of Honor: Nobility and Monarchical Construction in the Eighteenth Century," in *Tocqueville and Beyond: Essays on the Old Regime in Honor of David D. Bien,* ed. Robert A. Schneider and Robert M. Schwartz (Newark, Del., 2003), 71–85.
4.  Marisa Linton, *The Politics of Virtue in Enlightenment France* (Houndmills, U.K., 2001), 153–70.
5.  See Daniel Wick's analysis of the attack on the court by the courtiers who dominated the Society of Thirty in 1788. Wick, "The court nobility and the French Revolution: the example of the Society of Thirty," in *The French Revolution in Social and Political Perspective,* ed. Peter Jones (London, 1996), 214–30.

outside the nobility, found the all-encompassing label of nobility both useful and relevant to their assessments of the changing conditions of the
eighteenth century. Despite the considerable evidence of fragmentation
and adulteration—or perhaps because of such evidence—many continued to write and think about "the nobility" as though it stood for something essential to the existing social and political order.

The second source of surprise, in my reading of the published commentary that treated the subject of honor, was the prominent place that
the theme of equality occupied in so many of the texts. Few of the authors
who introduced the theme, moreover, opposed equality to honor or simply denounced honor as an antisocial property of the elites. Instead, the
most innovative authors sought to redefine honor, and reconfigure its social functions, to make it compatible with a certain understanding of equality. Initially the effort struck me as curious, even self-defeating, since, as
Hans Speier explained in his classic essay on honor and social structure,
"it is inevitable that the process of honoring creates hierarchical distinctions," and the ideal of equality necessarily stands as an implicit challenge
to the differentiating function that honor plays in any social system.[6]

Further reading revealed, however, that my eighteenth-century subjects
were probably less confused by this contradiction than I happened to be.
Indeed, the most fascinating aspect of the entire published discussion
about honor in the eighteenth century was the writers' awareness of the
tension between the ranks established by honor, on the one hand, and
pressures tending toward equality, on the other hand. The injection of the
theme of equality into debates about honor's meaning enabled some to
test the nobility's special claim to honorable status, sometimes openly so,
and writers on all sides of the issue were quite conscious of the redrawing
of social boundaries that their speculations often implied. In other words,
public discussion of honor provided a medium for assessing France's social and political structures and the assumptions on which they were based.

The reassessments carried out in the course of discussions about honor
led to conservative attempts to bolster the condition of the nobility, on the
one hand, and to various projects of social inclusion tending to efface the
dividing line between noble and *roturier,* on the other hand. To my mind,
these opposing efforts cast doubt upon another assertion that had been integral to the standard revisionist account of social life under the old
regime. In their attempt to render untenable the old "social interpreta-

6. Hans Speier, "Honor and Social Structure," in Speier, *The Truth in Hell and Other Essays on
Politics and Culture, 1935–1987* (Oxford, 1989), 50–69, esp. 55.

tion" of the coming of the Revolution, with its central hypothesis about growing class conflict, revisionists had not only emphasized the lack of unity and outlook among the nobility of the old regime, but they had also stressed the increasing cultural homogeneity connecting *all* literate and well-to-do members of French society in the eighteenth century. The Enlightenment, it was famously argued, had created a form of "horizontal solidarity" in which vaguely liberal political principles, a commitment to the idea of personal merit, and disdain for superstition had come to undermine consciousness of rank and residual corporate prejudices.[7] My reading of contemporary debates about honor suggested, to the contrary, that the broad, civil exchange of ideas that characterized the Enlightenment "public sphere" served to reinforce and revitalize some traditional divisions and prejudices even as it may have defused others. The confrontation with the principle of equality elicited the articulation and refinement of a variety of reformist ideas. Some of the projects to which they gave shape sought to undermine the existing model of a corporate social order, but others sought to conserve and strengthen that same order.

Prescriptive literature on the subject of honor in the eighteenth century, which I had initially regarded as background for an examination of an honor rooted in local circumstance, thus turned out to contain a dynamic, and to possess an intrinsic intellectual interest, of its own. Contemporary conceptions of honor, it seemed, could not be studied in isolation from other moral and social categories in which issues of status, esteem, and social standing were necessarily implicated. In the texts I had encountered, attempts to define honor led inevitably to discussion of nobility and to a broader consideration of French social structure, and authors' recognition of the principle, or at least the widening social appeal, of equality disclosed a tension in the eighteenth century's long conversation about honor that promised to reveal something important about the changing world of the old regime.

But what was the source of this tension? How had the notion of equal-

---

7. See Furet, *Interpreting the French Revolution,* 115; and Lucas, "Nobles, Bourgeois," 121. For particularly strong statements of this now conventional view see Chaussinand-Nogaret, *The French Nobility,* passim; Simon Schama, *Citizens: A Chronicle of the French Revolution* (New York, 1989), 112–21; and J. F. Bosher, *The French Revolution* (New York, 1988), 45–59. William Doyle offers a subtle and updated version of the story—stressing both intra-estate divisions and inter-estate commonalities—in *Origins of the French Revolution* (New York, 1999), 13–21. For instructive critiques of the revisionist line of argument, see Alison Patrick, "The Second Estate in the Constituent Assembly," *JMH* 62 (1990): 223–52; and Timothy Tackett, "Nobles and Third Estate in the Revolutionary Dynamic of the National Assembly, 1789–90," *AHR* 94 (1989): 271–301.

ity come to infiltrate discussion of a subject that would seem to have excluded it by definition? Many broad historical forces can be cited to account for the increasing relevance of the principle of equality in the eighteenth century. Between the 1680s and the 1750s, the combined processes of administrative leveling and fiscal innovation, an influx of commercial wealth, the formation of a wide reading public, and the emerging theory and practice of economic liberalism helped to narrow the social gap between traditional elites and common citizens and contributed to the perception that France comprised a single social community.[8] At the same time, the development of new norms of sociability and intellectual exchange in reading rooms, salons, and other venues, as described in the work of Daniel Gordon, Dena Goodman, and Margaret Jacob among others, established mutual respect and disregard for hierarchy as basic expectations of "enlightened" social intercourse.[9] The philosophes, of course, made inherited status a prime target of their satire from the 1740s, and the growing attraction of natural law theory, as developed from Locke's *Two Treatises on Government* to Rousseau's *Second Discourse,* made the concepts of individual rights and natural equality a standard feature of intellectual discussion in the second half of the eighteenth century.[10]

All of these developments certainly gave the concept of equality increasing salience in the eighteenth century, both as a philosophical ideal and as a set of everyday habits, and they help to explain why writers would have been inclined to use the term, or to allude to the idea, even in unlikely contexts. There are reasons to assume, however, that a more direct and specific impulse lay behind the association between honor and equality in the minds of eighteenth-century writers and social observers. After all, very few extended discussions of honor failed to offer a defense, a

8. On the reading public see, for example, Roger Chartier, *The Cultural Origins of the French Revolution,* trans. Lydia Cochrane (Durham, N.C., 1991), 20–91; on administrative leveling the classic work remains Alexis de Tocqueville, *The Old Regime and the French Revolution,* trans. Stuart Gilbert (New York, 1955); for fiscal innovation see Michael Kwass, "A Kingdom of Taxpayers: State Formation, Privilege, and Political Culture in Eighteenth-Century France," *JMH* 70 (1998): 295–339; on the economy see Colin Jones, "The Great Chain of Buying: Medical Advertisement, the Bourgeois Public Sphere, and the Origins of the French Revolution," *AHR* 101 (1996): 13–40; and Cissie Fairchilds, "The Production and Marketing of Populuxe Goods in Eighteenth-Century Paris," in *Consumption and the World of Goods,* ed. John Brewer and Roy Porter (London, 1993), 228–48.
9. Daniel Gordon, *Citizens without Sovereignty: Equality and Sociability in French Thought, 1670–1789* (Princeton, 1994); Dena Goodman, *The Republic of Letters: A Cultural History of the French Enlightenment* (Ithaca, N.Y, 1994); Margaret Jacob, *Living the Enlightenment: Freemasonry and Politics in Eighteenth-Century Europe* (Oxford, 1991).
10. And not only the discourse of intellectuals. See Michael Sonenscher, *Work and Wages: Natural Law, Politics, and the Eighteenth-Century French Trades* (Cambridge, 1989).

reevaluation, or a critique of established hierarchies. In fact, almost from the beginning of the century, consideration of the challenge of equality became central to the process of rethinking honor and its meaning. Certainly by 1748, with the publication of Montesquieu's *Spirit of the Laws*, the topics of honor and equality had become mutually and inextricably linked.

Powerful intertextual and intratextual evidence suggests that the originary link between the subjects of honor and equality was rooted in another development distinct from, though related to, the wide cultural phenomena just mentioned. I refer to the efflorescence of French patriotism, or love of the *patrie,* in the eighteenth century.[11] David A. Bell, in a stimulating book that charts the early rise of nationalism in eighteenth-century France, has argued that the French developed stronger attachments to the *patrie* and the nation, beginning in the later seventeenth century, in order to fill the void left by God's receding presence in the realm of human affairs. *Patrie* and nation, he contends, became important "foundational concepts" that allowed people to conceive of the "human terrestrial order" as autonomous, self-regulating, and no longer "subordinated to exterior (particularly divine) determinations."[12] He also points to changes in the "realm of material organization" that made it possible to imagine France as a cohesive community; he particularly cites the absolutist state's new administrative efficiency, the spread of print journalism, and the emergence of a "bourgeois public sphere."[13] But the development of a patriotic sensibility in France depended above all, in Bell's view, on the grand reconceptualization of the relationship between the human and the divine spheres that occurred in the later seventeenth and early eighteenth centuries.

11. The terms *patriotisme* and *patriote* did not appear in the *Dictionnaire de l'Académie Française* until the edition of 1762, and were not a standard feature of the French political lexicon much before the 1750s. Still, the terms were defined in 1762 as being derived from "amour de la *patrie,*" a phrase in circulation at least since the late seventeenth century. The phrase had appeared in the first edition of the *Dictionnaire de Trévoux* of 1704, for example, as one of the expressions of "amour." The expression implied not only love for one's country, which might be passive and largely unreflective, but also an active commitment to the country's well-being—Trévoux specifically cited the ancient Romans, "who sacrificed themselves for their love of the *patrie.*" For purposes of simplification, I will use "patriotism" to convey virtuous love of the *patrie* throughout the book, though I am aware that the term is slightly anachronistic for the early part of the century. For the definitions see *Dictionnaire de l'Académie Française* (Paris, 1762), vol. 2: 325; *Dictionnaire universel françois et latin* (Paris, 1704), vol. 1, unpaginated.

12. David A. Bell, *The Cult of the Nation in France: Inventing Nationalism, 1680–1800* (Cambridge, Mass., 2001), 26. Bell counts five of these foundational concepts, including civilization, public, and society, but he stresses the importance of *patrie* and nation.

13. Ibid., 34.

A fundamental shift in religious values may indeed have provided one of the preconditions for the new orientation toward the nation in early eighteenth-century France, but efforts to define the character of the *patrie*, and to promote its well-being, also represented a creative and critical response to political disillusionment. The new call to patriotism was both conceived and presented as a critique of existing practices, and it therefore advanced an array of competing political claims.[14] The assertion, or recovery, of patriotism around the turn of the seventeenth century thus involved more than the renegotiation of relations between the worldly and the divine, and it represented much more than the belated cultural expression of changing "material" realities. The articulation of French patriotism was experienced as a self-consciously political process that derived from, and was premised upon, the renegotiation of three relationships that pertained inescapably to "this" world: the relationship between modernity and antiquity, the relationship between the monarchy and the nobility, and the relationship between the various constituent members, or citizens, of the *patrie*.

The French assertion of love of the *patrie* required a rethinking of the relationship between antiquity and modernity because patriotism's new appeal partly reflected a discomfort with certain perceived features of the modern world—the increased role of money and finance, the growth of commerce, social mobility, egoism—and also because the most compelling models of patriotic civic culture all came from Greek and Roman antiquity. Even at the time, the promotion of patriotism was understood to involve a process of appropriation; self-styled patriots knew that they adapted ancient ideals to modern purposes. Those who sought to define patriotism for a modern context inevitably compared, and translated between, ancient values and mores and the values and mores of the eighteenth century.[15]

14. A traditional form of patriotism, "at once monarchical, Christian, and . . . aristocratic," had marked the language of noble servants of the crown, and of the royal agents who praised them, even before the 1690s. See Jean-Pierre Labatut, "Patriotisme et noblesse sous le règne de Louis XIV," *RHMC* 29 (1982): 622–34, esp. 633. The patriotism that informs political discussion after 1685 and the Revocation of the Edict of Nantes, by contrast, assumes an explicitly critical tone. As Hélène Dupuy has noted, "the revival of the idea of the *patrie* [in the early eighteenth century] was inscribed in a movement for moral renewal that manifested itself through a political radicalization." All "across the [eighteenth] century, the idea of the *patrie* became the vector of political contestation." See Dupuy, "Genèse de la patrie moderne: La naissance de l'idée moderne de la patrie en France avant et pendant la Révolution" (Mémoire de Doctorat, University of Paris I, 1995), 17.

15. On the eighteenth century's cult of antiquity, see, for example, Chantal Grell, *Le dix-huitième siècle et l'antiquité en France* (Oxford, 1995).

The articulation of French patriotism also entailed a rethinking of the relationship between monarchy and nobility. In large part this was because the self-denying virtue associated with ancient patriotism came to be conceived by noble critics of monarchical "despotism" in the later seventeenth century as forming part of an alternative political morality in France, one that could restore the proper values and the proper people to the center of French political life. Those who began to promote, or ponder, the promise of patriotism in the early eighteenth century had in mind the apparent defects of the monarchical regime and the role that a now-marginalized nobility could or should play in alleviating those defects.[16]

The third relationship renegotiated through the articulation of French patriotism, that between the nobility and commoners, was entangled both in the modern confrontation with antiquity and in the nobility's confrontation with absolute monarchy. The ancient polities whose patriotic examples inspired modern admiration had all assumed more or less "republican" form, after all, and eighteenth-century students of ancient patriotism had to contemplate not only the duties and rights of republican citizens, and the link between patriotic feeling and the status of citizen, but also the moral and legal distance separating the modern subject of a monarchy from the republican citizen of antiquity. At the same time, those who imagined a new civic role for the nobility understood that the redefinition of its role would alter not only its political position vis-à-vis the monarchy but also its social position vis-à-vis the other subjects of the crown. The imperative to restore, appropriate, or create a patriotism suitable for eighteenth-century France, in other words, required an all-encompassing evaluation of the rights, duties, and obligations of French subjects/citizens.

The need to renegotiate the relationship between nobles and non-nobles also emerged, however, from the often unspoken social premises implied by the very use of patriotic rhetoric. After all, the recourse to a language of patriotism necessarily implicated all the constituents of the *patrie*. The invocation of inclusive terms such as patriot, citizen, and Frenchman appealed implicitly to a community defined by common loyalties, and the identity of the patriot therefore transcended that of the noble, or, for that matter, that of the merchant or the cobbler. No one, with the possible exception of a few conservative noble theorists, assumed that the features of the patriot were identical to the features of any particular corporate group. Patriotism, as the chevalier Jaucourt would explain in the 1760s,

16. Cf. Bell, *Cult of the Nation*, 18, 24.

was understood as a "sentiment" rather than the product of specialized knowledge, and in his eyes this implied that "the lowliest man in the state can have it just as well as the leader of the republic."[17] The collective process of defining the ideal qualities and characteristics of the modern French patriot therefore inevitably entailed a reassessment of corporate boundaries, and it ultimately challenged the nobility's claim to social and political preeminence.

Linda Colley has written, in her magisterial analysis of the contemporary British scene, that the rising patriotism of the eighteenth century implied "a much broader access to citizenship," and that it provided formerly excluded people a way of "claiming the right to participate" in political life.[18] The process of forging a new civic consciousness had similar effects even in "absolutist" France, and historians who have begun to study the circulation of classical republican ideas in France have detected signs of patriotism's implicit threat to established hierarchies. Marisa Linton has noted the "radicalism and egalitarianism always potentially present" in the eighteenth century's attention to virtue. Johnson Kent Wright, in his penetrating study of the "classical republican" Mably, has discussed the abbé's concerns about material inequality and his flirtation with communist utopian ideas. Keith Michael Baker, in a study of the pamphleteer Guillaume Saige, observed that "claims to equality" were "inherent" in the political arguments developed by this "patriot" opponent of ministerial despotism in the 1770s.[19]

The notion of equality implied by patriotic rhetoric, however, was not a universal, limitless equality that placed all human beings on the same political and cultural plane. Even Greek and Roman equality had applied only to the certified citizens of the polity, and the ancient republics had established their form of equality against a background of moral differentiation and rigid class differences that highlighted the civic qualities of an elite. Similarly, partisans of patriotism in the eighteenth century generally conceived of "equality" through the prism of civic virtue, that is, a capacity for extraordinary selflessness that did not belong to all people in equal measure. For this reason, honor and virtue were rarely taken to be

---

17. *Encyclopédie, ou Dictionnaire Raisonné des Sciences, des Arts et des Métiers, par une Société de Gens de Lettres,* vol. 11 (Neuchâtel, 1765; repr. Parma, 1970), P 37.

18. Linda Colley, *Britons: Forging the Nation, 1707–1837* (New Haven, Conn., 1992), 5.

19. Linton, *The Politics of Virtue,* 16; Johnson Kent Wright, *A Classical Republican in Eighteenth-Century France: The Political Thought of Mably* (Stanford, 1997), 94–105; Keith Michael Baker, "A Classical Republican in Eighteenth-Century Bordeaux: Guillaume-Joseph Saige," in Baker, *Inventing the French Revolution: Essays on French Political Culture in the Eighteenth Century* (Cambridge, 1990), 148.

antithetical terms. In fact, eighteenth-century admirers of the ancients commonly evoked the example of the legendary Roman consul Marcellus, who had constructed a temple to honor that could be approached only through a gate leading first through the temple of virtue. Precisely because virtue carried its own hierarchical implications, and because no one associated it with a pure or absolute form of equality, the rhetoric of patriotism proved to be the ideal vehicle for mediating and renegotiating the relationship between nobles and non-nobles in the imaginations of the eighteenth-century French.

Sarah Maza has recently argued that the rise of patriotic sensibilities in the eighteenth century should not be associated with the rise of putatively "bourgeois" values, or with the displacement of noble values—such as generosity, selflessness, service—that actually continued to exercise a strong hold over the French "social imaginary" well into the nineteenth century.[20] Analysis of the terms through which patriotic attitudes were conceived and promoted under the old regime helps to substantiate Maza's claim, and to explain the continuing allure of the noble ideal. Patriots of all stripes continued to respect moral hierarchies, and they invariably regarded patriotic citizenship as an expression of moral excellence. Patriots writing from different social locations and institutional contexts also agreed on the desirability of expanding the circle of patriotic fellowship. Disagreement arose not over the existence but over the extent and nature of rank and distinction within the patriotic polity. The prescriptions of patriotic writers inevitably engaged two questions that framed the entire patriotic project in the eighteenth century: *Who* are the patriots? *How* equal are they?[21] "Love of the *patrie*" constituted a vast playing field over which a complicated contest of tug-of-war attracted new participants throughout the century. Pulling in this direction were those drawn to the importance of rank (honor), pulling in that direction were those emphasizing the importance of equality (virtue). The French *thought* their way to the construction of a patriotic nation by renegotiating the relationship between rank and equality, and by reimagining the meaning of nobility.

This book focuses on published commentary concerning a highly specific topic—the ways in which the concepts of honor and virtue informed

20. Sarah Maza, *The Myth of the French Bourgeoisie: An Essay on the Social Imaginary, 1750–1850* (Cambridge, Mass., 2003), 10–11, 53–61, 195–204.
21. See Jean-Fabien Spitz, *L'amour de l'égalité: Essai sur la critique de l'égalitarisme républicain en France, 1770–1830* (Paris, 2000). Although the book focuses too narrowly on Rousseau's impact, Spitz helpfully draws attention to the debate in philosophical circles over the form of equality most appropriate to a "liberal" state (54).

and reflected the structure of social and political relations. And although I have consulted a wide array of sources, the book's evidence is largely drawn from overtly "political" writings; I concentrate especially on those authors for whom honor and virtue had a specifically political resonance and who had in mind clear civic objectives. Needless to say, then, virtually all the voices registered here are those of well-educated and mostly urban males. Despite the relatively narrow range of themes, people, and contemporary problems directly engaged by the evidence presented, however, the book throws new light on several issues important to the study of eighteenth-century France and, more generally, to historians testing new methods for investigating processes of cultural change. Two issues in particular stand out, and I need to address each of them separately and at some length.

## ORIGINS OF THE REVOLUTION

Anyone familiar with the constitutional disputes that dominated the preceding months and opening weeks of the Estates-General of 1789, or aware of the inflammatory rhetoric used by writers such as the abbé Sieyès, knows that the French Revolution was inaugurated by a heated public dispute over the rights and prerogatives of the nobility. Despite the pivotal nature of the constitutional conflict that raged from the fall of 1788 through the early summer of 1789, however, specialists of the eighteenth century are now challenged to explain the origins and fury of this protracted argument about the relationship between nobility and nation. According to the older Marxist perspective, now discredited, societies carried a built-in mechanism for conflict and, thus, historians always had a ready explanation for decisive political confrontations and other catalysts for social transformation. Having eliminated class conflict as the central motor of change in the eighteenth century, the revisionists bequeathed to future specialists of the period a distinctly "political" interpretation of the inter-estate hostility that erupted in the "pre-Revolution" (1787–89), an interpretation that stressed the determining power of political circumstance. According to the now-standard view, misunderstandings and miscalculations arising from the immediate political context—most notably, the vacuum of power left by a delegitimized monarchy—led to recriminations, outrage, and obstinacy that could not have been predicted on the basis of the social and political relations, and the forms of conflict, that had characterized the old regime. The animosity between the second and third estates, even if it crystallized the meaning of certain prior experiences, was unnecessary and unexpected, and it became decisive mainly because the heat of political contest accentuated differences of perspective and magnified the import of every choice and event.

This "classic" revisionist interpretation of the developing revolutionary crisis suppresses, ignores, or lightly dismisses a number of troubling questions. If the society of orders had really become largely irrelevant on the eve of the Revolution, and if the nobility had been superseded in importance by a socially heterogeneous "elite," as many revisionists claimed, why did the demand for ennobling venal offices remain high to the end? Why were two royal genealogists convinced, on the eve of the Revolution, that France was in need of a new *recherche de la noblesse* modeled after those of Louis XIV, one that would finally separate the authentic nobles from the frauds?[22] Just as important, if the parlement's famous decree of 25 September 1788—one that declared that the coming Estates-General should meet according to its traditional forms, with the nobility and clergy meeting separately from the third estate and enjoying veto power—really came as a startling reminder that the society of orders retained meaning in a liberal era, as some have suggested, why were participants in the ensuing public debate able to draw quickly and extensively from a variety of arguments both for and against the nobility's special claims?

Over the past ten years, social and cultural historians have sought to reintegrate social change into the story of the coming Revolution, and they have exposed the inadequacies of narrowly political and event-driven accounts of the old regime's collapse. Timothy Tackett has highlighted the starkly different material circumstances, legal powers, and cultural expectations that distinguished nobles from commoners in the later eighteenth century. Michael Kwass has shown how eighteenth-century debates over taxation, which pitted the nation against the crown, eventually exposed the nobility to criticism because of the expectations of equity and fairness that informed the construction of a "fiscal" nation. Colin Jones and John Shovlin, reflecting on the rise of commercial society in the eighteenth century, have suggested new ways of conceiving how middle-class sensibilities may have emerged as an alternative to traditional corporatism, even in the absence of a self-consciously capitalist bourgeoisie.[23]

22. See chapter 5.
23. Timothy Tackett, *Becoming a Revolutionary: The Deputies of the French National Assembly and the Emergence of a Revolutionary Culture, 1789–1790* (Princeton, 1996); Colin Jones, "The Great Chain of Buying," and "Bourgeois Revolution Revivified: 1789 and Social Change," in *Rewriting the French Revolution,* ed. Colin Lucas (Oxford, 1991), 69–118; John Shovlin, "Toward a Reinterpretation of Revolutionary Antinobilism: The Political Economy of Honor in the Old Regime," *JMH* 72 (2000): 35–66; Michael Kwass, *Privilege and the Politics of Taxation in Eighteenth-Century France: Liberté, Egalité, Fiscalité* (Cambridge, 2001).

These and other historians working from a post-revisionist perspective have established intriguing connections between the broad social developments of the old regime and the political arguments of the early Revolution. Several mysteries remain to be explored, however. Discrepancies in wealth and status, the rise of economistic modes of thought, the emergence of new commercial markets, and the increasing intensity of tax disputes may all help to explain how and why some commoners began mobilizing arguments against noble privilege well before the Revolution, but the *simultaneous* appearance of robust and theoretically subtle arguments both for and against nobility and the society of orders in 1788–89 is still hard to account for. Defensiveness and residual traditionalism are inadequate explanations for noble intransigence in the Estates-General or for the wider defense of noble prerogatives evident in both Paris and the provinces. The defenders of nobility, or at least many of those who wrote in the nobility's behalf, countered their opponents' claims with a variety of arguments with deep roots in the old regime. Noble participants in the great constitutional conflict of 1789 had evidently given much thought to the relationship between nobility and nation long before the pre-Revolutionary crisis forced the choosing of sides and the drawing of battle lines.

Still, even if one grants the possibility that the dramatic clash between estates in 1789 resulted not from political contingency and a disorienting vacuum of power but from a confrontation between pre-formed, sincerely held, and unalterably opposed ideological perspectives, another question poses itself. How had such conflicting arguments—both for and against nobility, for and against the society of orders—gestated in the context of the last decades of the old regime, when the natural leaders and self-appointed spokesmen of nobles and non-nobles seem to have enjoyed harmonious social relations, and when the estates cooperated politically in the struggle against ministerial "despotism"? And why had those conflicting perspectives not clashed openly before? Recent work suggests that the revisionist thesis about the merger of elites under the old regime exaggerated or misread some phenomena and overlooked others, but the larger revisionist argument about the absence of tension between a "nobility" and a "bourgeoisie" was certainly well founded.[24] Despite disagreements over

24. Recent works emphasizing hostilities between segments of the elite include Rafe Blaufarb, "Noble Tax Exemption and the Origins of the French Revolution: The *Procès des Tailles* of Provence, 1530s–1789," and Thomas E. Kaiser, "Nobles into Aristocrats, or How an Order Became a Conspiracy," both in *The French Nobility and the Eighteenth Century: Reassessments and New Approaches,* ed. Jay M. Smith (forthcoming); Daniel Wick, *A Conspiracy of Well-Intentioned Men: The Society of Thirty and the French Revolution* (New York, 1987); and Blaufarb, "Nobles, Aristocrats, and the Origins of the French Revolution," in *Tocqueville and Beyond,* 86–110.

tax policy and general resentment toward the court, virtually no one called for the destruction of the nobility as such. Besides, noble audiences laughed at performances of Beaumarchais's *Marriage of Figaro* (1784), with its sympathetic common characters and its unflattering representation of Figaro's antagonist, the noble count Almaviva. Readers from the nobility and third estate admired many of the same authors and attended the same salons. Especially from the 1770s, all expected and wished for thorough political reform. In such a context, how could the future combatants of 1789 have developed starkly opposing perspectives on the future of the French social and political order?

Analysis of the negotiations over the meaning of honor and virtue in the eighteenth century provides a mechanism for addressing these questions. Because discussion about the meaning, function, and social implications of honor and virtue was carried out within the framework of a general patriotic awakening, authors understandably used a unifying rhetoric aimed at the well-being of France as a whole and designed to bring together the disparate elements of the polity in a common civic project. The use of a common vocabulary—honor, virtue, and especially patriotism—served to mask or deflect important disagreements even as it expressed the existence of a set of shared premises. Historians studying the operation of the concept of "merit" in the old regime and Revolution have already shown the varying and sometimes opposing assumptions that lay behind use of the word in specific institutional settings.[25] Patriotism functioned similarly in eighteenth-century culture. The habitual use of a patriotic idiom, and the widely shared assumption that some form of "nobility" would play a vital role in the regeneration of the *patrie*, created an illusion of consensus, or at least the rising anticipation of an achievable consensus, even as the umbrella of patriotic sentiment nurtured different understandings of patriotism's social implications. The phenomenon helps to explain how opposing social visions of a reformed France could develop and coexist amid the general call for an end to selfish "abuses" and the wide proclamation of the rights and claims of the nation.

The outlines of those opposing social visions of a reformed France were discernible at least from the middle of the century. The central argument of this book is that the rethinking of the meaning of honor and virtue—a process that necessarily accompanied the rise of the patriotic polity—even-

25. See Rafe Blaufarb, *The French Army, 1750–1820: Careers, talent, merit* (Manchester, 2002); Nira I. Kaplan, "A Changing Culture of Merit: French Competitive Examinations and the Politics of Selection, 1750–1820" (Ph.D. diss., Columbia University, 1999); and Jay M. Smith, *The Culture of Merit: Nobility, Royal Service, and the Making of Absolute Monarchy in France, 1600– 1789* (Ann Arbor, Mich., 1996).

tually yielded two opposing conceptions of nobility in French political culture. In one of these conceptions, nobility remained a social category formally distinct from, and necessarily elevated above, the mass of the citizenry. From this perspective, articulated most often by individuals from older noble families with military backgrounds, the nobility had a natural tendency toward patriotic thought and action because of its traditions of selfless service and because its inherent sense of honor predisposed it to sacrifice base pleasures in the pursuit of greater goods. From the other perspective, articulated largely though not exclusively by writers outside the second estate, nobility became an essentially moral category that symbolized civic excellence. Nobility, from this perspective, was rooted in traditions of "French" honor, and it remained open to all citizens who possessed the requisite virtue and demonstrated the proper patriotic spirit. This definition of nobility actually incorporated the principle of equality, since all citizens touched by patriotism had the same chance to distinguish themselves as true nobles, just as all ran the same risk of dishonoring themselves through base egoism. For some, in fact, the irreducibly moral basis of noblesse meant that all citizens of a patriotic nation were to be considered as presumptive nobles. Conflict between these differing visions could not be deferred indefinitely, even in spite of their proponents' wide area of common ground. As soon as "patriots" were empowered to confront "despotism" in August 1788, with the announcement of the coming Estates-General, the challenge of actually executing the victory of the nation and its citizens invited the aggressive articulation of incompatible principles of social organization.

Because it leads unavoidably to consideration of contemporary attitudes toward nobility and the society of orders, analysis of the meanings of honor, virtue, and patriotism under the old regime thus provides a new way of understanding both the initial conflicts and the long-term origins of the French Revolution. Because this book also assesses pre-Revolutionary developments partly in the light of later Revolutionary events, some might complain that the project is teleological by design. If true, this would constitute a grave offense indeed, especially within the current historiographical climate, because ever since the revisionists expelled Marxist determinism from the field of Revolutionary studies, teleology—that is, the assumption that history moves toward a predetermined end—has stood as the one unpardonable sin for all self-respecting dix-huitièmistes.[26]

26. In 1971 François Furet condemned "the teleological philosophy" that had guided Marxist analysis (reproduced in Furet, *Interpreting the French Revolution,* 92), and since the 1970s historians of the Revolution have struggled mightily to avoid "the snares of teleological interpretation" (Chartier, *Cultural Origins,* 6). The imperative has shaped general histories of

A natural aversion to teleology, however, must not discourage the historian from asking, and seeking to explain, how a society moved from point A to point B in the course of its history. One can avoid teleology and still explain why the historical course actually taken made perfect sense in the context of its unfolding. To make sense of the eighteenth-century French past, and to understand why the Revolution was both meaningful and intelligible to those who had lived its prehistory, one needs first to understand how the French people came to reevaluate, and finally to denounce, the moral and social hierarchies that had always sustained their existing corporate society. This book, by highlighting the way in which the absorption of patriotic values forced the reconfiguration of honor, virtue, and nobility, represents one effort to gain access to that cognitive process.

To be sure, *Nobility Reimagined* offers only a partial view of the large-scale transformation of attitudes that served as the chief precondition of the Revolution. A full account of changing attitudes toward nobility, hierarchy, and society would necessarily consider relations between peasants and seigneurs, tensions between the various kinds of venal officeholders in the cities, the philosophes' assault on superstition, and much more besides (including the legal contests over honor that formed the initial focus of my research). Such a comprehensive investigation, however, would have required the integration of widely disparate forms of evidence, it would have produced an enormous and little-read book, and it might have required a lifetime of work. In any case, there are good reasons for initiating an investigation into the century's attitudes toward nobility, hierarchy, and society by probing the published sources sampled here. These sources are valuable not only because of what they reveal about the evolution of French attitudes in particular, but also, I think, because collectively they happen to exemplify the processes of conceptual and historical change.

## IDEAS, AGENCY, AND CHANGE

From the 1960s to the early 1990s, study of the old regime and the French Revolution was shaped by three interpretive paradigms that dominated the

---

the period, such as Daniel Roche's *France in the Enlightenment,* trans. Arthur Goldhammer (Cambridge, Mass., 1998), which admonishes those who would "sacrifice to the idol of teleology" (6), and specialized studies such as Edmond Dziembowski, *Un nouveau patriotisme français, 1750–1770: La France face à la puissance anglaise à l'époque de la guerre de Sept Ans* (Oxford, 1998), which urges "vigilance in face of indices that could be construed too hastily as representing 'announcements' of the coming revolutionary era" (5).

field in succession. The "social" interpretation of the Revolution and its origins, associated with but certainly not limited to Marxist historians, particularly stressed the power of economic processes, competition for resources, and the changing distribution of power among various social groups. The "political" approach, championed by the revisionists of the late 1960s and 1970s, explained the Revolution by highlighting the influence of political structures, political contingencies, and the role of personalities in the unfolding of the Revolutionary drama. By the 1980s, a second generation of revisionists, much indebted to the political perspectives developed in the 1970s, developed an essentially "discursive" approach to the old regime and the Revolution. This approach focused especially on rhetoric, linguistic structures, patterns of meaning, and their constraining and enabling effects on human thought and action. Skilled and powerful advocates of the "social" and "political" approaches remain active in the field, but most would agree that the practitioners of "discursive" history have been responsible for some of the most exciting and seminal work that has appeared over the last two decades.[27]

*Nobility Reimagined* pays careful attention to language and meaning, and some may see the book as an elaboration, or perhaps as tiring repetition, of the "discursive" methods developed by pathbreakers in the field.[28] Like many social and cultural historians in recent years, however, I have grown increasingly frustrated by the inability of discursive analysis to yield a satisfying account of human agency.[29] Too often, "languages" and "discourses" are represented as autonomous actors in history, determining the out-

27. On the "political" see, for example, Doyle, *Origins,* and Munro Price, *Preserving the Monarchy: The Comte de Vergennes, 1774–1787* (New York, 1995). See also the discussion by Dale K. Van Kley, "Pure Politics in Absolute Space: The English Angle on the Political History of Pre-Revolutionary France," *JMH* 69 (1997): 754–84. On the "social" see, for example, Tackett, *Becoming a Revolutionary;* Donald Sutherland, *The French Revolution and Empire: The Quest for a Civic Order* (Oxford, 2003); John Markoff, *The Abolition of Feudalism: Peasants, Lords, and Legislators in the French Revolution* (University Park, Pa., 1996); and Gwynne Lewis, "Rethinking the Debate," in *The French Revolution in Social and Political Perspective,* 118–125.

28. Among the trailblazers: Furet, *Interpreting the French Revolution;* Mona Ozouf, *Festivals and the French Revolution,* trans. Alan Sheridan (Cambridge, Mass., 1988); Baker, *Inventing the French Revolution;* Lynn Hunt, *Politics, Culture, and Class in the French Revolution* (Berkeley, 1984); and William H. Sewell, Jr., *Work and Revolution: The Language of Labor from the Old Regime to 1848* (Cambridge, 1980) and *A Rhetoric of Bourgeois Revolution: The Abbé Sieyes and What Is the Third Estate?* (Durham, N.C., 1994).

29. For commentary specific to the French Revolution, see Vivian Gruder, "Whither Revisionism? Political Perspectives on the Ancien Régime," *FHS* 20 (1997): 245–85; Jack Censer, "Social Twists and Linguistic Turns: Revolutionary Historiography a Decade after the Bicentennial," *FHS* 22 (1999): 139–67; and Suzanne Desan, "What's after Political Culture? Recent French Revolutionary Historiography," *FHS* 23 (2000): 163–96. For broader discussion

come of historical processes and leaving little space for the motives and desires of purposeful human actors. How can the historian acknowledge the
power of language to define the parameters of the thinkable but also explain, at the same time, why individuals become motivated to change the
world around them? How does one appreciate the constraining influence
of Nietzsche's "prison house of language" while also signaling respect for
the individual initiative always necessary to cultural innovation?

The "revival of the social" advocated by various critics of the linguistic
turn, and some disillusioned cultural historians, stands as one possible alternative to analysis of discourse, but I fear that recent promoters of "the
social" seek, either consciously or unconsciously, to resuscitate problem-
atic working assumptions about the relationship between experience and
action.[30] They crave the existence of historical causes, or meta-causes, that
lie beyond language-encased processes of interpretation, and they seek
these causes in a putative "social" realm, where experience resides and
whence agency derives.[31] Thus, to take one example, Vivian Gruder seeks
to explain French writers' appeals to various philosophical authorities in
1788 by anchoring their ideas and rhetoric in their perception of "actual
and unfolding problems—the empirical moment."[32] Unfortunately, such
approaches rest on the convenient fiction that some "moments" are more
"empirical" than others, that they contain inherent and immediately recognized meanings, and that they therefore require no processing of information, no reformulation of ideas, on the part of the thinking agent.
Those who "revive the social" in the sense here described, that is, by con-
stituting a realm of the social held to be distinct from or analytically prior

---

of methodological issues, see Richard Biernacki, "Language and the Shift from Signs to Practice in Cultural History," *H&T* 39 (2000): 289–310; William H. Sewell, Jr., "Whatever Happened to the 'Social' in Social History?" in *Schools of Thought: Twenty-Five Years of Interpretive
Social Science* ed. Joan W. Scott and Debra Keates (Princeton, 2001): 209–16; Miguel Cabrera, *Postsocial History: An Introduction* (Lanham, Md., 2004); and Jay M. Smith, "No More Language Games: Words, Beliefs, and the Political Culture of Early-Modern France," *AHR* 102
(1997): 1413–40. Also see the theme issue of *H&T*, "Agency after Postmodernism" (December 2001).

30. The "revival of the social" was hailed by Jack Censer in "Social Twists and Linguistic
Turns," 161, and the social's "revitalization" has also been heralded by the editors of, and
contributors to, *Beyond the Cultural Turn: New Directions in the Study of Society and Culture*, ed.
Victoria E. Bonnell and Lynn Hunt (Berkeley, 1999). For critical discussion of the return to
the social, see Rebecca L. Spang, "Paradigms and Paranoia: How Modern Is the French Revolution?" *AHR* 108 (2003): 119–47. For stimulating reflections from a disillusioned cultural
historian, see Sewell, "Whatever Happened to the 'Social' in Social History?"

31. Also see my "Between Discourse and Experience: Agency and Ideas in the French Pre-
Revolution," *H&T* Theme Issue 40 (2001): 116–42.

32. Gruder, "Whither Revisionism?," 252.

to a realm of intellection, will most likely substitute one form of determinism for another, and thus they, too, will fail to detect and to explore the actual process whereby people engage, evaluate, and remake their world over time. Calls to examine "the social context" or "the political context" of an idea or an action generally serve only to divert attention from the intricate workings of the mind, where historical change invariably begins.

In spite of my discomfort with some of the tendencies built into discursive analysis, I do not assume, then, that the historian in search of agency should subordinate evidence of linguistic change to other evidence that can be safely deemed foundational, and therefore determinative of human action.[33] On the contrary, the reasons that lie behind human action are divulged *only* through analysis of language, because only language provides access to the interpretive environment in which individuals and groups make their way through life. The interpretive environment that effectively constitutes an individual's world is partly comprised by the features of the inhabited topography (as represented, for example, by institutions, social relationships, and formal constraints on action) but also by personal tastes, convictions, and inclinations, all of which can help to determine one's choices and priorities, and none of which are entirely determined by existing cultural paradigms or relations of power. This "interpretive environment," where individuals meet and navigate their way through the worlds they encounter, is therefore neither a definable set of structural "givens" nor a purely subjective realm of invention, but rather a space of endless interpretation penetrated by interrelated and ever-evolving *ideas.*

---

33. The ensuing discussion of agency draws from my previously published article "Between Discourse and Experience." My thoughts on the issue have been decisively influenced by recent practitioners in the broad field of cultural/intellectual history who seek the middle ground between "objective" and "subjective" accounts of human agency and are therefore drawn toward examination of cognitive processes. See especially Mark Bevir, *The Logic of the History of Ideas* (Cambridge, 1999); Siep Stuurman, "On Intellectual Innovation and the Methodology of the History of Ideas," *RH* 4 (2000): 311–19; William Reddy, *The Navigation of Feeling: A Framework for the History of Emotions* (Cambridge, 2001) and "The Logic of Action: Indeterminacy, Emotion, and Historical Narrative," *H&T* Theme Issue 40 (2001): 10–33; Gareth Stedman Jones, "The Determinist Fix: Some Obstacles to the Further Development of the Linguistic Approach to History in the 1990s," *History Workshop Journal* 42 (1996): 19–35 and "Une autre histoire sociale?" *AHSS* 53 (1998): 383–92; Anthony J. La Vopa, "Doing Fichte: Reflections of a Sobered (but Unrepentant) Contextual Biographer," in *Biographie schreiben,* ed. Hans Erich Bödeker (Göttingen, 2003), 107–71; Charles Taylor, *Sources of the Self: The Making of the Modern Identity* (Cambridge, Mass., 1989); and W. V. Quine and J. S. Ullian, *The Web of Belief* (New York, 1978). Also see the seminal text whose title partly inspired my own: Dror Wahrman, *Imagining the Middle Class: The Political Representation of Class in Britain, c. 1780–1840* (Cambridge, 1995).

These ideas, which provide the raw material of human agency, can be glimpsed only through the language inevitably used to apprehend, order, and express them.

The ideas I propose to place at the center of historians' investigation of human agency bear little resemblance to the subject matter of an older "history of ideas" practiced by intellectual historians who studied great thinkers and the intellectual traditions to which they gave voice. Ideas are not the exclusive province of "thinkers," and they have no necessary relationship to philosophical principles or systems of thought. They often lack coherence, and they have indistinct boundaries that make them permanently vulnerable to absorption, enlargement, transformation, or extinction. Ideas, to put it simply, are the mediating substance through which all people confront, construe, and act upon the world around them. They constitute, in the words of Daniel Wickberg, "the stuff of human reality itself."[34] They saturate the relationships, the institutions, the conversations—in short, they inform every context—in which people maneuver and through which they make meaningful lives for themselves. They can take the form of fully articulated principles, half-conscious assumptions, unassimilated insights, reprocessed memories, or unspoken expectations. Ideas are as integral to the preparation of dinner, or the operation of a jackhammer, as they are to the elaboration of a political philosophy.

Informing every context, ideas are also invariably informed by context. But to capture and communicate the intricate dynamics of human agency in the historical past, one must refrain from assigning primacy to a particular type of context—for example, the economic, social, demographic, or linguistic—when discussing the formation and evolution of ideas. In fact, the most immediate, and meaningful, context for any idea is the set of other ideas that surround, condition, and invite its inception and elaboration. The interpretive environment in which life takes place encompasses the whole range of interactions between the mind and all that is perceived to be outside the mind, and consequently no single interaction can have an unmediated impact on the consciousness of the interpreting agent. No form of "experience," in other words, is uninterpreted.[35] Indeed, no experience can even penetrate the human consciousness unless

34. Daniel Wickberg, "Intellectual History vs. the Social History of Intellectuals," *RH* 5 (2001): 383–95, esp. 393.
35. For a compelling philosophical statement of this position, see Michael Oakeshott's classic *Experience and Its Modes* (1933; Cambridge, 1966), 9–69. The touchstone essay in modern historiography is Joan Scott, "The Evidence of Experience," *Critical Inquiry* 17 (1991): 773–97.

it becomes attached to the networks of ideas through which people make sense of all stimuli. These networks of ideas simultaneously filter and express an individual's attitudes toward economic and social structures, sexuality, music, yesterday's news, parental authority, the weather, race, etiquette, ice cream, war, footnotes, and so on, and they mediate between the thinking agent and the phenomena that historians like to think of as the "social," the "political," or multiple other contexts for action. Awareness of "context" is indeed essential to the historian, but as an analytical category, context is unfortunately exceptional for its vulnerability to thoughtless abuse. The invoking of context can assist in explaining what people say, think, or do only if context is understood to involve the wide-ranging cognitive process through which people determine the meanings of, and improvise their responses to, the events that impinge on their lives.

Evidence of linguistic change, then, should be seen not as a reflection of changes occurring in "the world," but as a reflection of changing understandings of the ever-shifting worlds, or interpretive environments, that people inhabit. The creativity of the active human consciousness, and the very nature of human agency, are to be found precisely in the construction of these altered understandings. To prevent paralyzing incoherence, the mind organizes ideas into loose webs, or constellations, that join priorities of purpose and hierarchies of assumption into something like an interpretive disposition. Like the ideas of which they consist, interpretive dispositions are never fixed; they are susceptible to expansion, alteration, and transformation, and they always include potentially conflicting or even contradictory suppositions. Nevertheless, they order the swirl of ideas constantly emerging from the interpretive environment into coherent, or semi-coherent, webs of belief and inclination that determine how individuals apprehend the world and also understand their place within it. New ideas, whether they arise from a social exchange, the reading of a book, a teacher's lesson, or participation in a riot, are inevitably perceived through and assimilated to one's existing interpretive disposition, thus enriching or expanding one's stock of beliefs and sometimes complicating one's perspective on the interpretive environment. People are moved to enact change—that is, they alter their vision of the world and of the actions that are desirable and appropriate within it—when, in the quest to reestablish a coherent fit between the various ideas to which they feel attached, they reevaluate, rearrange, and reconstitute their hierarchy of beliefs, without whose existence no meaningful action is possible.[36] Their new way of see-

36. Bevir rightly asserts that "all actions are the product of beliefs" (*Logic of the History of Ideas,* 134). Bevir overstates the need for coherence within a given web of beliefs, as Siep Stuurman

ing themselves and their world—their new interpretive disposition—expresses itself in the language they employ, that is, in new words, new patterns of meaning, and new inflections that they give to traditional terms and symbols.

Some might be tempted to describe the impulse that leads to the rearrangement of beliefs, and to the construction of a new social vision, as the undeniable force of "interest." The quest for power, control, or economic advantage, one might argue, inevitably creates a rationale, an ideology, and a language to explain and excuse the pursuit of personal interests.[37] But although divergent interests obviously enter into the fabric of everyday life, interests, too, are conceived and understood in relation to a wide web of beliefs that encompass the totality of one's existence. The factory worker is motivated to strike for better wages and benefits not because her bare "interests" dictate it, but because of her attachment to a whole range of ideas, which might include the necessity of fairness, the dignity of work, the unacceptability of arrogance, the thrill derived from taking risks, memories of past indebtedness, the emotional satisfaction of bonding with one's associates, a sense of moral obligation to union organizers, the shame in seeing one's children dress in tattered clothing, admiration for teachers or for baseball players who happen to have waged noted and successful strikes in the past, and, not least, the historically specific idea that labor and management are supposed to battle over such issues as wages and working conditions. To recognize the ideational complexity of human motivation is not to deny that social groups have opposing interests. Rather, it merely draws attention to the need to begin analysis of personal, and historical, change by moving "from the mind out," from the constellation of ideas and assumptions that dispose individuals to see, and act upon, their interests in certain ways.[38]

The imperative to relate historical agency to the evolution of ideas may seem to pose a greater challenge to historians interested in collective

---

has observed ("On intellectual innovation"), and he underestimates the degree to which beliefs are arranged in hierarchies, but his important book offers a compelling account of the way in which beliefs mediate between the individual and social life.

37. On the dangers of interpreting ideas as "smokescreens to hide interests" (Wickberg, "Intellectual History," 394) see, in addition to Wickberg, Simona Cerutti, "La construction des catégories sociales," in *Passés recomposés: Champs et chantiers de l'histoire,* ed. Jean Boutier and Dominique Julia (Paris, 1995), 224–34; Gareth Stedman Jones, *Languages of Class: Studies in English Working Class History, 1832–1982* (Cambridge, 1983), 94–107; William Reddy, *The Rise of Market Culture: The Textile Trade and French Society, 1750–1900* (Cambridge, 1984), 4–11; and Smith, "No More Language Games."

38. Wickberg's felicitous phrase: "Intellectual History vs. the Social History of Intellectuals," 394.

processes than to, say, biographers. The analytical methods required in each case are really not so different, however, especially if the ideas studied happen to concern the organization of society itself. As others have noted, ideas about morality, on the one hand, and social categories, on the other hand, inevitably play a central role both in the apprehension of personal identities and in the construction and understanding of social relationships.[39] Moreover, such ideas are by nature intersubjective; their articulation always implies communion with other minds. Social categories represent claims to organize and distribute collectivities, after all, and discussion about them can proceed only on the basis of an existing and widely recognized template that locates individuals in relation to a host of others. Similarly, as Charles Taylor has noted, people first learn their "languages of moral and spiritual discernment" by being brought into "an ongoing conversation" by parents, relatives, and members of the wider social network in which they inevitably find themselves. The settling of moral priorities, which is essential both to the formation of a sense of identity and to the exercise of agency, inevitably takes place in "webs of interlocution" that transmit and sustain the moral categories recognized by the community or communities to which one belongs.[40]

The writings of individuals, then, can be used as a point of entry into the interpretive dispositions of a larger collectivity, especially if those writings explicitly address the social and moral structures that help to make up what Mark Bevir calls the "inherited background" against which innovative thought inevitably occurs.[41] Such was the case in eighteenth-century France, as the chapters of this book will show. Beginning in the early years

39. Simona Cerutti, in an essay urging a new approach to the study of social identity, has called for historians to seek "to understand *from the inside* the forms adopted by a society's social stratification, and the reasons behind these forms" [italics added]. Steven L. Kaplan has observed that "the eighteenth century suffered from an acute identity crisis" because of "the breakdown of its social taxonomy." Charles Taylor has written that the "self" can exist only "in a space of moral issues," and that moral frameworks that define "what is good, or valuable, or what ought to be done," are integral both to the formation of identity and to the exercise of agency. John Martin, in an article treating late-medieval and early-modern conceptions of the relationship between self and world, has underlined the importance of a "shift in moral vocabulary" for the Renaissance "discovery of the individual." Cerutti, "La construction des catégories sociales," esp. 234; Kaplan, "Social Classification and Representation in the Corporate World of Eighteenth-Century France: Turgot's 'Carnival'," in *Work in France: Representation, Meaning, Organization, and Practice,* ed. Steven Laurence Kaplan and Cynthia Koepp (Ithaca, N.Y., 1986), 176–228, esp. 176; Taylor, *Sources of the Self,* esp. 27, 49; Martin, "Inventing Sincerity, Refashioning Prudence: The Discovery of the Individual in Renaissance Europe," *AHR* 102 (1997): 1309–42, esp. 1312.
40. Taylor, *Sources of the Self,* 35, 39.
41. Bevir, *Logic of the History of Ideas,* 224.

of the century, the integration of patriotic ideals into systems of belief traditionally organized around respect for inequality and hierarchy stimulated in many minds a searching reassessment of the inherited social and moral categories that helped to order life and thought. I contend that, over the course of the eighteenth century, politically engaged writers and readers dealt simultaneously and unavoidably with three pressing issues. 1) They sought to define a patriotism, or love of the *patrie,* that fit within their understanding of French historical traditions but also set out new standards of moral excellence; 2) in traversing the crowded and unsettled moral terrain occupied by the ideal of patriotism, they sought to determine the proper balance between honor and virtue in a monarchical state; 3) finally, in settling on the proper relationship between honor and virtue, they founded their visions of the patriotic nation on a nobility reimagined.

Some of the participants in this century-long discussion were and still are well known—Fénelon, Boulainvilliers, Montesquieu, Coyer, Target. Others enjoyed only fleeting fame or existed in everlasting obscurity. This book casts all of their ideas in a new light by underscoring the degree to which they participated, however unwittingly, in a common, long-term project: the rethinking of nobility under the pressure of the patriotic imperative.

The best place to begin the story of the moral and social reconceptualization of eighteenth-century society is within the milieu of the aristocratic critics of Louis XIV during and after the closing years of his reign. The growth in the power and influence of the monarchy since the 1660s prompted not only a reevaluation of the role of the nobility in contemporary politics and society but also a reconsideration of the moral basis of French public life. The first attempts to recover the patriotic spirit of the ancients, and to rethink the character and value of the nobility's existing code of honor, sought to highlight the power and continuing relevance of virtue in modern society. By the 1740s, at least, the fusion of honor and virtue in the moral commentary of the times had also brought to light the moral challenge of equality in a still corporate society. Much of the political writing of the second half of the eighteenth century expressed the nation's effort, partly conscious and partly not, finally to come to terms with that challenge.

*Chapter One*

## NOBILITY AND THE APPEAL TO VIRTUE
## IN EARLY EIGHTEENTH-CENTURY FRANCE
## (1700S–1740S)

Because of the great triumphs and wretched excesses of Louis XIV's absolutist regime (1661–1715), the aristocratic "state of mind" in the early
eighteenth century recalled earlier periods of noble anxiety and unrest.
Beginning in the middle of the sixteenth century, displeasure over the
spread of venality of office and the rise of the *noblesse de robe* had led various spokesmen of the old nobility to decry the declining fortunes of the
second estate.[1] From the death of Henri IV (1610) to the Fronde (1648–
52), the presence of dynamic first ministers and the adoption of novel
fiscal policies aggravated existing tensions, and expressions of noble resentment filled the pages of pamphlets, histories, and family genealogies.[2]

Although the early eighteenth century witnessed no "crisis of the aristocracy" of the kind historians once described for the earlier period, much
evidence of heightened self-awareness, and of deep reflection about the

1. The standard works are Davis Bitton, *The French Nobility in Crisis, 1560–1640* (Stanford,
1969); Arlette Jouanna, *L'idée de race en France au XVIe et au début du XVIIe siècle (1498–1614)*,
3 vols. (Paris, 1976), esp. 1: 588–613, and "Les gentilshommes français et leur rôle politique
dans la seconde moitié du XVIe et au début du XVIIe siècle," *Il Pensiero Politico* 10 (1977):
22–40; and André Devyver, *Le sang épuré: Les préjugés de race chez les gentilshommes français de
l'ancien régime, 1560–1720* (Brussels, 1973), 56–109. For the seventeenth-century consequences of this late sixteenth-century anxiety, see, for example, Robert Descimon, "The Birth
of the Nobility of the Robe: Dignity versus Privilege in the Parlement of Paris, 1500–1700,"
in *Changing Identities in Early Modern France*, ed. Michael Wolfe (Durham, N.C., 1997), 95–
123.
2. For discussion of these public expressions of disgruntlement, see Smith, *The Culture of
Merit*, 11–123.

place of the nobility in a world remade by the absolutist government of the Sun King, dotted the political and cultural landscape. The battle over judicial protocol in the "affaire du bonnet" (1715–16) and the temporary establishment of government by aristocratic council during the Polysynodie (1715–18) expressed the new sense of vigilance, and self-importance, of the great nobility in the years after Louis XIV's death.[3] The writings of Fénelon, Boulainvilliers, the duc de Saint-Simon, and the marquis d'Argenson provide evidence of the serious intellectual ferment that preceded and followed the brief political offensive of the high aristocracy during the Regency (1715–23). Also, the appearance of new venues for the discussion of political and cultural matters—the Tuesday salons of the marquise de Lambert beginning in 1710, the short-lived Académie Politique (1714–20), the celebrated Club de l'Entresol (1724–31), which was designed in part as a successor to the defunct Académie Politique—signaled an eagerness, at least in certain aristocratic circles, to engage in discussion of contemporary social, political, and moral issues.[4]

Many of the themes broached by noble writers and discussants in the early eighteenth century were reminiscent of earlier periods of noble angst. Commentators worried about the corrosive effects of money in the management of social and political relations, they revisited the historical role of the nobility, and noted its recent transformation, they lamented the cheapening of noble status, and they underlined in various ways the difference between formal nobility and the "true" nobility of virtue.[5] These perennial themes would recur, and repeatedly find their way into print, throughout the century. Despite some rhetorical similarities, though, eighteenth-century discussion about nobility differed significantly from earlier debates because of the larger moral context in which it occurred. By the

---

3. On the "affaire du bonnet," see Harold Ellis, *Boulainvilliers and the French Monarchy: Aristocratic Politics in Early Eighteenth-Century France* (Ithaca, N.Y., 1988), 119–68. On the various jurisdictions of the councils that made up the *polysynodie*, and on the system's eventual demise, see Henri Leclercq, *Histoire de la Régence*, 3 vols. (Paris, 1922), 2: 51–78, 189–207.

4. For the schedule and content of Lambert's salon, see Robert Shackleton, *Montesquieu: A Critical Biography* (Oxford, 1961), 55–61; and Suzanne Delorme, "Le salon de la marquise de Lambert, berceau de l'Encyclopédie," in *L'"Encyclopédie" et le progrès des sciences et des techniques*, ed. Suzanne Delorme and René Taton (Paris, 1952), 20–24. On the Académie Politique, see Joseph Klaits, "Men of Letters and Political Reform in France at the End of the Reign of Louis XIV: The Founding of the Académie Politique," *JMH* 43 (1971): 577–97. On the Club de l'Entresol, see Nick Childs, *A Political Academy in Paris, 1724–1731: The Entresol and Its Members* (Oxford, 2000); and Shackleton, *Montesquieu*, 63–67.

5. To read earlier iterations of these themes, see Ellery Schalk, *From Valor to Pedigree: Ideas of Nobility in France in the Sixteenth and Seventeenth Centuries* (Princeton, 1986); and Jouanna, *L'idée de race*, 1: 588–613.

early years of the century, one of the key terms through which observers discussed nobility and society—virtue—had become inextricably linked to, and representative of, a developing program of political and social reform. Virtue no longer referred, at least not automatically, to Christian principles, or to the highest standards of ethical conduct to which an individual could aspire.[6] In the eighteenth century, virtue came especially to signify a selfless devotion to the political community at large, a political and moral disposition perhaps best defined by the opposing force that gave the word new salience at the end of the seventeenth century: despotism.[7]

The nomenclature of "despotism"—despot, despotic, despotism—was little used in the centuries between the ancient Greeks and the High Renaissance. In his *Six Books of the Republic* (1576), however, Jean Bodin provided an intriguing gloss on the concept of despotic rule, and in the seventeenth century his typology of governments attracted the attention of a series of theorists of sovereignty and natural law, including Grotius, Pufendorf, and Hobbes.[8] In France, by the time of the mid-century civil disturbances known collectively as the Fronde, critics of the ministerial "usurper" Mazarin coined the term "despotic monarchy" to discredit the recent and allegedly unjust concentration of powers in the hands of the crown and its agents.[9] Consciousness of the political model of monarchical despotism only increased in the second half of the century, as France's deepening diplomatic engagement with the Ottoman Turks provided occasions for extensive cultural comparison of eastern and western forms of rule and gave new currency to the stereotype of the "oriental despot."[10]

6. Religious impulses of course also contributed to the renewed focus on virtue at the end of the seventeenth century. Fénelon's doctrine of pure love, which was transposed to the political sphere, was partly inspired by the Quietist piety of Madame de Guyon, and Louis XIV's concern to regulate behavior owed something to his spiritual turn in the 1680s. On Guyon, see Marie-Louise Gondal, *Madame Guyon (1648–1717): Un nouveau visage* (Paris, 1989), and Louis Cognet, *Crépuscule des mystiques: Le conflit Fénelon-Bossuet* (Tournai, 1958); on Louis XIV's moral transformation see Philip F. Riley, *A Lust for Virtue: Louis XIV's Attack on Sin in Seventeenth-Century France* (Westport, Conn., 2001).

7. For discussion of the contemporary rhetorical assault on Louis XIV's despotism, and the monarchy's reaction to it, see Joseph Klaits, *Printed Propaganda under Louis XIV: Absolute Monarchy and Public Opinion* (Princeton, 1976); Lionel Rothkrug, *Opposition to Louis XIV: The Political and Social Origins of the French Enlightenment* (Princeton, 1965); and Thomas E. Kaiser, "The Abbé Dubos and the Historical Defence of Monarchy in Early Eighteenth-Century France," *SVEC* 267 (1989): 77–102.

8. Melvin Richter, "Despotism," in *Dictionary of the History of Ideas: Studies of Selected Pivotal Ideas*, ed. Philip Wiener (New York, 1973), 2: 1–18; R. Koebner, "Despot and Despotism: Vicissitudes of a Political Term," *Journal of the Warburg and Courtauld Institutes* 14 (1951): 275–302.

9. Koebner, "Despot and Despotism," 293.

10. On the importance of the Turk and of "Oriental despotism" in the literary imagination

Aristotle had declared in his *Politics* that, in contrast to the forms of governance appropriate to communities of free men, the despot exercised power over "men who are by nature slave." Even if they enjoyed the tacit consent of the governed, kings who ruled despotically ruled "according to their own judgment," and without regard for the common interest. In fact, despots recognize no common interest, since despotism never rests on "the partnership of free men."[11] In the sixteenth century Bodin continued this theme. Seeing the despot's power over the dominated as analogous to that of the conqueror over the conquered, Bodin announced that private rights and property rights effectively did not exist under despotism, since the despot could properly regard himself "as the legal owner of all individuals and goods."[12] In theoretical terms, at least, true despotism required the absence of freedom among those subjected to the despot's yoke and the lack of any common interest connecting the governor(s) to the governed.

Crown policies had been controversial, and had elicited much criticism, throughout the seventeenth century, but in the last decades of Louis XIV's reign, mounting evidence suggested that the monarchy had indeed moved in the direction of the "despotism" described by theorists of sovereignty. The crown's intensification of devious fiscal practices, the king's seemingly arbitrary abandonment of religious toleration in 1685, his construction of an elaborate universe of courtly etiquette that revolved around the needs and pleasures of the royal person, and Louis's vain and costly involvement in the Wars of the League of Augsburg (1689–97) and of the Spanish Succession (1701–14) had all helped to create the widespread perception that France itself had fallen victim, at the very least, to the whims of a king who resembled a despot. In reaction to the king's overweening power, critics therefore came to crave, and to promote, precisely those elements of political culture that they had come to think of as incompatible both with self-centered despots and with oppressive despotism, namely, liberty, the existence of free subjects, and an object of political loyalty—the state, the nation, or increasingly, the *patrie*—capable of focusing common interests and inspiring affectionate devotion. As La Bruyère remarked in his incisive reflections on the character of politics and society under Louis XIV, a people that lets itself be "put to sleep" by pomp, spectacles, vanity, and luxury unknowingly takes "great steps" toward "despotism." "There is no *patrie* in a despotic [government]," he observed, because other objects—"inter-

---

of later seventeenth-century France, see Michèle Longino, *Orientalism and French Classical Drama* (Cambridge, 2002).

11. Richter, "Despotism," 2.

12. As explained in ibid., 4.

est, glory, the service of the prince"—are permitted to take its place.[13] La Bruyère's sentiments, though they were expressed in his typical aphoristic style, reflected the impulses of a broader movement, for indictments of despotism in late seventeenth-century France called regularly, even if sometimes only implicitly, for the resuscitation of patriotic vigor among subjects of the French crown.

The dichotomous pairing of despotism and the virtues of the free patriot in the imagination of French social and political observers inspired, and was also partly propelled by, a new fascination with the civic culture of the ancients. The celebrated address of the chancellor Henri-François d'Aguesseau, delivered before the parlement of Paris in November 1715, has already attracted much attention from historians.[14] In delivering this ceremonial speech, just weeks after the death of Louis XIV, d'Aguesseau celebrated "love of the *patrie*," and wondered aloud whether monarchies could inspire the same attachments as republics, where "perfect equality" united all "citizens" in devotion to the commonweal. Despite the attention it has received, however, d'Aguesseau's address can hardly be considered singular or innovative. As Marisa Linton has noted, the words "virtue," "*patrie*," and "republic" actually saturated the discourse of parlementary magistrates in the early eighteenth century.[15]

Moreover, interest in the ancients, and especially in the political examples provided by the classical republics, actually extended well beyond the ranks of the magistracy. Already in the 1670s, for example, numerous disaffected nobles, including the chevalier de Rohan, Gilles du Hamel, sieur de La Tréaumont, the chevalier de Préaux, the comte de Guiche, and others, had become attracted to the ideas of a radical expatriate from Amsterdam, Franciscus Van den Enden. A brilliant teacher of Latin and author

13. Jean de La Bruyère, *Les caractères de Théophraste, traduits du grec, avec les caractères, ou les moeurs de ce siècle,* ed. Robert Pignarre (Paris, 1965), 242.

14. Marcel Marion used an extract from d'Aguesseau's speech to exemplify the custom of the *mercuriale,* the chancellor's inaugural address to the assembled parlement of Paris. See Marion, *Dictionnaire des institutions de la France aux XVIIe et XVIIIe siècles* (Paris, 1923; repr., Paris, 1984), 372. Robert Shackleton surmised that Montesquieu would have known about the content of d'Aguesseau's speech, and that the similarity between their definitions of patriotism can partly be attributed to d'Aguesseau's influence. See Shackleton, *Montesquieu,* 275–76. David Bell has hailed the oration as "the beginning of a new era in French political culture." See Bell, *Cult of the Nation,* 50–51. The speech was not actually published until 1759, when d'Aguesseau's complete works appeared. See D'Aguesseau, *Oeuvres,* 13 vols. (Paris, 1759), 1: 205–13.

15. Linton, *The Politics of Virtue,* 46. Isabelle Storez has noted, however, that a thorough-going commitment to the philosophical principle of the equality of man was one of the distinguishing features of d'Aguesseau's thought. See Storez, *Le chancelier Henri-François d'Aguesseau (1668–1751): Monarchiste et libéral* (Paris, 1996), 501–16.

in the 1660s of a subversive text titled *Free Political Institutions*, Van den Enden was steeped in the lessons of Machiavelli's *Discourses* on Livy, and he actively proselytized new adherents of egalitarian republicanism. In 1674, after Van den Enden had relocated to Paris, the crown uncovered plans for a major insurrection inspired by "republican political theory" and designed with the purpose of establishing a "free republic" in the province of Normandy. Betrayed by another young nobleman who had studied Latin with Van den Enden, La Tréaumont, Rohan, Préaux, and their teacher were quickly rounded up and eventually executed at the Bastille in November 1674.[16]

More innocent intentions motivated other expositors of republican ideas. The exiled nobleman Charles de Saint-Evremond (d. 1703) published in 1684, as part of his collected works, his *Reflections on the Spirit of the Roman People in the Various Ages of the Republic*.[17] As a free-thinker and libertine, whose belief in the power of innate interests would later be used to buttress materialist arguments in favor of commerce, Saint-Evremond exhibited political proclivities that were ambiguous to say the least.[18] Augustus appears in the *Reflections* as the savior of the Roman people, and Saint-Evremond may well have intended to demonstrate the advantages of the monarchical form of government in his retelling of Roman history. Nevertheless, his moral history of the Roman republic, deliberately modeled after Machiavelli's *Discourses*, celebrated the Romans' simplicity, their rustic independence, and their "great love of the *patrie*."[19] Saint-Evremond attributed the fall of the republic to the waning of the Romans' "spirit of equality" and their gradual abandonment of virtue.[20] One at least wonders if the free-thinker's long exile in post-Revolutionary England shaped in some way his prefatory comment that "kings played such little part in the grandeur of the Roman people that I am not obliged to say much about them."[21]

---

16. The story of Van den Enden and his noble co-conspirators is told with colorful detail in Jonathan Israel, *Radical Enlightenment: Philosophy and the Making of Modernity, 1650–1750* (Oxford, 2001), 175–84.

17. Charles de Saint-Evremond, *Réflexions sur les divers génies du peuple romain dans les divers temps de la République,* ed. Bertrand Hemmerdinger (Paris, 1795; repr., Naples, 1982). The *Réflexions* first appeared in Saint-Evremond's *Oeuvres meslées* (Paris, 1684), which went through four more editions between 1688 and 1692.

18. Saint-Evremond, *Réflexions*, 121–29.

19. Ibid., 18. On Saint-Evremond's debt to Machiavelli, see the remarks of Hemmerdinger, pp. xi–xii. For other discussions of the historical sources used by Saint-Evremond, and of his influence on Montesquieu, Gibbon, and others, see Patrick Andrivet, *Saint-Evremond et l'histoire romaine* (Orléans, 1998).

20. Saint-Evremond, *Réflexions*, 92.

21. Ibid., 4. Saint-Evremond acclimated quickly to English literary and cultural life. He in-

Other writers also conjured memories of the ancients' political virtue for the edification of modern readers. Jean Du Pradel called "all of antiquity" as his witness in a lengthy diatribe against luxury published in 1705.[22] Du Pradel confidently asserted that the banishing of luxury in France would "reestablish virtue in all parts of the state," and thereby reestablish "love of the *patrie*."[23] The anonymous author of the widely circulated pamphlet *Lamentations of Enslaved France, Which Aspires to Liberty* (1689) similarly urged his "compatriots" to adopt a new "love for the *patrie*," and a "desire for the return of liberty."[24] The *Lamentations*, likely written by an exiled Huguenot, especially decried the "despotic empire" of Louis XIV because of the king's usurpation of religious authority and his meddling in matters of conscience, but the *patrie* to which the author appealed included all who had been harmed by the Sun King's extravagance and irresponsibility.[25]

This longing for love of the *patrie* and political virtue in Ludovican France suggests French familiarity not only with classical authors such as Livy, Tacitus, and Plutarch, but also with the "civic humanist" idiom that served as an important vehicle for transmitting the values of the ancient republics to the early-modern Atlantic world.[26] Much evidence indicates

volved himself in the English version of the quarrel between the Ancients and the Moderns, for example. See Joseph M. Levine, *Between the Ancients and the Moderns: Baroque Culture in Restoration England* (New Haven, Conn., 1999), 113–58; see also Paul Chaponnière, "Les Premières Années d'Exil de Saint-Evremond," *Revue d'Histoire Littéraire de la France* 29 (1922): 385–408.

22. [Jean Du Pradel], *Traité Contre le Luxe des Hommes et des Femmes, et contre le luxe avec lequel on élève les enfans de l'un & de l'autre sexe* (Paris, 1705), 237.

23. Ibid., preface, 57.

24. *Les Soupirs de la France Esclave, qui aspire après la liberté* (Amsterdam, 1689), 3–4.

25. Ibid., 8. For example, the author highlighted the depredations suffered by the parlements and by the "true nobility." For discussion of the pamphlet's provenance, and its "aristocratic" character, see Nannerl Keohane, *Philosophy and the State in France: The Renaissance to the Enlightenment* (Princeton, 1980), 316–19.

26. J. G. A. Pocock and others have described in a series of studies the set of assumptions that informed the patriotic thought and action of the "civic humanists" of sixteenth-century Italy and their many readers and admirers in seventeenth-century England and elsewhere. Attention to the phenomenon of early-modern classical republicanism began with Z. S. Fink, *The Classical Republicans: An Essay in the Recovery of a Pattern of Thought in Seventeenth-Century England* (Evanston, Ill., 1945), but the decisive study was Pocock, *The Machiavellian Moment: Florentine Political Thought and the Atlantic Republican Tradition* (Princeton, 1975). See also Pocock, *Virtue, Commerce, History: Essays on Political Thought and History, Chiefly in the Eighteenth Century* (Cambridge, 1985); *The Languages of Political Theory in Early-Modern Europe*, ed. Anthony Pagden (Cambridge, 1987); and *Machiavelli and Republicanism*, ed. Gisela Bock, Quentin Skinner, and Maurizio Viroli (Cambridge, 1990). For the French case specifically, see Viroli, *Jean-Jacques Rousseau and the "Well Ordered Society"* (Cambridge, 1988); Wright, *A Classical Republican in Eighteenth-Century France;* and Linton, *The Politics of Virtue.*

that, long before the French Revolution, French observers had begun to
construe political change through categories either wholly or partially derived from what J. G. A. Pocock has called the "classical republican" tradition. This tradition had been revived by Italian humanists, most notably
Machiavelli, and then appropriated by radical proponents of political reform in England during the seventeenth century. According to the standard chronology, the civic humanist tradition spread to the broader
Atlantic world in the course of the eighteenth century, when the political
development of the American colonies and England's deeper cultural engagement with the European continent provided new avenues of intellectual migration and new contexts in which republican ideas could resonate.
In Pocock's own work, for example, the advent of French civic humanist
thought is represented in the person of Montesquieu, and by the publication in 1748 of *The Spirit of the Laws*.[27] Much earlier evidence suggests, however, that patriotic ideals influenced by classical examples had taken root
in France by the last years of the seventeenth century, and that the source
of these ideals lay not in England per se—though fruitful cultural interactions between France and England certainly occurred in this period—
but in France's own confrontation with the prospect of "despotism," and
with the social changes that Louis XIV's absolutist rule had already
introduced.

The Van den Enden affair notwithstanding, few nobles critical of Louis
XIV's use of power would have considered themselves outright republicans. Jean-Pierre Labatut has found, *pace* La Bruyère, that private correspondence and administrative documents from the period often
combined expressions of loyalty to the *patrie* with more traditional expressions of personal fidelity between the king and his servants.[28] More generally, historians in recent years have underscored the many ways in which
Louis XIV's policies and mode of governing appealed to aristocratic
elites.[29] Even the boldest critics of the Sun King's absolutist style remained,
for the most part, convinced monarchists.[30] In any case, classical republi-

27. Pocock acknowledges, for example, that Boulainvilliers belongs to the "republican lineage" (*Machiavellian Moment*, 476), but in his discussion of the eighteenth century, the only
significant French representative of classical republican thinking is Montesquieu, whom he
categorizes with "Machiavelli, Cato, [and] Bolingbroke" (484).

28. Labatut, "Patriotisme et noblesse sous le règne de Louis XIV."

29. My own earlier work reflected and contributed to this historiographical trend, which is
summarized in Smith, *The Culture of Merit*, 8–9, 125.

30. For a particularly skillful discussion of the ways in which Louis XIV's most prominent critics combined loyalty to the basic institutions of the monarchy with zeal to transform many of
those same institutions, see Ellis, *Boulainvilliers and the French Monarchy*.

can language hardly constituted a single idiom, and writers who drew from the ancients for political purposes united around no single ideology. The term "classical republican" at best captures a loosely defined set of inclinations in favor of virtue and patriotic feeling, and a desire to revive certain ancient values. Such inclinations and concerns could appeal to a wide variety of people for an equally wide variety of reasons.

The new appeal of classical republican models of politics and morality around 1700 was nevertheless critically important to the process of reimagining nobility, and the larger process of rethinking the foundations of corporate society, because it coincided with an aristocratic reassessment of nobility's place within a transformed political landscape. The second half of the seventeenth century had tested the nobility's traditional terms of self-definition in many ways.[31] Louis XIV had called on the active military support of his royal vassals, through the feudal levy of the *ban et arrière ban,* for the last time in the history of the French monarchy in 1674 during the Dutch War, and had thereby allowed the already attenuated formal identification between nobility and military service to expire.[32] Even before the installation of the royal court at Versailles, chivalric bravery and gallantry had been largely overtaken by new signs of social excellence—wit, grace, conversational skill—in salons and other alarmingly feminized social gatherings.[33] Under Louis XIV the nobility also saw its claims to social and political preeminence eroded or challenged in a variety of ways. The king and his ministers deliberately sought to recruit men of "talent" and "exactitude" for bureaucratic and other posts, thus subtly altering the definition of merit that royal servants had to recognize.[34] The legal status of nobility became, more than ever, a marketable commodity, and seemingly indiscriminate recruitment into the corps of nobility threatened to undercut the rationale for social hierarchy itself. Even the principle of noble exemption from taxation was directly challenged by "universal" taxes on persons and wealth introduced in 1695 and 1710.[35]

These and other developments ensured that many nobles experienced

31. Jonathan Dewald has discussed the impact of these changes on the noble sense of self in the seventeenth century. See *Aristocratic Experience and the Origins of Modern Culture: France, 1570–1715* (Berkeley, 1993).
32. John Lynn, *Giant of the Grand Siècle: The French Army, 1610–1715* (Cambridge, 1997), 369–71.
33. On conservative reactions to these changes in manners and morals, see Carolyn Lougee, *Le Paradis des Femmes: Salons and Social Stratification in Seventeenth-Century France* (Princeton, 1976).
34. Smith, *The Culture of Merit,* 164–80.
35. Kwass, *Privilege and the Politics of Taxation,* 33–38.

their encounter with "despotism" as a dislocating phenomenon in which the fate of their estate seemed to be directly implicated. One sign of the sense of displacement that Louis XIV's rule created in many minds, and of the flights of imagination that it stimulated, was the appearance in 1713 of the abbé de Saint-Pierre's utopian vision of "perpetual peace" in Europe. The second of five sons from an old noble family, and the former first almoner to the king's sister-in-law Charlotte Elizabeth, the idiosyncratic abbé expressed a desire to make himself "useful to my *patrie*" at the close of the War of the Spanish Succession.[36] Hoping to avoid in the future the kind of violence and social devastation incurred in the course of Louis XIV's recent wars, Saint-Pierre looked for a method to defuse destructive international rivalries. The pacifistic plan that he elaborated involved the creation of a unified European authority that would resolve disputes between sovereign states by means of arbitration rather than armed conflict.

The success of such a project, Saint-Pierre realized, would effectively strip the nobility of the military functions that had long been considered its chief raison d'être. But the abbé expressed confidence that the nobility would adjust to, and ultimately benefit from, the reorganization of the state's priorities. Specifically, nobles from the military would need to recognize that honors, distinctions, and status would now flow toward positions in "justice, police, finance, commerce, the arts and sciences, the only [vocations] that can make a state happy and flourishing." Part of the financial windfall derived from the elimination of warfare could be used to provide pensions for former military officers, and nobles might be permitted to purchase certain "offices of peace," just as they now frequently purchased "offices of war," but the nobility as a whole would need to become integrated into a new regime in which "those who render the greatest services to the state will receive the greatest recompense." With honors accruing only to those "in whom one recognizes the most goodness, justice, ability, and application," the motive force of emulation would be activated "to the benefit of the public," and "the state will be well served." Nobility still had a place in Saint-Pierre's "Republic of Peace," but its new service functions and expansive social definition would have made it virtually unrecognizable to the feudal progenitors of France's largely military early-modern nobility.[37]

In all likelihood, such a radical transformation of the nobility lay be-

36. Charles Irénée Castel de Saint-Pierre, *Projet pour rendre la paix perpétuelle en Europe*, ed. Simone Goyard-Fabre (Paris, 1981), 129.
37. Ibid., 274–75.

yond the imagination of most of Saint-Pierre's contemporaries in the early years of the eighteenth century, but his project for perpetual peace is indicative of the fluid interpretive environment in which many nobles engaged the antique ideals of civic virtue. Troubled by the social fluidity made possible by the crown's fixation on finance, disturbed by the over-concentration of authority in the hands of an often capricious king, and still coming to terms with the centralization of the state's administrative apparatus, politically engaged aristocrats sought simultaneously to correct unhealthy political practices and to articulate a new role for nobility in a reformed French society.[38] Not all aristocratic writers necessarily looked to the ancients for guidance—Saint-Pierre, for one, had little use for the ancients—and among those who did, not all studied ancient mores with a scholar's care or intensity. Nevertheless, the ancient ideal of love for the *patrie* ultimately proved to be the most potent and compelling tool of political and moral criticism available to the nobility in the first half of the eighteenth century. The invocation of the *patrie* highlighted the imbalance of powers and interests characteristic of a distorted absolutism, which was particularly important for those working in the long shadow cast by Louis XIV. Just as significant, the assumption that love of the *patrie* required the active ingredient of virtue also focused attention on the issue of moral leadership *within* the polity, and it thus offered a new rationale for asserting the utility and importance of nobility.

I argue in this chapter that the growing preoccupation with virtue, and with the political and social implications of its presence or absence, gave birth to two powerful impulses of moral reform that projected different futures for the French nobility and for the society of which it formed a part. One of these impulses associated virtue's absence with the degradation of the second estate and its values, and it therefore joined patriotism to the reform, and reconstitution, of the traditional nobility. The other impulse, which emphasized the nobility's moral responsibility for the historical failure of virtue, brought into question honor's continuing relevance to the requirements of a changing society, and it therefore challenged the nobility's viability both as an institution and as an ideal. The first reformist impulse, tending toward the moral and political reconstitution of the second estate, found its earliest expression in the writings of Boulainvilliers and Fénelon, two noble authors whose biting critiques of Louis XIV's regime happened to owe a great debt to the broad civic humanist engagement with the ancients.

38. On the psychic effects of centralization, see Smith, *The Culture of Merit,* 191–95.

## BOULAINVILLIERS, FÉNELON, AND THE RECOVERY OF VIRTUE

As a "sincere" man "who loves his *Patrie*," the proud Norman gentleman Henry de Boulainvilliers, whose important works appeared in print only after his death in 1722, spent the last two decades of his life developing his own distinctive critique of French politics and society.[39] Although he remained loyal to the monarchy and would never have dreamed of proposing a republican form of government for the French, Boulainvilliers was clearly influenced and inspired by the civic humanist mode of argument and historical criticism. This mode of criticism, focused on the centrality of virtue and on the forces tending to support or undermine it, shaped his understanding of nobility, monarchy, and society.

As an associate of the "Burgundy circle" in the first decade of the eighteenth century, Boulainvilliers, like Fénelon and the dukes of Chevreuse, Beauvillier, and Saint-Simon, had high hopes that the duke of Burgundy would eventually ascend to the throne and implement purifying reforms that would correct the abuses of Louis XIV. Those hopes were dashed when Burgundy died in January 1712, but the strongly anti-despotic rhetoric marking the governmental history that Boulainvilliers wrote for the duke between 1709 and 1711 was clearly meant to make an impression on the man whose character and inclinations might decide the future. Recent innovations, Boulainvilliers reported, had had no other purpose than to create "a despotic power more suited to the spirits of the Persians, the Turks, and other oriental peoples." The intendants created by Richelieu, for example, could be considered "oppressors of the *Patrie*" who obeyed no principle of government "other than that of pure despotism." They received valuable assistance in their oppressive work, moreover, from the tax farmers and financiers, those other "instigators of despotism."[40]

Despite his repeated condemnations of modern despotism and his search for institutional correctives, however, one of the principal themes of Boulainvilliers's historical analysis emerges from the story of the nobility's loss of virtue and its gradual alienation from its moral roots. The comte's identification of the Frankish conquest of the Gauls with the establishment of the French nobility, his promotion of the original rights of the Frankish "nation," and his criticism of the usurpations of kings and

---

39. Boulainvilliers, *Histoire de l'ancien gouvernement de la France: avec XIV lettres historiques sur les parlements ou états généraux*, 3 vols. (Amsterdam, 1727), 1: xi. Boulainvilliers had written the manuscript for this history between 1709 and 1711, possibly on the orders of the duc de Bourgogne himself. See Ellis, *Boulainvilliers and the French Monarchy*, 64–65.

40. Boulainvilliers, *Histoire de l'ancien gouvernement*, 1: xxv, xiii–xiv, 168.

their ministers in the later Middle Ages and Renaissance are of course well known.[41] Less appreciated, however, is Boulainvilliers's originality in situating the demise of the French nobility within a narrative frame most often associated with histories of the Roman republic. Underlying Boulainvilliers's specific political claims about the nobility, the Estates-General, and the original constituents of the French nation was a historical analysis of political decadence that fixated on the same problems that had bedeviled the Italian and English civic humanists: corruption and its seeming inevitability. Boulainvilliers merely changed the stage on which the great drama of corruption and loss was played out over time, and the chief actors, or victims, of the piece became the "true" nobles who had formerly enjoyed respect as "the honor and the glory of their *Patrie.*"[42]

Classical republican influences can especially be detected in the history that Boulainvilliers drafted for his young sons around the year 1700, a work that would later be published as *Essays on the Nobility of France* (1732).[43] The original Franks, according to Boulainvilliers, had been a simple people of "unpolished morals [*moeurs*]," but they had guarded their independence and liberty fiercely and courageously.[44] Even after their conquest of Gaul, all Franks of a certain age carried arms in anticipation of new battles to come, and they regarded the right to elect their kings as an important feature of their natural independence. "At the start," Boulainvilliers would later write, "the French were all free and perfectly equal and independent."[45] In most respects, then, the Franks resembled the earliest Romans as they had been described by Livy, or, for that matter, by Saint-Evremond in his *Reflections on the Spirit of the Roman people.*[46] Eventually, however, some

41. André Devyver, for example, portrayed Boulainvilliers as a knee-jerk reactionary and progenitor of modern "racism." More sympathetic scholars, who have also focused on the "national" dimension of his historical arguments, have emphasized his contributions as a constitutional theorist. See Devyver, *Le sang épuré;* 353–91, 432–37. Among the "constitutional" historians, see esp. François Furet and Mona Ozouf, "Deux légitimations historiques de la société française au XVIIIe siècle: Mably et Boulainvilliers," *AESC* 34 (1979): 438–50; Franklin Ford, *Robe and Sword: The Regrouping of the French Aristocracy after Louis XIV* (Cambridge, Mass., 1953), 222–45; and Keohane, *Philosophy and the State,* 346–50.

42. Boulainvilliers, *Essais sur la Noblesse de France, contenans une dissertation sur son origine & abaissement* (Amsterdam, 1732), v.

43. Although the *Essais* was not published until 1732, the "Dissertation sur la noblesse ancienne" on which it was based was actually written in 1700, when Boulainvilliers began to prepare for the education of his two sons. See Ellis, *Boulainvilliers and the French Monarchy,* 24–27.

44. Boulainvilliers, *Essais,* 18. For the morals and customs of the Franks: 17–27.

45. Boulainvilliers, *Histoire de l'ancien gouvernement,* 1: 26.

46. Saint-Evremond had written that the earliest Romans observed a "severe virtue" incompatible with "politeness and charm," a virtue that took patriotic disinterest "almost to excess." See *Réflexions,* 32.

nobles began to usurp special privileges and powers denied to others, and the appearance of unjust hierarchical divisions within the nobility ultimately enabled kings to encroach on the rights of the Frankish nation as a whole.[47]

The later chapters of Boulainvilliers's *Essays on the Nobility of France* certainly include accounts of the many wrongs and misdeeds committed against the nobility—Louis XI appears as one of the great villains—but the nobles' seduction by the attractions of material splendor and the powerful lure of the king's court form an equally important part of the larger story. Boulainvilliers observed that the introduction of luxury, magnificence, and Italian customs to the French court under Francis I "softened all hearts." Nobles "quit the countryside" and henceforth thought only of "advancing in positions at court and in the army." "The road to fortune," he wrote, "no longer conformed to the old ways. Until then one needed an essential merit grounded in high birth; afterwards it became necessary to add *pleasantness,* next *accommodation,* which soon degenerated into *baseness* and the total *subjugation of self.*" The desire for "present fortune" had led nobles to embrace "the phantoms of the Court and of favor," and to forget their own natural dignity.[48] A virtue anchored in family glory and self-awareness had been replaced by a shameful thirst for ephemeral goods.

In a rich passage that anticipated by half a century the style and some of the content of Rousseau's *Discourse on the Sciences and the Arts,* Boulainvilliers went beyond the standard expression of scorn for luxury to lament the subtle moral sacrifices that accompanied the loss of "ignorance" and "simplicity" and the gains represented by the "sciences." Do the sciences offer "real" advantages or only imaginary satisfactions, Boulainvilliers asked? "The license of the mind, the abuse of knowledge, false opinions, ambition, luxury, the unsettling of conditions, are these not greater evils than simplicity and ignorance?" The sciences served only to excite the "passions," and in particular the destructive passion of ambition, which, with the help of the sciences themselves, makes it possible for individuals to fashion "a mask of virtue" to hide their iniquity and injustice. Thanks to the "sciences" and the "politeness that they nurture," all now hoped to rise above their natural station, and to create personal and familial fortunes whose very edifice would be founded on the "disguise" afforded by the sciences.[49]

---

47. On Boulainvilliers's objections to the pretensions of the dukes and peers, and his commitment to equality within the nobility, see Ellis, *Boulainvilliers and the French Monarchy,* 51–56.
48. Boulainvilliers, *Essais,* 221–22, 227.
49. Ibid., 297–98.

Boulainvilliers expressed hope, at the end of his *Essays,* that future princes would recognize the "true and incommunicable nobility" of the families whose status predated the rise of the luxury-laden impostors. But pessimism pervades Boulainvilliers's reflections on the history of the nobility, and much of that pessimism can be attributed to his close study of the ancients. "We are meeting the same destiny as that of ancient Rome, where all the distinguished families were either extinguished or relegated to obscurity when the form of the government was changed."[50] At the height of the Republic, he wrote, Rome enjoyed a perfectly balanced social structure that granted distinctions and special status to noble families, but simultaneously enabled "each Roman [to regard] himself, with respect to other peoples, as the master of all Nations." (Later Boulainvilliers would say that, among the Franks, "each regarded himself as the master of the country and of all subject peoples.")[51] The title of "citizen" had been respectable even in the eyes of the kings of Rome. Unfortunately, "it would not remain brilliant for long, because it was granted too easily to cities and to whole provinces." Eventually the emperors abolished the distinction between citizens and noncitizens "and gave everyone the rights of the city."

In so doing, Boulainvilliers asserted, the emperors introduced "a kind of equality that undermined the nobility," and soon the empire itself became the prey of rapacious army officers, most of them "foreigners and barbarians." The city of Rome, meanwhile, focused on distributing bread and entertainments to swelling crowds now "vested with the Roman name." Perhaps intentionally, Boulainvilliers blurred the line that separated the fate of the Roman nobility from the fate of the Roman citizenry as a whole, but his general message was clear: easy access to higher status ensured the loss of civic spirit and the debasement of society's most distinguished citizens. Comparison of the cases of Rome and France showed that "we must recognize that such a destiny is common to all states of long duration. The world is a play-toy for the cycle of change. Why should the Nobility, with its advantages and possessions, be exempt from the common rule?"[52]

Boulainvilliers's desperate attempt to counter corruption and despotism by resuscitating the rights of the original Frankish "nation," and by asserting the necessarily ancestral origins of "true" nobility, recalled efforts among the English parliamentary gentry, both before and after the Puritan Revolution, to ground civic life in an immovable body of "custom."[53]

50. Ibid., 300, 227.
51. Ibid., 4, 22.
52. Ibid., 4–5, 227–28.
53. Pocock, *Machiavellian Moment,* esp. 340–41. For a full discussion of the way in which re-

Both Boulainvilliers and his English counterparts sought a new rationale for the defense of "liberty," and, like other writers wrestling with the civic humanist challenge of perpetuating a healthy polity through the vicissitudes of historical time, they sought an antidote to corruption and the abuse of power in the incontestable moral claim of precedent. In the civic consciousness of Boulainvilliers, constitutional safeguards took the place of republican love of the laws, and an authentic and pure nobility stood in for a generally virtuous citizenry in the ongoing battle against civic decrepitude and natural tendencies toward despotism. His quest to revive the spirit of the old nobility, and thereby to reestablish love of the *patrie*, continued to the end of his life, even though the death of the duke of Burgundy and the later disappointments of the Regency probably convinced him that the virtuous and pre-despotic model of government that he admired had been "irretrievably lost."[54]

The works of Boulainvilliers were often republished and read widely among what one scholar calls the broad "cultivated elite" in the eighteenth century, and his historical arguments would be a touchstone of political debate down to the Revolution.[55] But surely the most influential figure involved in the "return to the antique" at the dawn of the eighteenth century was François de La Mothe-Fénelon, author of "the most read literary work of eighteenth-century France," the *Adventures of Telemachus*.[56] Fénelon, the pious archbishop of Cambrai, was appointed tutor to the duke of Burgundy in 1689, and from that point until the duke's death in 1712, Fénelon worked to shape the morals and governing principles of a prince whom he expected one day to be king. The close relationship between the tutor and the pupil continued even after Louis XIV dismissed Fénelon from his post and exiled him from court in 1697 after the archbishop's controversial defense of the Quietist piety of Madame Guyon.[57]

Like Boulainvilliers, Fénelon remained a loyal monarchist despite his displeasure with Louis XIV's excesses, but his criticisms of despotism

liance on "custom" constituted a distinctive "mode of civic consciousness" in seventeenth-century England, see 333–400.

54. As Ellis has noted, *Boulainvilliers and the French Monarchy*, 206. In 1719, Boulainvilliers wrote a "Discours sur la noblesse" that repeated and refined many of the themes of the "Dissertation" of 1700. See Ellis, 199–206.

55. See Olivier Tholozan, *Henri de Boulainvilliers: L'anti-absolutisme aristocratique légitimé par l'histoire* (Aix-en-Provence, 1999), 25–26.

56. The estimate is that of Patrick Riley, ed. and trans., *Telemachus, Son of Ulysses* (Cambridge, 1994), xvi. The "return to the antique" is noted by Alfred Lombard, *Fénelon et le retour à l'antique au XVIIIe siècle* (Neuchâtel, 1954).

57. Elie Carcassonne, *Fénelon: L'homme et l'oeuvre* (Paris, 1946), 75, 93–98.

were based on an idealized vision of ancient virtue, and the allegorical tale
he composed as a guide for the grandson of the Sun King decisively shaped
the eighteenth century's cult of antiquity.[58] Montesquieu would refer
to *Telemachus* as the "divine work" of the century; Vauvenargues rated
Fénelon, with Newton and Pascal, as one of the greatest geniuses that the
seventeenth century had produced; Rousseau, according to Bernardin de
Saint-Pierre, "preferred Fénelon to all others."[59] Even as late as the 1780s,
the spectacularly successful *Telemachus*, which was published in 48 editions
in French and translated into virtually every European language between
its first publication in 1699 and 1789, went through nine new French editions (Figure 1).[60]

Fénelon's work tells the story of Telemachus, the loyal son of Ulysses,
who, while under the guidance of Mentor (a disguised Minerva), travels in
search of his wandering father in the years after the Trojan War. In fact,
*Telemachus* concerns less the search for Ulysses than the lessons on good
kingship that Mentor provides the young prince and future ruler in the
course of their travels and adventures. The work was widely recognized to
be an implicit critique of Louis XIV, whose "science of governing," according to Fénelon, was based on little more than brazen selfishness and
the systematic "banishment of virtue."[61] "Love of the people, of the public
good, [and] of the general interest of society is the immutable and universal law of sovereigns," Fénelon would write in his "Fundamental principles of a wise government," and his repudiation of self-interest led him to
characterize political virtue as a form of "pure love" similar to that binding recipients of grace to the Christian God. That kind of love, devoid of
all personal interest, he later explained, had guided "the wise Mentor" as
he sought "the happiness of the *patrie*" in a well-ordered society.[62]

58. Fénelon is one of the central figures, for example, in Renato Galliani's provocative study
of Rousseau's intellectual roots, *Rousseau, le luxe, et l'idéologie nobiliaire: Etude socio-historique* (Oxford, 1989), 141–49, 221–24, and passim. On Fénelon as champion of the aristocracy see
Gilbert Gidel, *La politique de Fénelon* (Paris, 1906; repr., Geneva, 1971), ix–x, 72–75; Ford,
*Robe and Sword*, 226–27; Ellis, *Boulainvilliers and the French Monarchy*, 60–61.
59. Albert Chérel, *Fénelon au XVIIIe siècle en France (1715–1820): Son prestige, son influence*
(Paris, 1917), 326–27, 396.
60. The numbers are based on the holdings of the Bibliothèque Nationale de France, as reflected in the *Catalogue général des livres imprimés de la Bibliothèque Nationale*, vol. 50 (Paris,
1912), 734–43.
61. Fénelon, *Ecrits et Lettres Politiques*, ed. Charles Urbain (Paris, 1920), 144. Fénelon made
this accusation in an anonymous letter sent to Louis XIV himself in 1694. On the close similarities between the letter of 1694 and the content of *Telemachus*, see Gidel, *La politique de
Fénelon*, 13–50.
62. Fénelon, *Ecrits*, 92, 96.

FIGURE 1. "Telemachus Explaining the Laws of Minos" (1782). This engraving of the wise Telemachus comes from one of nine French editions of Fénelon's work published in the 1780s. Bibliothèque Nationale de France

In response to the horrors of "despotism," Fénelon proposed not the establishment of a republic—he feared "excessive liberty" and the "despotism of the multitude" as much as the tyranny of a single sovereign—but the moral reform of the despotic ruler.[63] A belief in the power of moral instruction lay behind Fénelon's composition of *Telemachus*, and his faith in the possibility of personal redemption suffused the content of the story. Fénelon's desire to shape the thinking of a just king meant that Mentor's lessons inevitably revolved around the opposition between virtue and love of self, a moral defect that always leads to vanity, self-indulgence, and all the destructive delusions to which selfishness inevitably gives rise. The wise Mentor gradually educates the wicked king Idomeneus, for example, so that Idomeneus, who had been expelled from the isle of Crete, ultimately sees the error of his ways and governs his new kingdom of Salente strictly out of a virtuous concern for the general welfare. Telemachus, on seeing the many positive changes wrought by the reformed king, recognizes the meaning of "true glory."[64]

Fénelon's philosophical understanding of virtue, which he elaborated in a noted essay on "Pure Love," involved him in a long and increasingly populated discussion about the passions, the nature of human self-interest, and the possibility of selflessness. This discussion ranged from the pessimistic accounts of human nature by La Rochefoucauld and Pascal in the middle of the seventeenth century on to Mandeville, the philosophes, and the effort after about 1740 to rehabilitate the image of human society by naturalizing inclinations to sociable "virtue."[65] But perhaps Fénelon's most important contribution to the eighteenth century's understanding of patriotic virtue was his argument that both despotism and unregulated social mobility were known by the same symptoms: falsity and illusion. Both political and social order thus found their antithesis in luxury—a phenomenon based essentially on deception and disguise. "As arbitrary power is the bane of kings," Mentor declared, "so luxury poisons a whole nation."

63. In a text titled "Principes fondamentaux d'un sage gouvernement," Fénelon wrote that "a people ruined by an excessive liberty is the most insupportable of all tyrants." See ibid., 93.
64. Fénelon, *Telemachus*, 298.
65. See Linton's discussion of the efforts by Shaftesbury, Hume, Diderot, and others to elevate "sociability" to the status of natural virtue. *The Politics of Virtue*, 51–128. See also Gordon, *Citizens without Sovereignty*, 129–76. For discussion of the seventeenth-century roots of this strain of moralist thought, see Keohane, *Philosophy and the State*, 262–311, and E. G. Hundert, *The Enlightenment's Fable: Bernard Mandeville and the Discovery of Society* (Cambridge, 1994), 16–61. Mark Hulliung has persuasively argued that the unresolved debate concerning human nature and the possibilities of selflessness defined the entire Enlightenment project. See *The Autocritique of Enlightenment: Rousseau and the Philosophes* (Cambridge, Mass., 1994).

The contagion wastes no time in extending "to the very dregs of the people."

> The near relations of the king want to imitate his magnificence; the gran-
> dees, that of the royal family; those in the middle ranks of life, that of the
> grandees; for who is it that keeps within his own sphere? And those in low
> life will affect to pass for people of fashion. Thus all live above their rank and
> income, some from vanity and ostentation, and to display their wealth; oth-
> ers from a false shame, and to hide their poverty. . . . A whole nation goes to
> wreck; all ranks are confounded . . . wealth is the sole pursuit, and poverty is
> accounted scandalous.[66]

In a society overcome by this "almost incurable" disease, even "though
you should instruct mankind, gain victories, save your country, and sacrifice your all for its honor and interest, yet you will be despised, if your talents are not set off by luxury."[67] Morally corrosive luxury guaranteed the
social ascendancy of men whose only merits were wealth and the pomp and
deception that it enabled. Such men promoted "politeness" and the magnificence of buildings, furnishings, and retinues, but they showed their
true worth when the despot faced fiscal crisis.[68] "How can you expect venal souls who have fattened themselves on the blood of the people to ruin
themselves for [the people's] benefit? That would be expecting interested
men to act without interest."[69] A political system that encouraged the blind
pursuit of selfish interests would inevitably fall victim to the moral torpor
on which it thrived.

In Fénelon's eyes, the return of virtue necessarily implied the restabi-
lization of the social order. Mentor informed Idomeneus, for example,
that rank should be "regulated by birth," with the first rank always assigned
to "those of the most noble and illustrious birth" and marked off by distinctive, though inexpensive, dress.[70] This theme of social conservatism
reappeared in Fénelon's later writings. In 1711, for example, when the
duke of Burgundy became the heir to the French throne for one brief and
hopeful year, Fénelon and his collaborators drafted plans for the imminent
installation of a new government. Many of his fragmentary proposals

---

66. Fénelon, *Telemachus*, 297.
67. Ibid., 297–98.
68. Mentor notes that luxury also goes by the names of "good taste, the perfection of the
arts, and the politeness of a nation." See ibid., 297. "Magnificence" is condemned, 152–53.
69. Fénelon, *Ecrits*, 176.
70. Fénelon, *Telemachus*, 162.

showed a distaste for the parvenus who had acquired their fortunes under Louis XIV, and they aimed to put back in their place the flatterers and *anoblis* who had flourished in recent times. "No more financiers," he bluntly declared in a brief essay on taxation and the interior administration of the realm.[71] "Do not allow all courtiers to continue in military service," and there should be "no venality" in the army under any pretext.[72] Ennoblements should be prohibited, except in the case of "signal services rendered to the state," and the state should undertake new "investigations of the nobility" for the purpose of weeding out usurpers and undeserving newcomers. A general registry of noble families would be compiled in Paris, and "no branch will be recognized [as noble] without registration."[73] Finally, as part of a wider effort to eliminate ostentatious display and unhealthy spending, Fénelon called for "sumptuary laws like those of the Romans."[74] Had Fénelon's wishes come true, the reformed France constructed after the death of Louis XIV would have resembled in all its essentials the Salente reorganized by Mentor and Idomeneus.[75]

For Fénelon, then, the defeat of despotism and the recovery of long-lost political virtue in France would necessarily return the true nobility to its rightful position of preeminence in the social and political order. Because of the nature of virtue's opposites—selfish ambition, the deceptive masking of frivolity and vice, the blind pursuit of wealth, egoism, and scorn for the interests of the *patrie*—Fénelon defined virtue's recovery as the removal of "artful, mercenary men", and the restoration of men who hated "all falsehood and disguise."[76] Only men with simple and authentic moral qualities and well-established public identities could offer candid counsel to the king and assist him in presiding over a country defined by "simplicity of manners," a form of prosperity that did not entail gross inequalities of wealth, and a body of citizens whose "love of equitable laws" made them prepared "to fight and defend these lands cultivated by their own hands."[77] For Fénelon, the possessors of what the comte de Boulainvilliers had called "true and incommunicable nobility" not only ranked among the most ag-

---

71. Fénelon, *Ecrits*, 103.
72. Ibid., 98.
73. Ibid., 116, 118.
74. Ibid., 101.
75. Mentor, too, introduced sumptuary laws and distinctive dress for the "seven different ranks of freemen" in Salente. "Thus will every individual be distinguished according to his degree without expense, and all those arts that are subservient to pomp and luxury be banished from Salente." See *Telemachus*, 163.
76. Ibid., 158, 186.
77. Ibid., 295–96.

grieved victims of "despotism," but they, along with the king himself, also stood out as the most likely vehicle for the restoration of virtue in French political life.

Thanks largely to Fénelon, noble readers and political observers in the first half of the eighteenth century came to recognize ancient patriotism as a moral model appropriate for use by all modern opponents of the twin afflictions of despotism and luxury. *Télémaque* also established, or reaffirmed, a powerful association between the aristocracy and the moral high ground, an association that fit naturally with the traditional self-image of an old nobility that had always taken pride in its courage, fidelity, and commitment to honor. Mentor's final injunction to Telemachus to teach his people the ways of virtue and to "reform their morals" inspired the noble as well as the non-noble political reformers of the eighteenth century, vast numbers of whom sought to implant in the hearts of their fellow citizens the patriotic ardor characteristic of the ancient republics. In the waning years of Louis XIV's reign, the French engagement with ancient history and with the civic humanist celebration of virtue, patriotism, and moral independence eventually led some French aristocrats to imagine themselves to be the moral heirs of the Roman and Greek patriots of ancient lore.

The new attention to virtue, however, also coincided with, and helped to fuel, a wide reassessment of the nobility's code of honor, a reassessment that pointedly called into question any association between the nobility and the moral high ground of contemporary French society. On the one hand, the association of selfless qualities with the nobility made a great deal of sense, given the nobility's traditional scorn for profit-seeking and its proud record of generous sacrifice on the field of battle. But on the other hand, utter selflessness hardly seemed the chief characteristic of a class of people whose genealogical pride and disproportionate power and wealth distinguished it from other classes and promoted the elevation of familial honor above all other concerns. Although he supported established hierarchies, and carried himself with "the proud dignity of a *gentilhomme*," even Fénelon emphasized the importance of preventing conspicuous inequalities of wealth in a society, and he expressed nothing but contempt for the vain pursuit of personal glory.[78] The celebration of antique virtue in the

78. The description of Fénelon is that of Urbain, in Fénelon, *Ecrits*, 17. In *Telemachus*, Mentor laments that "it is the pride and luxury of certain individuals that involve so many of their fellow creatures in all the horrors of poverty." The rule must be that "the nobles will not be able to aggrandize themselves at the expense of the poor" (ibid., 168–69.) Later, Mentor insisted that true glory came only from the promotion of virtue, and that gratification of the "passions" and of "vanity" constituted a mere "false glory" (324).

early eighteenth century, especially the Fénelonian version, incorporated a critique of self-satisfaction, ostentation, and pride in rank that moralists elaborated with increasing self-consciousness in the wake of Fénelon's popular success. Their exploration of the tensions between virtue and honor shows that, even though it may have justified the reassertion of the traditional social order, the idealization of the ancients also subtly called into question the moral fitness of the French nobility. Eventually, the resuscitation of ancient virtue would also open to criticism the nobility's moral and social relationship to the larger society of which it formed a part.

## DEBATING ARISTOCRATIC MORALS, 1710S–1740S

Interest in the ancients, the revival of an aristocratic politics, and a concern for moral reform could not have converged in a culturally creative compound in the early eighteenth century if a critical mass of moralists, political observers, and interested readers had not already taken shape in the wake of Louis XIV's death.[79] But various personal and intellectual networks, many of them formed around a common admiration for the work of Fénelon, assured the continuation of the moral and political discussion that had been launched in earnest by the archbishop of Cambrai. Madame de Lambert, for example, was an ardent admirer of Fénelon, and her salon, "the most important salon in Paris" until the mid-1730s, attracted many of the eighteenth century's most influential commentators on nobility.[80] Her guest list included Montesquieu, Fontenelle, the marquis d'Argenson, the parlementary président Charles-Jean-François Hénault, and the marquis de Lassay, whose remarks on noble honor, republished in an essay of 1754, would later provoke the abbé Coyer to launch a controversial attack on the second estate, one that faulted the nobility for its lack of patriotic virtues.[81]

Other chains of intellectual contact and reciprocal influences can also be traced back to Fénelon. For example, the Scottish Chevalier Andrew Michael Ramsay, who had befriended Fénelon during a visit to Cambrai in 1709, became his first biographer in 1723, and his hagiographic work helped turn Fénelon into a kind of mythic hero.[82] Ramsay, too, had strong

79. The following discussion of Paris's intellectual milieu draws heavily from Shackleton, *Montesquieu*, 8–13, 55–67.
80. This according to the editor of Madame de Lambert, *Oeuvres*, ed. Robert Granderoute (Paris, 1990), 18.
81. See chapter 3.
82. A. M. Ramsay, *Histoire de la vie de M. François de Salignac de la Motte-Fénelon* (Paris, 1723). For details of Ramsay's own life see Chérel, *Fénelon au XVIIIe siècle*, 31–75.

interests in ancient history, and his own Telemachus-inspired edition of
*The Travels of Cyrus,* "famous for the applause it has received," according to
the *Journal de Trévoux,* ran through ten editions by 1789.[83] Among those
influenced by Ramsay's work was the editor of Boulainvilliers's *Essays on
Nobility,* J.-F. de Tabary, whose heavily annotated text cited Ramsay in support of Boulainvilliers's fatalistic remarks about the introduction of luxury
and the inevitable fall of great empires.[84] Another admirer of Fénelon,
Nicolas Fréret, collaborated with Ramsay on later editions of both *Telemachus* and Ramsay's life of Fénelon. But Fréret played the intermediary in
more ways than one. A gifted historian of the ancient world, he had been
the pupil of Charles Rollin, the former rector of the University of Paris,
one of the most accomplished classicists of the eighteenth century, and
one of the chief popularizers of Spartan educational ideals after the publication of his influential *Treatise on Education* in 1726–28. Moreover,
Rollin's pupil Fréret was the friend of both Boulainvilliers and Montesquieu, whom he had probably introduced to one another during the latter's first sojourn in Paris between 1709 and 1713.

The point is not that all of these luminaries became uncritical disciples
of Fénelon, or that they served as a direct conduit between Fénelonian
ideas and the larger culture of the developing Enlightenment. Rather,
their presence in many of the same Parisian circles and their similar interests in moral and political reform attest to the creation of a literary and
cultural environment in which comparison of ancient and modern values,
the weighing of the meanings of virtue, and contemplation of the connections between morals, on the one hand, and the structure of political
constitutions, on the other hand, had become ongoing concerns. For noble writers and intellectuals in particular, these concerns were undoubtedly sustained through conversations at Lambert's salon and, later,
through the vehicle of the abbé Alary's Club de l'Entresol, which was dis-
banded by the suspicious chief minister Fleury in 1731. Recent work has
shown that this highly aristocratic group included many of the habitués of
Lambert's salon as well as other men of political prominence, including
for a short time the exiled English Tory viscount Bolingbroke, an admirer
of the Romans who styled himself a new Fabricius and whose writings on
patriotism exercised a wide influence on French thinkers of the 1730s–
1750s.[85]

83. For the review, written about a later edition, see *JT,* May 1731, 755–73, esp. 755.

84. "Valor, conquest, luxury, anarchy: there, says [Ramsay], you have the fatal circle and the
different periods in the life of almost all states." See Boulainvilliers, *Essais sur la Noblesse de
France,* 211, n. 224.

85. On the high aristocratic character of the Club de l'Entresol, and on Bolingbroke's early

Whatever the precise relationship between intellectual creativity and new modes of sociability, the period from the 1710s to the 1740s produced many literary, political, and pedagogical works that explored, either directly or indirectly, the prospects for the nobility's moral rehabilitation and for wider patriotic reform in France. These efforts tended to focus on the status of noble honor in the modern world, and, often reflecting the influence of Fénelon, they expressed an emerging consensus that honor should either be replaced by virtue in the moral imagination of the nobility or be redefined in light of virtue's more demanding civic requirements. One of the most compelling statements of the nobility's need for moral readjustment came from the pen of the *roturier* Charles Rollin, whose admiration for the classical republics came close to incorporating elements of republicanism itself (Figure 2). Although he had been dismissed from his post as university rector in 1712 for his avowed Jansenism, Rollin actually began work on his *Treatise on Education* at the request of the university, which set out to reform and standardize its teaching methods in the more relaxed atmosphere of the Regency in 1719.[86] The *Treatise* influenced French pedagogical thought for more than a century, and it also helped to establish the widely held assumption in eighteenth-century France that the ancients far surpassed the moderns in their methods of civic instruction.

Rollin believed that "virtue alone puts men in a position to fill public offices. . . . It is virtue that gives [a man] the taste for true and solid glory, which inspires in him love of the *patrie* and the desire to serve it well, which teaches him always to prefer the public good to private good." Only virtue, he continued, "makes a man disinterested . . . and raises him above flattery, reproach, threats, and misfortunes."[87] A learned historian who published seminal works on both the Greeks and the Romans, Rollin believed, with Fénelon, that through systematic use of proper "examples from antiquity," instructors could counter the "love of wealth and pleasures" that

presence, see Childs, *A Political Academy*, 8–10, 87–93. On the enthusiastic reception of Bolingbroke during his two separate exiles in France, and on his posturing as Fabricius, see the introductory remarks of Bernard Cottret in *Bolingbroke's Political Writings: The Conservative Enlightenment*, ed. Cottret (Houndmills, 1997), 11–12, 30.

86. Louis Henri Ferté, *Rollin: Sa vie, ses oeuvres, et l'université de son temps* (Paris, 1902), 66–67. Rollin even served a second brief stint as rector of the university in 1720. On Rollin's engagement with Jansenism, see Grell, *Le dix-huitième siècle*, 10–16.

87. Charles Rollin, *Traité des Etudes. De la manière d'Enseigner et d'Etudier les Belles Lettres, par rapport à l'esprit et au coeur*, 4 vols. (Paris, 1805), 1: 121. On Rollin's admiration for Sparta and his influence on later advocates of Spartan values, such as Rousseau, see Michel Legagneux, "Rollin et le 'Mirage Spartiate' de l'Education Publique," in *Recherches nouvelles sur quelques écrivains des lumières*, ed. Jacques Proust (Geneva, 1972), 111–63.

A cet air vif et doux, à ce sage maintien, Mais croi-moi, cher Lecteur: médite son Ouvrage,
Sans peine de Rollin on reconnoit l'image. Pour connoitre son cœur, et pour former le tien.

FIGURE 2. Charles Rollin. Rector of the University of Paris, prolific classicist, and one of the chief historians of Greece in eighteenth-century France, Rollin influenced readers especially through the *Traité des Etudes,* in which he advanced an educational model based on the Spartan premise that "children belong more to the Republic than to their parents." Bibliothèque Nationale de France

had become the "dominant taste" of the century. They would thereby "rectify and regulate [students'] hearts by principles of honor and probity, and make them into good citizens."[88]

For Rollin, however, the imperative to instill virtue and to form good citizens implied that education should take place not in the privacy of the home but in public institutions, where all citizens would be sure to receive the imprint of a disinterested and public-spirited morality. The ancients' "capital maxim," he asserted, was that "children belong more to the republic than to their parents," since only the state can properly inspire in them "love of the *patrie*, respect for the laws of the country, and a taste for the principles and maxims of the state in which they live." Lycurgus had known that laws were never sufficient to regulate behavior, and that the mores of a society had to be "imprinted on the morals of citizens" so that the conscience would become an "ever-present legislator" in the minds of men. The Spartans had therefore arranged that "everything inspired [in the young] the love of virtue and the hatred of vice," and Sparta's robust military, and its long-enduring greatness, showed "how important it is for the state to ensure that the young are raised in a manner guaranteed to inspire love of the laws of the *patrie*."[89]

In Sparta, an instinctive respect for one's fellow citizens and the impulse to celebrate virtue wherever it appeared went hand in hand with love of the *patrie*. Lycurgus had therefore taken pains "to banish every sort of inequality" between citizens. Inequalities of wealth and landholdings were not permitted, and even furniture and movable property were shared so as to prevent the development of possessiveness and self-love. Just as important, the Spartans agreed never to grant "preeminence and honors except to virtue and merit."[90] In other words, love of the *patrie* and its laws, which was considered the basis of Sparta's civic health and the guarantee of its survival, rested on a prior foundation of moral and material equality between citizens, an equality that ensured that universal commitment to autonomy, courage, and self-sacrifice which civic humanists from Machiavelli to Boulainvilliers had also seen as the chief civic characteristic of republican Rome.

Acutely aware of the value that the Spartans had placed on equality, Rollin paid particular attention to the prejudices of the nobility in his discussion of the moral instruction imparted to students. Like other moralists of the time, he criticized the shameful self-love captured in the custom

88. Rollin, *Traité des Etudes*, 1: 107.
89. Ibid., 3: 353–55, 368.
90. Ibid., 1: 346–47.

of the duel, and he pointed out that neither victories nor reputation nor "nobility of extraction" constituted "solid glory and true grandeur."[91] But Rollin went further than other champions of virtue by proposing to correct, through the normative lessons administered in the public schools, the prideful habits and assumptions of the typical noble student. "He talks about himself often, always with pride and self-satisfaction. At every opportunity he boasts about the nobility of his family, the dignities of his relatives, their wealth, the magnificence of their carriages, their furnishings, their dinners; he has only scorn for everyone else."[92] The young noble's assumption of his personal superiority presented an obstacle to virtue that had to be overcome through conscious effort.

In "public" schools, fortunately, the intellectual merits of all students, of whatever background, could be forged through competitive fires that touched everyone equally. With praise and rewards, instructors could motivate students by exploiting their innate "love of glory," and all would strive to excel because of the "shame of ceding to one's equals." A "noble emulation" would help to eliminate "disrespect, envy, [and] pride" and lead all students toward "great virtues and difficult challenges."[93] According to Rollin, however, "public lessons" alone would not suffice to expunge dangerous self-love. The principal of each *collège* would also have "private conversations" with each student on a regular basis. In private dialogue, where the students "can open themselves to [the principal], and speak with liberty," he would be able to teach the students "to know themselves, not to become angry when their faults are pointed out, to discover them themselves, admit them honestly, and work on correcting them." The prideful student would be made to see the "deformity" of his attitudes, as well as the justice of the remedies proposed: "No longer to speak of himself, nor of his relatives, nor of their wealth and dignities; never to place himself above others in his own mind; never to have scorn for anyone; to speak well of his companions."[94]

In time, all students would recognize that nobility of extraction paled in importance to "nobility of sentiments," which one expressed by "preferring the public good to everything, [and] sacrificing for its benefit one's

---

91. Ibid., 3: 68. Rollin observed, "among neither the Greeks nor the Romans, those conquerors of so many peoples, who were certainly good judges of the point of honor, and who knew of what true glory consists, was there ever, throughout the centuries, any example of a duel between individuals" (1: 136–37).

92. Ibid., 4: 463.

93. Ibid., 3: 366.

94. Ibid., 4: 465.

property, one's tranquility, one's life, even one's reputation if necessary. This is what makes a man great, and truly worthy of esteem." Underlining the social implications of his elevation of "sentiments" over extraction, Rollin cited an episode of French heroism from the Hundred Years' War that would come to acquire mythological status in the course of the eighteenth century. "Can we admire enough the rare generosity that inspired love of the *patrie* and a view of the common good among the bourgeois of Calais?" After a long siege, the city had fallen to the English in 1347, and Edward III had demanded the sacrifice of six of its notable residents. "When the city assembled [to discuss the demand], one of the principal bourgeois, Eustache de Saint Pierre, rose to speak. He spoke with a courage and firmness that would have done honor to those ancient Roman citizens in the time of the republic, and he offered to be the first victim in order to spare the rest of the people." Five other citizens quickly volunteered, and they bravely offered themselves to the English, secure in the knowledge that their sacrifice would save the city from further destruction. Only the compassionate intervention of the English queen saved them from certain death.[95] For Rollin, as for the many future admirers of the bourgeois of Calais, the patriotism of these common citizens proved that superior virtue had no necessary correlation to superior rank.

Rollin came from a common background, but his critique of noble morals certainly reflected no hostility toward the aristocracy per se. Like Fénelon and Boulainvilliers, he railed against luxury and the social instability and corruption that followed in its train, and his dismissal of the traditional point of honor was intended not to offend the established nobility but rather to define the higher moral standard toward which nobles, especially, should aspire.[96] Elsewhere he noted that the whole population need not absorb the "sentiments" and "maxims" of the ancients. Even if only "a small number" profited from the effects of careful moral instruction, "this small number would undoubtedly be very useful to the Republic."[97] Rollin wished only to ensure that "the homage that one renders to the nobility is a true homage." It must be "voluntary, and from the heart. Because the moment one claims to demand [respect] as a kind of debt, or tries to extract it by force, one loses whatever right one had to it, and it changes into hatred and scorn." The noble desirous of the esteem of other citizens must base his reputation, then, not on birth or "the elevation of

95. Ibid., 3: 98, 103–4.
96. For the argument against luxury, see ibid., 3: 46–58.
97. Ibid., 1: 139–40.

his rank," but on that "nobility of sentiments" that expressed itself in virtue, love of the *patrie,* and true selflessness.[98]

Despite its considerable heft, Rollin's *Treatise on Education* proved to be so popular with readers that production of the second edition began even before the final volume of the first edition had been released in 1728.[99] The work went through eight full or partial editions in the twenty years after its initial release, and Rollin acquired such esteem, as an educator and as an ancient historian, that by 1780 the abbé Lucet could justify publishing a collection of Rollin's aphorisms.[100] Rollin's influence can be seen in the works of lesser figures who wrote about education or moral reform, or who became otherwise engaged in the eighteenth-century effort to revive the ancients' civic values. One can imagine, for example, that Charles Dutot had in mind Rollin's discussion of the bourgeois of Calais when he insisted, in his *Political Reflections on Finance and Commerce* (1738), that "Bourgeois Heroes" and "Military Merchants" also deserved respect for their faithful attachment to the *patrie.* They, after all, provided more useful services to the state than did the nobility, "a large portion of which remains idle in its chateaus."[101] Similarly, authors of educational treatises—a surprising number of them nobles or preceptors working on behalf of nobles—repeated Rollin's basic precept that "a citizen's life belongs more to the *Patrie* than to himself."[102]

Rollin depicted civic virtue as a moral challenge to the nobility's traditional attachment to honor, but not every admirer of the ancients saw the relationship between virtue and honor in opposing terms. A prime example of the early eighteenth-century effort to reconcile the two qualities is found in the work of the moralist Vauvenargues (d. 1747), a Provençal no-

98. Ibid., 3: 75.
99. Ferté, *Rollin,* 228.
100. Abbé [Jean-Claude] Lucet, *Pensées recueillies de l'Histoire Ancienne et du Traité des Etudes de M. Rollin* (Paris, 1780). Full editions of the *Traité des Etudes* were released in 1726–28, 1728–31, 1730–31, 1736, 1741, and 1748. A "supplement" was published in 1734, and a condensed two-volume version appeared in 1740. The work was also translated into English, Italian, and Russian. Rollin's influence also extended beyond Europe. See William Gribbin, "Rollin's Histories and American Republicanism," *William and Mary Quarterly* 29 (1972): 611–22.
101. [Charles Dutot], *Réflexions politiques sur les finances et le commerce,* 2 vols. (The Hague, 1738), 2: 329–30.
102. M. le chevalier de Brucourt, *Essai sur l'éducation de la noblesse,* 2 vols. (Paris, 1748), 1: iv, vii. On "belonging to the *Patrie*" see also vol. 1: 3, and vol. 2: 203. Other noble educational treatises inspired in part by Rollin include *De l'éducation d'un jeune seigneur* (Paris, 1728), see 4, 342, and preface, and Bonneval, *Les Elémens et Progrès de l'Education, par M. de Bonneval* (Paris, 1743), see iv, 89. See also 92–93 of the 1751 edition.

bleman whose disfigurement by smallpox led him to spend the last years of his short life contemplating morals, manners, and the state of contemporary society in the privacy of a modest Parisian apartment.[103] An admirer of Boulainvilliers and a close friend to his fellow countryman the marquis de Mirabeau, Vauvenargues belonged to a long and unbroken line of sophisticated theorists of aristocratic morals, and aristocratic supremacy, in the eighteenth century, but he celebrated nobility more as a moral necessity than as a social caste.[104] His subtle exploration of the content of a noble morality led him to articulate a hybrid form of honor/virtue, thus setting a precedent that many others would later follow. Like the marquise de Lambert, whose contemplative "Advice from a Mother to Her Son" (1727) he may well have read, Vauvenargues insisted on making a distinction between corrupting self-love and legitimate self-regard, and he specifically sought ways to combine the call to virtue with the affirmation of personal and familial pride.[105] Those who scorn glory and admire only virtue, wrote Vauvenargues in an essay on glory addressed to an anonymous friend, "deprive virtue itself of its recompense and its firmest support." Virtue's opposite was not glory, but rather "vanity and weakness."[106] Just as Sulla and Pompey would have scoffed at anyone who dared to preach contempt for glory in ancient Rome, he continued, "I wish to speak to you of glory as I might have spoken to an Athenian in the time of Themistocles or Socrates."[107]

Vauvenargues's defense of "glory" surely reflected in part his belief in the necessity and utility of rank, it being "impossible to maintain equality of conditions and of fortunes in a powerful State." Elsewhere, in an essay on inequality of wealth, he wrote that "inequality of conditions" was an "indispensable necessity." The emergence of inequalities was such an inevitable aspect of the human condition, he wrote, that even "ancient legislators condemned it without effect."[108] His willingness to accept, and even to applaud, a certain degree of self-conscious pride in rank and sta-

103. Paul Souchon, *Vauvenargues: Philosophe de la gloire* (Paris, 1947), 98–139.

104. Fernand Vial notes that Vauvenargues was "deeply touched" by Boulainvilliers's *Histoire de l'ancien gouvernement*. See *Une philosophie et une morale du sentiment. Luc de Clapiers, marquis de Vauvenargues* (Paris, 1938), 63.

105. Madame de Lambert's categories, which she had worked out in 1710 when the letter was first written, reappeared in only slightly altered form in Vauvenargues's essay "De l'Amour-Propre et de l'Amour de Nous-Mêmes," in *Oeuvres complètes de Vauvenargues*, ed. Henry Bonnier, 2 vols. (Paris, 1968), 1: 227–28.

106. Vauvenargues, *Oeuvres complètes*, 1: 73–74.

107. Ibid., 1: 79.

108. Ibid., 1: 197, 104.

tus explains why Vauvenargues had Fénelon confess, in an imaginary dialogue with Bossuet, that he had "erred" in condemning human vices "too severely."[109] For Vauvenargues, as for Boulainvilliers, the embrace of virtue must not lead to the total "subjugation of self."[110]

Still, Vauvenargues agreed with the basic thrust of Fénelon's arguments, and in an essay on the passions he forthrightly declared that one should "prefer virtue to all else," since true glory could only follow from virtue. "Men are tired of virtue," he complained, and he suggested that those who tried to discredit glory actually had an ulterior motive: that of avoiding the stain of dishonor while they wallowed shamelessly in vice. Like Fénelon, he rejected the argument of La Rochefoucauld that all human action derived from self-interest and that true virtue lay beyond the reach of sinful man. Virtue was indeed possible, but in order to pursue it, he insisted, the conscientious individual had to reject outright "the maxims that reign today in high society [*le grand monde*]." Those maxims, "by devaluing merit and virtue, and by recognizing nothing but appearances among men, make good and evil equivalent." Vauvenargues's condemnation of vice, and his own appeal to virtue, focused especially on the familiar targets located at and around the royal court. To find true glory, he informed his friend, ignore the "bizarre prejudices" of those insincere dandies always so generous with their ridicule, "those who take pride in having soft skin and in entertaining the women." The "extravagances" of these people, who felt "mortal chagrin" if they happened to be ignored at a supper, should not be permitted to interfere with the young noble whose eyes were focused on a "more reasonable ambition." Although most Frenchmen would find it impossible to imitate the virtues of the Romans, wrote Vauvenargues, "nature always produces some men superior to the spirit and prejudices of their century," and virtue and true glory remained attainable for those who directed their passions toward worthy ends.[111]

As Vauvenargues's own contemptuous attitude toward "society" suggests, the widespread perception that the meaning and value of honor itself had been perverted by decades of inattention and careless self-indulgence on the part of nobles and society at large necessarily compli-

109. Ibid., 2: 362. "I wished too much for princes to constrain men to live by rules, and I condemned vices too severely. To impose such a yoke on men, and to repress their weaknesses by severe laws, at the same time that one recommends mutual support and charity, is to contradict oneself."

110. Boulainvilliers, *Essais*, 222. On the contrary, for Boulainvilliers the nobility's historical loss of its self-respect stood as a chief symbol of the triumph of luxury and vice, not the apotheosis of virtue.

111. Vauvenargues, *Oeuvres*, 1: 70, 102, 75, 79.

cated the effort to strike a proper balance between selfless virtue and self-affirming honor. Luxury and the establishing of so many false symbols of status during the reign of Louis XIV had promoted what Vauvenargues called a vain cult of "appearances among men," and the moral laxity of the Regency period had exacerbated the problem by leading some to confuse elegance, sexual conquest, and infamy with legitimate social standing. Montesquieu, in his *Persian Letters* of 1721, had already satirized the aristocratic desire to have a "reputation for being witty." He also poked fun at the silly excesses of the "point of honor," and he had one of his two perplexed Persian travelers, Rica, express amazement at the indifference with which French husbands and wives typically confronted one another's sexual infidelities.[112] In the decades that followed publication of the *Persian Letters,* the critique of aristocratic honor grew in volume and intensity.

Novelists participated actively in the discussion. In *Manon Lescaut* (1733), for example, the abbé Prévost tells the story of a young noble scion, the chevalier des Grieux, reduced to the depths of depravity through his romantic involvement with the title character, a mercenary harlot of low birth. The central theme of the story forms around the discrepancy between the chevalier's life as a wastrel—he cheats at gambling, lies to his friends, swindles a fellow noble, shames his family, and eventually commits murder—and the traditional code of honor that he both recognizes and finesses in an attempt to save his own dwindling self-respect. Through the adventures of Grieux, Prévost simultaneously held up for criticism a code of honor built around the cultivation and maintenance of mere appearances and faulted those nobles who knowingly exploited the loopholes in honor's public code in order to pursue their own blind passions. Even from his jail cell, for example, Grieux still finds it possible to console himself that "there was nothing in my behavior, taken all around, which was completely dishonorable." The disapproval of his own father could be attributed to the older man's "fantastic notions of honor," and his lack of appreciation for the dangerous power of true love. In the end, after exile to America, the death of Manon, and his own involvement in a near fatal duel, Grieux is in fact reconciled to the code of honor that he has so egregiously violated. The novel ends with Grieux awaiting a ship back to France, and harboring "thoughts worthy of my birth and upbringing."[113] Despite the evidently happy ending, however, Prévost's tale invited reevaluation of both the traditional code of honor and the behavior of those who ostensibly obeyed that code.

112. Montesquieu, *Lettres Persanes,* ed. Laurent Versini (Paris, 1986), 173–77, 241–42.
113. Abbé Prévost, *Manon Lescaut,* trans. Leonard Tancock (New York, 1991), 125, 154.

Charles-Pinot Duclos's *Confessions of the Comte de* \*\*\* (1741), "one of the greatest publishing successes of the century," raised similar questions about the contemporary meanings of honor.[114] In a very lengthy epistle written to a friend who is incredulous that anyone would willingly abandon the delights of "le monde," the unnamed comte tells the story of his own sexual depravity and eventual redemption after years of scandalous license. "Destined by my birth to live at court," the comte explains that he received the typical, "that is to say, very bad," education of the high nobility. Raised by a governor who set poor moral examples at every turn, the comte went off to court as a young man dreaming only of sexual dalliance. Buoyed by thoughts of "my happiness and my glory" after he conquered his first "woman of condition," the comte, overcome by "the senses and by vanity," wished for nothing more than to share his conquest with the public. Disappointed, and "not feeling my honor engaged" by his pledges to the unlucky marquise, the comte moved on to another lover, initiating a pattern of deceit and depravity that continued for many years. The comte turned his back on vice only after meeting the virtuous and recently widowed comtesse de Selve. Sweet, forgiving, simple, unprepossessing, and lacking all ambition to impress, the comtesse finally touched the comte's heart and filled it with "a more tender sentiment" than the ephemeral passions of love. After marrying, they abandoned the court for the country, knowing that "society, far from being necessary to our happiness, could only importune us." Elevated by "this union of hearts, which is the fruit and the principle of virtue," the comte was now prepared to live out his days enjoying the greatest happiness "to which an honorable man [*honnête homme*] can aspire."[115]

The chief message of Duclos's novel, a message articulated almost at the same moment by Vauvenargues, emerged from the exposure of the false values represented by the court and its denizens. The pursuit of true glory, Duclos suggested, could not be carried out at court or among courtiers, for the preoccupation with appearances and a commitment to earning and ruining reputations through manipulation of perceptions and the playing of games corrupted all who came in contact with the court. Of course the

---

114. Duclos, *Les Confessions du Comte de* \*\*\*, ed. Laurent Versini (Paris, 1969), xlvii. The novel went through fifteen editions between 1741 and 1783, and was the fifth most often owned French novel of the eighteenth century, judging by a survey of the holdings of large private libraries. See both the remarks of Versini, pp. xlviii–liv, and Daniel Mornet, "Les Enseignements des bibliothèques privées," *Revue d'Histoire Littéraire de la France* 17 (1910): 449–96, esp. 460.

115. Duclos, *Les Confessions*, 4, 11–12, 167–68.

anti-court argument placed Duclos in a tradition of moral criticism that went back to Fénelon, La Bruyère, and the first formal critiques of luxury and courtliness in the sixteenth and seventeenth centuries. But Duclos's novel also formed part of a new strain of moral criticism directed squarely at nobles themselves, a criticism focused on the misuses of honor and, more specifically, on the separation of honor's ever more conspicuous and misleading signs from its forgotten or misunderstood substance.

The marquis d'Argenson (1694–1757), who wrote what was in some ways the most devastating critique of nobility penned before the Revolution—the *Considerations on the Ancient and Present Form of French Government*—also cited the use of counterfeit forms of honor as one of the chief causes of the second estate's degradation. The subtle moral criticism that lay behind d'Argenson's radical social and political program has rarely received the attention it deserves. The marquis's championing of representative institutions has marked him, in the eyes of historians of political thought, as a progressive thinker far ahead of his time, one who dismissed nobility and cherished democratic principles long before it became fashionable either to promote republicanism or to denounce "aristocrats."[116] But the reasoning behind d'Argenson's project of reform, which he freely circulated in manuscript by the late 1730s, indicates his embeddedness in the broad moral discussions of the early eighteenth century, and close reading of the text shows that his attitude toward nobility was actually far more ambivalent than his angriest pronouncements would seem to suggest.[117]

D'Argenson's unflinching support for strong monarchy shows that the political and moral ferment of the first decades of the eighteenth century had been elicited not by dissatisfaction with monarchy per se, but by the peculiar social and institutional forms that absolute monarchy had come to assume by 1715. In fact, d'Argenson's forthright promotion of democratic forces—which he saw developing within the framework of France's absolutist government—needs to be understood in the context of his analysis of the state of the monarchy, which he saw suspended between the competing forces of "aristocracy" and "democracy." His characterization of those competing forces underlines the long-term political importance of the eighteenth century's rethinking of honor and virtue.

---

116. Chaussinand-Nogaret, *French Nobility in the Eighteenth Century*, 19–20. Halévi, "The Illusion of 'Honor'"; Neal Johnson, "L'idéologie politique du marquis d'Argenson, d'après ses oeuvres inédites," in *Etudes sur le XVIIIe siècle*, ed. Roland Mortier and Hervé Hasquin (Brussels, 1984), 21–28.

117. R. L. de Voyer de Paulmy, Marquis d'Argenson, *Considérations sur le gouvernement ancien et présent de la France* (Amsterdam, 1765). This text is a reprint of the original 1764 edition.

D'Argenson expressed respect for "legitimate aristocracy," in which "men distinguished by their birth and wisdom govern for the common good." After noting that "it will always be presumed" that nobles of extraction are born with distinguished sentiments of courage and virtue, which are continually reinforced by examples and the power of emulation, d'Argenson also averred, in anticipation of Montesquieu, that nobles' "interior sentiment" of their social superiority "approaches" in its outward effects "the honor that we render to virtue." The great disadvantage of aristocratic government, however, is that the corps of nobility, "being separated from the other citizens," affects scorn and disdain for the commoners, who are nonetheless "the most numerous and hard-working [citizens.]" While the commoners suffer in silence, "the nobility adds to its privileges each day and consummates its separation from the rest of the state." As this occurs, government by nobility can degenerate into "false aristocracy," where "a small number of citizens usurp all authority for themselves and relate everything to their own interests and passions."[118]

Significantly, however, d'Argenson made it clear that in France the "false aristocracy" that had usurped authority since the time of Louis XIV was not a pure aristocracy of the nobility but an aristocracy of ministers, court grandees, financiers, and the rich.[119] Echoing the "country" rhetoric of his friend Bolingbroke, with whom he met frequently in the years when the *Considerations* was composed, d'Argenson remarked that the "simple nobility," like most other citizens, had become victims of the illusory reign of "circulation and credit" that financiers and self-interested royal ministers had ushered in following the premature death of the visionary Colbert.[120] Simple nobles, most of them serving in the military, had been lured into a race to acquire the signs of what d'Argenson called "illustra-

118. Ibid., 3–6, 207.
119. The times of feudal usurpation in the Middle Ages had represented a false aristocracy of nobility, but it was not feudalism that the marquis resisted in the eighteenth century. D'Argenson explained that "under Louis XIV, our government was completely rearranged around a new system, which consisted of the absolute authority of the ministers of each department." The biggest winner in this transformation had been the department of "finances." He added that "among the members of the aristocracy, all rich people must be included. . . . If the kings take umbrage at the [claims of the] *grands* in the state, they find all the same reasons to oppose excessively rich Citizens." D'Argenson, *Considérations,* 175, 191.
120. Ibid., 208, 264. The terms "circulation" and "credit," he wrote, were actually "devoid of meaning," and had consistently been misrepresented as the causes, rather than the mere effects, of "abundance" (264). "Pernicious errors" had resulted from the myth that these things were vital to the health of the state (266). On the friendship between d'Argenson and Bolingbroke, see Isaac Kramnick, *Bolingbroke and His Circle: The Politics of Nostalgia in the Age of Walpole* (Cambridge, Mass., 1968), 150–52.

tion," that is, public representations of honor. Consequently, they became locked in an ever-losing battle against the "false" aristocrats, who actually controlled the means of "illustration" and inevitably left their lowly competitors indebted, demoralized, and dishonored. Many, thinking to maintain the image of honor that had become so pathetically dear to them, ironically "dishonored themselves" by contracting unworthy marriages for financial reasons.[121]

In opposition to the unjust system of this new false aristocracy, which threatened both the monarchy and the citizens from whom the aristocrats had become so conspicuously "separated," d'Argenson thus advocated the expansion of "democratic" principles. D'Argenson defined democracy as a "popular government in which all the people have an equal part, without regard to the distinction between nobles and commoners," and he articulated plans for a national network of consultative bodies that would cripple the power of the false aristocracy, thus uniting all the citizens of the state and replacing the "interests and passions" of the selfish few with a collective commitment to the public good.[122] D'Argenson's goal of having a virtuous citizenry united through equality and the right of participation in government prefigured the patriotic designs of countless later theorists, including Rousseau, who cited d'Argenson's work in *The Social Contract*.[123] D'Argenson suggested, already in the 1730s, that the time was ripe for governmental reform in France, in part because both "religion and honor are [now] coming to resemble virtue, which is the enemy of tumultuous passions."[124]

D'Argenson's *Considerations* is a revealing document because of the way it characterizes the mutually opposing forces at work on the political horizon of the eighteenth century. As shown by the title of his one chapter of genuinely constructive criticism, "Arrangements for extending democracy in France," d'Argenson regarded unjust inequality and civic equality, false

---

121. Ibid., 207–8.

122. Ibid., 7. D'Argenson envisioned the creation of "magistrats populaires," in numbers proportionate to the population, for each city, town, and village of the realm. Selected annually through a complicated process involving both popular nomination and administrative appointment, the magistrates would have power over general administration and tax collection. Royal officials would play a loose supervisory role in the localities, though they would also have a say in the selection of the magistrates. The system would not establish true democracy, but a consultative form of monarchy in which the interests of the people informed royal decision-making. "A king worthy of the title will listen to the interests of his people, and will have no other organ through which to learn [those interests] than their own voice, no other mechanism than their own free activity" (263).

123. Rousseau cites the marquis in his chapters on "different systems of legislation" and "civil religion." See *Du contrat social*, ed. Pierre Burgelin (Paris, 1966), 89, 178.

124. D'Argenson, *Considérations*, 187.

"aristocracy" and inclusive "democracy," as polar opposites attracting competing forces in an unacknowledged battle to determine the future of the French monarchy. D'Argenson's text cannot be considered representative by virtue of the political outcomes it proposed; with the possible exception of Dupont de Nemours's famous essay on municipalities in the 1770s, it proposed a leveling assault on privilege more systematic than that of any other influential political text of the old regime. Nevertheless, *Considerations* is emblematic of its time because it captured in stark terms the social and political alternatives contemplated by the moralists and political thinkers of the eighteenth century, and because it exemplified the common predilection to mediate between those alternatives through a reformulated language of honor and virtue.

D'Argenson's criticism focused not on nobility as such, but on "false" values and the social inequities that those values had promoted and insidiously concealed. Nobility appeared in his story not only as a historical perpetrator of falsity, but also as its most prominent victim. And just as d'Argenson regarded the fabrication of artificial "honor" by the wealthy as a symbol of the unjust form of social separation that had characterized French politics after Louis XIV, he saw the increasing similarity between "virtue" and the residual honor of the socially excluded as the portent of a political solution that would end this unhealthy separation and establish greater equality between citizens. In d'Argenson's mind, "separation" between citizens led to, and was inevitably perpetuated by, the perversion of honor, and only an honor that came back to its roots in virtue could dispel the false shadows that had overtaken the eighteenth century and create a state whose structure promoted the legitimate interests of all. D'Argenson awaited a "great change in the morals of the Nation."[125]

D'Argenson made a special effort, in the concluding chapter of his work, to assure noble readers that they had nothing to fear in the system he proposed. "In considering this system, the French nobility should feel no wistful longing for an Aristocracy that it considers to be favorable to the Nation. [The system] actually entails the extirpation of an odious despotism of commoners, one that spreads evil each day while perverting our morals."[126] By mounting proper "efforts toward equality," the state would

125. Ibid., 277.
126. Ibid., 312. He described the abusive system to be destroyed as "une Satrapie roturiere & odieuse qui augmente chaque jour les maux, en pervertissant nos moeurs." After describing the prejudices, arrogance, and indolence of much of the nobility, d'Argenson asked, "Should we then abolish this famous order?" "Certainly not," he answered. "In truth, I say that we should strive toward equality, but we will never achieve it" (310).

bring an end, above all else, to the rapid proliferation of nobles. "We will especially abolish the entry into the corps of Nobles of unworthy people, [who gain access] by way of finance."[127] Nobility would then no longer be an instrument of "separation" that introduced scorn, arrogance, and falsity into the social relations of the polity.

## VIRTUE AND THE SOCIAL ORDER

Despite his promise of a brighter future for both nobility and nation, d'Argenson's endorsement of new "efforts toward equality" underscored the disruptive potential that the much desired "change in the morals of the Nation" held out for the second estate. Reflecting upon the recent adulteration of the nobility through the influx of unworthy parvenus, and the suspect morals that characterized life at court and in the highest social circles in the early eighteenth century, all conscientious patriots could agree that honor, and the nobility that supposedly embodied it, needed reform. All could further agree that, in the struggle against the "odious despotism" of a deformed royal court, both the nobility and the nation would benefit from a fresh infusion of virtue. But the structural consequences of this desired infusion of virtue were construed differently. For Vauvenargues, as for Fénelon and Boulainvilliers before him, the return of virtue implied the reconsolidation of an existing social hierarchy, one in which nobles would behave according to the virtuous norms of a "true" honor based on commitment to the commonweal. Rollin, on the other hand, understood both honor and virtue to be the expression of a patriotic commitment that assumed the moral homogeneity of a vigorous citizenry. When reading Rollin, one could not always be sure that the "Republic" to which he so often alluded did not invoke a polity with a constitution very different from that of eighteenth-century France. Indeed, Rollin provocatively declared that if long lineage made nobles, "we are all equally noble," since all people have "equally ancient" origins.[128] In identifying the coming triumph of virtue with the nullification of the nobility's formal political role and the rise of civic equality, d'Argenson merely elaborated the social message that lay implicit in Rollin's moral lessons.

The existence of divergent plans for integrating virtue into the eighteenth-century social order should come as no surprise. As Pocock's study of the Italian and English cases has shown, the very adaptability of the "clas-

127. Ibid., 310–11.
128. See Rollin, *Traité des Etudes,* 3: 75.

sical republican" tradition meant that civic humanist thought always contained an inherent tension reflecting disagreement over the internal organization of the virtuous polity. The problem of the optimal balance of powers between "the few and the many," a problem inherited from Aristotle's *Politics,* occupied all of the formulators of early modern civic humanist thought as they tried to conceive the foundations of a virtuous and stable government.[129] For some, such as Guicciardini or many of the promoters of English "country" ideology, the sustaining of virtue required the special moral devotion of the select "few," even if the "many" played an indispensable role in critically and actively judging the performance of exalted officeholders.[130] For others, such as Machiavelli and Harrington, virtue required "equality," meaning not only a more genuinely republican form of government, but, even more so, a perfectly equal commitment to virtue and personal independence among all the citizens, or "citizen-warriors," of the state.[131] The republican tradition, as it had developed in the sixteenth and seventeenth centuries, had forged consensus around the desirability of virtue, independence, and patriotism, and all civic humanists agreed that corruption, luxury, and dependence should be avoided at all costs, but the question whether virtue should be considered the special attribute of "popular" or "aristocratic" governments remained open to discussion.

The leveling potential inherent in the call to virtue may explain why M. de Chansierges, one of Fénelon's many imitators, declared in 1723 that "wise kings . . . know well that it is not necessary to bring back antique morals so foreign from our own in order to revive the golden age. It suffices to renew good morals."[132] The proper means of renewing "good morals" nevertheless remained a subject of debate throughout the eighteenth century. The single most influential attempt to define the good morals appropriate to modern France, Montesquieu's *Spirit of the Laws,* was written very much in the spirit of Chansierges's warning, for it described a moral regime distinct from that of antiquity and connected organically to French monarchical traditions. Instead of ending debate, however, *The Spirit of the Laws* served both to frame it and to accelerate it. Evidence sug-

---

129. Pocock notes that "the Aristotelian polity" stood as "the ultimate paradigm of all civic humanism" (*Machiavellian Moment,* 478).

130. On Guicciardini, see ibid., 131–34, 219–71; for country ideology and the importance of the "landed" interest, see 416, 462–64, 478–86.

131. On Machiavelli, see ibid., 196–211, esp. 210; on the adaptation of Machiavellian principles by Harrington and other English thinkers, see 333–60, 383–400.

132. [M. de Chansierges], *L'Idée d'un Roy Parfait. Dans laquelle on découvre la véritable Grandeur, avec les moyens de l'acquérir* (Paris, 1723), 114.

gests that Montesquieu, too, recognized the potential for social leveling inherent in the resuscitation of ancient virtue, and that he saw that potential as a threat to hierarchical principles he found useful and convenient. But his solution to the challenge represented by the turn to antique morals—the relegation of patriotism and virtue to an ancient and alien past—struck most of his readers as patently unacceptable. Consequently, the publication of *The Spirit of the Laws* set off an avalanche of political writing that aimed to define anew the moral and social contours of French patriotism. It is to Montesquieu's opus, and the powerful impact it made after 1748, that we now turn.

*Chapter Two*

===

# NOBILITY AND THE LONGING FOR VIRTUE
## Patriotic Possibilities from Montesquieu to Mirabeau

"Among all the books that have caused a stir in our time," wrote J-B. Crevier in 1764, some sixteen years after its appearance, "none have succeeded more brilliantly than The Spirit of the Laws."[1] The reasons for the broad and lasting appeal of Montesquieu's work are easily identified. The book's innovative argument about the influence of climate on morals and manners, its analysis of the English constitution, its exploration of the principle of the separation of powers, and its learned discussions of both ancient and medieval history secured it a wide and attentive readership. The rich diversity of its arguments ensured that traces of Montesquieu's influence would be "dispersed throughout all the literature of the age."[2]

The powerful impact of Montesquieu's opus, however, also needs to be placed in the context of the emerging patriotic consciousness of the early eighteenth century. Montesquieu deserves the title of "Newton of the moral world" because he managed to reduce to a system the often conflicting ideas that had shaped civic thought since the age of Fénelon.[3] Honor, virtue, patriotism, despotism, nobility: the meanings of all these terms and the relationships among them were given definitive shape in Montesquieu's analysis of the types of government and their respective

1. Jean-Baptiste Crevier, *Observations sur le Livre de l'Esprit des Lois* (Paris, 1764), 1.
2. Elie Carcassonne, *Montesquieu et le problème de la constitution française au XVIIIe siècle* (Paris, 1927; repr. Geneva, 1978), 177.
3. This title was conferred by Bernard Manin, "Montesquieu et la politique moderne," *Cahiers de Philosophie Politique* 2–3 (1984–85): 157–229, esp. 159.

principles. Clearly indebted to Fénelon, intrigued by Boulainvilliers, and undoubtedly familiar with the works of Rollin, Vauvenargues, and d'Argenson, among others, Montesquieu developed a guide to political morality more subtle and systematic than that of any of his illustrious forebears.

The wide and lasting impact of *The Spirit of the Laws* can also be attributed, however, to the provocative nature of its political and moral arguments. Montesquieu helped to clarify many of the issues at stake in the eighteenth century's growing infatuation with the civic life of the ancients, but not all writers and readers of the time were willing to accept his treatment of those issues. Chapter 3, which is devoted to the uproar surrounding the abbé Coyer's text *La noblesse commerçante* (1756), will address the reaction to Montesquieu's handling of one of these key issues—his attempt to limit, if not suppress, the principle of equality that, according to Montesquieu himself, had always accompanied the sentiment of civic virtue among the ancients. Chapter 2 addresses the reaction of three important moralists of the 1750s—Rousseau, Duclos, and Mirabeau—to Montesquieu's redefinition of the role of the nobility in French civic life.

I argue that all three accepted, in one way or another, Montesquieu's decision to place nobility at the center of a project of moral and political restoration in modern France. But all three also agreed that Montesquieu's structural maneuver came at too great a moral cost. In different ways they insisted, in spite of Montesquieu, on the viability of a genuinely virtuous patriotism in the eighteenth century, and their divergent understandings of patriotism necessitated the reimagining of nobility's moral, social, and political functions. In opposition to Montesquieu's narrow nobility of honor, all three constructed nobilities of virtue, though the social implications built into their moral constructions differed in essential ways. Rousseau and Duclos were both drawn to an image of moral nobility, a nobility that, in the case of the former, found expression only in qualities of the heart and, in the case of the latter, retained only the most tenuous link to its formal embodiment in the second estate. Mirabeau, in contrast, found the vital morals of nobility in the sentiments of the authentic second estate, whose traditional commitment to honor bore all the marks of civic virtue as practiced by the ancients.

The works of Rousseau, Duclos, and Mirabeau, when considered in the light of Montesquieu's towering masterpiece, attest to the continuing process of conceptual readjustment that the growth of patriotic feeling had initiated at the beginning of the eighteenth century. Montesquieu's effort at systematization hardly brought an end to the sorting and weighing of ideas that the reconsideration of ancient values, and the confrontation with "despotism," had inspired among politically engaged readers and writers since the time of Fénelon. Indeed, the appearance of Montesquieu's work provided a new impetus to the wide cultural project of balancing between the conflicting tendencies of equality and rank, virtue and honor, selflessness and pride. Rousseau, Duclos, and Mirabeau illuminate this process with special clarity because, unwittingly, they forecast what would become, in the course of the next thirty years and more, the three principal approaches to defining the patriotic polity. Before discussing their texts, however, let us consider the work of the master theorist who did so much to inspire, and to provoke, their reflections.

## MONTESQUIEU AND THE CONTAINMENT OF VIRTUE

Long before his permanent relocation to Paris from Bordeaux in the 1730s, and even longer before the publication of *The Spirit of the Laws* (1748), Montesquieu had expressed admiration for the political values of the classical world. Both in his capacity as a parlementary magistrate (from 1714 to 1726), and as an active member of the Academy of Bordeaux, Montesquieu had had occasion to study the legal and political history of the ancients, and he fastened on the selfless patriotism of the ancient citizen as the distinguishing feature of pre-modern societies. In the *Persian Letters,* for example, Montesquieu had a French acquaintance of the Persian traveler Usbek declare that "the sanctuary of honor, reputation, and virtue is to be found in republics, and the lands where one can speak of 'my *patrie.*' In Rome, Athens, and Sparta, honor alone was the reward for the greatest of services."[4] In a "Treatise on Duties," written in 1725, Montesquieu called "love for our fellow citizens" the greatest virtue, and he observed that "it is love of the *patrie* that gives the histories of the Greeks and Romans a nobility that our histories lack."[5]

Montesquieu's fascination with the ancients was reinforced during his stay in England (1729–31), where he regularly read Bolingbroke's journal *The Craftsman,* became reacquainted with Machiavelli's *Discourses* on Livy, imbibed the patriotic language of the country party, and began comparing the natures of modern and ancient liberty.[6] After his return from England, he devoted himself single-mindedly to an analysis of Rome's de-

4. Montesquieu, *Lettres Persanes,* 240.
5. As cited in Shackleton, *Montesquieu,* 75–76.
6. Ibid., 151–53. On Montesquieu's connection to Bolingbroke, see also D. J. Fletcher, "Montesquieu's Conception of Patriotism," *SVEC* 56 (1967): 541–55, esp. 549–55; Childs, *A Political Academy in Paris,* 98–99; and Kramnick, *Bolingbroke and His Circle,* 144–50.

cline, and his *Considerations on the Causes of the Greatness of the Romans and of Their Decadence* appeared in 1734. Clearly indebted to Machiavelli, and at times strikingly reminiscent of Boulainvilliers, the *Considerations* particularly emphasized the importance of equality in Roman civic culture. As Montesquieu saw it, the "equal sharing of land" had been one of the preconditions of Rome's rise to greatness, and the universal frugality that characterized the early Romans had ensured, for example, that all Roman soldiers were "proud, determined," and "sure of their command over others."[7] The pivotal struggle of the orders during the early history of the Republic merely symbolized the Roman instinct for autonomy. The people's "jealousy toward the power of the Senate and the prerogatives of the great, always mixed with respect, was nothing other than a love for equality," and Rome's demise became inevitable only when the citizens' determination to preserve civic equality waned.[8]

Montesquieu, like Boulainvilliers before him, traced the decline of the Romans' love of equality, and their devotion to the *patrie,* to a legal innovation that had the ostensible purpose of extending the cherished principle of equality: the Republic's granting of citizenship status to all Italians. "From that point [88 BCE], Rome was no longer this city whose people all had the same spirit, an identical love of liberty, [and] the same hatred for tyranny." Citizenship itself had become a fiction, since citizens no longer worshiped the same gods, recognized the same laws, obeyed the same magistrates, or lived within the same walls. By replacing moral equality with a deceptive legal equality, the government had mistakenly ensured that people "no longer had the same love of the *patrie,* and Roman sentiments were no more."[9]

Montesquieu's obvious admiration for Roman virtue, and the tone of lament with which he pronounced the demise of Roman ways, could lead one to think that the former parlementaire retained hope that aspects of the ancients' political virtue could still be recovered for use in the modern world, just as Fénelon had sought to cultivate a "pure" love of the *patrie* and Boulainvilliers had dreamed of reestablishing, among the nobility at least, the primitive equality of the Romans/Franks. Soon after publishing the *Considerations,* however, Montesquieu began writing the early chapters of *The Spirit of the Laws,* particularly those that dealt with the types of government and their respective principles, and the typology he devel-

7. Montesquieu, *Considérations sur les causes de la grandeur des Romains et de leur décadence* (Paris, 1987), 43, 50.
8. Ibid., 105.
9. Ibid., 105–6.

oped seemingly had the effect of relegating political virtue to what one historian has called "an all but irretrievable past."[10] Departing from the standard political categories of Aristotle (monarchy, aristocracy, democracy), Montesquieu identified three types of government: despotism, whose activating principle was fear, republics, which were inevitably based on virtue, and monarchy, which incorporated honor as its core principle. In chapter five of book three of *The Spirit of the Laws,* Montesquieu made clear his assumption that virtue could rarely be found among the subjects of a monarchy.[11]

Specialists of eighteenth-century political thought have explained Montesquieu's excision of virtue from modern political life in a number of ways. Harold Ellis, Thomas Pangle, and Bernard Manin have emphasized, from different angles, Montesquieu's faith in the possibilities of modernity and his historicist skepticism about the compatibility of rustic simplicity and modern civilization.[12] Pierre Rétat has argued that Montesquieu absorbed and transformed Mandeville's principle about the inadvertent public benefits of private vices, and thereby found a new means of rationalizing the nobility's social preeminence.[13] Others have stressed Montesquieu's mistrust of republicanism, with its demanding moral standards and its inherent instability, and have described his "aristocratic liberalism" as the best and most realistic modern alternative he could devise to prevent the despotism that he dreaded.[14]

All of these interpretations ring true. Montesquieu regarded the onward progress of modernity as an inalterable historical reality, one that offered benefits as well as losses. The impact on his thinking of Mandeville's *Fable of the Bees,* which is cited twice in *The Spirit of the Laws,* is undeniable.[15] Like other political philosophers of the eighteenth century, Montesquieu

10. Harold A. Ellis, "Montesquieu's Modern Politics: The Spirit of the Laws and the Problem of Modern Monarchy in Old Regime France," *History of Political Thought* 10 (1989): 665–700, esp. 690.

11. Montesquieu, *De l'Esprit des Lois,* ed. Laurent Versini, 2 vols. (Paris, 1995): 1: 120–22.

12. Ellis, "Montesquieu's Modern Politics;" Thomas Pangle, *Montesquieu's Philosophy of Liberalism: A Commentary on "The Spirit of the Laws"* (Chicago, 1973); Manin, "Montesquieu et la politique moderne."

13. Pierre Rétat, "De Mandeville à Montesquieu: Honneur, luxe et dépense noble dans l'"Esprit des Lois,'" *Studi Francesi* 50 (1973): 238–49.

14. Jean-Jacques Chevallier, "Montesquieu ou le libéralisme aristocratique," *Revue Internationale de Philosophie* 9 (1955): 330–45; Judith Shklar, "Montesquieu and the New Republicanism," in *Machiavelli and Republicanism,* 265–79; David Lowenthal, "Montesquieu and the Classics: Republican Government in *The Spirit of the Laws,*" in *Ancients and Moderns,* ed. Joseph Cropsey (New York, 1964), 258–84.

15. The point has recently been reaffirmed by Hundert, *The Enlightenment's Fable,* 21.

doubted that democracy could work outside of small states, and his identification of honor as the principle of monarchy surely reflected his perception of the inescapably hierarchical character of the society and mores
of modern (that is, postclassical) France. Montesquieu ended *The Spirit of
the Laws,* for example, with an extended discourse on French medieval history in which he defended Boulainvilliers's effort to establish the nobility's
historical and legal independence from the monarchy.[16] Although he
questioned Boulainvilliers's historical judgment, and pointedly dismissed
his claim that the Frankish nation had reduced the Gauls, the purported
ancestors of the third estate, to abject servitude, Montesquieu accused
Boulainvilliers's principal critic, the abbé Dubos, of basing his arguments
on "poor sources."[17] Montesquieu developed an interpretation of the early
medieval past that supported his argument that inequalities of status were
linked essentially to monarchical government. He insisted, in opposition
to Dubos, that nobility had existed before the institution of the monarchy,
and that the principle of social preeminence that nobility represented had
served as the necessary grounds from which legitimate monarchy, as opposed to a mere usurping tyranny, was able to emerge in France.[18]

Montesquieu's elaboration of a new typology of governments, however,
must also be placed within the context of the broad early eighteenth-century effort to confront the twin menace of despotism and social corruption
with one or more updated versions of antique virtue, an effort in which he
had long participated. As a close reader of Machiavelli and Harrington,
Montesquieu recognized that an impulse toward moral and social equality
followed as a necessary corollary to the principle of virtue, and he therefore
saw with disconcerting clarity the difficulties entailed in attempts to reconcile virtue with aristocratic honor.[19] Unlike Fénelon and Boulainvilliers,
whose willful blindness toward the perception of commoners allowed them
to imagine a purified aristocracy reconstituted in "republican" morals, or
Lambert and Vauvenargues, whose critical reevaluation of honor led them
to prescribe the incorporation of selflessness and humility into the nobility's traditional consciousness of rank, Montesquieu saw the destabilizing

---

16. Montesquieu, *De l'Esprit,* 2: 1052 (book XXX, chapter x).

17. Ibid., 2: 917 (XXVII, iv).

18. Ibid., 2: 1105–7 (XXX, xxv).

19. Rebecca Kingston has argued that Montesquieu broke new ground both by associating
virtue with self-sacrifice and by defining it as a sentiment that "all citizens can share in"
equally. Subordination of the self and the equal obligations of citizenship, however, had always been implied by the civic humanist expositors of virtue, even if those themes were
brought out more explicitly in some texts than in others. See Kingston, *Montesquieu and the
Parlement of Bordeaux* (Geneva, 1996), 185–87.

potential inherent in the eighteenth-century call to virtue. Jonathan Israel has provocatively characterized the figures of the High Enlightenment as moderates who sought to contain or refute the radical claims articulated in the early Enlightenment by Spinoza and others inspired by him.[20] Although Israel's analysis focuses especially on the perceived threat of atheism, and he probably deploys too narrow a definition of "radical," his perspective on the mature Enlightenment helps to underscore Montesquieu's transformative, and grudgingly conservative, impact on contemporary moral discourse. For in his approach to the problem of French political morality, Montesquieu portrayed virtue—and equality—as a tempting extravagance that the modern world ultimately could not afford.

Montesquieu insisted, for example, that public schools—the schools where Rollin aspired to instill an equalizing love of the *patrie* in every student—should not be regarded as the true institutions of learning in monarchies, where "le monde" served to instruct the young in the ways of honor.[21] For similar reasons, he also rejected the idea that nobility should be permitted to engage in commerce, a practice that would destroy the specific prejudices central to the self-image of the nobility and also undercut the competition for honor that served as the glue of civic life in a monarchy.[22] Torn between his admiration for classical virtues and his doubts about the wisdom and applicability of egalitarian values in modern monarchies, Montesquieu separated virtue from honor categorically, and thereby sought to preclude the tensions and opposing imperatives that would necessarily mark a political culture organized by rank but nevertheless motivated by a universal patriotic fervor.

Montesquieu's categorical solution to the problem of virtue laid down clear definitions of terms, principles, and structures, but it failed to eliminate the ambiguities surrounding the notion of virtue, and it ultimately failed to suppress Montesquieu's own ambivalence toward the solution that he had devised. Montesquieu celebrated honor, nobility, rank, and the passions nurtured by the modern world; he even justified luxury as a kind of necessary evil that kept the social order in proper balance and represented the inequality he considered essential to the spirit of monarchy.[23] At the same time, however, Montesquieu refused to relinquish all hope that virtue could be resuscitated in his own time.[24] The ambivalent attitudes he

---

20. Israel, *Radical Enlightenment*, 6–13.
21. Montesquieu, *De l'Esprit*, 1: 131 (IV, ii).
22. Ibid., 2: 629–31 (XX, xxi–xxii).
23. Ibid., 1: 237 (VII, iv).
24. On this point see the analysis of Nannerl Keohane, "Virtuous Republics and Glorious

harbored toward both antiquity and modernity emerge through comparison of his various clarifications of the respective meanings of virtue and
honor.

"What I call virtue in a republic," wrote Montesquieu in an explanatory
note added to the 1757 edition of *The Spirit of the Laws*, "is love of the *patrie*, that is to say, the love of equality."[25] Where virtue reigns, the individual's only ambition "is to render to the *patrie* greater services than the other
citizens." In republics, distinctions are born from the principle of equality
itself, since superior talents and signal services—the only basis for distinctions—come to light only against the background of the universal obligation that motivates all citizens to sacrifice themselves for the good of the
*patrie*. Because virtue required "a renunciation of the self," virtuous citizens
took for granted the equality that united them in their commitment to the
greater good.[26]

By contrast, "no one aspires to equality in monarchies and despotic
states; the idea never even comes to mind." In states lacking in virtue,
"everyone strives for superiority. People of the basest conditions desire to
leave their station only in order to become the masters of others." The
"virtues" learned in monarchical societies "are not those that draw us
closer to our fellow citizens, but those that distinguish us from them."[27]
This is why Montesquieu could assert that the true "homme de bien," that
is, one who "loves the laws of his country . . . and acts on the basis of this
love for the laws of his country," scarcely existed in France.[28] Honor, which
took the place of virtue in monarchies, always reinforced the "prejudice
[attached to] each person and condition," and it therefore gave birth to
ambition of a different sort from that operative in republics. Honor, instead of focusing attention on one's obligations to the *patrie*, guaranteed a
continual search for "preferences and distinctions."[29]

In establishing this seemingly unbridgeable distance between the modern French monarchy, on the one hand, and political virtue and the love
for equality that characterized it, on the other hand, Montesquieu nevertheless sought to show that the motivations guiding public behaviors in
monarchies could have effects similar to those produced by patriotic

Monarchies: Two Models in Montesquieu's Political Thought," *Political Studies* 20 (1972):
383–96.
25. Montesquieu, *De l'Esprit*, 1: 79 (avertissement).
26. Ibid., 1: 149 (V, iii), 137 (IV, v).
27. Ibid., 1: 150–51 (V, iv), 131 (IV, ii).
28. Ibid., 1: 122 (III, v), and 1: 79 (avertissement).
29. Ibid., 1: 122–23 (III, vi–vii).

virtues. Honor had "good effects" in a monarchy, and proved "useful to the public" because of the actions it inspired. The desire for reputation, after all, could lead men to perform "all manner of difficult acts" without hope of any recompense "other than the renown of [their] actions," and such bravery and fortitude surely deserved credit. Drawing on Mandeville, Montesquieu pointed out that honor even had the power to produce "good citizen[s]" who worked inadvertently toward the political ends dictated by "virtue itself." To preserve the "good effects" produced by the principle of honor, however, the laws must "work to sustain this nobility that is both the father and the child, so to speak, of honor." Nobility "enters in some fashion into the essence of monarchy, whose fundamental maxim is *no monarch, no nobility; no nobility, no monarch.*"[30] Because it supported the independent existence and necessary self-consciousness of the nobility and other "intermediary powers," honor not only produced citizens that bore some resemblance to virtuous republicans, but also played a critical role in moderating a monarchy's natural despotic tendencies. Honor, in short, could be as effective as virtue in repelling the threat of despotism.

Despite Montesquieu's effort to contain virtue's equalizing effects by consigning it to an alien and unrecoverable past, and his appreciation for the positive effects of honor, his own characterizations of honor and virtue inevitably raised doubts about his deepest intentions.[31] Surprisingly, in light of his defense of modern institutions, Montesquieu never bothered to disguise his higher opinion of the ancients. Like a child forced to make a difficult choice between two sources of amusement, Montesquieu continued to look with longing at the object left behind, and his submerged resentment toward his chosen political model bubbled to the surface with regularity. Ancient peoples, because they lived under governments that had virtue as their principle, "accomplished things we no longer see today, and which would astonish our puny souls," he wrote in a chapter devoted to the education of the ancients. He claimed that the modern monarchical state, in contrast to virtually all ancient governments, "subsists inde-

30. Ibid., 1: 123–24 (III, vi–vii), 168 (V, ix), 109 (II, iv).
31. Mark Hulliung has argued, in fact, that Montesquieu "dreamed of nothing less than a national republic and a democratic society in France." See Hulliung, *Montesquieu and the Old Regime* (Berkeley, 1976), ix. Pangle, too, has noted "the necessity of the implication" that political change was both expected and enabled by the text of *The Spirit of the Laws.* Pangle, *Montesquieu's Philosophy of Liberalism,* 23. Elie Carcassonne also emphasized "the difficulty of defining" Montesquieu's later influence, in large part because of the varied and conflicting uses to which his magnum opus could be put (*Montesquieu et le problème de la constitution française,* 176–77). The conflicting messages of *The Spirit of the Laws* seem to have reflected Montesquieu's own ambivalence about the choice he felt compelled to make.

pendently of love of the *patrie*, of the desire for true glory, of renunciation of the self, of the sacrifice of one's own interests, and of all those heroic virtues we find among the ancients and about which we [today] have only heard spoken." Meanwhile, his defense of luxury did not prevent Montesquieu from complaining that, unlike the Greeks, who "recognized no force to sustain them other than that of virtue," modern statesmen "speak to us only of manufactures, commerce, finances, wealth, and even luxury."[32]

The attitude of barely concealed contempt with which Montesquieu discussed modern politics even extended to his description of aristocratic honor, the principle that he claimed to be offering as a substitute for unattainable virtue. "Morals," he declared bluntly, "are never as pure in monarchies as in republican governments," and the reasons for this lay in the peculiar, and often offensive, logic of honor. The "false" and "bizarre" logic of honor defines "virtue" in its own way, and often in direct conflict with the laws. In "society," where honor reigns, "the actions of men are not considered good, but impressive, not just, but grand, not reasonable, but extraordinary." The need to acquire the self-serving veneer of elegance and to project the image of nobility meant that "gallantry" would always be praised, even if mere conquest had been its motive. In conversation, discussants esteemed candor not because of any love for the truth, but because "a man who is accustomed to speak candidly appears to be bold and independent." Naturally, then, the people of "society" disregarded the candor of simple folk, since their honest speech "has only truth and simplicity as its object." "The whole manner of the court," Montesquieu noted, "consists in setting aside one's own grandeur and assuming a borrowed grandeur" which "flatters" the courtier more than genuine qualities of soul ever could.[33]

Montesquieu's most biting condemnation of the "borrowed," "false," and "bizarre" nature of honor appeared in the chapter where the principle was compared most directly to virtue, a chapter focused on the value and behavior of courtiers. To show, as his chapter heading indicated, that "virtue is in no way the principle of monarchical government," Montesquieu used the "miserable character of courtiers" to exemplify the character of the people as a whole.[34] "Ambition mixed with idleness, baseness

---

32. Montesquieu, *De l'Esprit*, 1: 136 (IV, iv), 120 (III, v), 117 (III, iii).
33. Ibid., 1: 131–35 (IV, ii).
34. Ibid., 1: 121 (III, v). "I hope that none will be offended by what I say; all the histories agree with me. I know well that it is not rare for a prince to be virtuous, but I maintain that, in a monarchy, it is very difficult for the people to be [virtuous]."

amid pride, the desire to enrich oneself without working for it, an aversion for the truth, flattery, betrayal, perfidy, disregard for all engagements, scorn for the duties of the citizen, fear of the prince's virtue, hope for his weaknesses, and, more than anything, perpetual ridicule directed at virtue form, I believe, the character of the greatest number of courtiers, in all times and all places." Worse, the court could be regarded as representative of the nation at large. "Now, it is very unlikely that most of the principal [citizens] of a state can be dishonest, while their inferiors are people of integrity [*gens de bien*], that the former would be connivers, and the latter would consent to be their dupes." In a chapter that explicitly relegated virtue to an ancient past and to nonmonarchical societies ("how true it is that virtue is not the mainspring of this government!"), Montesquieu had depicted a community that even the most charitable reader would necessarily perceive as shallow, destructively selfish, and corrupt.[35]

Confusion about Montesquieu's true sentiments—did he mean to defend and promote honor or to satirize and discredit it?—unfortunately could not be dispelled by reference to the preface to *The Spirit of the Laws*, where he laid out his general objectives and offered readers guidance in approaching his work. His wistful statement of purpose would have clouded, rather than facilitated, comprehension of the arguments developed in the body of the text. In the first five books of his opus Montesquieu identified patriotism with virtue, love of the laws, and love of equality, and he went to great lengths to show that those political qualities, embraced instinctively by the ancients, could not be grafted onto a monarchical system based instead on honor, rank, and self-regard. In his preface, however, Montesquieu nevertheless enjoined his readers to "cure themselves of their prejudices," and he confidently declared that "it is not an indifferent matter that the people should be enlightened." Echoing his own "Treatise on Duties" of 1725, where he had praised the patriotism of the ancients and declared "love for our fellow citizens" the greatest virtue, he urged the practice of "that general virtue that encompasses the love of all." In fact, his closing remarks seemed to imply that even patriotic virtue still lay within reach. "If I could arrange that everyone would find new reasons to love one's duties, one's prince, one's *patrie,* one's laws, and that each would find contentment in his own country. . . . I would consider myself the happiest of mortals."[36] Montesquieu specified, in the 1757 edition of his work, that the citizens of a *republic* expressed virtue

35. Ibid., 1: 121–22 (III, v).
36. Ibid., 1: 82–83 (preface).

through love of the *patrie,* which he further defined as "the love of equality." By expressing hope that his own readers might develop love for the *patrie,* the prince, and the established laws of the nation, Montesquieu seemed to leave open the possibility—either consciously or inadvertently—that a nonegalitarian form of patriotic virtue could yet take root in monarchical soil.

In light of his own noble lineage, and his text's embeddedness in a moral discussion that, until mid-century, had been carried on largely by and for fellow aristocrats, one might plausibly assume that Montesquieu's satirical descriptions of honor, coupled with his admiring accounts of virtue, were intended to offend and thereby to provoke his noble readers. By highlighting the shameful aspects of aristocratic "honor," and brazenly declaring nobles' unattractive egoism a structural requirement of monarchy, perhaps Montesquieu wished to promote patriotic urges among those citizens he believed most in need of the selfless dispositions that vigilance against despotism required. Such limited rhetorical objectives, however—even assuming Montesquieu entertained them—could not possibly contain the power of his analysis, especially given the timing of the text's publication. In the burgeoning publishing world of the mature Enlightenment, a long series of interventions into contemporary moral debate would show that nobles were not the only readers moved to action by Montesquieu's various provocations. As one of his later critics would point out, "printed works are conversations with the public. Every reader takes part in [the discussion], and proposes his or her own ideas as well," and few books launched as many conversations as *The Spirit of the Laws.*[37] By linking the fate of French patriotism so closely to the moral character and institutional existence of the nobility, Montesquieu invited an outpouring of critical reflection on both the state of the nobility and the prospects for patriotic renewal in France. Most of the participants in this discussion showed a determination, in answer to Montesquieu, to lay claim to patriotism for the modern world. Three of the earliest and most thoughtful treatises written in Montesquieu's wake offered up new formulations of the connection between patriotic sentiment and nobility, and they redefined nobility in ways that made it well suited to the particular patriotic designs imagined by their authors.

37. *Projet d'Ecoles Publiques, qui répondront aux voeux de la nation, & dont l'exercice n'exige que quatre professeurs* (Bordeaux, n.d.,), 88.

## ROUSSEAU, DUCLOS, AND THE HISTORY OF MORAL CORRUPTION

The background and general argument of Rousseau's *Discours sur les sciences et les arts* (the *First Discourse*) are well known. In response to the Academy of Dijon's invitation for essays addressing the question whether the development of the arts and sciences had contributed to the purification of morals, the obscure and struggling Rousseau submitted a scintillating essay that repudiated all of the accoutrements of civilized society, and won first prize in the Academy's competition.[38] The appearance of the *First Discourse* in November 1750 created a literary sensation, and it launched a brilliant and controversial career passionately devoted to the critique of modernity, the celebration of rustic simplicity, and the promotion of individual autonomy and virtue. Rousseau's emphasis on authenticity, moral transparency, and the corrupting effects of society, often delivered with a self-righteous air, eventually alienated his good friend Diderot and other former comrades in the parti philosophique.[39] But his relentless critique of society's conventions brought him public acclaim and won the heartfelt devotion of countless readers touched by the model of subjectivity he provided.[40]

The *First Discourse* can easily be read for signs of what would come later in Rousseau's career: his break with the philosophes, his diatribe against the theater in the famous letter to d'Alembert, his creative recycling of Spartan ideals in *Emile,* his prescription for the cultivation of virtue in *La Nouvelle Heloïse,* in short, the development of his distinctive form of moral criticism. But when one considers the *First Discourse* squarely within the context of its time, one is struck by the degree to which the text surreptitiously entered into dialogue with Montesquieu's *Spirit of the Laws.*[41] Rousseau borrowed liberally, either consciously or inadvertently, from many

38. See the richly informative critical introduction in George R. Havens, ed., *Discours sur les sciences et les arts* (New York, 1946), 1–88. For the discussion of Rousseau, I also consulted Roger D. Masters, ed., *The First and Second Discourses* (New York, 1964) and, with few exceptions, have followed the translations of Roger D. and Judith R. Masters.

39. The antinomies between Rousseauean thought and the assumptions of the philosophes against whom he reacted should not be exaggerated, however. See Hulliung, *The Autocritique of Enlightenment,* 9–37.

40. See Jean Starobinski, *Jean-Jacques Rousseau: Transparency and Obstruction,* trans. Arthur Goldhammer (Chicago, 1988), 81–113; Robert Darnton, "Readers Respond to Rousseau," in *The Great Cat Massacre,* 215–56, esp. 228–35.

41. Rousseau is known to have read *The Spirit of the Laws* within the first year after its publication, because he served as copyist to the author who wrote one of the first, and sloppiest, critiques of Montesquieu's opus. See Shackleton, *Montesquieu,* 358.

parts of Montesquieu's analysis, and the similarities between the two texts were not lost on contemporary readers, one of whom would later accuse the upstart Rousseau of having plagiarized his illustrious predecessor.[42] But accusations of plagiarism or imitation really miss the point, for one of the marks of Rousseau's originality, and one of the early signs of his vexing talent for paradox, was the way in which he managed, despite his indebtedness to *The Spirit of the Laws,* to overturn or simply ignore Montesquieu's central claims.

Rousseau's critique of the arts and sciences focused on their concealed moral effects. For the individual, the arts and sciences assisted the wasteful and delusional pursuit of standing, reputation, and personal comfort.[43] For the polity, they inevitably supplanted the healthy values of authenticity, generosity, and self-reliance and put in their place the counterfeit values of urbanity, sociability, and skillfulness. To illustrate these differences, Rousseau exploited a series of contrasts between ancient and modern cultures that Montesquieu had already sketched out in *The Spirit of the Laws.* Repeating Montesquieu almost word for word, he complained, for example, that whereas ancient statesmen spoke only of "morals and virtue," those of the modern world spoke exclusively of "business and money."[44] Not surprisingly, the focus on trade and profit meant that love of the *patrie,* the animating principle of ancient politics, existed in the modern world as little more than a dim memory, an alien and nearly unimaginable principle.[45] One sign of this loss was the modern world's celebration of mere talent, which, like Montesquieu before him, Rousseau characterized as a deceptive and superficial substitute for virtue and the qualities of heart that had marked the ancient patriot.[46]

42. Pierre-Claude-Rigobert Lefebvre de Beauvray, *Dictionnaire Social et Patriotique, ou Précis Raisonné de Connaissances relatives à l'Economie Morale, Civile & Politique* (Amsterdam, 1770), 486. "[Rousseau's] prize-winning Discourse on the abuses of the arts and sciences has been much praised until now, but no one has gone to the trouble to mention that all of the basic ideas belonged to Montesquieu."

43. "Let us remain in obscurity," wrote Rousseau in the penultimate paragraph of his treatise. "Let us not chase after a reputation which would escape us, and which in the present state of things would never be worth what it cost, even if we had all the qualifications to obtain it" (*The First and Second Discourses,* 64).

44. Ibid., 51. See Montesquieu, *De l'Esprit,* 117 (III, iii).

45. Rousseau complained that "I see everywhere immense institutions where young people are brought up at great expense, learning everything except their duties. . . . that sweet name *patrie* will never strike the ear (Masters, 51)." In monarchical states, wrote Montesquieu, "the state subsists independently of love of the *patrie* (*De l'Esprit,* 1: 117)."

46. Rousseau associated the "distinction of talents" with the "debasement of virtues (Masters, 58)." In an ideal state, wrote Montesquieu, "one would measure men not by talents or frivolous attributes, but by real qualities (*De l'Esprit,* 1: 601)."

Of the many parallels between the texts of Rousseau and Montesquieu, perhaps the most fascinating involves a phenomenon that they condemned in identical terms but ultimately used for different purposes: the modern rituals of politeness and etiquette. For Rousseau, polite manners exemplified the artifice and falsity that characterized modern social and political relations. Ever since the "art of pleasing" had been reduced to a set of rules to be mastered, he observed, a "deceptive uniformity" had come to prevail in relations between individuals, with the result that "one will never know well those with whom one deals." The "false veil of politeness" provided a mask behind which people inevitably pursued their selfish designs, nursing suspicions, hatreds, and petty concerns that would never have occurred to pre-civilized men. Worse, the illusory ideals of refinement and sophistication ensured that many vices had even come to be "dignified with the name of virtues." The triumph of urbane manners and the art of conversation had marked the eclipse of authentic virtue, a correlation that Rousseau noted with biting irony: "such is the purity our morals have acquired."[47]

The context of Rousseau's remarks make it clear that the court stood out in his mind, as it had for Montesquieu, as a principal site of the moral corruption that they both associated with politeness.[48] But despite the similarity of attitudes informing their discussions, Rousseau's brief allusions to the court did not perform the same rhetorical function as Montesquieu's extended critique of courtiers. Montesquieu had highlighted the moral deficiencies of courtiers to dramatize the "false" and sometimes "bizarre" nature of the thirst for reputation and status that always underlay the sentiment of honor.[49] By discussing honor's most absurd manifestations, and by associating them directly with the widely reviled institution of the court, Montesquieu simultaneously cast light on the "good effects" that honor could produce when responsible men managed their sensitivity to honor in ways consistent with the "common good." Montesquieu conceded the possible ill effects of honor, but by localizing its latent corruptive potential in that peculiar enclave of the court, he rescued honor for the nobility at large, and thereby encouraged his conscientious readers to embrace those aspects of honor that resembled "virtue itself."[50]

---

47. Rousseau (Masters), 38–39.
48. "It is in the rustic clothes of a farmer and not beneath the gilt of a courtier that strength and vigor of the body will be found. Ornamentation is no less foreign to virtue, which is the strength and vigor of a soul" (ibid., 37).
49. "This bizarre honor defines virtues as it wants to define them; by its own authority, it imposes qualifications on all that is prescribed to us" (Montesquieu, De l'Esprit, 1: 133).
50. Ibid., 1: 123–24.

Rousseau's scorn for the court and for polite manners may have held great appeal for the many nobles resentful of courtiers, but it invited a moral response very different from that implied by the analysis of Montesquieu. For Rousseau, courtly behavior represented not the misuse or distortion of *honor* but the tragic loss of *virtue,* and the tacit narrative of loss that he constructed in the *First Discourse* paralleled in striking ways the by-then familiar narrative of aristocratic decline in absolutist France. Through his language and his sparing use of examples from modern history, Rousseau left his readers to believe that Europe's vanished virtue could be found by turning back the clock on the unfortunate history of its beleaguered nobility.

The language through which Rousseau described virtue's disappearance from modern culture would have resonated widely among the many noble families who, for generations, had seen themselves as the bearers of traditional military values. According to Rousseau, the rise of the sciences, luxury, and egoism had entailed the inevitable loss of "courage," "magnanimity," "military virtues," "military exercise," "robust" bodies, and the willingness to "shed blood" for the *patrie.*[51] If this use of the nobility's self-defining vocabulary of generosity and sacrifice failed to grab the attention of noble readers, the before and after images that framed Rousseau's history of declining virtue would surely have set off sparks of recognition. Sparta deserved praise, Rousseau wrote, because its "noble youths" had absorbed only the lessons of "valor, prudence, and justice." They learned to "ride and hunt" at the age of seven, formed "handsome and healthy" bodies, and, in addition to hearing of the importance of honesty and duty, learned to "fear nothing."[52] Consequently, virtue had come to seem as natural as the air to the Spartans, who regularly produced "heroic actions."[53]

Unfortunately the same could not be said of Italy in the fifteenth century. There "the rise of the Medicis and the revival of letters" had meant the inevitable fall of the Italians' "warlike reputation." Proof of the decline came at the time of the French invasion of 1494, when Charles VIII conquered Tuscany and Naples with stunning ease. The king attributed the victory "to the fact that the princes and nobility of Italy had enjoyed themselves becoming ingenious and learned more than they exerted themselves becoming vigorous and warlike." In time, though, the same process of moral enervation had come to affect the French as well. The "scientifically disciplined" modern warrior occasionally showed real valor, but only

51. See Rousseau (Masters), 56, 54, 37, 41, respectively.
52. Ibid., 57, note.
53. Ibid., 43.

in fleeting moments. "I hear their bravery on a single day of battle highly praised, but I am not told how they bear overwork, how they endure the rigor of the seasons and the bad weather. Only a little sun or snow, or the lack of a few superfluities, is necessary to dissolve and destroy the best of our armies in a few days." Throwing in the face of the modern French soldier this damning charge of moral and physical deficiency, Rousseau declared, "it is not with you that [Hannibal] would have crossed the Alps and [Caesar] conquered your ancestors."[54]

Rousseau's intention to have his French audience read their own history in light of ancient developments becomes clear in his treatment of Rome's decline. Like all readers of Plutarch, Tacitus, and Livy, Rousseau knew unquestioningly that the Roman republic had been brought low by the introduction of luxury and elegance. He dramatized this tragedy by reviving and transplanting into the period of Roman decadence the figure of Fabricius, the legendary consul of the third century B.C. who had been idolized for his simplicity and incorruptibility. "'Gods,' you would have said, 'what has become of those thatched roofs and those rustic hearths where moderation and virtue used to dwell? What disastrous splendor has succeeded Roman simplicity? . . . Madmen, what have you done?'" At the heart of the republic, in the Senate itself, Fabricius would have been shocked to discover that "wealth" and "frivolous eloquence" had supplanted virtue.[55]

Leaping over the interval of time and space separating the ancients from the moderns, and remarking "what has happened in our countries and under our own eyes," Rousseau noted that he could spare himself "the trouble of repeating the same things under different names. It was not in vain that I called up the shade of Fabricius; and what did I make that great man say that I might not have put into the mouth of Louis XII or Henry IV?"[56] The periods following the reigns of those warrior kings, in the sixteenth and seventeenth centuries respectively, had seen an upsurge in elegance, refinement, and taste. But the eras of Francis I, Louis XIII, and Richelieu, to which the development of venality of office, financial speculation, court manners, and administrative centralization could all be traced, had also provided disappointing and ominous evidence of greed, self-indulgence, and lassitude. What Rousseau did not say, perhaps because there was no need for it, was that the middle sixteenth and early seventeenth centuries had also been a time of noble discontent, when alarmed

54. Ibid., 54–56.
55. Ibid., 45–46.
56. Ibid., 46.

spokesmen of the second estate worried openly about the nobility's fate, spoke bitterly of the devaluation of true merit and virtue, and complained at length of the deleterious effects of money, ambition, and luxury.[57]

Others have noted the mutual affinities between the ideas of Rousseau and that portion of the nobility nostalgic for feudal mores and the memory of its lost power and prestige.[58] And indeed, the *First Discourse*, like Boulainvilliers's *Essays on the Nobility of France*, validated the patriotic self-image undoubtedly embraced by many of its noble readers. By evoking the historical causes of modern corruption, and by specifying the qualities that had been lost in the process of moral decline, Rousseau permitted readers to believe that it had been the nobility, in particular, that embodied the authentic virtues of the past. The broad importance of the *First Discourse*, however, lay not in its representation of the nobility and its history, which is addressed only in the most allusive terms, but in its representation of patriotism itself. Unlike Montesquieu, who responded to the threats of despotism and corruption by reconciling himself to at least some of the features of modernity and by offering a complex and controversial apology for honor, Rousseau openly aspired to "revive love of virtue in the hearts of citizens."[59] Moreover, because he eschewed the political and moral typologies that structured Montesquieu's text, he effectively denied the existence of special structural barriers to the French pursuit of virtue. To the contrary, his account suggested that traces of virtue had been present on French soil as recently as the seventeenth century and the age of Henry IV. Patriotism was alive and well in the eighteenth century, at least as a moral ideal worth pursuing, and Rousseau associated it with noble mores reminiscent of the virtues of the ancients and available for emulation by all conscientious readers. Nobility functioned in his text as a synonym for virtue itself.

The nobility's moral and historical relationship to lost virtue, which readers had been able to infer from Rousseau's *First Discourse*, rose much closer to the surface in a widely read moral treatise published in February

57. See Jouanna, *L'idée de race*, 1: 588–613; Devyver, *Le sang épuré*, 56–109; and Smith, *The Culture of Merit*, 11–56.
58. See Jean Biou, "Le Rousseauisme, idéologie de substitution," *Roman et lumières au 18e siècle*, Centre d'Etudes et de Recherches Marxistes (Paris, 1970), 115–28; Roger Barny, "Les aristocrates et Jean-Jacques Rousseau dans la Révolution," *Annales Historiques de la Révolution Française* 50 (1978): 534–68, and *Prélude idéologique à la Révolution française: Le Rousseauisme avant 1789* (Paris, 1985); Jean Fabre, "Jean-Jacques Rousseau et le prince de Conti," *Annales de la Société Jean-Jacques Rousseau* 36 (1963–65): 7–48; Bluche, *La vie quotidienne de la noblesse*, 244–46; and, especially, Galliani, *Rousseau, le luxe, et l'idéologie nobiliaire*.
59. Rousseau (Masters), 59.

1751, Charles-Pinot Duclos's *Reflections on the Morals of Our Century.* Like Rousseau, whom he soon befriended, Duclos focused his critical attentions on the problem of moral decay in the modern era.[60] Like Montesquieu, who expressed excited admiration for Duclos's work just weeks after its appearance, Duclos respected hierarchy and regarded honor as the true opposite of the corruption that he decried.[61] But this novelist, academician, and officially named "historiographer of France" did not merely appropriate and combine the disparate ideas of his better-remembered contemporaries. Duclos synthesized the concerns expressed by Montesquieu and Rousseau and thereby formed a distinctive perspective on the need for moral reform. Duclos associated honor with nobility, as Montesquieu had, and he believed that the sentiment of honor was crucial to the future moral life of the nation. But the weakened status of the nobility as an institution nevertheless led Duclos to represent honor less as a fixed attribute of a particular estate and more as a marker of moral excellence and inner nobility of soul, a nobility characteristic of all "patriots."

The title of Duclos's first chapter, "On morals in general," betrayed the influence of Montesquieu, whose magnum opus had first inspired Duclos to examine the relationship between morals and manners. But Duclos's divided sympathies are apparent from the opening pages of the text. His allusion to distinct layers of historical development, and to the distinction between politeness and virtue, clearly evokes Rousseau's critique of the arts and sciences. "The most polite people are not also the most virtuous," Duclos declared. "Simple and severe morals are found only among a people tempered by reason and equity, [a people] that has not yet sunk into corruption through the indulgence of the mind. Well-ordered peoples [*les peuples policés*] are superior to polite peoples. Among barbarians, laws are needed to shape morals, but in a refined society, morals perfect and supplement the laws; a false politeness merely ensures that [laws] are forgotten."[62] This picture of historical progress—from barbarism to a basic and desirable level of refinement to corruption—provided the underlying framework for Duclos's analysis. Working on a canvas much smaller and more focused than that of Montesquieu, Duclos provided a carefully delineated theory of moral autonomy, and he identified the moral resources required to recover that autonomy in a corrupting environment.

60. Jacques Brengues, *Charles Duclos (1704–1772), ou l'obsession de la vertu* (Saint-Brieuc, 1971), 91–104.
61. Ibid., 83.
62. Charles-Pinot Duclos, *Considérations sur les moeurs de ce siècle,* ed. F. C. Green (Cambridge, 1939), 12.

Duclos's arguments rested on a complicated anthropological analysis of morals. Human experience, he maintained, was divided into two dimensions, one physical and the other moral. "Men are destined to live in society, and they are even obliged to do so by the need that they have for one another; one can say that they live in a state of mutual dependence. But their material needs are not all that unites them. They have a moral existence that rests on the reciprocal regard they have for each other." Despite the inescapable duality of the human condition, individuals balanced their moral and material needs in different ways. "Few men are so confident and satisfied with the opinion that they have of themselves that they can be completely indifferent to [the opinions] of others; and some are more preoccupied with meeting the demands of opinion than with meeting the needs of life itself."[63] For Duclos, this natural but unevenly manifested instinct to cultivate the opinion of the community at large ensured the stability of human society.

History had shown, after all, that laws addressed only those problems that "openly attack" society. To forestall the many indirect and invisible threats to their well-being, the inhabitants of the earliest communities had had to establish, "by tacit convention, a set of expectations that, through usage, assumed the force of law for all conscientious people, and supplemented the positive laws." These conventions, derived from the mutual recognition of informal but powerful obligations between people, were continually reinforced by the threat of "scorn and shame" that inevitably followed their violation. The force of "public opinion" so impressed upon sensitive minds the moral logic of society's agreed-upon conventions that it eventually created another judge of individual behavior: that "interior sentiment that one calls *conscience*."[64] The cohesion of human society was maintained, in Duclos's view, not by the exchange of goods or by the formal elaboration of legal or constitutional structures, but by the self-imposed and internalized moral constraints that arose from the needs of human interconnectedness.

The measurement of moral excellence, for Duclos, needed to be linked to the gradations of intensity with which people devoted themselves to satisfying the demands of "opinion" and "conscience." Probity stood out as the minimum requirement of the reputable citizen. The quality implied honesty, the quiet observance of duty, respect for the laws, and consistent compliance with public mores. In contrast to mere probity, which was per-

63. Ibid., 64.
64. Ibid., 44, 48.

fectly compatible with the pursuit of self-interest, and which "almost consists of inaction," virtue implied positive moral exertion, an active "inclination toward the good." Virtue expressed itself in "the generous effort one makes to sacrifice one's own well-being for that of others. History contains many examples of these heroic efforts. The degrees of moral virtue are measured, more or less, by the sacrifices one makes to society." Genuine virtue was acquired, according to Duclos, through the glory that accrued to its exterior signs. Any person who performed "some act of generosity," even if only by accident, would find that the satisfaction and esteem derived from the deed inevitably made subsequent gestures of generosity "less taxing." Soon the inclination toward beneficence, and a "love for humanity," would become ingrained in the conscience, and generous behavior would require "no effort" at all. Virtue may have its origin in self-regard [*amour-propre*], but "it continues through honor, and it perseveres by habit."[65]

Virtue, then, was a product of rational reflection, the cumulative moral result of many conscious and deliberate decisions to act in the interests of all. Honor, however, because it had no roots in rational calculation, represented the highest expression of the individual's moral investment in the community. Its effects were virtually identical to the effects of virtue, but honor had the added advantage of proceeding from reflex. "[Although] honor is different from probity, it really may be not at all different from virtue; but it lends brilliance to virtue, and seems to me a quality more grand." Duclos tried to clarify the point by differentiating between the various kinds of moral action. "The man of probity conducts himself according to [the lessons of] education, or by habit, interest, or fear. The virtuous man acts from goodness. The man of honor thinks and feels with nobility. It is not laws that he obeys; it is not reflection, and still less imitation, that guides his behavior. He thinks, speaks, and acts with a certain loftiness, and gives the impression of being his very own legislator." The man of honor performed generous actions naturally, often with an impetuous ardor. His "instinct for virtue" always emboldened him to act. "He never examines the issue, he acts unreflectively, even imprudently, and has none of that timidity or circumspection that stifles so many virtues among weaker souls."[66] Honor exemplified the "moral existence" whose state of atrophy Duclos wished to address because it had a self-generating logic entirely independent of laws or of the other exterior forces devised to shape and regulate human behavior.

65. Ibid., 51–53, 55.
66. Ibid., 56–57.

Unfortunately, though, the eighteenth century's moral crisis expressed itself in a general shamelessness. Duclos complained that behaviors formerly reputed to be dishonorable no longer received collective and public rebuke; emerging from the shadows where they had once hidden, they now thrived unchecked. "I am persuaded that virtues and vices are distributed more or less evenly throughout the world; but in different historical periods, it is certainly possible that [virtue and vice] would be shared unequally from nation to nation, from people to people. Eras, too, can be more or less brilliant, and ours certainly does not appear to be the age of honor, at least not when compared to an earlier time." Duclos called up for rhetorical effect the distant ideals of a pre-civilized age. "It is often said that in olden times a fanatical form of honor reigned among us, a happy mania that goes back to the centuries of barbarism. If only that mania could be revived in our own day! The enlightenment that we have acquired would help to control the enthusiasm [for honor], without smothering it."[67]

Significantly, and perhaps surprisingly, in light of honor's centrality in Duclos's moral analysis, the remedy that he proposed for French corruption differed markedly from the position laid out in *The Spirit of the Laws*. In contrast to his eminent friend from Bordeaux, who believed that the protection and nurturing of the sentiment of honor required a strong nobility, in addition to the institutional support of lesser intermediary bodies, Duclos placed all of his hopes in "general education." Echoing Rollin, he argued that all men, "of whatever profession," must be raised to be "patriots." For Duclos, this imperative meant that all must "become accustomed to find their own personal advantage within the larger context of the general good."[68] In other words, the French should receive an education designed to instill that "instinct for virtue" that Duclos regarded as the defining attribute of honor itself.

Patriotism's implicit link to the sentiment of honor resurfaces later in Duclos's text, in a chapter devoted to probity, virtue, and honor, where his concern for "general education" leads him to a discussion of the need to inculcate honorable sentiments. After describing the reflexive character of honor, the possession of which supposedly proved that one was naturally accustomed to act virtuously, Duclos went on to acknowledge honor's other-than-natural foundations. "Although honor is a natural quality, it is developed through education, it is sustained by principles, and it is forti-

67. Ibid., 57, 61–62.
68. Ibid., 20.

fied by examples. Consequently, no effort should be spared to arouse the ideas [of honor], to excite the sentiment, to stress its glory and its advantages, and to attack anything that might diminish it."[69] Duclos's program for the education of the patriot, which he neglected to sketch out in detail, would clearly have entailed a concerted and widespread effort to promote, or perhaps to revive, a national culture of honor in France.[70] Rather than select the nobility as his chosen instrument of moral reform, however, Duclos preferred to launch a socially indiscriminate discussion of the values appropriate to France's struggle against corruption.

Duclos was no social leveler, despite his own common roots. He claimed that he had no desire to "devalue an order as respectable as the nobility."[71] As the son of a Breton merchant who had gained entry, by dint of talent, to the most exclusive salons and academies, Duclos remained convinced that families of illustrious birth and rank deserved customary demonstrations of respect.[72] But even so, as his own earlier novel had shown, Duclos had been struck by the unsettling separation of the form from the content of nobility in the modern era. The second estate, it seemed, had developed no particular immunity against the shamelessness of the age. Even among those nobles otherwise inclined to do good, the confusion between signs and signified had inevitably corrupted behavior.

Far too many nobles, for example, talked about their birth as though it were a "merit," rather than a fortunate accident. They failed to appreciate that the "publicity of their names" preceded them, and that they had no need to tastelessly draw attention to their family backgrounds.[73] Still worse were the great lords who, having become spoiled courtiers, studiously affected an ostentatious grandeur and racked up disastrous debts for the sole purpose of maintaining what they regarded as a "noble air." In connection with this subject, Duclos paused to offer some general comments on the significations of the term "noble." "This term, in its general usage, signifies that which is distinguished, elevated above other things of a similar type." The word could be applied to all things physical and moral, to birth

69. Ibid., 57.
70. In a comment on the French national character, Duclos accentuated the historical continuities that linked the modern French to their earliest ancestors, including especially those who had lived in the "barbarous" age of honor. "Of all peoples, the French is the one whose character has changed the least over time; one perceives the Frenchmen of today in their forebears who went on crusade, and, if one goes back even farther to the Gauls, the resemblance is still striking (ibid., 98)."
71. Ibid., 29.
72. Ibid., 185.
73. Ibid., 28.

and bearing, for example, but also to manners, actions, speech, style, customs, and more. But according to Duclos, the meaning of the phrase "noble air" had undergone a revealing historical transformation. "In [the] nation's infancy, a noble air was an exterior that demonstrably announced strength and courage. These qualities conferred on those endowed with them a superiority over other men." But the children of those superior beings, free to enjoy the fruits of their ancestors' labors, eventually grew soft. As a result, the typical descendant of those primordial heroes "exhibits a weak and delicate bearing, especially if he is decorated with many marks of dignity; it is principally by this [appearance of weakness] that one now recognizes a noble air." Alas, concluded Duclos, the phrase could no longer be heard, as it had formerly been, to describe men of athletic figure.[74]

From Duclos's perspective, then, the nobility as an institution did not seem an especially promising place to find that "instinct for virtue" that characterized true honor and informed the attitudes of the patriot. Courtiers, far from acting impetuously on behalf of virtue, bore the marks of the "timidity" that plagues "weaker souls" and "stifles so many virtues." The *grands,* and the other nobles who habitually brandished their genealogical credentials, acted not "unreflectively" for the good of society but with affectation and calculation for the good of themselves. Duclos certainly recognized the nobility's organic connection to the honor that he sought to revive—nobles' fanatical attachment to honor in the age of barbarism provided the moral standard against which Duclos measured contemporary corruption—but its current state only underlined the historical degradation of honor that now pushed France toward the edge of the moral abyss. To find anew the seeds of a vigorous moral autonomy, and to create citizens who "think and feel with nobility," Duclos focused his attentions not on the nobility per se, but on a plan of general reform that would broadcast patriotic lessons and cultivate virtuous inclinations in all the professions.

**MIRABEAU AND NOBLE IDENTITY**

Duclos's concern to revive moral sensibilities that had been deadened by mercenary pursuits reappeared in a similar framework within the classic text of the marquis de Mirabeau, *The Friend of Man.* This highly influential book, which went through twenty printings in the four years after its initial publication in 1756, is now known mainly as an early physiocratic text, a

74. Ibid., 88.

work whose last chapters announced the pivotal partnership of Mirabeau with the physician Quesnay, the great theorist of physiocratic reform.[75] Many elements of mature physiocratic theory, as articulated during its period of political ascendancy in the 1760s, were already present in Mirabeau's relatively unsophisticated economic analysis: the celebration of farmers as the "most useful class of society," the focus on agriculture as the source of true wealth, and lengthy speculations about the relationship between agricultural production and fluctuations in population.[76] Quesnay supplied the vital scientific formulas, but the noble Mirabeau's agrarian and seigneurial sensibilities also helped define the essence of physiocracy.

Less widely appreciated, however, is the depth of Mirabeau's engagement in ongoing debates about nobility, morality, and the possibilities of French patriotism.[77] Although he found inspiration in *The Spirit of the Laws,* he responded to the provocation of Montesquieu's categories and characterizations in the way that Rousseau and Duclos had already done and many others would later do; he rearranged or modified them to fit his own narrative of French corruption and recovery. The nobility's history in the age of absolutism, and the second estate's moral resilience despite the forces arrayed against it, occupied a crucial position in that narrative.

Like Duclos, whose exposition of the "moral existence" had focused on the importance of a distinctly moral realm of experience, Mirabeau emphasized the dual character of the social bonds uniting humanity, bonds that were conveniently captured by the term "commerce." "Commerce is the useful and necessary relationship that every sociable being establishes with others. In this sense, its territory is moral as well as physical, and everything constitutes commerce in this world. . . . At the first moment when two men came together, there existed between them a reciprocal commerce of services and utility; there has never been society without commerce."[78] But the two elements of commerce did not exist in perfect

75. Though it was printed in 1756, the book's distribution was delayed until the middle of 1757, possibly because of the strictness of the censorship during the Seven Years' War. See Elizabeth Fox-Genovese, *The Origins of Physiocracy: Economic Revolution and Social Order in Eighteenth-Century France* (Ithaca, N.Y., 1976), 134, n. 1.

76. Victor de Riqueti, marquis de Mirabeau, *L'Ami des Hommes, ou Traité de la Population,* 2 vols. (Avignon, 1756; repr., Darmstadt, 1970), 1: pt. 1, 87. Volume 1, from which I draw all the material for the following discussion, is divided into three parts, each paginated separately.

77. A noteworthy exception to the rule is Michael Kwass, who has discussed the "classical republican" elements of Mirabeau's thought in both *Privilege and the Politics of Taxation,* 232–38, and "Consumption and the World of Ideas: Consumer Revolution and the Moral Economy of the Marquis de Mirabeau," *Eighteenth-Century Studies* 37 (2004): 187–213.

78. Mirabeau, *L'Ami des Hommes,* 1: pt. 2, 5.

symmetry. Mirabeau argued that "physical goods" possessed a value much inferior to that of "moral goods," which, because they could be expanded infinitely, provided the true foundation for all commerce.[79] Heading Mirabeau's list of the "moral goods" that underlay social exchange were qualities that Duclos had also emphasized: "disinterest, honor, glory, generosity, and all that arises from magnanimity." Greatness of soul was not apparent or required in every instance of commerce, however, since moral experience also manifested itself in less conspicuous "goods." Mirabeau included among them "probity, justice, fidelity, and all that pertains to truthfulness," as well as "peace, charity, and love for all those sentiments important to the cohesion of society." Together, the "moral goods" amounted to "virtue . . . that general term that comprises all of the goods of this world, whose every expression is so beautiful and worthy that even the most corrupt man cannot stop himself from admiring it in others."[80]

Commerce, then, as a phenomenon essential to sociability itself, integrated the full range of human virtues. Unfortunately, though, sociability was only one of two natural instincts that drove human behavior. Sociability's "contrary" instinct, cupidity, always threatened to overwhelm the virtues because it led to "all of the vices that dishonor humanity," including envy, pride, fraud, and cruelty.[81] Cupidity reflected humanity's susceptibility to the illusory attractions of material possessions and other mere "signs" of substance, and if it was not held in check through careful molding of humans' "acquisitive ardor," the virtues of sociability would inevitably be supplanted by a narrow, delusional, and ultimately antisocial self-indulgence.[82] Mirabeau's vision of this Manichean struggle between the moral life of sociability and the magnetic pull of cupidity colored his perceptions of France's political history and shaped his intervention in the eighteenth century's developing discussion about nobility, patriotism, and the prospects for French moral reform.

In terms reminiscent of the historical perspectives of both Rousseau and Duclos, Mirabeau represented an earlier period in the history of the French nobility as an age of lost purity. The Franks had "recognized few virtues that were not rooted principally in valor: generosity, directness, good faith, hospitality, [and] nobility, precious virtues . . . [that] found

79. Mirabeau defined the "physical goods" as follows: "health, youth, strength, beauty, wealth, dignities" (ibid., 1: pt. 2, 50).
80. Ibid., 1: pt. 2, 50.
81. Ibid., 1: pt. 1, 5–6.
82. For Mirabeau's allusion to "l'ardeur d'acquérir," see ibid., 1: pt. 2, 49.

their source in strength of body and soul, and in the independence of the mind." From the heart of "barbarism" itself came customs and habits that reflected the "most mature wisdom of the human mind," and an understanding of "natural law" that put to shame the vain claims of "modern philosophy." Mirabeau particularly cited the principles of honor that underlay "ancient chivalry," the medieval warriors' instinctive disdain for mercantile activity, and the regulated social harmony provided by "feudal laws." The signs of these rustic habits, still "lamented by the most civilized nations," were still evident as recently as the sixteenth century, when even Parisian nobles who attended the royal court remained "accustomed to the sobriety of ancient morals" and, consuming little, typically lived in modest quarters, or even in "stables on the outskirts of town."[83]

Mirabeau's patriotic reading of the French past led him to develop a pointed critique of Montesquieu's analysis of governmental types and its implicit anatomy of corruption. The mere existence of corrupt courtiers, for example, did not support Montesquieu's broader argument that the French monarchy lacked patriotism, an assertion contradicted both by logic and by history. Montesquieu had relegated patriotism to the ancient past in part because of the pervasiveness of "fantastic ideas that the stories of antiquity, possibly exaggerated, and circulated since childhood, have led us to associate with that grand phrase, 'love of the *patrie*.'" Mirabeau preferred to demystify the words by assigning them a simple definition. "Let us say that ardor for the public interest constitutes [love of the *patrie*], and that a preference for one's own personal interest is its opposite." If patriotism were understood in those straightforward terms, wrote Mirabeau, many examples of it could be found in the history of the French monarchy. "I maintain that love of the *patrie* can exist in a monarchy, since it has been vigorous [here] in the past. I know of no better proof than that residing in facts. [One need only] recall to memory the infinite number of heroic feats performed by our soldiers in the service of a king whom they had never seen and had no hope of ever seeing." This willingness to fight and die for a king "never seen" proved that the affective bonds connecting soldiers to the monarch transcended the realm of the immediate and the personal. For a "hundred years" or more, wrote Mirabeau, the French had not really known their kings, who appeared infrequently even in Paris and the major cities of the realm. Kings were known only by their edicts, by their images, and by the agents who worked in their name. Yet, "we all love

83. Ibid., 1: pt. 1, 31, 107.

the king just the same," because all recognized implicitly what the majesty of the throne represented. "It is the *patrie* . . . that one sees in the person of the king and in his family."[84]

Montesquieu had seen honor and patriotism springing from different sources, and he believed that feats of honor, because they reflected the search for distinctions, were qualitatively different from genuinely selfless demonstrations of patriotism. Mirabeau responded to that argument by decrying the rigidity of Montesquieu's basic distinction between personal interests and the interest of all. Appropriating for his own use currents of thought then associated with those who defended the morality of commerce and extolled the virtuous effects of human vices, Mirabeau argued that the personal and the social were in fact nearly indistinguishable.[85] Individuals inevitably recognized that their own particular interests were caught up in the interests of the whole, since "everyone has something to lose in times of trouble and anarchy. The interest that we all take in the maintenance of order is actually love of the *patrie*, [a love] similar to that shown by the care with which we guard the keys to our homes." Montesquieu's representation of honor as "a personal sentiment detached from any idea of patriotism" therefore obscured the complexity of human motivations. Mirabeau observed that even the "heroes" and "fanatics" of the ancient republics, "while devoting themselves to the *patrie*," had also had in mind "their personal glory."[86] After describing Roman patriotism as a "superstitious mélange" of religion, respectfulness, "tenderness for one's friends and fellow citizens, and a pride mixed up with the glory of the *patrie*," Mirabeau confidently affirmed that the French were susceptible to the very same sentiments.[87]

Mirabeau's dual convictions—that France had reached an advanced state of corruption, and that the French people had a great and even unique capacity for patriotic virtue—gave his text a schizophrenic quality, as it alternated repeatedly between tones of pessimistic condemnation and resilient optimism. The evidence of Mirabeau's conflicted perceptions is nowhere more clear than in his lengthy prognosis of France's prospects for patriotic renewal. Although he had faith in the patriotic character of the

---

84. Ibid., 1: pt. 2, 75–78.
85. The first and most arresting argument to this effect was Bernard Mandeville's essay of 1723, *The Fable of the bees; or, Private vices, public benefits*, ed. Douglas Gorman (London, 1974). Key translations of works by Shaftesbury and Hume in the 1740s and 1750s may have been more influential in the French context. See Linton, *The Politics of Virtue*, 51–128.
86. Mirabeau, *L'Ami des Hommes*, 1: pt. 2, 76.
87. Ibid., 1: pt. 2, 73–74.

French, Mirabeau did not believe that all possessed the same degree of patriotic potential. In Mirabeau's view, selflessness and selfishness coexisted and intermingled on the same moral continuum, with "ardor for the public interest" situated at one end of the spectrum, and "preference for one's own personal interest" defining the other. Those best able to resist the human instinct for cupidity tended to find their own interests in the virtues of sociability and in the satisfaction that came from making socially beneficial sacrifices. Those more susceptible to the vices of cupidity satisfied shallow desires for ephemeral goods, and they did so without regard to the claims of the public interest.

Patriotism thrived best in countries that nurtured and rewarded generous inclinations while simultaneously discouraging and containing the desire to seek empty personal gratification. In France, unfortunately, historical trends dating to the seventeenth century had worked to reinforce the wrong set of inclinations. As he surveyed the contemporary scene, Mirabeau concluded that the future prospects for French patriotism were then being decided by a silent war between the two human "instincts" of sociability and cupidity, each pulling in an opposite direction and necessarily projecting its own distinct political culture. This momentous struggle for the soul of France could be glimpsed through the changing nature of the exchange of service and recompense that bound king and people.

The reciprocal affections between the king and his people constituted, in Mirabeau's view, the surest means of planting in all hearts "love of the *patrie*." But in order to cultivate those affections, and the virtuous sentiment that grew out of them, kings needed to remember that the greatest powers of a government consisted in its "moral" rather than its "physical" goods, and that the moral qualities and gestures of those who served kings must be repaid in kind. If the person of the king, and his council, showed themselves to be "occupied only with physical interests," destructive lessons would penetrate down to the lowest reaches of the social hierarchy, and the monarchy would soon find itself with "no more obedience, unless forced and phony, no more love, unless false and feigned, no more patriotism, and no more bonds of society." Tragically, the reigns of the four Bourbon kings had coincided with the progressive squandering of the French monarchy's own moral goods. Despite the "great virtues of those princes as individuals," it could not be denied that in the previous century and a half "we have become extremely corrupt."[88]

Mirabeau laid particular blame for this development on Louis XIV,

88. Ibid., 1: pt. 2, 73, 52–53.

whose determination to make himself the source of all power and the fount of all beneficence directed all human energies toward "decoration of the edifice" that surrounded his person. In the effort to have his full majesty represented by all who served him, he "boosted the emoluments attached to offices and positions," and arranged that most of his gifts went to meet the "expenses of magnificence." Soon, instead of having one's emulation piqued by the "dignity and consideration" associated with the king's offices, or by the opportunity they offered "to gain attention through great services," attention "turned visibly toward remuneration, and the actual functions were disdained." Louis XIV, as well as other kings, had permitted "services to be measured by their weight in gold," and had even honored "moneyed men" by granting them their "familiarity, credit, attention, in short, all those things that attract the consideration [of others.]"[89] By ignoring vital distinctions in this exchange of service and reward, they had violated the venerable principle that "the type of service rendered determines the form of recompense. Friendship is rewarded with friendship, confidence with confidence, honor with honor, money with money."[90] Royal policy had opened the door to moral confusion.

That door, once opened, let in the nearly uncontrollable powers of luxury. Kings had failed to see that "once money enters a nation, bringing corruption in its wake, all distinctions based on honor are ordinarily debased, on the one hand because of their multiplicity, and on the other hand because of their poverty." Efforts to offset the declining respect shown for honorable positions and distinctions, by raising their monetary value in proportion to the level of respect to which they were supposedly entitled, only exacerbated the problem by "destroying all that is honorific and essential about the positions and making esteem a matter of finance." Mirabeau worried that the unacknowledged abandonment of the mechanism of honor, and the related surrender to luxury, would sap the moral vitality of the nation.

> From this mercenary spirit, spread throughout all the classes of society, comes the extinction of every noble principle and, consequently, of every generous action. One comes to scorn all prerogatives that cannot be translated into gold, and to avoid all functions where gold has no place, both for oneself and on behalf of one's family and relations. Now, since operations reducible to the value of gold represent in essence nothing other than ra-

89. Ibid., 1: pt. 2, 80–81, 53.
90. Ibid., 1: pt. 1, 130.

paciousness, profiteering, and usury, regardless of the disguises they may take, this gangrene soon enough overtakes the entire body of the state, and in a manner all the more incurable for having emanated from its noblest part.[91]

If allowed to proceed unchecked, Mirabeau suggested, the monarchy's unspoken policy of replacing honor with money would inevitably smother all patriotic inclinations among the French. "Once a state reaches a point where no one recognizes distinctions, recompenses, and prerogatives except those paid in gold, it will no longer have any heroes, or even any citizens; the nation will soon be nothing but a mass of mercenaries and usurers." Troubling evidence of this change had been mounting for years. In the nation's period of youth, before the eighteenth century, "who would have ever believed of the French nobility (which really constituted the Nation in those days) that its children would engage in commerce, and even in speculation, that it would speak of little other than commerce and finance, that it would scarcely concern itself with the real happiness of the people?" Perhaps alluding to his own failed attempts to secure a suitable military appointment at the court of Louis XV, Mirabeau asked, "Who could have told my ancestors that I would be writing this treatise?"[92]

Mirabeau, like both Duclos and Rousseau, looked past recent developments to find optimism in the traditions and instincts of the French. The "love of the people toward their sovereign" burned as strongly as ever. The "sociable virtues," and the taste for "generosity and nobility of morals," though they had taken new and attenuated forms in the modern age, were still "more natural to us than to any other nation;" they would provide an important foundation for the nation's "convalescence."[93] For Mirabeau, however, the chances for full recovery ultimately hinged on the historical core of the "nation," the group that had naturally proven most resistant to the seductive power of money and luxury, the nobility. The nobility demonstrated its atavistic inclination toward virtue through its ever stronger attachment to the profession of arms. "We are undoubtedly less warrior-like than we once were," Mirabeau ironically noted, "but we are more military." Although rash and instinctive displays of virtue happened infrequently in the modern age, the desire for a military career had become an "exclusive" passion among the majority of the nobility, and the noble impulse toward self-sacrifice had clearly survived the ravages of time.

91. Ibid., 1: pt. 1, 128–29.
92. Ibid., 1: pt. 2, 79, 144.
93. Ibid., 1: pt. 2, 145–46.

Unfortunately, like the country as a whole, the nobility as an institution had suffered corrosion since the seventeenth century. The paths to ennoblement had multiplied so profusely that "ridicule has now become mixed up with [noble status], a mortal wound to the French." Mirabeau mockingly noted the "general ambition of everyone in France to make his son a nobleman."[94] Meanwhile, even the greatest families of the nobility behaved with the greed of tax-farmers, and they were presumptuous enough to continue demanding honors as well as the money that they sought in the liberality of the prince. The mirage of moneyed wealth had mesmerized the nation, and with their attention diverted, both the nobility and the nation at large had neglected the moral resources essential to the health of the polity.

Despite the dire circumstances, Mirabeau expressed confidence that the nation's unhealthy habits could be reversed, just as the old and healthy customs still in force during the reign of Henry IV had been overturned in the course of the seventeenth century. "I know my nation; skilled at melting down and spending [precious] metals, it is not predisposed to honor them through the cult of habit; the faintest signal would find [the nation] ready to return to its ancient idols." The "signal" that Mirabeau awaited would involve both a concentrated effort to elicit and reward feelings of honor and a determination to bolster traditional social hierarchies. The "absolute debasement" of the old seigneurial families, and the general "obliteration" of hierarchies, represented "a prelude to total anarchy and the delirium of a people who, before vanishing from the face of the earth, [will] impudently reenact the monstrous festivals of Saturnalia." To forestall this calamity, the government needed to stifle luxury, underscore through its own actions the importance of modesty, restraint, and respect for one's superiors, and thus revive the natural regulatory capacities of honor and shame.[95]

Mirabeau did not doubt that the portion of the citizenry most responsive to the new enticements of honor and emulation would be that part of the nation "to which the prejudice of valor and fidelity is most particularly confided," the nobility.[96] He himself had had critical things to say about certain segments of the nobility—specifically, the great lords at court and the newly ennobled—and he even conceded that the distinction between noble and *roturier* may be based on an "absolute illusion," but the preju-

94. Ibid., 1: pt. 1, 93, 97.
95. Ibid., 1: pt. 2, 79, 80, 95, 108.
96. Ibid., 1: pt. 1, 87.

dices that informed the culture of the nobility were all too real, and they required protection.[97]

> I have said . . . that honor must enter into all the professions; but there are several [professions] in which one does not allow oneself to think of honor until after the profit [has been collected]. . . . Whatever amount of ridicule that two centuries of European affluence and gold have thrown upon devalued honor, and even though the source of corruption grows endlessly, it is nevertheless true that nothing would be easier than to inspire the poor nobility to content itself with honor and to do without money, especially as long as the nobility is kept separate from those professions whose purpose is to earn money.[98]

Reprising one of Montesquieu's principal themes, Mirabeau identified the noble taste for honor as the monarchy's most indispensable moral ingredient. "The prejudices that constitute honor form the real foundation of the Treasury of State, [a resource] that lessens the need for the other elements within it. It is therefore important to conserve and protect as much as possible that portion of the people in whom this form of money has the greatest currency, that is, the nobility."[99] Because morals "have infinitely more influence in society than laws," the government should act to shore up the nobility and its distinctive culture, which tended to encourage trade in "moral" rather than "physical" goods. By taking measures to preserve the most selfless and reflexive form of honor, the state would promote all the vital "virtues of sociability," patriotism prominent among them.

### REASSERTING PATRIOTISM, REDEFINING NOBILITY

In their respective assessments of the modern condition, Rousseau, Duclos, and Mirabeau all detected a troubling gap between reality and appearances, the authentic and the fraudulent, the lasting and the ephemeral. As Mirabeau put it, "corruption slips in dressed in the fine names of expertise, ability, taste, etc. I repeat, *there is nothing in the world but the true and the*

---

97. In response to the argument that the process of ennoblement replenished the ranks of a nobility depleted by losses in war and the failure of some families to reproduce, Mirabeau retorted that "if you mix vinegar with wine, you ruin both" (ibid., 1: pt. 1, 96).

98. Ibid., 1: pt. 1, 87–88.

99. Ibid., 1: pt. 3, 180.

*false, and they are what constitute good and evil.*"[100] Concerned by the effects of luxury on social and political habits, and by the rising empire of "business and money" in the modern consciousness, Rousseau, Duclos, and Mirabeau all concluded that the bonds of society had come to rest on illusory foundations. Despite some differences in emphasis, each of them sought to peel back the evil veneer of modern mores and visualize the stable ground on which a healthy society could flourish.

The authors' common preoccupation with the difference between mere appearances and underlying realities explains their close engagement with the arguments of *The Spirit of the Laws,* for Montesquieu had been the first to draw attention to the complicated relationship between deeply ingrained morals and formal laws. But despite their obvious intellectual debt to Montesquieu, Rousseau, Duclos, and Mirabeau could not be fully satisfied by *The Spirit of the Laws* because the text appeared to condone aspects of that false consciousness that all three took to be the root of modern corruption. The problem went well beyond Montesquieu's limited endorsement of luxury.[101] By arguing that the damaged institution of nobility, and the philosophically "false" honor that it embodied, formed the best available substitute for genuine virtue and patriotism in a monarchy, Montesquieu capitulated to a moral failure, and he therefore inspired a search for authentic moral purity in a misguided modern age. Rousseau, Duclos, and Mirabeau realized that mission, and stayed true to humanity's fading moral ideals, by challenging the content and configuration of three of the key analytical categories in Montesquieu's work: honor, virtue, and nobility.

As read by his three successors, Montesquieu's argument about the political inappropriateness of the principle of virtue in modern monarchies was contradicted by the very nature of the corruption that the modern age confronted. Recognition of the illusory character of eighteenth-century morals was made possible, after all, only by memories of the realities that they had replaced, memories indelibly inscribed in the habits, manners, and institutions whose deficiencies social critics now decried. If modern corruption were read as a tragic history of negation, its progress could be traced in the rise of those hollow opposites that the elemental virtues had perversely engendered. Legal titles and an emasculated "noble air" had supplanted true nobility of soul. The internal and autonomous laws of honor had been transmuted into a reflexive search for empty markers of

---

100. Ibid., 1: pt. 2, 54.
101. On Montesquieu's defense of luxury, see *De l'Esprit*, 1: 236–38 (VII, iv).

status and wealth. Courage, austerity, and military virtues had migrated to court and city, where they had been tamed and transformed into polite conversation, affectation, and cupidity. All three authors continued to believe that virtue and patriotism remained within reach because they each traced virtue's decline to historically specific, and thus reformable, institutions, processes, and developments.

Rousseau, Duclos, and Mirabeau broke down Montesquieu's distinction between honor and virtue by placing the concepts in the purifying solution of noble sentiment. But the techniques they used to redefine Montesquieu's key terms, and the social assumptions built into their arguments, differed in significant ways. In fact, what makes comparison of their texts so relevant to the long-term context of French patriotic thought is that together they represent the full range of ideas and assumptions out of which virtually all subsequent reflections on patriotism and nobility in pre-Revolutionary France would be elaborated. Although they all sought the revival of patriotic attitudes, and all took for granted that such attitudes bore the mark of nobility, they interpreted differently the impact that modern corruption had had on the essential meaning of nobility, and this subtle variation in perspective created the potential for widely divergent visions of social and political hierarchy.

Rousseau identified patriotic values with the values of the traditional nobility through an intricate process of narrative attachment. By insinuating that the story of the nobility's historical emasculation overlapped the story of declining virtue, Rousseau suggested that the nobility's bygone values of honor and military prowess were fully compatible with patriotism, and that moral renewal in the modern world would inevitably involve a resuscitation of those values. He established this identification of values, however, without ever mentioning either honor or the nobility explicitly by name. Through a sly reversal of the analysis of Montesquieu, Rousseau effectively disengaged the idea of nobility both from its institutional embodiment and from Montesquieu's semantically restricted concept of honor, and thus freed it to function as a virtual synonym for virtue. Nobility figured into Rousseau's vision of patriotic renewal, but his nobility was rooted in unrealized ideals and the shadows of memory rather than any existing social or institutional form. Nobility represented for Rousseau a set of distant moral qualities that, though particularly recognizable to some, remained equally available for the emulation of all.

Duclos expanded on certain aspects of Rousseau's theme, but the social ambiguities of his ideas ultimately expressed a greater deference toward both the established nobility and Montesquieu's moral vocabulary. In terms more explicit than those of Rousseau, Duclos distinguished between the institution of nobility, which he clearly believed had been implicated in and compromised by the phenomenon of moral decay whose progress he lamented, and those who actually "think and feel with nobility" and therefore exemplified the calling of the moral existence. He also discreetly challenged Montesquieu's definition of honor by declaring that it was "not at all" different from virtue. But despite this movement toward an ideal of nobility that transcended conventional social boundaries, Duclos also sent reassuring signals to those who feared that the solidity of the social order had been the prime casualty of modern corruption. In Duclos's scheme, honor still remained the quality that differentiated the truly noble from the merely respectable and virtuous, and it surely was no coincidence that he placed honor at the top of a familiar three-tiered hierarchy that distinguished the most common form of morality from the most rare. Moreover, his belief that birth and rank deserved customary marks of respect indicates that Duclos's simultaneous promotion of patriotism and virtuous honor remained consistent with a desire to solidify and purify, rather than to undermine, the traditional social hierarchy. By alternating between general moral condemnation and selective praise, Duclos tacitly informed his readers that a craving for moral nobility was perfectly compatible with the strengthening of a formal one.

Mirabeau, who similarly attempted to reconcile honor and virtue, went beyond Duclos in his effort to salvage the traditional social hierarchy. For him, too, the patriotic regeneration that he considered both possible and desirable in the eighteenth century depended on the reemergence of true nobility in French political culture. But because the desire for renewal and the temptation to corruption sprang from opposing human instincts arrayed along the same moral continuum, the cultivation of true nobility required strict social delineation and the careful separation of the dominant motivations underlying the different orders and professions. Honor, and the virtuous patriotism to which it was related, could indeed be found in "all the professions," but honor functioned as a way of life only among those insulated from the inevitably corrupting preoccupation with mere "physical" goods. Realization of a true, moral nobility required the existence of a formal, socially constituted nobility whose commitment to the selfless virtues could be sustained by both the reality of its separate activities and the illusion of its distinct moral identity. To be sure, Mirabeau did not represent the true nobility and the contemporary legal nobility as perfectly identical—great nobles figured among the most egregiously corrupt—but the forces of corruption could be defeated, and the sentiments of patriotism and virtue fully revived, only if the nobility regained its place of honor within a stabilized social hierarchy.

The impact of Montesquieu's *Spirit of the Laws* reverberated throughout the period stretching from the Seven Years' War to the early 1780s, as his admiring but often indignant readers sought to define a distinctly French patriotism appropriate to the modern world. The imperative to define French patriotism continued to gain momentum from the 1750s as the result of a series of dramatic political and cultural events, including the Seven Years' War (1756–63) and its demoralizing consequences, the expulsion of the Jesuits (1762–64) and the prospect of developing a genuinely "national" system of education, and the Maupeou coup of 1770–71, which inspired a new and self-consciously patriotic resistance to despotism in its ministerial form. These efforts to define patriotism took as their common starting point Montesquieu's controversial assertions about the moral character of the modern world.

The patriotic projects that appeared in such profusion in the 1750s–70s were also loosely united by an assumption that had lain behind the work of the moralists discussed in this chapter, namely, that the articulation of a French patriotism, in the wake of Montesquieu, depended on the rehabilitation of honor, or nobility, or both. The means and the precise meaning of such rehabilitation, however, varied from author to author, as each pondered the social parameters of patriotic feeling and adjusted his or her prescriptions accordingly. Some followed the precedent of Rousseau and imagined a nobility of sentiments unbounded by formal lines of stratification and characterized only by a commitment to virtue. Others echoed Mirabeau in linking patriotic renewal and the return of virtue to the reinvigoration of the second estate and its traditional code of honor. Still others, perhaps even a majority, adopted the tone of Duclos and searched for a middle road between a patriotism based on the moral equality of all virtuous citizens and a patriotism defined by the moral excellence of a few. Perhaps the most self-conscious, and certainly one of the most renowned, efforts at patriotic inventiveness in the eighteenth century was the abbé Coyer's *Noblesse commerçante* of 1756. The debate that rose up around that text provided stark demonstration that the craving for patriotism among the French, no matter how widely dispersed, was bound to engender very different recipes for social and moral reform.

# Chapter Three

## PATRIOTISM AND SOCIAL TAXONOMY IN
## THE DEBATE OVER *LA NOBLESSE COMMERÇANTE*

The 1750s gave rise to an expansive, conceptually adventurous, and long-lasting discussion about nobility's place in the social and political order, a discussion that ultimately involved scores of writers and attracted the attention of a wide reading public. Despite the great influence it exerted on the shape of that discussion, however, Montesquieu's *Spirit of the Laws* can hardly be seen as the sole, or even the primary, cause of this rich fermentation in social thought. The years around the middle of the eighteenth century saw a number of developments that focused new attention on the state of the French nobility and created the widely held perception that the second estate had ceased to resemble that honorable and honored corps of nobility that existed in the not too distant past. Three developments in particular warrant mention, because they combined to call into question the legal definition of nobility and raised doubts, at least in some minds, about the viability of the second order as an institution.

The sale of ennobling offices had gradually become an indispensable part of crown finance over the course of the later seventeenth and eighteenth centuries. The systematic marketing of ennobling offices, which had already formed part of the specter of "despotism" against which Boulainvilliers, Fénelon, and others had reacted in the 1690s, happened to reach unprecedented levels of efficiency and productivity after about 1730. In the sixty years before the Revolution of 1789, a period that one leading historian of the old regime has called the "golden age" of legal ennoblements, the much-satirized office of *secrétaire du roi* alone produced an average of about thirty-five new nobles each year.[1] Another recent estimate holds that, between 1725 and 1789, ennobling offices in their entirety created approximately 500 to 700 new nobles annually.[2] In the eyes of the more established nobility and of many disinterested observers, this influx of the newly ennobled, many of them exorbitantly wealthy financiers, accelerated the dilution and fragmentation of the second estate, and established what one commentator referred to in 1756 as a "multitude of modern nobilities."[3] The state's unacknowledged but enduring challenge to the genealogical character of noble status, and the proliferating routes of entry into the second estate, created anxiety and uncertainty about the integrity of the institution that Montesquieu had deemed to be the most vital support of monarchical government.

The crown probably aimed to offset the appearance that the king no longer valued or respected the long records of service compiled by ancient noble families when, in 1732, Louis XV adopted a strict genealogical hierarchy in regulating the distribution of honors at court. Henceforth only nobles of old stock could be formally "presented" to the king, gain entry to the royal carriage, or seek an audience with other members of the royal family. The sliding scale of genealogical requirements would be adjusted, and made even more stringent, in 1759.[4] As an experiment in soothing wounded pride and satisfying the nobility's thirst for recognition, the attentiveness to genealogy had at least some limited success, as hundreds of obscure provincial nobles flocked to Versailles to lay claim to the "honors of the court."[5] But the crown's increasing fastidiousness in the matter of legal proofs also offered further evidence of its skewed priorities. The institution of the honors of the court, by prizing families who boasted the longest genealogies, seemed in many ways consistent with a fiscal regime that bestowed honors on those possessing the largest sums of ill-gotten wealth. Both reinforced the perception, articulated aggressively by Mira-

1. David D. Bien, "Manufacturing Nobles: The Chancelleries in France to 1789," *JMH* 61 (1989): 445–86, esp. 478–79. Bien observes that with the beginning of the War of Spanish Succession, when "all restraint disappeared," royal edicts created close to a thousand ennobling offices in the provincial chancelleries alone (467–68).

2. William Doyle, *Venality: The Sale of Offices in Eighteenth-Century France* (Oxford, 1996), 165. Doyle estimates that the nobility expanded by "something like two per day" throughout the period 1725–89.

3. J. H. Marchand, *La Noblesse Commerçable ou Ubiquiste* (Amsterdam, 1756), 41.

4. In 1732, when lists of the honored first began to be compiled, the noble aspirant needed to show proof of 300 years of military nobility. In 1759, the standards were raised; henceforth, a noble needed to show, with original legal proofs, nobility dating at least to the year 1400. See François Bluche, *Les honneurs de la cour* (Paris, 1957), nonpaginated.

5. In all, only 942 families met this stringent requirement before 1789. Ibid.

beau, that the king and his court were vulnerable to deception, and unable or unwilling to recognize the true essence of merit, good character, and virtue. The rise to prominence in 1745 of Madame de Pompadour, the protégée of a financier who became, as mistress of the king, one of the most influential power brokers at the court of Louis XV, contributed to the perception of social disruption at the center of the French polity. Already by 1747–48, Pompadour herself had become the object of a "general campaign of vilification," and from the 1740s to 1789, the court became a locus of published criticism onto which a multitude of reformist visions would be projected.[6]

Apprehensions about taxonomical upheaval also received powerful reinforcement at the close of the War of Austrian Succession. In 1749, the crown began a decades-long effort to impose permanent universal taxes on its subjects, taxes that ostensibly measured only quantitative differences of wealth and disregarded qualitative differences of status. The concept of the universal tax was not new, for the *capitation* (head tax) had been established in 1695, and the *dixième* tax that Louis XIV imposed during the War of the Spanish Succession had been collected intermittently for decades. But beginning in 1749, the relentless efforts of successive finance ministers to render the taxes permanent, and to ensure their fair distribution, sparked disputes that focused critical attention not only on the state's taxing authority but also on the rationale underlying the tax exemptions of the privileged orders.[7] Resistance to ministerial efforts to create a permanent *vingtième* tax provided one of several issues around which the noble magistrates of the parlements—who were empowered to register, or to refuse to register, new royal legislation—formed a nascent oppositional ideology in their dealings with the crown in the 1750s.[8]

The convergence of these various phenomena at mid-century inspired a wide public critique of noble status and of the strange courtly environment that had seemed to intensify both the genealogical consciousness and the frivolity of the most exalted elites. The new tone of mockery was perhaps best expressed through the biting irony of Voltaire, who introduced on the first page of his satirical *Candide* (1759) the absurd baroness Thunder-ten-Tronckh. Voltaire's readers learned that, although the baron-

---

6. Thomas Kaiser, "Madame de Pompadour and the Theaters of Power," *FHS* 19 (1996): 1025–44, esp. 1029.
7. For discussion of the origins of the "vingtième" and other universal taxes, and the abundant published commentary they generated, see Kwass, *Privilege and the Politics of Taxation*, 33–38, 117–252.
8. On parlementary opposition see Jean Egret, *Louis XV et l'opposition parlementaire, 1715–1774* (Paris, 1970).

ess had been perfectly willing to fornicate with a certain "gentleman of the region," she had refused to marry him because "he could prove only seventy-one generations of noble lineage, the rest of his family tree having been lost in the shadows of time."[9] Around mid-century, many joined Voltaire in ridiculing the misplaced pride and arrogance of much of the nobility. Noting sarcastically that the prerogatives of nobility had been "reduced to a rather modest pecuniary value," in 1756 the economic theorist Forbonnais mockingly addressed the prospect that "we will all soon be nobles."[10] In a new *Essai sur les moeurs* of the same year, the lawyer Jean Soret insisted that "one more degree of merit will always be of greater value to society than ten centuries of nobility."[11]

Amidst this critical atmosphere, in which formal hierarchies were being subjected to new and often disapproving scrutiny, the editor of the *Mercure de France* decided to publish, in December 1754, some scattered reflections of the late marquis de Lassay, a noted free thinker and former member of the Club de l'Entresol who had died in 1738.[12] The reflections comprised only fifteen pages, and in some ways they were refreshingly unorthodox; the noble Lassay more or less accepted, for example, the defense of luxury propounded by Mandeville and especially associated, in France, with Jean-François Melon's controversial *Political Essay on Commerce* (1734).[13] But Lassay also represented the moral relationship between nobility and commoners in a way that touched a nerve with at least one of his readers, the abbé Gabriel-François Coyer. Referring to the oft-repeated suggestion that nobles be permitted to engage in commerce, Lassay insisted that the nobility should remain tied to the military vocation. He claimed that it was only the presence of the nobility in the army that had assured the superiority of French arms in the past, since "the [common] soldiers of other nations are at least as good as ours, and more accustomed to work." Lassay represented the nobility as a morally superior class whose sentiments of honor and "warrior spirit" made it especially inclined toward selfless sacrifice on the field of battle.[14]

9. Voltaire, *Candide,* ed. Daniel Gordon (Boston, 1999), 41.

10. François Véron Duverger de Forbonnais, *Lettre à M.F., ou examen politique des prétendus inconvéniens de la faculté de commercer en gros, sans déroger à la noblesse* (n.p., 1756), 17, 79.

11. Jean Soret, *Essai sur les moeurs* (Brussels, 1756), 129.

12. "Réflexions de M. le marquis de Lassé, mort en 1738," *MF,* December 1754, vol. 2: pp. 86–101.

13. For the long debate on luxury, which Melon's essay reignited in France, see John Shovlin, "The Cultural Politics of Luxury in Eighteenth-Century France," *FHS* 23 (2000): 577–606; Ellen Ross, "Mandeville, Melon, Voltaire: The Origins of the Luxury Controversy in France," *SVEC* 155 (1976): 1897–1912; and M. R. de Labriolle-Rutherford, "L'évolution de la notion du luxe depuis Mandeville jusqu'à la Révolution," *SVEC* 26 (1963): 1025–36.

14. "Réflexions de M. le marquis de Lassé," 86–87.

Coyer had good reasons to resent Lassay's dismissal of commerce as a profession antithetical to generous values.[15] The son of a merchant draper from Franche-Comté whose literary talents and progressive thinking earned him a position as tutor to the son of the philosophically-minded duc de Bouillon, Coyer had become involved with the so-called Gournay circle of economic theorists in the early 1750s.[16] The Gournay group, led by the intendant of commerce Vincent de Gournay, sought new ways to promote commerce and to erase France's traditional prejudices against it. Already in 1754, one of Coyer's associates in the Gournay group, Plumard de Dangeul, had published a treatise that compared England's favorable treatment of commerce to France's lamentably backward attitudes. He complained that in France "all operates by honor or vanity," and he provocatively charged that French nobles were unworthy of the title of citizen.[17] Coyer, in his retort to Lassay, likewise advanced the Gournay program by highlighting the social and political benefits of a thriving commerce.

Coyer attracted wide public attention, however, not because he promoted commerce or showed a willingness to criticize nobility, neither of which would have seemed novel in the mid-1750s, but because he conspicuously joined consideration of those subjects to the larger challenge of thinking through the meaning of French patriotism. Coyer had already expressed his interest in the subject in an essay of 1755, where he complained hyperbolically about the French abandonment of *patrie* as both word and concept.[18] Recent content analyses of political writing in the

15. For the outlines of Coyer's biography, see Leonard Adams, *Coyer and the Enlightenment* (Banbury, U.K., 1974), 19–25.
16. On the rising influence of Gournay, and his innovative circle of economists, see Antoin E. Murphy, "Le développement des idées économiques en France (1750–1756)," *RHMC* (1986): 521–41; and Gustave Schelle, *Vincent de Gournay* (Paris, 1897; repr. Geneva and Paris, 1984;), esp. 227–52. On the growing interest in commercial and broadly economic subjects in the published literature of the 1750s, 1760s, and 1770s, see also Jean-Claude Perrot, "Nouveautés: L'économie politique et ses livres," in *Histoire de l'édition française*, vol. 2, *Le livre triomphant, 1660–1830*, ed. Henri-Jean Martin and Roger Chartier (Paris, 1984), 240–57; Edgard Depitre, "Le système et la querelle de la noblesse commerçante (1756–1759)," *Revue d'Histoire Economique et Sociale* 6 (1913): 137–76; Henry Lévy-Bruhl, "La noblesse de France et le commerce à la fin de l'ancien régime," *Revue d'Histoire Moderne* 8 (1933): 209–35; Loïc Charles and Philippe Steiner, "Entre Montesquieu et Rousseau. La Physiocratie parmi les origines intellectuelles de la Révolution française," *Etudes Jean-Jacques Rousseau* 11 (1999): 83–159; and Shovlin, "Toward a Reinterpretation of Revolutionary Antinobilism."
17. Plumard de Dangeul, *Remarques sur les Avantages et les Desavantages de la France et de la Grande Bretagne, par rapport au commerce* (Leyden, 1754), 31, 43–46, 48.
18. Coyer's text, the "Dissertation sur le vieux mot de patrie," has been re-edited by Edmond Dziembowski: *Gabriel-François Coyer, Jacob-Nicolas Moreau: Ecrits sur le patriotisme, l'esprit public, & la propagande au milieu du XVIIIe siècle* (La Rochelle, 1997), 41–53.

eighteenth century have underscored the inaccuracy of his claims, because it was precisely in the period when he was writing that the words *patrie* and *nation* came to saturate published literature in France.[19] Nevertheless, Coyer's concern was genuine enough, because *La noblesse commerçante* (1756) focused as much on the need for patriotic sensibilities in France as on the desirability of supporting commerce and the vocation of the merchant.

During his time as a tutor in the home of Bouillon, Coyer had made the acquaintance of the Fénelonian chevalier Ramsay, and it was perhaps through his involvement with Ramsay that Coyer had initially developed his quasi-classical understanding of French patriotism.[20] In any case, showing an alert appreciation for the moral leveling implicit in the embrace of virtue, Coyer constructed a spiritual and inclusive definition of nobility rooted in feelings of commitment to one's country. He elaborated his vision of nobility through an extensive reworking of the concept of honor, an effort that inevitably led him to engage Montesquieu's earlier analysis of the competing "principles" of republican and monarchical governments. The visions of patriotism and nobility that emerged from Coyer's work elicited a fierce response from a more conservative defender of Montesquieu's analysis, the chevalier d'Arc, and after a rejoinder by Coyer in 1757, the debate over commercial nobility (*noblesse commerçante*) came to involve dozens of writers and continued unabated for several years.[21] Echoes of the debate could be heard, in fact, to the very end of the old regime.[22]

---

19. See the discussion of Dziembowski, *Un nouveau patriotisme français*, 350–68; see also Bell, *The Cult of the Nation*, 56–57.

20. See Adams, *Coyer and the Enlightenment*, 23–24. Expressions of respect for the patriotic virtues of the Romans and Spartans would be a hallmark of Coyer's writing to the end of his career. See, for example, his *Plan d'Education Publique* (Paris, 1770), iii.

21. Gabriel-François Coyer, *La noblesse commerçante* (London, 1756); Philippe Auguste de Sainte-Foy, chevalier d'Arc, *La noblesse militaire, opposée à La noblesse commerçante: Ou le patriote français* (Amsterdam, 1756). The chevalier's name is often spelled Arcq, and the title pages of his works bear that spelling. Confusion about the spelling of his name arose from the very beginning, however, and the variation continues to this day. The name was spelled Arc by Alès de Corbet, for example, in his *Nouvelles Observations sur les Deux Systèmes de la Noblesse Commerçante ou Militaire* (Amsterdam, 1758), 4. Among modern authors, William Doyle follows the custom in *The Oxford History of the French Revolution* (Oxford, 2002), 30, as does Colin Jones, *The Great Nation* (Oxford, 2002), 331. For the sake of consistency within my own published work I have opted for the shorter spelling.

22. For example, Mably made allusions to Coyer and the debate he had inspired in his widely read *Entretiens de Phocion* of 1763, when he referred unfavorably to "those who speak only of extending commerce and enriching the state." Gabriel Bonnot de Mably, *Entretiens de Phocion, sur le rapport de la morale avec la politique* (Amsterdam, 1763), 238.

In a recent discussion of the Coyer-Arc debate, Pierre Serna represents the conflict between the abbé and the chevalier as a confrontation between enlightened values (Coyer) and defensive, nostalgic fantasy (Arc).[23] Reprising the "revisionist" theme that the nobility lacked any coherent sense of itself in the eighteenth century, Serna argues that, after about 1720, "winds of intellectual reform" forced a diffuse and fragmented nobility to redefine itself. Challenged by an "enlightened discourse" that promoted talent, merit, professional achievement, and the natural equality of man, nobles responded either by recognizing and celebrating the legitimacy of the critique directed against them, or by improvising new justifications for noble status. In this new "struggle for classification," Arc and others who took up the "defense" of nobility worked under the illusion that by adapting "the form of the new discourse," they could "mask the conservation of ancestral values." Their efforts to articulate a "coherent" and "positive" image for the nobility provided some noble readers a new sense of legitimacy and security, suggests Serna. But in fact, the fictional and ideological unity that they created through their emphasis on historical traditions, pedigrees, and inherited principles only ensured that nobility came to be "ideologically discredited," and thus vulnerable to righteous anger, well before the Revolution.[24]

Several debatable assumptions inform this analysis, but perhaps the most misleading involves the ideational dynamics shown to be driving discussion over *noblesse commerçante*. As Serna explains it, Arc, like the nobility as a whole, was aroused to consciousness by the presence of an external threat—the "enlightened discourse" deployed by Coyer—and Arc responded defensively by inventing a new rationale for noble status and by disingenuously appropriating new language to "mask" traditional claims. By asserting the existence of mutually opposing languages, and by representing Arc and Coyer as battling to determine the dominance of one discourse over another, Serna obscures the fascinating processes of negotiation internal to each text and integral to the broader "struggle for classification" in which they were engaged.

Interpretive dispositions are never closed or impermeable, and words, concepts, and ideals are not the exclusive property of a social group or an intellectual current such as the "movement of Enlightenment."[25] Merit, utility, and the pursuit of the general good were part of a common stock of ideas open to the use and rearrangement of any and all individuals en-

23. Serna, "Le noble," esp. 68–74.
24. Ibid., 68.
25. Ibid., 68, 71.

gaged in public discussion in the eighteenth century. Moreover, one of the express purposes of Coyer's supposedly "enlightened" text was to demonstrate that honor, glory, and status did not comprise a language specific to the nobility. The Coyer-Arc exchange, then, should not be seen as a debate between a proponent of Enlightenment, on the one hand, and a traditionalist suddenly awakened to the need to find and justify a new role for his class, on the other hand. Sustained and creative reflection on the role, function, and definition of the nobility had characterized political and moral discussion since the beginning of the century. The "struggle for classification" to which Arc and Coyer gave voice arose from the ambiguous moral imperatives inherent in a developing French patriotism, and the immediate context most relevant to their discussion was the dissemination throughout the 1750s of the categories and arguments of Montesquieu.

Alluding subtly but repeatedly to the framework laid out by Montesquieu in *The Spirit of the Laws*, Coyer argued, in effect, that the cultural choice between honor and virtue also implied a choice between an open, expansive nobility and a narrow, exclusive one, between a civic culture based on the common quality of citizenship and one based on the differentiating qualities of rank. By pointing directly to the possible social remapping that lay implicit in the push for patriotic revival, and by making his own strong case for the widening of nobility, Coyer threw open for discussion the social configuration of a patriotic monarchy. In his response to the abbé, Arc defined the morality of patriotism in a way that demanded the maintenance of a corporate social order. The abiding importance of these differing perspectives, with their shared patriotic roots, would be demonstrated in dramatic fashion in 1789.

## COYER: HONOR, UTILITY, AND THE *PATRIE*

The eighteenth century's upsurge in international commercial activity, and the wave of discussion that grew up around the subjects of commerce and political economy from the 1730s, formed part of the context that helped to produce the abbé Coyer's controversial ruminations on the relationship between nobility and commerce. Equally present in Coyer's thinking, however, were the new semantic vulnerability of the concept of nobility and the evidently shifting foundations of the French social order. Coyer distinguished between "the brilliant nobility that lives in palaces" and the "obscure nobility that sees each day the châteaux of its fathers fall into ruin," the "new men who have risen by their work" and the "ancient nobles who have fallen into indolence," the nobles who lived "in the center of luxury" and those who labored alongside the poorest peasant farmers.[26] In the elaborate defense of his system published in 1757, he also noted that, unlike centuries past, "today the nobility is a dispersed corps, having no occasion to assemble, no representation, and no influence in public affairs."[27] For Coyer, this recognition of the nobility's fragmented and weakened condition gave rise not to nostalgia or sympathy, but to feelings of anger and disgust. The second estate's failure to sustain its own moral ideals, and the seduction of a large segment of the nobility by the forces of luxury and selfishness, induced Coyer into articulating a social argument that would reach full maturity only in 1789. According to the terms of this argument, the existence of an enclosed and privilege-laden nobility stood as an affront to the nation because it perpetuated an unjust and anachronistic form of inequality among citizens. Coyer justified his stance by building his argument around a confrontation of categories: the useful citizen versus the honorable noble.

Coyer (Figure 3) sought to underline the illegitimacy of noble privilege by systematically contrasting the characteristics of the current nobility with the characteristics of the nation at large. "There are in general," wrote Coyer in his work of 1757, "two classes in the nation. One, the active class, produces constantly; it consists of farmers, workers, artisans, sailors, and merchants." This collection stood in sharp contrast to the unproductive groups who made up the second class—clergy, men of war and justice, rentiers, lackeys, beggars, idlers, and *grands seigneurs*. "This second class, . . . created only to consume, produces no wealth at all."[28] By placing beggars and idlers in a broad class of undesirables that also included soldiers, magistrates, and noble landlords, Coyer achieved the same rhetorical sleight of hand managed in 1789 by the abbé Sieyès, whose incendiary *What Is the Third Estate?* constituted a nobility "foreign to the nation by its idleness."[29] Indeed, like Sieyès, who specifically condemned noble idleness as "treason against the public good," Coyer averred that the refusal to work for one's living represented "a continual crime committed against the Nation."[30]

This contrast between a grasping nobility and a victimized nation also

26. Coyer, *La noblesse commerçante*, 7, 34, 35.

27. Coyer, *Développement et défense du système de la noblesse commerçante*, 2 vols. (Amsterdam and Paris, 1757), 1: 92.

28. Coyer, *Développement et défense*, 1: 37–38.

29. Emmanuel Joseph Sieyès, *Qu'est-ce que le tiers état?*, ed. Roberto Zapperi (Geneva, 1970) 125.

30. Ibid., 123; Coyer, *La noblesse commerçante*, 46.

GABRIEL FRANÇOIS COYER,
Des Académies de Nancy
de Rome et de Londres

FIGURE 3. Gabriel-François Coyer (1782). Known for his light-hearted satires in the late 1740s and early 1750s, Coyer moved to acquire a weightier literary reputation in the middle 1750s after falling in with the Gournay circle of economic thinkers and having become convinced that the patriotic virtues held out great promise for a country in need of reform. Bibliothèque Nationale de France

underlay Coyer's general perspective on French history and the slow march of progress. He admitted that the very idea of a commercial nobility would have seemed absurd "in the barbarous times of feudal government, when the nobility held half of France in abject servitude."[31] In that benighted age, when land and labor formed the essential ingredients of material well-being, the French nobility put no effort into the cultivation of its fiefs because "it had under its hand an enserfed people that labored on command." Fortunately the balance of power, and the needs of the nobility, had gradually changed. "The nation, in throwing off its barbarism, liberated itself in several respects, and today if the nobility wants to reap its produce, it must first hire workers and spend money in order to till the ground."[32] Following the argument of Hume's recently published *Political Discourses,* Coyer asserted that the rise of a money economy and the spread of political liberty constituted a single historical development discernible in the changing relations between the nobility and other classes. As peasants acquired the means to farm more land, they became "independent of those petty tyrants" known as "*Seigneurs.*" Meanwhile, "merchants and traders acquired property and brought some measure of authority and consideration to this middling order of men, which is the best and firmest base of public liberty."[33]

In light of these improvements, plans to remilitarize the nobility and to purge the army of ignoble blood represented nothing more than a perverse design to turn back the clock. "That was the arrangement in the earliest days of the Monarchy. The Franks, who were stronger, declared themselves *Nobles* and made the natives of the land *Commoners.* The nobles fought and the commoners worked and practiced the useful arts." Some military reformers, charged Coyer, sought to renew "this order of things" by keeping the nation divided into two distinct parts. "The entire nobility would be stationed on the frontiers; and with its valor serving as a rampart, the rest of the realm, that is to say, the essential part of the Nation [*le fonds de la Nation*], would be engaged in agriculture, the arts, the sciences, finance, commerce, law, and religion. . . . The French people would vivify everything, while the nobility defends everything."[34] For Coyer, the nobility's modern decline only underscored how much it had benefited from the Franks' unjust usurpation of privileged status at the dawn of the monar-

31. Coyer, *La noblesse commerçante,* 8–9.
32. Ibid., 49–50.
33. Coyer, *Développement et défense,* 1: 50.
34. Ibid., 2: 187–89. "Le peuple François suffiroit à tout vivifier & la Noblesse à tout défendre."

chy's history. Lassay and the other promoters of a fully aristocratic military merely sought to give new form to an ancient injustice.

As an expression of the principle of division of labor, the idea of separating the military profession from the various "useful arts" did not especially offend Coyer.[35] What bothered him was the implicit moral hierarchy that underlay this traditional form of professional segregation. The hierarchy of honor that served as the justification for noble preeminence and the prestige of the military profession no longer corresponded to modern realities—in part because the value of honor was now regularly betrayed by nobles themselves, and in part because the value needed to be redefined to reflect the needs and sensibilities of an increasingly self-conscious nation. "It is quite unfortunate for monarchies, and especially for ours where the prejudice of honor dominates so completely, that they tend to be guided only by this principle [of honor] and not by virtue, as one finds in republics. Honor does not operate ceaselessly as virtue does."[36] The two sources of personal motivation had something in common, to be sure, but the "republican" principle entailed genuine subordination of self-interest and therefore produced more widely beneficial effects. "Condé won battles with no regard to the cost in blood, and that was *honor.* Turenne was also victorious, but he lost ten thousand fewer Frenchmen; that was *virtue.*"[37] Claims to distinction should arise not out of a selfish concern for one's own glory, but from a truly patriotic selflessness reminiscent of republican virtue.

To outgrow its old-fashioned and ineffective attachment to honor, and to develop the instinct for virtue, the nobility needed to orient its attention toward the needs of the country and away from the person of the king. Coyer had already grumbled, in 1755, that soldiers invariably described themselves as servants of the king rather than the *patrie.*[38] In *La noblesse commerçante,* he continued to harangue noble readers about the need to recognize the needs of the nation, and to direct the vaunted "generosity" of the nobility toward the needs of the entire country. Every young noble, he remarked, wishes "to lay down his life in the service of the king." But the king, he observed, "does not need so many servants; the state needs them."[39]

35. Cf. Coyer's *Plan d'éducation publique.*
36. Coyer, *Développement et défense,* 1: 137.
37. Ibid., 1: 138.
38. Coyer lamented the king-centered notion of service and civic duty that seemed to exclude in France any consideration of the *patrie.* "I ask one of these citizens who always goes about armed: What is your occupation [*emploi*]? 'I serve the king,' he says. But why not the *Patrie?*" See Dziembowski, ed., *Ecrits sur le patriotisme,* 41.
39. Coyer, *La noblesse commerçante,* 12.

By measuring service and sacrifice through the lens of state requirements rather than through the eyes of the king, the nobility could come
to see the patriotic value of engaging in commerce. The activity would help
to enrich the nation at large, decrease unemployment, increase the population, and, moreover, help to "prevent the ruin of the nobility."[40] Pointing out the irony that young nobles, in their quest to be "something,"
frequently had to be content to do "nothing," Coyer urged them to shed
their prejudices and become involved in this traditionally non-noble profession that accomplished so much good for the *patrie*. He concluded his
exhortation with the reminder that "the Nation awaits your services."[41]

In attempting to establish the moral equivalence of military and commercial activities, Coyer underscored the virtuous dimension of commerce
and asserted an abstract notion of the public good as the ultimate arbiter
of merit and service. But he did not stop there. He also attacked the deficit
in merchants' prestige from the other direction, and argued for the in-
herently "honorable" character of merchants and their work. In other
words, he attempted, in a manner comparable to the conceptual tinkering
carried out by Duclos and Mirabeau, to merge the values of honor and
virtue in a patriotic mix that yielded the highest noble sentiments and, consequently, the only truly justifiable claims to noble status.

The prospect of a commercial nobility had become thinkable in the
eighteenth century, wrote Coyer, because commerce itself "has begun to
acquire nobility in the eyes of the public."[42] This social mobility of the
imagination had begun to occur not only because of the recognized utility of the merchant's profession but also because of the moral character of
those who practiced it. Commoners had frequently shown that "one can
be brave without being noble," and Coyer noted that individuals of "bourgeois birth" had repeatedly shown evidence of "a noble soul" in the king's
armies.[43] But merchants, in particular, did not require access to the theater of war in order to express their admirable qualities. Contrary to prejudice, the moral impulses that drove commercial activity were fully
analogous to those more often associated with military service. Coyer invited his readers to compare the *grands* of the court, and their outdated
prejudices, to merchants, "these active citizens whose wealth produces that
of so many others, these nurturers of the arts and of men. Which side possesses honor, decency, importance, dignity, and true nobility?"[44] Here

40. Ibid., 35.
41. Ibid., 214.
42. Ibid., 8.
43. Coyer, *Développement et défense*, 1: 80; *La noblesse commerçante*, 13.
44. Coyer, *La noblesse commerçante*, 110.

Coyer did not contest the conventional association of honor with nobility, but he announced that the time had come to reconsider the forms through which these high moral ideals were expressed.

Coyer acknowledged that, according to tradition, honor was exemplified through the search for glory on the battlefield. He nevertheless aimed to persuade his readers, through creative clarifications of meaning, that the detection of true honor required a much larger perspective. "Glory, this passion that characterizes elevated souls, this motive for grand actions, is not always well understood." Nobles of the sword, for example, based their exalted reputations and their own self-respect on their record of "services, dangers, and blood. And without doubt, it is admirable to suffer and die for one's *patrie*. But do you think that commerce does not have its own services, its own dangers, its own combats?" Merchants and soldiers followed different careers, but these were simply separate paths toward a similarly glorious end. "Is there no glory in exploiting the natural advantages of one's homeland, in putting men to work, in making the land productive, in seeing that money circulates through the body of the state, in establishing public credit, in expanding the realm's wealth into a new world that nature had wanted to conceal?" Credit for the settlement of New France clearly belonged to the merchants "who made the first discoveries," who went to the trouble of comparing the economic needs of France and America, and who "conquered the natives of the land with kindness and the attractions of commerce."[45] In pursuing their work, moreover, merchants had also established new friendships between foreign peoples and the kingdom of France. By "procuring allies for the *patrie*," they had earned added glory and demonstrated the value of their profession.

Coyer challenged nobles' convictions about their moral superiority by using their own vocabulary of self-identification—honor, blood, combat—to describe the activities of the merchant class, and by ascribing new meanings to that vocabulary in the process. Unlike the great nobles who consistently identified honor with "titles and vanity," the merchant based his claim to prestige on possession of "this other honor, less brilliant, that consists in the knowledge of needs, in the perfection of the arts, in application, frugality, probity, public credit, in the pursuit of enterprises that are peaceful but useful to one's family and to the state."[46] An ingrained sense of duty shaped the merchant's attitudes toward all activities, including leisure. "If [the merchant] gambles, it is only after having applied himself seriously; if he pursues pleasure, it is only after work; if he spends, he

45. Ibid., 131–32, 150.
46. Coyer, *Développement et défense*, 1: 139.

spends wisely; if he gives, it is only after having paid his debts."[47] With this undisguised jab at the frivolity and ostentatious display that characterized much of the nobility, Coyer identified true honor—the "less brilliant" kind—with vigilant attachment to one's domestic and civic responsibilities, and a broad-minded concern for the general well-being. Although it lacked occasions for spectacular display, the merchant's honor was wholly admirable for being directed in all ways toward the good of the state.

Coyer's analysis, which drew its rhetorical power from its emphasis on the gap between official marks of status and the moral qualities that high status supposedly signified, contained multiple contradictions of its own. "I speak of utility," Coyer had declared near the conclusion of *La noblesse commerçante*.[48] He expressed this commitment to the principle of utility by drawing a distinction between productive and unproductive citizens, by describing money and commerce as positive forces of historical progress, and by incorporating Mandeville's arguments about the virtuous effects of private vices.[49] But Coyer's utilitarian and materialist arguments could not be easily reconciled with schemes of social differentiation based on scales of morality, which inevitably assessed degrees of selfishness and accorded the greatest esteem to those who denied their own self-interest. Hence Coyer's contradictory characterization of the value of the merchant's profession. On the one hand, he argued that the merchant's "dangers" and "combats" were as selfless and ennobling as the risks run by soldiers on the field of battle. But on the other hand, he acknowledged that merchants' patriotism often arose from their will to defend their wealth and possessions, and that they "only see the *patrie* where they see their own happiness."[50] Such a fundamentally ambiguous account of the patriotic character of merchants would have held out little appeal to the likes of Rousseau, Duclos, or Mirabeau, all of whom associated patriotic virtues with the triumph of moral instinct over merely physical appetites.

The basic contradictions in Coyer's thinking also shone through in his attitude toward the nobility. In many sections of his two works, Coyer barely

---

47. Coyer, *La noblesse commerçante*, 110–11.
48. Ibid., 207.
49. Coyer declared it necessary to "govern [men] by their passions, and draw good from the bad." See *Développement et défense*, 1: 56.
50. Ibid., 1: 128. Coyer wrote that "those who have much to defend are stirred by the sight of their possessions placed in danger." For the contemporary debates about the "passions," see Albert O. Hirschman, *The Passions and the Interests: Political Arguments for Capitalism before Its Triumph* (Princeton, 1977), esp. pt. I; Hundert, *The Enlightenment's Fable;* Wright, *A Classical Republican in Eighteenth-Century France,* 82–84, 89–90; Pocock, *The Machiavellian Moment,* 462–505.

contained his anger at the nobility's privileged status or his contempt for traditional noble values. To assure his noble readers that their involvement in commerce would not entail sacrifice of the privileges they cherished, he remarked, for example, that they could still "grouse about the bourgeois who assume [coats of arms], boast of your ancestors to those who would not dare question you, cling religiously to that precious first syllable [of your name]," and even preserve the exemption from the *taille*, "so long as you pay it under another name."[51] Elsewhere he hinted that the need "to preserve clearly the distinctive mark of each of the three orders" had vanished with the monarchy's practice of convening the Estates-General.[52] This willful mockery of noble pride, and skepticism of noble superiority, also colored Coyer's discussion of the second estate's military inclinations. In one passage, he had a fictional noble son describe the domestic formation of the future soldier: "We learned at an early age how to swear, to quarrel, to insult everyone who is not noble, to handle arms, to shoot at the scouts in rival hunting parties, to devastate the crops, to maim peasants . . . in short, we were trained for the army."[53]

But despite his utilitarian distaste for military values, and his precocious rhetoric of national liberation, Coyer nevertheless projected a new social and moral order that retained important features of the traditional one that he criticized so severely. He conceded, for example, that the modernized nobility should have the right to hold on to a set of identifying marks—"rights of precedence, prerogatives, privileges"—and even to "conserve its [distinctive] character."[54] Even more telling was Coyer's strategy for elevating the dignity of the merchants' profession in the eyes of those who disdained it. He argued that the profession had begun to "ennoble" itself through quiet display of its own patriotic virtues. In addition to hard work, productivity, responsibility, and modesty, those virtues also included honor, courage, generosity, and a taste for glory.[55] Indeed, according to Coyer, the possession of those common virtues explained why "commerce will not efface" the traditional moral identity of the nobility. Taking a page from Montesquieu, Coyer generalized the "self-love that searches for distinction," and confidently declared that "the characteristic of the Frenchman is honor itself."[56] As the very title of *La noblesse com-*

51. Coyer, *La noblesse commerçante*, 152.
52. Coyer, *Développement et défense*, 1: 92.
53. Coyer, *La noblesse commerçante*, 15.
54. Coyer, *Développement et défense*, 1: 100, 93.
55. Ibid., 1: 124–36.
56. Ibid., 1: 93, 144.

*merçante* indicates, he accepted the existence of a moral elite that possessed special status within the nation; he wished only to establish that the "nobility" to which distinguished individuals could justly lay claim actually derived from widely distributed abilities and inclinations found even among those professions traditionally deemed antithetical to the noble calling.

Coyer's apparent contradictions left him vulnerable to criticism on many fronts, as his detractors throughout the late 1750s took delight in pointing out. But the importance of his argument lay not in its inner coherence, which very few commentators on patriotism and nobility ever managed to achieve in the years before the Revolution, but in its creative attempt to balance the conflicting demands of a virtuous patriotism articulated within the legal and moral framework of a society of orders. Confronting the challenge of fraternal equality that lay implicit in the classical variant of patriotism— a challenge so daunting that it had led Montesquieu to construct for monarchies an entirely different civic principle whose very essence was hierarchy—Coyer devised a social system that combined hierarchical features with egalitarian ideals. By referring insistently to utility, the well-being of the *patrie,* and the hybrid characteristic of honor/virtue, Coyer elaborated a more widely accessible model of civic excellence and razed the putative moral barrier between nobility and nation. In proposing the establishment of a *noblesse commerçante,* he effectively told his readers that honor, decency, and "true nobility" lay in the practice of a utilitarian and patriotic morality embraced by all the "active citizens" in a shared community.

## ARC: HONOR, INTERESTS, AND THE CHARACTER OF THE NATION

The first and fullest critique of *La noblesse commerçante* appeared within months of its publication in January 1756. The chevalier d'Arc, a retired but decorated soldier who enjoyed the rare distinction of being the illegitimate son of one of the illegitimate sons of Louis XIV, responded to Coyer's idea for a *noblesse commerçante* by reasserting the traditional moral distinction between honor and profit.[57] In *La noblesse militaire,* Arc presented an argument largely derived from well-known sources. He reaffirmed the nobility's traditional association with the army, he predictably invoked the categories of Montesquieu, and he condemned commerce on

---

57. Arc entered the cavalry in 1737, and won the cross of Saint-Louis for his bravery at the battle of Fontenoy. He left the army in 1748, in part because his resources were inadequate to bear the expenses of leadership. See Jean-Pierre Brancourt, "Un théoricien de la société au XVIIIe siècle: le chevalier d'Arc," *Revue Historique* 250 (1973): 337–62.

grounds that it promoted the horrors of luxury. But despite the presence in Arc's work of these familiar points of reference, the carefully chosen wording of his title announced the author's intent to define both the "military nobility" and the "French patriot," and these dual objectives necessarily carried Arc onto the ambiguous terrain explored by his opponent Coyer. There he, too, confronted a troubling tension between the competing imperatives of equality and inequality—a tension that Coyer had resolved by offering a new and inclusive version of "true nobility." For his part, Arc sought a solution to the problem by developing a simultaneously traditional but endlessly elastic definition of noble honor.

Following Montesquieu, Arc insisted that the monarchical form of government required clear distinctions between the "three principal classes: the clergy, the nobility, and the third estate." Inequality of ranks, the "basis of monarchical government," preserved the prejudice of honor and prevented the monarchy from moving in the direction either of despotism or of republicanism. Coyer's plan to remove legal barriers between estates would open floodgates into the world of commerce, thus making the pursuit of financial gain the predominant motive of all citizens. The political result would be either an "equality of citizens" like that found in despotic and republican regimes, or "a sort of bizarre, volatile, stormy inequality" impossible to sustain. In time the nation would either lose all traces of nobility or, equally bad, become "a people of nobles"—a nation therefore destined to "deteriorate and fade into nothingness." The "disorder" of social homogeneity might well lead the state toward "a revolution that will change the form of its government."[58]

Although he recycled elements of Montesquieu in the early pages of his text, many other aspects of Arc's presentation reveal the same capacity for creative conceptual compromise that had defined Coyer's controversial proposal. Like the abbé, Arc responded to Montesquieu's tacit invitation to define a form of patriotism that would be appropriate within a monarchical system. Also like Coyer, he dealt explicitly with the tension to which that project necessarily gave rise—a tension between the desire for greater political fellowship, on the one hand, and the wish to retain clear hierarchical principles, on the other hand. Despite his stern opposition to that "equality among citizens so dangerous in a monarchy," Arc sought to define a common patriotism that "announces itself differently" in the different professions.[59] His attempt to define the moral attributes of the patriot

58. Arc, *La noblesse militaire*, 35, 38–40, 48–49.
59. Ibid., 46, 64.

demonstrated that the revival of classical patriotism could be fully compatible with the affirmation of traditional features of noble identity. But the effort also revealed the risks involved in justifying the nobility's distinctiveness by appealing to its superior patriotism.

From the beginning, Arc seemed eager to engage Coyer's argument on the abbé's own terms. Evidently responding to Coyer's claim, in his earlier *Dissertation on the Ancient Word Patrie* (1755), to have rediscovered the word *patrie* for a scandalously egoistic modern age, Arc asserted his own patriotic credentials and made clear his intent to contest the meanings that Coyer had assigned to the term. "No less qualified as a citizen than [Coyer], I too know this word *Patrie,* and I will attack his principles with the zeal of a Patriot and the simplicity of a soldier who says what he thinks, and does so without artifice." Arc was drawn to respond to Coyer not only because the abbé's plan would affect the nobility, but even more because it would affect "the Nation in general," and he therefore felt compelled to speak out "as a free man and as a citizen."[60]

Arc not only embraced the terms *patrie* and citizen, but also joined Coyer in holding the nobility to the leveling standard of utility. "The idle citizen," wrote Arc in a passage that echoed *La noblesse commerçante,* is "useless" and "criminal" in the eyes of his *patrie,* and he "steals all that he consumes. The *Gentilhomme* is a citizen before being noble, and the only privilege his nobility gives him is the right to choose among the important services that the state can and must expect of him. The moment he stops thinking in this way, he ceases to be noble." Conversely, Arc implied, commoners also ennobled themselves through devoted service to the well-being of the *patrie.* Arc laid out this rationale in his positive evaluation of the common soldier. "He is a commoner, it is true, but he is filled with bravery. Honor is his treasure. He obeys only discipline, that is to say, the laws of his *patrie.* He gives his life for the tranquility of his fellow citizens. He loves his king and his *patrie,* and serves both with zeal . . . . What more does the nobility offer?" In a passage surprisingly reminiscent of Coyer's discussion of the merchant's glory, Arc looked past the formalities of status to identify the common moral impulses underlying exemplary citizenship: "And if the French soldier has sentiments that one has a right to expect only of the nobility, is there really so much distance between a *gentilhomme* and him?" The chevalier even thought it desirable "in a state such as France" to confer "personal nobility" on brave and honorable soldiers of common status. The practice would nurture the "sentiments of honor so

60. Ibid., 10, iii.

suited to the profession of arms" and it would help to maintain those sentiments "among the French nation."[61]

In his assessment of the sentiments of the "nation," Arc did more than offer the traditional praise for the spontaneous bravery of the French soldier.[62] Having noted "certain analogies" between the life and work of the merchant and the soldier, Arc also remarked the incipient sense of "honor" in those merchant sons-turned-soldiers whose professional ambitions caused him such anxiety. These military novitiates were "all the more praiseworthy," he remarked, for having abandoned their own class "in order to elevate themselves into another whose prejudices run contrary to those surrounding them at birth, [a class] where honor counts for everything and interest counts for nothing." Although they lacked the "advantages of birth," their "patriotic spirit" and their desire to serve the *patrie* "should attract general esteem." Arc even conceded that the young man of commercial background "might be able to perform [a military] function as capably as a *gentilhomme*."[63] Here, in anticipation of the arguments of the abbé Sieyès, Arc effectively admitted that if professional performance were judged solely by the standard of efficiency, processes of professional recruitment would need to be opened to the skills and talents of all social estates.

Arc's reluctance to pursue the logic of that argument reveals his impressive capacity for compartmentalization. By measuring the worth of nobles, non-noble soldiers, and merchants through the same standards of honor, patriotism, and utility, Arc focused attention on the common duties and characteristics that bound the entire community of French citizens. Indeed, his suggestion that evidence of one's commitment to the good of the *patrie* should even have the power of altering one's legal status nearly brought his argument into alignment with that of his opponent Coyer, who above all wanted a nobility constituted through service to the nation. But in emphasizing the moral determinants of noble status, and in acknowledging that noble sentiment could sometimes be found even in those mercantile professions where one would least expect to find it, Arc actually reformulated older, more conservative arguments about the "true nobility" of virtues familiar to French readers since the Renaissance.[64] For

61. Ibid., 192–93, 179–80, 182–83.

62. This tradition dated at least to the early seventeenth century, when Richelieu, in an otherwise scathing discussion of the French character, praised the French people for their well-known "valor" and "impetuosity." See *Testament politique de Richelieu*, ed. Françoise Hildesheimer (Paris, 1995), 298.

63. Arc, *La noblesse militaire*, 163–64, 166–67.

64. Jouanna, *L'idée de race*, 1:253–62; Schalk, *From Valor to Pedigree*, 21–65.

Arc, as for many of his Renaissance predecessors, the admission that some commoners deserved to be granted noble status, and the related idea that "the *gentilhomme* who does not try to merit his nobility . . . does not deserve to maintain it," hardly constituted a challenge to the nobility's existence as a separate social entity.[65] Arc was perfectly happy to contemplate the movement of individuals into and out of the second and third estates; the kind of movement that he described represented a salutary form of social mobility with sound moral causes. He nevertheless insisted that the nobility represented a specific moral model indispensable to the life of the nation, and he tied the efficacy of that model to the social distinctiveness that Coyer had so carelessly sought to undermine. In proceeding to make his argument about the national benefits and national origins of the nobility's moral particularity, Arc threw into relief the often convoluted logic that suffused explanations of noble patriotism in later eighteenth-century France.

Arc confidently asserted that no Frenchman would ever "refuse the glory of serving the king and the *patrie*."[66] To Arc, this dual eagerness to serve the country and to acquire glory reflected the natural inclinations of the French "nation" or "people" toward honor, bellicosity, and valor.[67] Although he may have considered this assertion of the nation's honor to be an innocent extension of Montesquieu's analysis of governmental principles, his attempt to combine the taste for glory with a patriotic commitment to the community at large led to rhetorical contortions of the kind that Montesquieu, with his categorical definitions, never had to confront. The tensions created by Arc's conflicting objectives become apparent in his extended reflections on the meaning of the word "glory." Responding to Coyer's semantic challenge to the contemporary understanding of the term, Arc seemed to concede Coyer's, and Montesquieu's, point about the lamentable absence of genuine selflessness in modern France. By separating and contrasting the concepts of glory and virtue, Arc even cast doubt on the depth of French patriotism. "What, then, is this love of glory? Does anyone suppose that it can be separated from love of oneself? Does anyone suppose that Patriotism alone animates those who seek glory? Perhaps there have been, and still are, some few generous souls who, in everything and in every situation, consider nothing but virtue, who attend only to the good of humanity as a whole and the good of their *patrie* in particular, with-

65. Arc, *La noblesse militaire*, 191–92.
66. Ibid., 191.
67. These assumptions are laid out in a rich but painfully convoluted discussion of population and social structure in ibid., 48–63.

out being inspired or guided by any kind of personal interest." If not for the occasional appearance of a Turenne, however, people would be skeptical of the very existence of such heroes. "Without a doubt it would be desirable for all the citizens of a state to behave in such a way, but this cannot be hoped for. The happiest state is one where the love of oneself [*amour de soi-même*], or individual interest, leads citizens toward the general good."[68] Here Arc seemed to fall back on Montesquieu's position that honor should be regarded as the best available substitute for a patriotic virtue inappropriate to monarchies.

But Arc was not really prepared to accept honor's status as a mere consolation prize for the patriotism-deprived. Within the argument of the text as a whole, he used Montesquieu's typology to advance a larger claim about the reality of French patriotism and the nobility's special responsibility in sustaining it. After all, in answer to Coyer's charge that the nobles' fixation on the person of the king obscured all thoughts of the state in which they lived, Arc had opened his text with the declaration that "I am unable to distinguish, in the bottom of my heart, between the prince and the *patrie,* or [between] individual interest and the interest of the state." He repeatedly and conspicuously praised the nobility for wishing to be "useful to the *patrie,*" and he reminded his noble readers that their "true grandeur" came from "your ancestors, your virtues, and the services you have rendered the *patrie.*" By couching his own discussion of "glory" within the terms of Mandeville's argument about private vices and public virtues, Arc merely sought to highlight the peculiarity, and the fragility, of French patriotic sentiment, which was based on distinct moral prejudices and the special "character of the nation."[69] The "love of oneself" that lay behind the search for glory stood out as a particular kind of individual interest, a delicately crafted interest defined solely by the prejudices of the imagination. Fortuitously, and paradoxically, this "interest" consisted of a search for the glory that arose from the willful repudiation of self-interest. The search for glory could be construed as self-interested, and therefore as unpatriotic ("Does anyone suppose that Patriotism alone animates those who seek glory?"), but it derived from moral prejudices fully consistent with, and even synonymous with, the patriotism displayed by the ancients.

Unfortunately, because the self-interest that produced honor, valor, and glory sprang from moral prejudices rather than brute physical characteristics, it was "delicate" and unusually "susceptible to alteration."[70] To cul-

68. Ibid., 67–69.
69. Ibid., iii, 89, 202, 56.
70. Ibid., 60. The forms of valor, Arc wrote, were inevitably related to "the character of the

tivate and preserve it, society needed to ensure that it remained separate
from that other form of self-interest, the one that expressed itself not
through demonstrations of selflessness but through selfish acquisitive ardor. The presence of luxury inevitably threatened the simplicity, frugality,
moderation, and "purity of morals" that characterized a virtuous people.[71]
And since commerce made possible the impurities of luxury, its extent had
to be limited rather than broadened, and its practice had to be restricted
to the class of people already contaminated by the base motives that commerce implied. If all citizens contracted the moral virus of cupidity, the
country would be lost. What kind of men did commerce produce? "Mere
calculators, whose only goal is to enrich themselves while procuring for
their fellow citizens all the things that weaken their courage . . . men who
will do anything to increase the level of opulence, pomp, and luxury in
their country and [who do] nothing to conserve its liberty."[72]

The delicacy of honor meant that French renewal depended on strict
social and professional segregation. The differences between honor and
money, which implied forms of self-interest that were "completely opposed" to one another, corresponded in Arc's mind to irreconcilable social milieus inhabited by distinct kinds of people. The nobility "must
naturally, by its function, be the principal component of the French military," since the inclination to self-sacrifice defined the essence of the military profession. "Now, if the nobility is the class in which the nation's
military force principally resides, this class must especially be charged with
the conservation of this prejudice [of honor]," and the state must resist developments that would "attack this prejudice in [the noble] class." Above
all, the conservation of the nobles' prejudice of honor required that they
be kept separate from merchants and the base values that characterized
their profession. Coyer's proud talk about the "dangers" confronted by
merchants on the high seas really applied only to their underlings, or perhaps to their apprentices. The "consummate merchant sits behind a
counter, where he calculates continuously." His head filled with nothing
other than "different exchange rates, the price of goods, profits and
losses," he naturally lacked the courage necessary to handle arms and to

---

nation; if the nation is petulant, valor is a kind of impetuous fire animated by prejudice alone;
it is then possible, strictly speaking, to get by without nurturing robust bodies." And "however
little one may know about the French nation, it is not difficult to see that its valor is the kind
I have called valor based on prejudice. But the very name I give it conveys how delicate this
valor is, and that it is susceptible to alteration (56)."
71. Ibid., 47.
72. Ibid., 53.

confront true dangers. Facing the prospect of welcoming such a man into the most honorable of professions, the state could do nothing better than to "leave him to vegetate in the obscurity into which he was born, and to which his way of thinking condemns him."[73]

In the end, then, Arc asserted a basic moral difference between nobles and those not fortunate enough to be "born in your world."[74] Having declared his faithful adherence to the traditional principle of "inequality of ranks," which had been given a new rationale by Montesquieu, he also followed the master in describing honor as a principle of social differentiation, a principle whose practical effects "are not those that draw us closer to our fellow citizens, but those that distinguish us from them."[75] Yet what makes these assertions of basic social and moral inequalities so jarring, and so threatening to the overall coherence of Arc's argument, is his conflicting desire to depart from Montesquieu's line of reasoning by denying the antithetical character of honor and patriotism. Arc performed the feat by defining and justifying honor not in terms of corporate rank, but in terms of the character and inclinations of the nation. By pointing out the common possession of sentiments that seemed to draw the nobility "closer to our fellow citizens," he secured some of the rhetorical advantages that came from the nobility's inclusion in a larger political fellowship. But by defining honor in relation to a widely dispersed patriotic feeling, he also inadvertently raised doubts about the specificity of noble honor, and he showed how difficult it could be to preserve the integrity of one's hierarchical assumptions within the context of a patriotic idiom.

The contradictions are laid bare through comparison of the different parts of Arc's argument. Arc freely admitted, for example, that non-nobles, and especially non-noble soldiers, could possess honor, bravery, self-discipline, and other sentiments that one could "expect" only of the nobility. Their love of the *patrie* and of its laws—a form of selflessness that Montesquieu had identified as the chief criterion of patriotic virtue—entitled them to the same high status enjoyed by nobles. In fact, Arc's plan to create a thoroughly noble military incorporated a mechanism allowing the regular ennoblement of common soldiers who distinguished themselves by their services.[76] Arc credited the sons of merchants, meanwhile, with

73. Ibid., 64, 60–62, 167.
74. Ibid., 89. In encouraging his noble readers to flee the evils of luxury, Arc advised that they "leave all that useless pomp to those whom it can console for not having been born in your world."
75. Montesquieu, *De l'Esprit,* 1: 131.
76. Arc proposed establishing companies of "Volunteers" consisting only of *gentilshommes.*

displaying admirable "patriotic spirit," and for possessing the ability to perform well in military functions. They, too, were evidently capable of desir-
ing the honor that came from abandonment of selfish personal interests.
At the same time, Arc criticized the nobility in broad terms for having allowed itself to be seduced by the temptations of luxury.[77] Indeed, even his
assertion that the nobility "naturally" belonged in the military was belied
by the accompanying observation that its predisposition to honor could be
"attacked" in certain environments and therefore required special protection. Arc himself provided much evidence, in other words, that the moral
opposition between honor and lucre did not, by necessity, correspond to
a social opposition between different classes of citizens. His dichotomous,
and thoroughly traditional, pairing of grubby merchants and the pure *gentilshommes* who were "especially charged" with preserving honor conflicted
with his own patriotic strategy of promoting and recognizing honor widely
"among the French nation."

The rhetorical tensions that permeate *La noblesse militaire* arose from
Arc's valiant effort to link honor both to the natural identity of the nation
and to the historical identity of a distinct social class, and these tensions
are displayed with dazzling clarity in the peroration to Arc's essay, where
France's imminent war with England brings an urgent focus to his patriotic energies. France had suddenly to choose between two paths, one leading to luxury, the other to honor, and Arc expressed confidence in the
inclinations that would ultimately decide the issue. "I have spoken and I
await the choice of my *patrie*. . . . I hear the murmuring of the Nation; thousands of voices cry out, to arms! O Frenchman . . . yes, you are worthy of
the blood from which you have descended. You have the virtues of your ancestors, and some that they did not always demonstrate, such as moderation and humanity. The king is offended, the Nation is insulted; I see you
shedding all of your vain ornaments, these symbols of voluptuousness that
you permit yourself only in periods of repose." Then, turning briefly from
his representative "Frenchman" to address the English nation, Arc evoked
the terrible consequences that would follow this arousal of French fury.
"See our nobility impatient to punish your audacity, [which was only an]
effect of your jealousy. The fire that burns in noble eyes is the signal sent

---

But he also suggested that those companies should be opened to common soldiers who,
through actions of bravery and signal services, merited "personal nobility." In his view, "even
soldiers" should be able to see the prospect of future ennoblement. See *La noblesse militaire*,
183, 186–87.

77. Ibid., 89. "French nobility, do you desire riches?" he asked. "Then abandon this luxury
that degrades you. . . . When a *gentilhomme* dares to be great, he is rich."

to you by a people of heroes." Arc closed his treatise with a spirited expression of unifying national feeling: "France! See your children assemble
at the coast, ready to seek vengeance . . . . The last of your citizens would
defend you against the entire world armed to bring about your ruin. . . .
All of your children are new Bayards and Turennes. They want nothing of
riches, if it costs them honor; they covet no possessions that are not draped
in glory."[78]

In the name of an honor that must be kept pure, Arc had expressed horror at the prospect that France might eventually become a "people of nobles." Here, in the rousing conclusion to his essay, he proudly referred to
the French nation, again in the name of honor, as a "people of heroes" who
possessed ancestral virtues, disdained riches, and valued glory above all
else. His ambiguous emotional appeal—an appeal pitched both to a nobility "impatient to punish" French enemies, and to a nation of heroes *all*
of whose children followed in the honorable footsteps of Bayard—underscores the variety of patriotic purposes for which the concept of honor
could be used. It also demonstrates, along with the conflicted arguments
of Coyer, the social confusion occasioned by the eighteenth century's conceptual merger of patriotism and nobility.

Throughout the 1750s and early 1760s the debate between Coyer and
Arc attracted wide attention and generated a flood of books, articles, and
pamphlets either critical or supportive of the abbé's ideas. The writings of
Coyer and Arc both went through multiple editions in the 1750s, and journalistic commentary was plentiful.[79] The typically acerbic Grimm complained in July 1756 that too much paper had already been wasted on the
subject.[80] But the issues were apparently too compelling to ignore. Grimm
himself had initially responded to Coyer's treatise by writing a lengthy re-
ply of his own in the *Correspondance Littéraire.*[81] The marquis d'Argenson
wrote in his memoirs that he and others had been "charmed" by Coyer's
argument.[82] Public discussion of the debate continued intermittently and
in more oblique form throughout the 1760s and beyond, as historians, soldiers, clergy, lawyers, and merchants found new occasions to offer com-

78. Ibid., 210–13.
79. J. Q. C. Mackrell, *The Attack on 'Feudalism' in Eighteenth-Century France* (London, 1973),
92–98.
80. See *Correspondance Littéraire, Philosophique et Critique, par Grimm, Diderot, Raynal, Meister,
etc.,* 16 vols. (Paris, 1877–82), 3: 262.
81. Ibid., 3: 170–79.
82. As cited in Carcassonne, *Montesquieu et le problème,* 230.

mentary on the implications of Coyer's bold reevaluation of the French social hierarchy.

The taxonomical confusion addressed at the beginning of the chapter
helps to explain why the arguments of Coyer and Arc resonated as widely
as they did, but their debate also intersected with public parlementary
polemics over the nature of the French constitution, and this convergence
of controversial new claims to political and moral authority surely helps to
account for the enduring interest in the subject of *noblesse commerçante*. Beginning in the early 1750s, and continuing through the 1760s, the parlements locked horns with the king and his ministers over several thorny
issues, including the royally endorsed policy of denying church sacraments
to Jansenists, who happened to be disproportionately represented in the
magistracy, the crown's renewal and intensification of controversial procedures for levying and assessing taxes, and various jurisdictional quarrels.
In historical treatises, formal remonstrances (or written objections) to the
crown, and a vast private correspondence, the magistrates and their various spokesmen openly accused the king's ministers of "despotism," defended the interests of the "nation" against ministerial oppressors, and
claimed provocatively that the many parlements scattered across the realm
could legitimately act in unison to resist the unjust innovations of the
crown.[83]

These efforts propagated an image of the "nation" as a historical entity
possessing political rights distinct from those of the crown, as many historians of constitutional politics have noted, and they even expressed vaguely
"republican" sentiments.[84] Parlementary agitation over despotism, liberty,
and the rights of the nation helped to instill a more self-conscious sense of
national identity among the politically engaged classes between 1750 and
1770, as the evolving rhetoric of political dispute clearly demonstrates.[85]
Moreover, because this rhetoric of the nation emanated from various aristocratic corps of magistrates demonstrably playing the role of Montesquieu's "intermediary bodies," they also reinforced for the nobility—or
at least the juridical component of the nobility—its special political relevance as the likeliest standard bearer for national liberties.

83. Julian Swann, *Politics and the Parlement of Paris under Louis XV, 1754–1774* (Cambridge,
1995), 130–48.
84. On the rhetoric of the nation, and "republican maxims," see Dale K. Van Kley, *The
Damiens Affair and the Unraveling of the Ancien Régime, 1750–1770* (Princeton, 1984), 184–
202, esp. 194–98; David A. Bell urges cautious interpretation of this rhetoric in *Lawyers and
Citizens: The Making of a Political Elite in Old Regime France* (Oxford, 1994), 117–19.
85. See Baker, *Inventing the French Revolution*, 31–44; and Kwass, *Privilege and the Politics of Taxation*, 155–212.

The disputes between crown and parlement also played out against two other backdrops, however. During the Seven Years' War, the royal army, with its thoroughly noble officer corps, found itself repeatedly outclassed by the Prussian forces of Frederick the Great, creating consternation among officers themselves and, among the wider public, an eagerness to reevaluate military institutions.[86] Meanwhile, royal attempts to manage both the crisis of the war and the challenge from the parlements often foundered amid the exceptionally volatile politics of the court. There an increasingly fierce factionalism, and the image of a king fallen victim to the seductions of low-born mistresses and the corrosive luxury that they represented, presented an inviting target for all who were convinced that the political crisis of mid-century had moral and social roots.[87] The comte de Forges remarked in 1764, "I hear nothing except cries in favor of the *patrie*, I see nothing but works recommending patriotism," but the ubiquitous expressions of concern noted by Forges reflected unsettling anxieties about the civic health of the nation.[88] In this anxious context, the connection between the development of patriotic morals and the legal structure of social relations understandably remained an object of intense interest.

A survey of all published literature that addressed this issue in the later 1750s and 1760s would fill many pages, but the flavor of the ongoing discussion can be captured by an analysis of three representative texts. Comparison of the programs that they articulated is instructive not only because of the different social visions they projected, but also because of the shared assumptions that united them. Like Coyer and Arc, these authors had obviously given thought to the arguments of Montesquieu, and they also responded to the *président* by attempting to reconcile the principles of honor and virtue. Also like Coyer and Arc, they recognized that the difficulties attendant on that effort lay in the challenge of articulating a truly *national* patriotism that incorporated proper sensitivity to honor and distinction. Their respective attempts to meet that challenge led them to focus much of their intellectual energy on the moral characteristics of the commoner, whose status as a virtuous patriot all three authors wished to affirm.

86. For discussion of the criticism, see Smith, *The Culture of Merit*, 227–48.
87. On the factions, see Swann, *Politics and the Parlement of Paris*, 193–314; on the image of court and king see Thomas Kaiser, "Madame de Pompadour," and "Louis le Bien-Aimé and the Rhetoric of the Royal Body," in *From the Royal to the Republican Body: Incorporating the Political in Seventeenth- and Eighteenth-Century France*, ed. Sara E. Melzer and Kathryn Norberg (Berkeley, 1998), 131–61.
88. Forges, *Des véritables intérêts de la patrie* (Rotterdam, 1764), 20.

## JAUBERT, BELOT, AND M.C.C.A.: NEGOTIATING INEQUALITY

In promoting the value of merchants and commerce, the abbé Coyer had focused largely on the nobility's traditional prejudices against mercantile activities, and he especially set out to show the injustice and irrationality of those prejudices. His admirers in the later 1750s and 1760s often adopted a more aggressive posture, and they seized on the devaluation of legal nobility and the perversions of modern honor to challenge nobles' insistence on maintaining distance between the social orders. The anonymous author of *The Citizen Philosopher*, for example, observed that wealth alone was now responsible for making nobles, just as ambition, "tyranny, audacity, and force [had] made the first nobles." He added that it might have been historically preferable to have granted opulence the exclusive right to ennoble its favorites, since in that case "we would have seen fewer crimes, disorders, [and] horrors, and the land would not have absorbed the blood of so many of its children."[89] Jean-Baptiste Crévier, a printer's son who had been one of the most distinguished students of Charles Rollin, accused Montesquieu of having completely misread the moral condition of the French nation. He had effectively excluded virtue from the French monarchy because he had looked for it in the wrong place—among courtiers, whose false honor stood in stark contrast to the real character of the nation. "The bourgeoisie offers citizens whose fortunes protect them from the temptations of indigence, and whose modesty, in which they thrive, protects them from scandalous seductions. It is in this middling order that virtue, banished from courts, find its asylum."[90]

A self-conscious effort to contrast the "false" honor of the nobility to the virtuous qualities of common citizens characterized one of the principal rhetorical threads traceable to the Coyer-Arc exchange. One of the most provocative examples of this effort came from the pen of the Encyclopedist abbé Pierre Jaubert, who argued that commoners had moral resources not only equivalent to but actually superior to those of the nobility. Jaubert, who addressed the dedicatory epistle of his *In Praise of the Common Man* (1766) to all "virtuous commoners," advanced an argument for equality that clearly derived from multiple sources. The years preceding the appearance of his text had seen the publication not only of Coyer's incendiary pamphlet, but also of Rousseau's *Nouvelle Heloise* (1761), with its promotion of sentimental virtues and its rejection of outmoded expres-

---

89. *Le Citoyen philosophe, ou examen critique de La Noblesse Militaire. Dédié à M. l'Abbé Coyer* (n.p., 1756), 38.
90. Crevier, *Observations sur le Livre de l'Esprit des Lois*, 190.

sions of honor, Mably's *Observations on French History* (1764), with its scathing account of the "feudal" usurpations of the Middle Ages, and d'Argenson's *Considerations on the Ancient and Present Government of France* (1764), whose analysis of the decadent institution of nobility was discussed in chapter 1.[91]

For Jaubert, however, much of the moral force of the argument for greater equality came from the contemporary image of a corrupt nobility juxtaposed to that of a useful but dishonored class of commoners. A corporation that fails to regenerate itself through good morals, Jaubert wrote, is nothing but "a monstrous assemblage of individuals, appropriate more to the destruction than to the formation of a society."[92] In the context of an essay devoted to the praise of the third estate, Jaubert had no need to identify the "monstrous" corporation to which he referred, but his subsequent complaint about the nobility's selfish search for tax exemptions left no doubt about the identity of the monsters he had in mind.[93]

The opposite of monstrosity, however, could be seen in the "common estate, which is the principal force of the state . . . [and] without which, the state would cease to exist." Repeating a point made by others, Jaubert complained that common citizens' lack of renown resulted only from a lack of the right kind of attention. The assemblies of the people who, in the early history of human society, granted honors to the defenders of the *patrie* had certainly never imagined that "those whom they honored would be regarded as men of a different type." One would have to ignore the history of the human race, Jaubert proclaimed, to imagine that "virtue, valor, zeal for the *patrie*, probity, ability, talents, experience, scorn for dangers, the honor of becoming a martyr for one's *patrie* . . . in short, personal merit, are always hereditary in families." If only the "subaltern heroes had their historians, their panegyrists, and their defenders, in the same way that they have had witnesses to their bravery, there would be an infinity of commoners decorated with honors—honors that flattery, protection . . . and importunities allocate to some commander, to the prejudice of those beneath him." How unfortunate it is, he intoned, that these great men, in whom "true Nobility resides," have been rendered incapable of transmit-

---

91. Pierre Jaubert, *Eloge de la Roture, dédié aux Roturiers* (London, 1766). Some of the influences are obvious. For evidence of the historical thought of both Rousseau and Mably, see 18–21. For echoes of Rousseau's model of domestic harmony at Clarens see 48–51. For the allusion to Coyer see 73.

92. Ibid., 44.

93. Ibid., 55. In contrast to the nobility, he wrote, "[the commoner] finds through economy, in the resources of his own industry, and in his own zeal for the *patrie*, whatever [sum] the *patrie* requires of him."

ting "the greatness of their sentiments" to their posterity. Thanks to public silence and shameful neglect, their feats were destined to be forgotten, a credit only to their own characters.[94] For Jaubert, then, "virtue" was indeed integral to the French character, since it constituted the "true nobility" of the common classes, whose "zeal for the *patrie*" and sadly unrecognized honor constituted the firmest support of French patriotism and national well-being. Jaubert's message clearly resonated among some of his readers in the 1760s, for one of his reviewers criticized him for not having gone far enough in his celebration of the qualities of the "commoner."[95]

In contrast to Jaubert, whose insistence on the wide distribution of virtue in France led toward a socially leveling conception of patriotism, one of Coyer's most attentive critics made a strong case for preserving the corporate distinctiveness of the nobility. She did so, however, only after acknowledging the legitimate grievances of commoners who felt insulted or ignored by noble assertions of corporate pride. The resourceful Octavie Guichot, called dame Belot, had responded to the death of her first husband, a Parisian lawyer, by taking lessons in English so that she could become a translator of novels, histories, and philosophical texts. She eventually gained access to the exceptionally rich library of the parlementary magistrate Durey de Meinières, who—after Belot's brief romantic liaison with none other than the chevalier d'Arc—became her second husband.[96] Belot evidently acquired a reputation as a pretentious and pedantic bore in conversation, at least according to the correspondence of Helvétius, Madame de Riccoboni, and others who knew her, but her written work showed a thoughtfulness that few of the later contributors to the debate over *noblesse commerçante* possessed.[97]

Working in the library of Durey de Meinières, Belot undoubtedly became familiar with Montesquieu's theory of the "intermediary bodies" and other anti-despotic arguments drawn from history and political theory,

---

94. Ibid., 42, 23, 28, 31–32.

95. *JE*, 1767, vol. 2, pt. 3, 95–106, esp. 97–98. The reviewer faulted Jaubert for retaining even the theoretical distinction between noble and common. Jaubert had failed to recognize that "all men are noble by origin," as "anyone who goes to the trouble of researching the primordial title of nobility" would find.

96. The liaison with Arc was reported on two occasions in Bachaumont's *Mémoires Secrets,* in May 1764 and December 1765. See *Mémoires Secrets pour Servir à l'Histoire de la République des Lettres en France, depuis 1762 jusqu'à nos jours* (London, 1777), 2: 63, 298–99.

97. On Belot's status as a less than coveted dinner guest, see Marianne Fizet, "'Je n'ai aucun droit à votre confiance.' Réflexivité et stratégies de légitimation dans la correspondance de Madame Belot (1719–1804) avec la marquise de Lénoncourt," in *Dans les miroirs de l'écriture: La réflexité chez les femmes écrivains d'ancien régime,* ed. Jean-Philippe Beaulieu and Diane Desrosiers-Bonin (Montreal, 1998), 145–55, esp. 150–51.

which Durey de Meinières had been quietly amassing for years.[98] Her attempt to reconcile noble claims for privileged status with the rights and needs of the nation at large certainly showed the impact of Montesquieu's growing influence in parlementary circles, as well as the increasingly contentious relationship between the crown and the judicial bodies who had begun to speak out on behalf of the "nation." Belot's argument is especially impressive, though, because of its sustained attention toward, and great sensitivity to, the perspective of the third estate. By honestly addressing that perspective, Belot anticipated, and for some readers may have preempted, a host of moral objections to the legal rigidity of the society of orders.

Belot admitted, for example, that the hypothetical philosopher/architect who wished to found a new society would advise men "to consult one another without prejudice, to appreciate each other without ill will, to find one's place [in the social order] without pride or envy."[99] Society would have no hereditary castes, and all citizens would follow the careers for which they were personally suited. "But though my philosopher reasons well," Belot observed, "he predicts badly." In the early stages of a state's history, the common interest remains constantly in sight, and one finds it impossible to imagine personal interests distinct from general ones. But as the state grows larger, "the circle of the general interest becomes so vast that one pair of eyes cannot encompass it," and the increasingly distant "common interests" become subordinate to the more instinctive pursuit of personal interest. In large and mature states, therefore, rank, hierarchy, and nobility compensate for the loss of society's original patriotic vision by providing incentives to promote the qualified self-denial of at least certain individuals.[100]

Belot recognized, however, that some members of the third estate mourned the loss of equality and resented the compensating social conventions that served to perpetuate that loss. She revealed her sensitivity, which undoubtedly owed something to her close reading of Rousseau's discourse on the origins of inequality, by trying to wish away the divisive confrontation between rank and equality that the public debate between Coyer and Arc had unfortunately engendered.[101] "Has it been a good

98. For more on the activities of the magistrate and legal historian Durey de Meinières, see Baker, *Inventing the French Revolution*, 34–36, and Dale K. Van Kley, *The Jansenists and the Expulsion of the Jesuits from France, 1757–1765* (New Haven, Conn., 1975), 53–56.

99. Belot, *Observations sur la noblesse et le tiers-état* (Amsterdam, 1758), 32–33.

100. Ibid., 48–49, 24.

101. Two years earlier, Belot had written a lengthy commentary on the Second Discourse.

thing for the state to raise a question that draws commoners' attention to their so-called inferiority, and that draws the attention of poor nobles to their so-called deprivation? How is it possible to reconcile the pride of both [groups] with the facts of chance and prejudice?" The commentary that followed the publication of *La noblesse commerçante* had managed only to "awaken the self-regard of the commoner, buried until now beneath wealth and work, [it managed] to throw in his face the distance separating the commoner from the *gentilhomme,* and to make that interval all the more humiliating." If only luxury had been contained, and French morals had remained "pure," Belot lamented, there would have been no need to urge the nobility to support itself through commerce, or to "humiliate the commoner" by erasing all but the seemingly gratuitous legal difference separating the noble from the common citizen.[102]

Belot sought to placate the insulted and newly self-conscious members of the third estate by declaring that "nothing is more just" than the idea of ennobling commoners who, motivated by their courage, zeal, and ability, seek to serve the public. But she disagreed with those who would boldly ask, "What difference does it make, after all, whether there's a nobility, provided there are nobles; that is to say . . . provided there are always illustrious citizens?" She remained convinced that corporate organization, and the moral hierarchy it reflected, was important for its own sake. The "spirit of calculation" so antithetical to the "French genius" would inevitably conquer all hearts and minds if it invaded even those precincts where it was formally forbidden. The "military spirit" that had always sustained France would no longer be "the soul of the nation" if honor lost its force, and "this prejudice will have less force once the nobility, which was always its principal depositary, becomes disengaged from it." A vast realm needed a group of citizens that preferred by habit "the vanity of rank, public consideration, the immortality of one's name, [and] the favor of the Sovereign, to the tranquil pleasures of opulence."[103] Only the nobility's abandonment of luxury, and the reinvigoration of hierarchical principles, could guarantee the survival of such a group. "I have enough esteem for my Nation to believe that it is capable of [such] a virtuous and reasonable return to its roots."[104]

<hr />

See *Réflexions d'une provinciale, sur le discours de m. Rousseau, touchant l'origine de l'inégalité des conditions parmi les hommes* (London, 1756). Belot had refuted Rousseau on the grounds that the natural equality of the state of nature had been accompanied by a natural inequality of abilities and strengths. See 50, 81.

102. Belot, *Observations,* 20–22, 54–55.

103. Ibid., 73, 30–31, 6, 97, 24.

104. Ibid., xxi. Belot had devoted part of her preface to criticism of the nobility's own delusional pursuit of grandeur.

The appeal to unity embedded within Belot's apology for hierarchy and rank underscored the wide impulse to articulate the social basis for a common patriotic morality in the years following the Coyer-Arc debate. The impulse expressed itself through countless literary efforts to find a middle ground between Montesquieu's "principles" of virtue and honor, and in efforts to minimize or erase the formal distinctions between nobles and *roturiers*. The redefinition of honor in light of French "love of the *patrie*" and the desirability of a broadly shared civic virtue made it ever more difficult to define and sustain the moral barriers put in place by society's formal hierarchies of honor. One of the best illustrations of the ineluctable equalizing tendencies inherent in the appeal to patriotic virtues is found in an anonymously authored text of 1764, one that sought to strike a balance between the positions of Coyer and Arc. The author's uneasy integration of the principles of honor and virtue betrayed an overriding desire to establish a socially universal understanding of patriotism.

The author of *The Citizen Merchant* opened his/her text with a Coyeresque juxtaposition of the useful calling of the merchant with the destructive work of the soldier, who cannot act "without inflicting long-bleeding wounds on the *patrie*."[105] Because commerce contributed no less than the nobility to "the glory of the nation," the author observed, merchants deserved greater respect than they received. The increase in trade following the discovery of the New World had been largely responsible for the Renaissance itself, and further progress could now be expected among those nations that applied themselves to the principles of the agricultural and commercial arts.[106] Like the author of the *Dictionary of the Citizen* (1761), who believed that appreciation for French commerce would inevitably make "patriotic sentiments more common among us," M.C.C.A. stressed the great benefits that would accrue to the *patrie* through increased knowledge of and appreciation for commercial practices.[107]

The author nevertheless noted that "the two professions [of commerce and the military] must be distinct," and explained this necessity using a kind of reasoning that would have made perfect sense to the chevalier d'Arc. Since "honor and disinterest are the particular principle of the military profession, [and] good faith and a love of work are the principle of

---

105. M.C.C.A., *Le Négociant Citoyen, ou Essai dans la Recherche des Moyens d'augmenter les lumières de la Nation sur le Commerce & l'Agriculture* (Amsterdam, 1764), iii.

106. Ibid., 3.

107. In the preface to his *Dictionnaire du citoyen, ou Abrégé historique, théorique, et pratique du commerce*, 2 vols. (Paris, 1761), Honoré Lacombe de Prezel emphasized the "patriotic love that I have tried to inspire in my readers" by sharing details of French merchants' "laborious enterprises, so advantageous to the Nation" (pp. xx, xxiii–xxiv).

commerce," only separation could ensure the careful conservation of each of their respective principles. The distinction between the professions and their principles fostered a form of "emulation very advantageous to the state," guaranteeing that the soldier acquired from his compatriots an appreciation for "study and moderation," while merchants learned to add "disinterest and a love for real glory" to their other qualities. Equally active and useful to the state, one profession working vigilantly for its prosperity and the other for its defense, they both found in the execution of their respective duties that "their own glory is united to that of the *patrie,* for which they must always be ready to render sacrifices."[108]

To identify further the "glory" of the professions with that of the *patrie,* M.C.C.A. suggested increasing emulation by regularizing the recompense of recognition, thereby spreading honor throughout the social body. "We keep registers of Officers' names, listing their actions and their merit; it would be just as useful to do the same for enlightened merchants who distinguish themselves by their zeal for the *patrie.*" The attentions of a royal minister, "which would seem to associate the merchant with the administration of the state, would purge from his heart the self-interest for which he is so often reproached; he would identify [the interest] of the *patrie* with his own, and perhaps would even prefer it." Ideally, the system would eventually be extended to all professions, placing before the eyes of the government the names of all men of merit in every vocation. The "passions" may be impossible to destroy, the author noted, but "it is easy to direct men toward the good by managing their passions adroitly."[109]

Around the concepts of glory, professional pride, and emulation, M.C.C.A. had adopted a stance that seemed to combine elements of the patriotic positions of both Arc and Coyer. Like Arc, the author stated that honor and disinterest were particularly affiliated with the military profession, and argued that the military needed to be kept separate from commerce and the other civilian professions. But like Coyer, M.C.C.A. stressed the interdependence of the state's useful occupations and suggested the creation of parallel hierarchies of honor that would guarantee the recognition of outstanding services performed outside the military. Also like the abbé, who modulated between the standards of "utility" and "virtue" at considerable cost to the coherence of his argument, M.C.C.A. was eventually led by his/her all-consuming commitment to the well-being of the *patrie* to raise furtive doubts about the civic value of honor. Despite a stated optimism about the state's ability to manipulate the passions by linking them

108. M.C.C.A., *Négociant Citoyen,* 6–8.
109. Ibid., 10.

to the service of the *patrie,* the second half of *The Citizen Merchant* developed a contradictory repudiation of the passions that seemed closer to the Spartan ideals of Rousseau than to the negotiations over honor and citizenship carried out by Arc and Coyer.

The changing course of M.C.C.A.'s argument first becomes apparent in its surprising denunciation of sociability. The criticism diverged from the author's own earlier emphasis on commerce's positive impact on human relations, and it ran counter to the thinking of most other champions of commerce, who praised the peaceful forms of social interaction that commerce encouraged.[110] But to M.C.C.A., the true friends of society were not the habitués of social "circles," but rather "virtuous citizens."[111] "The wisest and most enlightened people of antiquity took no pride in being sociable," for they had had better uses for their time. "They assembled only for the interests of the *patrie,*" and their discussions inevitably "extinguished all other interests from their heart." In contrast, "the cold and sterile attachment" that the French evinced for "society" has "only the individual self for its object."[112]

M.C.C.A.'s unflattering contrast between the civic cultures of modern France and the ancient world revealed what seems to have been the chief objective of *The Citizen Merchant:* to revive in all social orders virtuous affection for the *patrie.* "Friends of Virtue and of the *Patrie,*" the author wrote, "show yourselves to be their defenders. Subjected to insults and ingratitude, they solicit your help; have the courage to defend them." Hardhearted citizens, distracted by frivolity and "sensual love," and "enslaved to their individual interest," naturally resisted the call to patriotism. The conscientious citizen must "penetrate their hearts" and "break their chains." Liberated from selfishness, all citizens would have the opportunity to cultivate virtue and that patriotic "disinterest" that M.C.C.A. had initially identified as a special feature of the military profession. Virtue, the author declared, was the source of all worthwhile action, as careful comparison of the professions inevitably revealed. Virtuous qualities motivated:

the honest courtier who is attached to his prince, the magistrate with integrity, the courageous warrior focused uniquely on the duties of his profession, the disinterested financier, the enlightened and upright merchant who

---

110. Forbonnais's article on commerce for the *Encyclopédie* stressed commerce's role in establishing "reciprocal communication." The word commerce, he wrote, "applies particularly to men's exchange of the products of their lands and of their industry." As cited in Murphy, "Le Développement de Idées Economiques," 533.
111. M.C.C.A., *Négociant Citoyen,* 46.
112. Ibid., 48, 53.

cannot separate his interest from that of the *patrie,* the man of letters who consecrates his talents to the celebration of virtue, the men of law who employ their eloquence in the interests of the truth, in sum, [virtue produces] in all the orders a strong attachment to one's profession and to one's duties, and the total sacrifice of everything that nourishes the passions.[113]

Like Coyer and Arc, M.C.C.A. produced a treatise marred by contradictions. After first advising that the state manipulate and manage the "passions" by creating honorific distinctions that would stimulate emulation in all professions, this author concluded by celebrating inner virtue and rejecting the passions, honor included, as an unpatriotic threat to the greater good. After first naming "disinterest" as the distinguishing mark of the military profession, the text ended by calling for disinterest on a national scale. After first echoing Hume and Voltaire with an emphasis on the human interconnectedness created by the historical rise of commerce, the author denounced "sociability" in Rousseauian terms. After first distinguishing professions by their particular principles, she or he closed the argument with a resounding declaration of the common principle of "virtue" that underlay the patriotic execution of all professional obligations.

Even allowing for the likelihood of M.C.C.A.'s intellectual mediocrity, or the possibility that the author combined disparate ideas and influences out of a strategic desire to please many audiences at once, the moral contradictions of *The Citizen Merchant* reveal the challenges inherent in the attempt to articulate a virtuous French patriotism in a society still persuaded of the utility and necessity of hierarchies of honor. M.C.C.A.'s text gave expression to two distinct moral schemes—individual moral autonomy *and* competitive emulation, honorific distinctions within professions *and* moral equivalence between professions, one profession characterized by disinterest *and* all professions characterized by disinterest. To put it simply, the author of *The Citizen Merchant* embraced both honor *and* virtue, with all of their conflicting implications for the structure of social relations.

The texts of Jaubert, Belot, and M.C.C.A. suggest the taxonomical possibilities glimpsed by patriotic writers in the wake of the celebrated Coyer-Arc debate. For all three, the historical separation of the "sign" of nobility from the "signified" of its moral content provided a key point of departure, as it had for the abbé, the chevalier, and other commentators since the middle of the century.[114] All simultaneously defined the healthy moral

---

113. Ibid., 53, note m, 55.
114. Jean-Jacques Garnier observed in 1756 that nobility did not consist of "titles and rank,"

ground on which the polity should rest and projected new visions of the social order that would reflect that morality. Belot's vision of reform included the suppression of luxury, a return to "pure" morals, and, especially, the reinvigoration of a nobility defined by the "prejudice" of honor, though she also wished to make conscientious commoners feel welcome in the new order that the return to tradition required. For Jaubert, a social order that recognized "true nobility" would confer equal honors on the commoners whose "virtue" and "zeal for the *patrie*" generally surpassed those of the legal nobility. M.C.C.A. focused on professions rather than social estates, and the absence of the nobility as a category in the text of *The Citizen Merchant* may explain why this author, unlike Coyer or Arc, was able to avoid making a clear choice between the moral standards of honor and virtue in the patriotic polity the work projected. But his/her emphasis on the common obligations of all "friends of virtue and of the *patrie*," and the moral equality that finally united all patriotic professions (at least those practiced by well-educated elites), showed the author's eagerness to define a universal standard of civic excellence that transcended social differences.

Recalling the different visions of nobility enunciated by Mirabeau, Rousseau, and Duclos, the authors of these three texts balanced, or combined, the qualities of honor and virtue in different ways, and they expressed conflicting attitudes toward hierarchy—in one case, the conflict appeared even within the same text. Despite their differing social predilections, however, each of their visions of the social order was elastic enough to accommodate the moral excellence of all civic-minded citizens. Their commitment to patriotism exerted a common pressure to articulate a civic morality intelligible and acceptable to all.

M.C.C.A.'s suspicious attitude toward honor—that dubious passion that harbored destructive traces of "individual interest" and therefore found itself superseded by virtue in the course of the text—provided one sign of the imperative toward moral equality that the enthusiasm for patriotic "disinterest" entailed in the 1750s and 1760s. Paradoxically, however, another sign of this phenomenon was the wide rehabilitation of honor as a national characteristic during and after the Seven Years' War. M.C.C.A.'s perspective on honor and virtue may still have been cast in the oppositional terms that Montesquieu had laid down in his own exposition of patriotism and the principles of government. But already by the late 1750s there was another, distinctly patriotic, way of talking about the value of honor in polit-

---

since good logic prevented taking "the sign for the thing signified." [Garnier], *Le Commerce Remis à sa Place: Réponse d'un Pédant de Collège aux Novateurs Politiques, adressé à l'auteur de la Lettre à M.F.* (n.p., 1756), 14.

ical and cultural debate. Some philosophes waged a "campaign" against honor beginning in the 1750s, as John Pappas has pointed out, but the nature of that campaign—which was directed precisely against the "false" honor that Montesquieu himself had disparaged even as he elevated it to the status of governing principle—was fully consistent with patriotic appeals to French honor.[115] In the course of the Seven Years' War, as the contest with England had drawn attention to the contrasting cultural characteristics of the two countries, the French taste for honor, and scorn for the mere profit-seeking that often seemed to drive the English, had increasingly come to stand as a marker of French national identity.[116] Many readers and writers were therefore inclined to associate honor with Frenchness and to assume that French patriotism must necessarily incorporate the sensibility of honor.

When the chevalier d'Arc responded to the abbé Coyer's call to virtue, and his clever recasting of the concept of "glory," by insisting on honor's centrality to the French national character, he struck a chord that resonated widely among educated readers of the period.[117] The chevalier surely did not anticipate, however, that the appropriation of honor for "national" uses would most often lead—at least in the imaginations of the writers and artists who represented the phenomenon—to the blurring of boundaries between estates rather than to their accentuation. In the wake of the disheartening events of the Seven Years' War, honor served as the basis for a new patriotic awakening that involved a widening cross-section of the French population. Instead of solidifying the image of the nobility as the moral standard bearer of the nation, as Arc would have expected, this nationalization of honor actually facilitated the nation's collective reabsorption of "noble" qualities. The nation's appropriation of honor expressed in new ways the moral equality that patriotism seemed inevitably to imply.

---

115. On the philosophes, see John Pappas, "La campagne des philosophes contre l'honneur," *SVEC* 205 (1982): 31–44. For examples of other social groups criticizing a traditional noble honor represented by the duel and misplaced genealogical pride, see Robert Nye, *Masculinity and Male Codes of Honor in France* (Oxford, 1993), 15–46; Chaussinand-Nogaret, *The French Nobility in the Eighteenth Century;* and George Armstrong Kelly, "Duelling in Eighteenth-Century France: Archaeology, Rationale, Implications," *Eighteenth Century: Theory and Interpretation* 21 (1980): 236–54.

116. Dziembowski, *Un nouveau patriotisme,* 59–110.

117. Cf. Norman Hampson, "The French Revolution and the Nationalisation of Honour," in *War and Society: Historical Essays in Honour and Memory of J. R. Western, 1928–1971,* ed. M. R. D. Foot (London, 1973), 199–212. Hampson refers to the process during the French Revolution whereby French armies were rhetorically endowed with an honor superior to that of other nations.

=========

# Chapter Four

# PATRIOTIC RESURGENCE AND
# THE NATIONALIZATION OF HONOR
## (1760s–1780)

France's demoralizing loss to the English and the Prussians in the Seven Years' War led to a collective soul-searching the likes of which the French had never experienced. Within a few short years, France had seen its standing in the world dramatically reduced. Its large overseas empire had nearly vanished, the British had emerged as the most imposing imperial power in Europe, and tiny Prussia, under the dynamic leadership of Frederick the Great, had inflicted a series of humiliating defeats on the largest and proudest army on the continent.[1] The challenge of repaying the debt incurred in the course of the war helped poison relations between the crown and the parlements throughout the 1760s, leading to the pivotal "Maupeou coup" directed against the courts in 1770–71. Meanwhile, the military and administrative lessons learned from the war inspired a series of reforms under the ministers of war Choiseul and Saint-Germain that opened the door to unending reformist agitation.

Among writers, soldiers, playwrights, historians, lawyers, and publicists of various kinds, the momentous defeat also inspired an extended examination of the moral condition of the French. As Edmond Dziembowski has noted, in the immediate aftermath of the war, many attributed the English victory to a more developed sense of patriotic feeling among the inhabi-

---

1. In proportion to its total population, Prussia, with a force of roughly 270,000 men, had a much larger army than France, but in absolute terms the French, with a force of well over 300,000, easily had the largest army in Europe. See Lee Kennett, *The French Armies in the Seven Years' War* (Durham, N.C., 1967), 77–78, 97.

tants of the island nation.[2] Despite the desperate calls for reform that appeared in the years after the war, however, one point seemed to arouse virtually unanimous agreement among the crown, its agents, and its subjects: the French had the capacity to be a passionately patriotic people.[3] "Patriotism, or love of the *patrie*" wrote M. Rossel in his *History of French Patriotism* (1769), "is nothing other than that zeal, that noble attachment, that every man feels for the land where he was born." Rossel knew that "there is not a single Frenchman who does not possess this feeling in the depths of his heart." In fact, "I would dare say that this sentiment is more vivid, more generous in the French Citizen than it ever was in the most patriotic Roman."[4] This theme of the natural patriotism of the French citizen echoed throughout the period. "In the shadow of the throne," wrote the historian and Encyclopedist Claude-Louis-Michel de Sacy, "[were] born citizens that Sparta and ancient Rome would have envied."[5] It is particularly in monarchies, added the lawyer Elie de Beaumont in 1777, "that Patriotism has its principal hearth, where it produces its most frequent and useful effects."[6]

As David Bell has shown, the patriotic revival that occurred during and after the Seven Years' War can be partly attributed to the deliberate efforts of the crown. Royal ministers, wishing to rally both moral and financial support for controversial crown policies, paid various publicists and artists to link the images of king and nation in printed literature and iconography, and much propaganda extolled the traditional love of the French for their king and their *patrie*.[7] Bell exaggerates, however, when he suggests that royal polemicists of the 1750s and 1760s were largely responsible for making the *patrie* "a central category in French political culture."[8] The insistence on the French capacity for patriotism during and after the Seven Years' War reflected the intensification of a broad and ongoing effort to define a distinctively French, and distinctively postclassical, patriotic moral-

---

2. Dziembowski, *Un nouveau patriotisme français*, 298–307.
3. Cf. David Bell, *The Cult of the Nation*, 140–54, and "The Unbearable Lightness of Being French: Law, Republicanism, and National Identity at the End of the Old Regime," *AHR* 106 (2001): 1215–35.
4. M. Rossel, *Histoire du patriotisme François, ou Nouvelle Histoire de France, Dans laquelle on s'est principalement attaché à décrire les traits de Patriotisme qui ont illustré nos Rois, la Noblesse, & le Peuple François, depuis l'origine de la Monarchie jusqu'à nos jours*, 6 vols. (Paris, 1769), 1: v–vi.
5. Claude-Louis-Michel de Sacy, *L'Honneur François, ou Histoire des Vertus et des Exploits de Notre Nation, depuis l'établissement de la Monarchie jusqu'à nos jours*, 12 vols. (2nd ed., Paris, 1783–84), 1: xxiii.
6. Elie de Beaumont, *Discours sur le Patriotisme dans la Monarchie* (Bordeaux, 1777), 5.
7. Bell, *The Cult of the Nation*, 63–68.
8. Ibid., 62.

ity capable of thriving in modern conditions. This celebration of the *patrie* in the late 1750s and 1760s led to a more appreciative engagement with French traditions and institutions, and it particularly involved a conscious and expansive program to redefine citizenship in light of respected French traditions of honor.

To refute the claim that France was a land hospitable to honor but *not* to patriotism—an idea associated with Montesquieu but reaffirmed by Rousseau himself in his widely read *Emile* (1762)—self-styled patriots set out to define a patriotism not merely compatible with but actually rooted in feelings of honor.[9] In 1763, for example, the author of an educational treatise designed for the nobility asked "why true honor, which is really virtue properly speaking, should not serve as the principle of monarchical government."[10] Some years later, the baron d'Holbach reiterated the point. "How can an enlightened philosopher distinguish honor from virtue?" he asked in reference to the esteemed author of *The Spirit of the Laws.* "In any reasonable government, honor and virtue must be inseparable," and the goal of the state should be to form "the heart and spirit of a citizen Nobility, for whom honor—always inseparable from virtue— would be the prime mover."[11]

Holbach's remarks are useful because they signal the broad social implications embedded in the patriotic rehabilitation of honor. The concept of honor attracted attention in two different ways after the middle 1750s. Many commentators continued to refine honor's meaning, in the manner of Duclos and Mirabeau, so that the word came to approximate more closely the virtue said to characterize the ancient republics. But the nation's collective appropriation of honor especially manifested itself in efforts to define a broad "citizen Nobility" that bore the moral characteristics of the heroic French nobility of ages past, including its legendary attachment to the sentiment of honor. Those who promoted the concept of a "citizen nobility" developed arguments drawn from different sources in philosophy, political economy, and history. But whatever the line of approach, their efforts always reflected a desire to forge a truly patriotic fellowship out of the different orders of royal subjects. Tellingly, the basis for

9. Rousseau declared that the words "*patrie* and citizen should be effaced from the modern language," in light of the absence of the free institutions that nurtured those entities. Jean-Jacques Rousseau, *Emile, ou de l'éducation* (Paris, 1966), 40.
10. [Poncelet], *Principes Généraux pour servir à l'éducation des enfans, particulièrement de la Noblesse Françoise*, 3 vols. (Paris, 1763), 3: 72–73.
11. [Holbach], *Ethocratie, ou le Gouvernement fondé sur la morale* (Amsterdam, 1776), 12–13, 59.

such a fellowship was increasingly sought in the imagined remnants of a traditional aristocratic culture.[12]

## A CITIZEN NOBILITY

Celebration of the moral qualities of the citizenry at large had actually begun in the years before the abbé Coyer's attention-getting mockery of traditional noble honor. In 1752, for example, a moralist critical of the custom of dueling had located true honor in social classes outside the nobility. "From whatever perspective one regards honor," the author Champdevaux declared, "one has to admit that honor is as important to civil life as fire and water are . . . to animal life." But sadly, the baron de Montesquieu's exposition of the vices of the court had proved all too well that "[honor] is a stranger there, entirely unknown. . . . Ambition, the divinity of those places, has attracted a people of slaves and banished honor." Courtiers retained only the mask of honor, which they found useful for concealing their perfidies.[13] Champdevaux responded to Montesquieu's implicit acknowledgment of the court's "banishment" of true honor by giving it a more diffuse social location. He found honor in the "heroic sentiment" of the soldier who cared more for his *patrie* than for his reputation, and in the virtue that abounded "in the lower as well as the higher [social] conditions."[14] Anticipating Diderot and other later champions of the *drame bourgeois*, Champdevaux even called on playwrights to abandon their attachment to kings and conquerors and to write tragedies that drew attention to the honor and virtue of commoners.[15] "Because their heroism would be unequivocal, our hearts would take an interest in their destinies;

12. Michael Mosher argues persuasively that the "ambivalent" Montesquieu had intended to inspire a "democratized version of honor," despite the accusations of his contemporary critics. Even as he upheld a definition of honor that led "toward intransigent pursuit of exclusivity," he offered another understanding of honor that "reconciles nobility and nation not by proclaiming exclusive aristocratic leadership of the nation, but by inviting the nation to assimilate the cultural norms of the nobility." Whether or not he intended it, the nation's conscious assimilation of the noble value of honor was clearly one consequence of debates over *The Spirit of the Laws*. See Mosher, "Monarchy's Paradox: Honor in the Face of Sovereign Power," in *Montesquieu's Science of Politics: Essays on The Spirit of Laws*, ed. David W. Carrithers, Michael A. Mosher, and Paul A. Rahe (Lanham, Md., 2001), 159–229, esp. 210–11.
13. Champdevaux, *L'Honneur considéré en lui-même, et relativement au duel* (Paris, 1752), ix, 48–49.
14. Ibid., 12–17, 58, 93.
15. On the development of the *drame bourgeois*, see Scott Bryson, *The Chastized Stage: Bourgeois Drama and the Exercise of Power* (Stanford, 1991); and Maza, *The Myth of the French Bourgeoisie*, 61–68.

moved by the remorse [inherent in] tragedy, we would weep with the same pleasure over the sad fate of a bourgeois Iphegenia, or the cruel anxieties of a *roturier* Andromachus."[16] This same motivation had inspired Claude Godard d'Aucourt's *Military Academy, or Subaltern Heroes,* a novel published in two editions in the late 1740s, after the rousing French victory at Fontenoy (1745). The novel highlighted the superior merits of "good bourgeois sons" who performed courageously in battle not for fear of being dishonored, or in "the hope of obtaining a more attractive post," but simply because they believed that "nothing could be more noble than to serve one's prince."[17]

By the 1760s, Godard d'Aucourt's phrase "subaltern heroes" had become part of the common vocabulary of novelists, playwrights, and moral critics who decried the injustice of honoring only those with distinguished names and illustrious genealogical credentials.[18] Pierre Jaubert's celebration of "subaltern heroes" in his *In Praise of Common Men* (1766) has already been noted, but the impulse to lift up from obscurity honorable men of low origins also penetrated the institutions of the monarchy itself. A reform proposal submitted to the ministry of war in 1762 or 1763, for example, showed the impact of the new ideal of the subaltern hero. The anonymous author recommended that "there be printed in times of war a military gazette which would contain only the actions of [common] soldiers. These Gazettes . . . [could then] be sent to all the regiments and all the cities and villages of the realm."[19] The idea of celebrating the generous sacrifices of individuals outside the nobility gained wider cultural currency in the years after the Seven Years' War, as attested by the continuing popularity of Godard d'Aucourt's work. The novel was adapted for the stage in 1766, and French readers greeted a new and expanded edition of the original text in 1777 (Figure 4).[20]

In the 1760s and 1770s, other popular literature provocatively called into question the supposed moral superiority of the nobility. Practitioners of the new *drame bourgeois* frequently contrasted the selfish and malevolent behavior of courtiers, *grands,* and the newly ennobled with the bearing of *gentilshommes,* who represented an older and purer noble morality. The su-

16. Champdevaux, *L'Honneur,* 91–93.
17. Claude Godard d'Aucourt, *L'Académie Militaire, ou Les Héros Subalternes,* 2 vols. (n.p., 1745–46). For discussion of this text, see André Corvisier, "Les 'héros subalternes' dans la littérature du milieu du XVIIIe siècle et la réhabilitation du militaire," *Revue du Nord* 66 (1984): 827–38, esp. 830.
18. See the examples in Corvisier, "Les 'héros subalternes,'" 834–38.
19· "Réflections sur la Constitution Militaire," [1762–63] (SHAT), MR 1709, no. 15, p. 19.
20. *Les Héros Subalternes, tragédie en trois actes* (Paris, 1766).

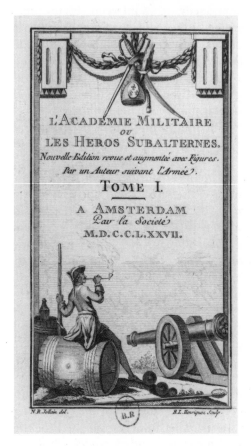

FIGURE 4. Title page from the first
volume of the 1777 edition of Godard
d'Aucourt's *Académie Militaire*. The
heroes of this novel were "subaltern"
officers—below the rank of lieuten-
ant—described as "good bourgeois"
sons. Bibliothèque Nationale de
France

perior moral standards of these "true" nobles were then further identified
with respectable characters from the upper reaches of the third estate. In
Bernard-Joseph Saurin's *Morals of the Times* (1761), the "good" noble Dorante plays the foil to the malicious Marquis, identified by shorthand as "a
man of court," that is to say, a man "without morals, without principles."
The two compete for the hand of Julie, the daughter of a financier, and in
a conversation with a mutual acquaintance, who is portrayed as a "frivolous
and conniving" comtesse puffed up with false pride, Dorante takes up the
task of defending men of finance, many of whom, he declares, are "very
respectable."[21] Fréron, in his *Année Littéraire*, applauded Saurin for having

21. Bernard-Joseph Saurin, *Les Moeurs du Temps* (Vienna, 1761), 5–8.

Dorante speak up for men of finance, whom the other noble characters treated offensively as mere "petty bourgeois."[22] Similarly, Michel Sedaine, in *The Unwitting Philosopher* (1765), uses the ambiguous social status of his main character to pose new questions about the meaning of honor. M. Vanderk is represented as a common merchant at the beginning of the play, but he is finally revealed to be a noble of long lineage, one who has to face the difficult moral prospect of his son's involvement in an illegal duel. In a long soliloquy in the middle of the play, Vanderk, who extols an honor expressed through moral conscience rather than display, explains to his son that the moral foundation of "integrity, honor, [and] probity" makes the merchant just as "respectable" as the *gentilhomme*.[23]

Other literature placed nobles in an unambiguously negative light, at least in comparison to the non-noble heroes who occupied center stage. Buirette de Belloy, whose patriotic play *The Siege of Calais* inspired a devotion bordering on "fanaticism," celebrated the humble social origins of his main protagonists (Figure 5).[24] Recounting the story of the selfless townsmen of Calais who offered their lives to Edward III in exchange for the safety of their fellow citizens, Belloy contrasted the common status of the bourgeois heroes of the drama with the noble status of the French villain of the piece, the traitorous comte d'Harcourt.[25] Audiences responded to the play with such enthusiasm that the king ordered free performances at the Comédie Française in Paris and at other theaters around the country.

The display of such social imagery, clearly designed to console and bolster the self-esteem of *roturiers* and others whose merits often went neglected, became common in the course of the 1760s. In a book charting the transformation of legal culture after mid-century, for example, Sarah Maza has studied the trial briefs, or *mémoires judiciaires*, written and disseminated by lawyers on behalf of their clients. Reform-minded lawyers frequently addressed "the Nation" in these briefs, and they endowed their texts with a melodramatic force by contrasting the simple and virtuous qualities of their common, innocent, or downtrodden clients with the arrogance, frivolity, and corruption of the high and mighty, a dispropor-

22. See the review of Saurin in *AL*, 1761, vol. 1, 145–66, esp. 149.
23. Michel Sedaine, *Le philosophe sans le savoir*, ed. Robert Garapon (Paris, 1990), 37.
24. The "fanaticism" was noted with amusement by Bachaumont in the *Mémoires Secrets* of February 1765. See *Mémoires Secrets pour Servir à l'Histoire de la République des Lettres en France*, vol. 2: 172.
25. For discussion of *The Siege of Calais* and its reception, see Dziembowski, *Un nouveau patriotisme*, 475–78, and Eric Annandale, "Patriotism in de Belloy's Theatre: The Hidden Message," *SVEC* 304 (1992): 1225–28.

FIGURE 5. "The Patriotic Devotion of the Six Bourgeois of Calais, 1347." From one of the rare editions of Moreau le Jeune's *Figures de l'Histoire de France*. The moving story of the bourgeois of Calais was used in the eighteenth century to represent both the social breadth and the historical depth of French patriotism. Bibliothèque Nationale de France

tionate number of whom were noble.[26] The briefs produced for high-profile cases often sold in the thousands, exceeding the print runs of most books.[27]

French sensitivity to the discrepancy between the exalted status of nobles and the neglected merits of honorable people from lower estates clearly had roots that penetrated beyond the loud public debates over honor, virtue, and nobility that had erupted in the mid-1750s. The inclination to anoint commoners as the upholders of "true" honor gained new impetus, however, from the abbé Coyer's criticism of noble mores, his figurative ennoblement of the merchant, and the taxonomical experimentation inaugurated by his text. Some of those who spoke on behalf of the commoner's claim to honor obviously had in mind the degradation of the institution of the nobility, a development discussed obsessively in the 1750s, and in light of the second estate's degradation they aggressively asserted the superior dignity of the commoner. In order for "noble emulation" to produce virtue "in all classes of Society," insisted the baron d'Holbach, the absurdities of the current system for distributing honors would have to be corrected. "Anyone from the inferior classes, even those most scorned by the haughty, who exercises with honor a useful profession must occupy in the mind of his fellow citizens a rank more esteemed than all these vicious courtiers, these ignorant Nobles, these *grands* who, without virtues or talents, devour the *Patrie* and threaten its ruin."[28]

The historian and lawyer Rossel, whose *History of French Patriotism* (1769) detailed the admirable patriotic traits of both "the Nobility and the People," adopted a tone less hostile to the established nobility. But Rossel, too, faulted the modern pattern of ennoblement for having spoiled the promise of patriotic unity that the practice of ennoblement had initially held out in the thirteenth century. Elaborating arguments first developed by the historians C.-J.-F. Hénault and the abbé Mignot de Bussy, Rossel represented the original precedent of royal ennoblement, set by Philip the Bold in the 1280s, as a remedial mechanism that allowed the "simple citizen" to compete again on the same plane with *gentilshommes* for supremacy of "sentiments, greatness of soul, courage, wealth, and generosity."[29] Philip

26. Especially for ambitious barristers of undistinguished origins, writes Maza, "the promise of such documents was social as well [as political], for they were touted as the nonprivileged's best answer to the great and influential. Those outside of the elite wanted to make trial briefs into the vehicles of *égalité* as well as *liberté*." Maza, *Private Lives and Public Affairs: The Causes Célèbres of Prerevolutionary France* (Berkeley, 1993), 120.

27. For discussion of publication figures and readership, see ibid., 123–28.

28. Holbach, *Ethocratie*, 183, 185.

29. Rossel, *Histoire*, 1:406; C.-J.-F. Hénault, *Nouvel abrégé chronologique de l'histoire de France*, con-

and his immediate successors, contended Rossel, had sought to reestablish the natural equality that had governed relations among the Franks, "who did not even know the word noble."[30]

Unfortunately this system, "so wise, so appropriate for stimulating noble emulation . . . in all French hearts," this plan that had established "reciprocal esteem and generous courage, this patriotic system, I say, was unable, because of the abuses to which it gave rise, to remove this horrible inequality that divides fellow citizens." The rise of venality had assured that "riches alone are decorated," and nobility had eventually become a mere "parchment" that gave the bearer title to "scorn [the citizen] who lacks one."[31] Modern developments thus obscured this "equality of natures and of liberty which ensures that a man of the people is no less suited to filling the offices of the realm than one who is called noble by birth and extraction."[32] In the concluding pages to the first volume of his work, Rossel hopefully opined that "one class of citizens will not have the right to look with disdain on the other class when the temple of nobility is equally open to all, when a certain amount of gold or silver is not required for entry, and when even the lowliest Citizen will be able to fly there on the wings of genius, renown, or victory."[33] Rossel's understanding of the moral equivalence of all citizens may have rested on a debatable rendition of medieval history, but reviewers found him "worthy of the greatest praise" because he revealed "love of the *patrie* as the principle and soul of all the revolutions that have strengthened the French monarchy."[34]

After the mid-1750s, even those writers who spoke particularly on behalf of merchants justified their visions of an honor beyond nobility by pointing first to the unappreciated moral resources of the commercial sector of the third estate. The young Bordelais merchant Louis-Hyacinthe Dudevant, who would go on to address the National Convention in 1794 on the importance of maintaining "republican morals," insisted in 1777 that merchants were "animated by [the] patriotic fire that makes all true citizens."[35] The "love of honor and glory" motivated all Frenchmen

tenant les Evénemens de notre histoire, depuis Clovis jusqu'à Louis XIV, les Guerres, les Batailles, les Sièges, etc. Nos loix, nos moeurs, nos usages, etc., 2 vols. (Paris, 1756 [first published 1744]), esp. 1: 238, 262–63; Mignot de Bussy, Lettres sur l'origine de la noblesse françoise, et sur la manière dont elle s'est conservée jusqu'à nos jours (Lyon, 1763), esp. 4, 115, 305, 337.

30. Rossel, Histoire, 1: 401.

31. Ibid., 1: 406–8.

32. Ibid., 1: 401.

33. Ibid., 1: 408–9.

34. For the "greatest praise" see JE, 1769, vol. 7, pt. 1, 30–41, esp. p. 41; for "love of the patrie" see AL, 1769, vol. 3, 341–54.

35. L. Dudevant, L'Apologie du commerce, essai philosophique et politique, avec des notes instructives:

equally, Dudevant maintained, and for that reason the government should consider granting "titles of nobility to all wholesale merchants whose families remain in the trade for three generations."[36] By regularizing recognition of their qualities through the promise of certain ennoblement, the state would discourage merchant families from pursuing narrow "interests"—a human temptation common to all the orders of society—and render them all the more "eager to acquire true glory."[37]

In 1779 the self-styled "patriotic merchant" Bedos praised the moral resources of merchants and bankers with words that similarly violated the presumed moral boundary between nobles and the commercial professions that they had been taught to scorn. In a pamphlet addressed to all the chambers of commerce throughout the realm, he declared that bankers possessed "true nobility" because they made their resources and expertise available to "sovereigns, generals, ambassadors," and others who looked after the general welfare.[38] Others in the commercial professions were similarly driven by moral motives. The merchant who went bankrupt by trying to pay his debts and standing by his friends would most likely console himself by saying, "at least I have honor, that bread of the soul. . . . I prefer honor to my own life."[39] Bedos thus reminded his readers that while they awaited the disappearance of the "unjust prejudices" arrayed against them, their "innate love for the Bourbons, the examples of our Ancestors, . . . [and] even our own prejudices invite us to sustain with dignity and brilliance the character of the Nation."[40] Their "physical and moral resources," he assured them, were more than sufficient to allow them "to cut a noble figure."[41] They could take satisfaction, meanwhile, in the inclinations of a young king who now stood ready "to inspire a unanimity of patriotic sentiments in all the Orders of the State."[42]

The impulse to accentuate the estimable moral qualities of royal subjects outside the nobility surely reflected the assumption, promoted assiduously by political economists, that all people craved the reward of public esteem and that all could be taught to emulate behaviors deemed honor-

suivi de diverses réflexions sur le commerce en général, sur celui de la France en particulier, & sur les moyens propres à l'accroître & le perfectionner. Par un jeune négociant (Geneva, 1777), 19–20. See also Dudevant, Stabilité et garantie de la république française, une et indivisible. Moeurs républicaines. Adressé à la convention nationale (Agen, Year III).

36. Dudevant, Apologie, 46, 49.
37. Ibid., 52.
38. [Bedos], Le négociant patriote (Brussels and Paris, 1779), xi.
39. Ibid., 224.
40. Ibid., 226.
41. Ibid., 227.
42. Ibid., 231.

able in the public eye. John Shovlin's recent work on the development of economistic thought in the last decades of the old regime has underlined reformers' attachment to the idea that the prospect of honor could be used to ensure greater productivity among the working and middling classes.[43] The influence of ministerial propaganda that dramatized the unjust usurpations of the "aristocracy"—especially that written in the course of the crown's frustrating disputes with the parlements over taxation policies in the late 1760s and early 1770s—should also not be underestimated. For immediate political reasons, royal agents and those who sympathized with the royal cause had an interest in challenging traditional noble claims to moral superiority and in appealing to the generous qualities of the "nation" whose support the king now actively sought.

Nevertheless, the broad-based effort to define what Holbach called "the heart and spirit of a citizen Nobility" also represented the search for a solution to a nagging problem peculiar to the phenomenon of French patriotism, a problem that cried out urgently for resolution after the psychological humiliations of the Seven Years' War. Promoters of patriotism accepted with virtual unanimity the premise that ancient-style political virtue could not serve as the sole basis for patriotic sentiment in France. Too austere in its moral demands, too little known to the inhabitants of the modern world, too alien to French subjects nurtured in the tradition of *amour-propre* (self-love), unalloyed virtue seemed an unstable foundation for a French patriotic revival. This is why even publicists who explicitly sought to restore sentiments of virtue to France, such as Coyer, the former army officer Rouillé d'Orfeuil, or even Rousseau, invariably incorporated honor into their discussions of French civic morals.[44] They assumed that

43. John Shovlin, "Toward a Reinterpretation of Revolutionary Antinobilism," and "Luxury, Political Economy, and the Rise of Commercial Society in Eighteenth-Century France" (diss., University of Chicago, 1998), 99–103. One author typically suggested in 1778, for example, that on an annual basis the king should simply grant titles of nobility to the most productive farmers of each *généralité*. See M. Fresnais de Beaumont, *La Noblesse Cultivatrice, ou Moyens d'élever en France la Culture de toutes les Denrées que son Sol comporte, au plus haut degré de production, & de l'y fixer irrévocablement, sans que l'Etat soit assujetti à aucunes dépenses nouvelles; ces Moyens portant sur le mobile de l'amour-propre* (Paris, 1778), 7, 14, 18–19.

44. *La Nouvelle Heloise* (1761) was not written for a specifically French audience, or to address French political conditions, but a French audience would have appreciated that Rousseau's celebration of simple virtues at Clarens involved not the rejection of honor but its modification. See, for example, pt. I, letter 57, in *Julie, ou La Nouvelle Heloise* (Paris, 1988), 133, 129. In 1773 Rouillé d'Orfeuil responded defiantly to Montesquieu that the inhabitants of the French realm should be "united by virtue," but he agreed with Rousseau that "honor . . . far from being disconnected from virtue . . . necessarily joins with it, since together they make one." See *L'Alambic des Loix, ou Observations de l'Ami des François sur l'Homme et sur les Loix* (Hispaan, 1773), 100, 103.

the French could embrace only a virtue tempered by sensitivities to honor and compatible with a respect for rank.

Yet in the eyes of many, honor, in its conventional form, also stood as an obstacle to true patriotic sentiment. Montesquieu himself, in proposing honor as a substitute for patriotism, had exposed the repulsive falsity of an honor oriented toward appearances and selfish pursuits. Moreover, the pride and arrogant self-regard that attention to rank seemed to encourage among those endowed with high status precluded the sense of fellowship and national solidarity that the appeal to patriotism necessarily implied. The deformed state of the modern nobility only exacerbated the problem, for the infiltration of the wealthy, the enervating effects of luxury, and the ever-changing composition of the second estate made all nobles, new and old, acutely sensitive to their own status and narrow privileges. Compromised by modern abuses, honor in its most familiar forms seemed inconsistent with the selflessness and love for the general good that patriotism required.

Confronting a population that could never embrace Spartan virtues, and a corporate nobility that increasingly gave honor a bad name, partisans of patriotism therefore compromised by excavating the venerable ideals of an honor that had flourished in earlier times. By resuscitating the "true" sentiments of honor that had been displayed throughout French history, the civically minded were able to offer a vision of an authentically French patriotism, one modeled by verifiably French heroes. Better still, by rooting these admirable sentiments of honor and patriotism in a distant past, where examples of selflessness abounded, writers made it easier to identify feelings of honor with the nation at large. Even the merchant Bedos, we have seen, could cite the "examples of our Ancestors" as he called on merchants to sustain "the character of the nation." In search of a sturdy basis for French patriotism in the troubled years following the Seven Years' War, writers of all kinds seized on the ideal of a pure honor that could be represented as characteristic of the French people as a whole.

The nation's appropriation of honor, then, did not simply reflect hostility to the nobility, or an eagerness to supplant corrupt nobles at the head of society's hierarchy of ranks. On the contrary, the appropriation of honor involved, on the one hand, a more appreciative engagement with the honorable history of the French nobility, and, on the other hand, the rhetorical diffusion of noble qualities across the social spectrum. When writers like Rossel claimed to see the seeds of "noble emulation" in "all French hearts," they expressed the conviction that both honor and nobility were innate to the French character, and that the flourishing of French patriotism depended on recognition of the "equality of natures and of liberty" that united all citizens. The nation's return to an older and authentic honor thus allowed the articulation of a common morality that avoided the divisive tendencies of modern honor but, at the same time, also separated French patriotism from the austere selflessness of the ancient republicans. The articulation of this common morality entailed the spiritual ennoblement of the nation.

## REVISITING THE MIDDLE AGES

Interest in the history of France did not arise suddenly as a result of the catastrophe of the Seven Years' War. Ever since the posthumous publication of Boulainvilliers's historical essays in the late 1720s, magistrates, historians, philosophes, and royal propagandists had debated the meaning of the Frankish conquest of the Gauls, and discussion of the French constitution—including especially the respective prerogatives of the crown, the nobility, and "the nation"—had filled the pages of historical works from Dubos's *Critical History of the Establishment of the French Monarchy in Gaul* (1734) to Mably's *Observations on the History of France* (1765). In the 1750s and 1760s alone, this tradition of historical reflection, often more philosophical than erudite, produced seminal theories of parlementary constitutionalism by the magistrate Le Paige, led to reactive royal legitimations of absolutism by the propagandist Jacob Moreau and his minions, and elicited an exchange between Mignot de Bussy and Alès de Corbet that was much informed by the debate over *noblesse commerçante*, an exchange that focused on the nature of the Franks' primitive "equality" and the implications of that equality for the social structure of eighteenth-century France.[45]

In addition to these largely polemical works, which often focused on the political prerogatives of the nobility, the parlements, or the "nation," other historical works directed attention not to the political but rather to the moral constitution of the French monarchy. In the second half of the century, the most influential of these works was undoubtedly the *Memoirs on Ancient Chivalry* by the medieval scholar La Curne de Sainte-Palaye. Sainte-Palaye, who came from a distinguished family of the robe nobility, aban-

---

45. See Mignot de Bussy, *Lettres sur l'origine de la noblesse françoise* (1763), and M. le vicomte d'Alès de Corbet, *Origine de la Noblesse Françoise, depuis l'Etablissement de la Monarchie, contre le système des Lettres imprimées à Lyon en 1763. Dédiée A La Noblesse Françoise* (Paris, 1766). Alès de Corbet referred directly, and mockingly, to the ideas of Coyer; see 10. On the ideological uses of history, see Chantal Grell, *L'histoire entre érudition et philosophie: Etude sur la connaissance historique à l'âge des lumières* (Paris, 1993); Dieter Gembicki, *Histoire et politique à la fin de l'ancien régime: Jacob-Nicolas Moreau, 1713–1803* (Paris, 1979); Furet and Ozouf, "Deux légitimations historiques"; and Baker, *Inventing the French Revolution,* 31–106.

doned his legal career at a young age and, after being invited to join the scholarly Académie des Inscriptions, devoted his life to an investigation of France's medieval past. But instead of focusing on the misty Frankish forests of the early Middle Ages, where eighteenth-century constitutional theorists battled over the origins of the monarchy and the rights of French subjects, Saint-Palaye analyzed the twelfth through sixteenth centuries, an age when chivalry molded the passions of the French nobility and determined the spirit of the times. In addition to his much-circulated manuscript, the *Dictionary of Antiquities,* and the highly popular *Memoirs on Ancient Chivalry,* which saw a second successful edition in 1759, Sainte-Palaye also published a *History of the Troubadors* in 1774.

As Lionel Gossman has shown, La Curne de Sainte-Palaye was hardly an uncritical apologist for the French old nobility or for feudalism.[46] He lamented the barbarism of the Middle Ages and considered the eighteenth century an age of progress. His work advanced no clearly discernible political agenda. He harbored ambivalent attitudes toward the Middle Ages, and, as Gossman notes, he intentionally arranged for his works to be "open to whatever interpretations their contemporary readers might wish to put upon them."[47]

Nevertheless, for all his ambivalence about the comparative advantages of medievalism and modernity, Sainte-Palaye consistently described chivalry as a coherent and admirable system of morals that had made true heroism possible and that put to shame the increasingly effete morals of the civilized eighteenth century. He analyzed various chivalric customs and mores, such as the tournament and the knightly ardor for damsels in distress, and he recounted historical anecdotes revealing the moral behavior and feats of arms of individual knights from the French past. In laying out this colorful tableau, the *Memoirs on Ancient Chivalry* represented medieval honor as a standard of moral excellence which had once come naturally to the French and which now seemed sadly beyond the reach of modern man. From the very beginning, Sainte-Palaye suggested, an internal sense of honor had regulated the hearts and minds of the medieval French. "No other *human* laws inforced, as Chivalry did, sweetness and modesty of temper, and that politeness which the word *courtesy* was meant perfectly to express. . . . Nor did any other human law insist, with so much force as that of chivalry, on the necessity of inviolable adherence to truth, and horror of deceit and lies. Adherence to their word was the hereditary virtue of the French, and was anciently esteemed the most honorable part of their char-

46. Lionel Gossman, *Medievalism and the Ideologies of the Enlightenment: The World and Work of La Curne de Sainte-Palaye* (Baltimore, 1968), 278.
47. Ibid., 343.

acter. Even in the judgment of the Romans and their enemies."[48] Some charged that chivalry had merely been the uncultivated product of cruel and barbarous times. But chivalry had actually yielded "the most accomplished models of public valour, and of those pacific and gentle virtues that are the ornament of domestic life. . . . [It] is worthy of consideration that in ages of darkness, most rude and unpolished, such examples were to be found, from adhering to the laws of an institution founded solely for the public welfare, as in the most enlightened times have never been surpassed, and very rarely equalled."[49]

Sainte-Palaye acknowledged that the English, too, had been "no less renowned" than the French for these honorable qualities in "the good old times," but patriotic intent clearly lay behind his celebration of chivalry, whose French cultural origins were known to all his readers.[50] He noted that courage and magnanimity of spirit, "engraven on the tenderest hearts," had been "the rich fruits of chivalry, which burst forth and nourished that multitude of heroes, who have [immortalized] the honor of the French nation."[51] For young nobles, the prospect of joining the knighthood "impressed sentiments so noble and elevated, and gave rise to actions so daring and heroic, as almost to exceed the ideas of mere humanity," and it was through the reverent ceremonies inducting one into the order of knighthood that "the squire was fully repaid for his services to his sovereign and to his country."[52] To ensure that their noble "emulations" would not become "fatal sources of division and discord," the knights had formed a "league of affection" that prevented them from pursuing personal ends to the detriment of the order as a whole.[53] Sainte-Palaye referred repeatedly, and appreciatively, to the knights' "fraternities of arms," their "kind and brotherly unions," and their inviolable "oaths of fraternity."[54] Chivalry, as presented by Sainte-Palaye, had not only encouraged the knight's quest for glory but also restrained all selfish impulses in the name of the common good.

In the final pages of his work Sainte-Palaye had sadly to report that "the declining age of Chivalry," which he located in the first half of the sixteenth century, "bears a strong resemblance to the present times." Despite "all the superior knowledge we boast in this enlightened period and country," the

48. La Curne de Sainte-Palaye, *Memoirs of Ancient Chivalry. To which are added, the anecdotes of the times, from the romance writers and historians of those ages. Translator of the life of Petrarch* (London, 1784), 68–69.
49. Ibid., 312.
50. Ibid., 374.
51. Ibid., 142.
52. Ibid., 39.
53. Ibid., 210.
54. Ibid., 212, 213, 217.

"increase of luxury and dissipation," and the failure to educate children in sound morals, threatened once again to bring the kingdom of France "to the brink of ruin." Sainte-Palaye offered no specific political solution to the problems of the times, but he had little trouble identifying the moral solution appropriate to the contemporary context. "Happy will it be, indeed, if that affectionate compact of youth and age, that discretion and modesty, and that noble hospitality of character and refinement of manners, shall revive in this nation, which, in the first years of Chivalry, were the foundation of its glory." If joined to, and tempered by, the superior knowledge of an enlightened age, the revival of chivalric values might "restore those principles of morality, order, and respect, which can alone insure solid virtue, real elegance, and public peace."[55]

From the 1750s to the end of the old regime, the Middle Ages, chivalry and chivalric literature, and the feats of honorable heroes from the French past indeed attracted the admiring attention of moralists, soldiers, painters, salonnières, royal ministers, lawyers, educators, musicians, and historians. The sensation caused by Buirette de Belloy's play *The Siege of Calais* was one of the more obvious examples of the vogue for the medieval French past, but signs of the new enthusiasm for the golden age of chivalry showed up everywhere after the middle of the century. In 1750 Marguérite de Lubert published a new four-volume edition of *Amadis des Gaules,* the history of the French hero of the early Middle Ages, and no less a sophisticate then Madame du Deffand confessed a "passionate enthusiasm" for the text, which inspired an opera in 1779. The prolific composer Grétry, always "closely in touch with drifts in cultural thought," teamed with the playwright and librettist Sedaine to stage *Richard the Lion-Hearted* in 1784. The production, set amid the romantic color of medieval Aquitaine, would become Grétry's most frequently played *opéra-comique.*[56]

Medieval or pseudo-medieval novels and verse also filled the pages of journals and special collected editions such as the *French Anthology* (1763), the *Almanach of the Muses* (1778), and the *Library of Epic Verse* [Bibliothèque des romans] (first published in 1775), which is known to have attracted the attention of Marie Antoinette.[57] Engravers were kept busy producing illustrations for historical works devoted to the signal events of French history, the social life of aristocratic courts, and the customs of medieval warfare (Figures 6 and 7). In the preface to the second edition of one such

55. Ibid., 373–74.
56. David Charlton, *Grétry and the Growth of Opéra-Comique* (Cambridge, 1986), 4, 250.
57. For Deffand, Marie Antoinette, and the revival of literary interest in the Middle Ages see Gossman, *Medievalism,* 257–58. On architectural fashions see René Lanson, *Le goût du moyen âge en France au XVIIIe siècle* (Paris, 1926).

FIGURE 6. "The Death of Bayard." Mortally wounded in 1524 at a battle near Romagnano in the Milanais, Bayard, "without fear and without reproach," urges his grief-stricken comrades in arms to abandon him in order to make their escape. Undated engraving by Jacques Couché. Bibliothèque Nationale de France

FIGURE 7. "The Death of Toiras" (1783). The maréchal de Toiras was fatally wounded in 1636 during the Thirty Years' War—coincidentally, in the same Milanais region where Bayard had met his end. Soldiers are here depicted mopping the hero's blood with their handkerchiefs, believing, as the caption proclaims, that "as long as they carried these handkerchiefs, they would vanquish their enemies." Engraving by Jacques Couché. Bibliothèque Nationale de France

work, the *Figures from the History of France* (1785), the engraver Moreau le Jeune explained to subscribers that the first edition of the multivolume history warranted revision because "knowledge of the national history cannot be too widely distributed," in light of the need "to nourish the patriotic spirit."[58] The editors never actually completed the work, but they carried

58. Moreau le Jeune, *Figures de l'Histoire de France, dessinées par M. Moreau Le Jeune, et gravées sous sa direction; avec le discours de Monsieur l'Abbé Garnier* (Paris, 1785), Avis sur les changemens et Additions que M. Moreau le jeune fait actuellement dans la Continuation des Figures de l'Histoire de France.

the narrative to the end of chivalry's age of glory and the prelude to the Hundred Years' War. Beginning in the 1770s, the crown also began to subsidize the production of paintings and sculptures that celebrated "great Frenchmen," including the heroes Bayard and DuGuesclin.[59]

A treatise against luxury published in 1783 communicated in vivid terms the fetishistic concern for the medieval past that consumed many readers and writers of the last decades of the eighteenth century. The moralist and social critic Saint-Hiappy described his own transports of joy on seeing chivalric armor displayed at the chateau of Chantilly. Saint-Hiappy reported that "when those cabinets of armor are opened before me, I am struck with admiration and respect at the sight of those enormous arm plates, those heavy gloves, those massive and formidable swords and lances that decorate them. My eye is all the more astonished when it studies attentively the extent, the size, and the weight of those complete sets of armor worn in so many tourneys and combats by the Dunois, the Henrys, the Bayards, and the Crillons."[60] A similar appreciation for the strength and fortitude of medieval knights seems to have informed an educational treatise of 1777. The author, M. de Bury, assumed that the nobility was "destined to sustain by its courage and glorious actions the honor and glory of the state," and because he believed that nobles constituted his likeliest readership, he appended to his essay a lengthy "Historical précis on the Order of Chivalry."[61]

Many motivations undoubtedly lay behind the investigation of medieval mores and historical details in the second half of the eighteenth century, including, for some, the desire to gather evidence demonstrating the past sins of the nobility, or to find examples of barbarism proving the superiority of modern civilization. Much textual evidence suggests, however, that contemporaries were drawn to the Middle Ages through a craving for moral lessons, and moral examples, that could speak to a culture convinced of its own corruption and urgently seeking grounds for a patriotic revival. Like La Curne de Sainte-Palaye, many found in the Middle Ages a system of morals evocative of a former age of innocence, representative of a distinctly French character, and therefore relevant to the moral needs of the eighteenth century. They translated the moral lessons of the medieval past to the context of their own times by rehabilitating the concept of honor as a foundation for French patriotic sentiment.

59. Bell, *The Cult of the Nation,* 107–19.
60. Saint-Hiappy, *Discours contre le luxe: il corrompt les moeurs, & détruit les empires* (Paris, 1783), 45.
61. M. de Bury, *Essai Historique et Moral sur l'Education Françoise* (Paris, 1777), 42, 432.

In some cases Sainte-Palaye's influence on the thinking of the times is unmistakable. In his highly influential work *The Citizen Soldier* (1780), for example, the military reformer Servan de Gerbey referred to medieval chivalry as an "institution particularly well suited to the genius of the nation," and he cited "the actions of Montmorency, Du Guesclin, and Bayard" as proofs of "the attachment of the French toward their country and their king."[62] At the end of a long passage plagiarized from Mirabeau's *Friend of Man,* Servan de Gerbey announced that "honor, that divinity of our ancient knights, which can still serve as a motive force in our own time, is merely another name for the ancients' love of the *patrie.*"[63] The achievements of the past remained relevant to the present and the future, he declared, since "we are all still French like our fathers, and the seed of their virtues was transmitted to us along with the blood that courses through our veins."[64] The similarly optimistic educator Poncelet had declared in 1763 that France teemed with "generous souls who, affected more by the glory of the state than their own interest, would sacrifice their fortune, spill their blood, [and] risk their lives to obey duty, all in order to conform to the laws of honor."[65]

Even less sanguine assessments of contemporary French morals invoked the model of medieval honor as the likeliest source of a general French recovery. The moralist Reboul echoed Duclos's lament that the eighteenth century scarcely appeared to be "the age of honor."[66] "One notices a man of honor today," Reboul observed, whereas "formerly one noticed a man who lacked honor." Honor now belonged to "this or that family, or this or that individual," instead of being the "common property" that it once had been.[67] Nevertheless, Reboul expressed optimism that feelings of honor and "patriotic enthusiasm" could once again become the common property of the "the mass of the nation" if only the young were led to contemplate France's historical record of heroism.[68] Instructors in the collèges, instead of focusing always on the ancients, should relate to their pupils the heroic stories of Turenne, Condé, Bayard, and the defenders of Calais, whose deeds were fully comparable to "the great feats of the Greeks and Romans, which perhaps would also be less prized if they were closer to us

---

62. [Joseph Servan de Gerbey], *Le Soldat Citoyen, ou Vues Patriotiques sur la manière la plus avantageuse de pourvoir à la Défense du Royaume* (Dans le Pays de la Liberté, 1780), 18, 51.
63. Ibid., 50. For the plagiarism, cf. Mirabeau, *L'Ami des Hommes,* 1: pt. 2, 73–74.
64. Servan de Gerbey, *Soldat Citoyen,* 51.
65. [Poncelet], *Principes Généraux,* 3: 76.
66. Duclos, *Considérations sur les moeurs,* 57.
67. [Reboul], *Essai sur les moeurs du temps* (London, 1768), 15–16.
68. Ibid., 281.

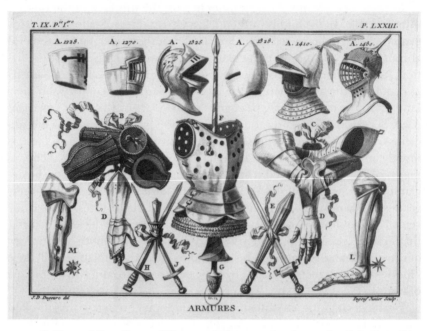

FIGURE 8. "Armor." One of a set of fifteen engravings completed around 1780 by Ingouf the young, after a sketch by J.-D. Dugourc. The image, intended for an evidently anonymous work "concerning antiquity and the Middle Ages," suggests the new fascination with all things medieval in the second half of the eighteenth century. See Yves Bruand and Michèle Hébert, *Inventaire du fonds français: Graveurs du XVIIIe siècle*, vol. 11 (Paris, 1970), 330. Bibliothèque Nationale de France

[in time]."[69] After learning of the burning "love of the *patrie*" that had distinguished "those illustrious and cherished names of Couci, Crillon, Duchâtel, Montmorency, etc.," a new generation of French citizens might prove themselves "worthy of those virile knights whose blood solidified the French monarchy, and of those good and generous Gauls who immortalized the French name!" (Figures 8 and 9)[70]

The decision to promote patriotic revival on the basis of honor, a moral quality identified closely with the nobility, potentially carried risks. Appeals to the exemplary character of noble feats of arms might alienate those disillusioned by the modern institution of the nobility or repelled by the violent customs of a barbaric age. Similarly, the idealization of an era marked

69. Ibid., 104.
70. Ibid., 279, 289.

FIGURE 9. "Tournament" (1785). From Moreau le Jeune's *Figures de l'Histoire de France*. The compilers of this illustrated history originally intended to span the medieval and modern periods, although none of the extant editions seem to have progressed beyond the Middle Ages. This image celebrates the rise in the twelfth and thirteenth centuries of the court tournament, which the authors described as "the principal school of the French nobility." Bibliothèque Nationale de France

by less ambiguous hierarchical divisions might discourage those who could not feel "worthy of those virile knights" who were said to have embodied French honor in the past. In the years after the Seven Years' War, commentators generally avoided these problems in two ways. They insisted on honor's status as a characteristic of the nation that expressed itself in many forms and, at the same time, they made honor a source of nobility that transcended social class. Increasingly they represented honor not only as a possession of *the* nobility, but as a sign of the underlying spiritual nobility of the nation. Several texts produced in the first decade after the war show how honor came to acquire some of the egalitarian resonance formerly associated with virtue itself.

### ENNOBLING THE NATION

Louis Basset de La Marelle's pamphlet *The Difference between the National Patriotism of the French and the English* (1762) can be said to have inaugurated the postwar effort to define French patriotism through the prism of honor. Although he wrote the text before the close of the war, Basset de La Marelle composed it in the aftermath of the war's major disasters, and like other texts of the 1760s it was designed to rally a disheartened populace by inspiring pride in the special moral resources of the French people. In its opening pages, the author reminded and reassured his readers that "patriotism, founded on the honor of the French name, has always sustained [the monarchy] against all of its external enemies."[71] In light of the monarchy's historically demonstrated ability to endure military calamity, there was reason to hope that French patriotism would carry the day once more.

The patriotic honor that Basset de La Marelle extolled, however, differed from the honor exemplified by the well-known image of the "warrior hero." The hero motivated by an "insatiable desire for glory" necessarily "sacrifices everything to vanity," even including the blood of his fellow citizens. He is never animated by "love of the *patrie*" since, for him, virtue is "nothing but a name."[72] By contrast, the "patriot hero," whose virtuous actions are founded on the "honor of the French name," is able to stifle the passions and work single-mindedly for the health of the *patrie*. Recalling the rhetoric of Montesquieu, even as he disputed the argument that it ex-

---

71. Louis Basset de La Marelle, *La Différence du Patriotisme National chez les François et chez les Anglois* (2nd ed., Paris, 1766.), 11.
72. Ibid., 9–10.

pressed, Basset de La Marelle explained that the true patriot hero "is more anxious to be a good man [*homme de bien*] than to appear as one."[73]

Although Basset de La Marelle alluded to the nobility through his caustic description of the warrior hero, he focused attention not on the moral characteristics of any particular social group but on the moral characteristics of the nation as a whole, and the real purpose of his text was to demonstrate that the honor underlying French patriotism had been a common if not universal characteristic since the founding of the monarchy itself. For example, he simply ignored the sticky debate about the early medieval origins of France and assimilated the Gauls and the Franks into a single people who had formed "a *patrie* that no foreign power would be able to destroy." He claimed that the Franks, in rushing to defend the Gauls against their Roman oppressors, had shown that, "instead of making slaves, they had only wished to make Patriots. Once the *patrie* was formed, they never permitted it to be invaded."[74] This same moral determination, this "patriotism of the French, founded principally on their love for their kings," had always assured the heroic defense of French territory in times of crisis.

The French had shown at the battle of Bouvines (1214), for example, "how patriotic zeal augments the courage of a people armed for the defense of their *patrie*."[75] Later, during the Hundred Years' War, the siege of Calais that followed the stunning loss at Crécy merely provided another opportunity to display "the honorable patriotism and the fidelity of the French!" In Basset de La Marelle's rendering, Calais had survived the siege thanks to a collaborative demonstration of grit and determination on the part of all residents of the city. "The Governor . . . and the inhabitants of Calais were animated by the same spirit and the same zeal for its defense: the same courage, the same resilience sustained them."[76]

Further evidence of the socially indiscriminate fervor of French patriotism could be gleaned through comparison of later crises and other episodes of French heroism. During the darkest hours of the fifteenth century, the monarchy had been saved by the patriotic devotion of its nobles. "The Ducs d'Alençon and Bourbon, princes of the blood; Artus, who became the Duc de Bretagne; Coitivy, Taneguy du Châtel, the famous Dunois, [La] Hire, Richemont . . . and so many others whose names, forever dear

---

73. Ibid., 7–8. On Montesquieu's definition of the *homme de bien,* and his assertion of the rarity of the type in monarchical states, see *De l'Esprit des Lois,* 1: 120–23.
74. Basset de La Marelle, *Différence,* pp. 11–12, 74.
75. Ibid., 20.
76. Ibid, 26.

to France, are consecrated in our history, listened only to the call of fidelity on which they based their glory, and [they] saved the *Patrie*."[77] Later, however, during the chaos that plagued the regency of Marie de Medicis, the nobles allowed themselves to be divided by faction and influenced by self-interest. Fortunately "the Magistrates and the People, always patriotic, generally avoided being seduced by any parties, and if by chance they did [enter into a party], they were soon compelled to abandon it by the force of this love for king and *patrie* with which the Frenchman is so naturally imbued." In the end, "patriotism reunited divided minds."[78]

Other commentators had debated the social extent of honor's reach and, as noted in chapters 2 and 3, many had argued about the precise relationship between honor and virtue. Even social conservatives such as the chevalier d'Arc had casually noted, and rhetorically exploited, the general French instinct toward honor. But Basset de La Marelle's ascription of honor to the nation at large signaled a new determination to awaken all French citizens to their universal moral legacy and to persuade them to identify actively with the honor that had historically been the strongest civic bond of the French. Francis I's dramatic declaration, after the battle of Pavia, that "all is lost save honor" became a sign, in Basset de La Marelle's text, that "the honor of the French name persevered even amid disaster." In France, he observed, "the glory of the prince and the honor of the nation have formed, ever since the origin of the monarchy, the great object of patriotism."[79] Unlike England, whose patriotism recalled the "Carthaginian spirit" through its unique focus on "the unjust gains of commerce," French patriotism "has for its basis only the honor on which it has rested for thirteen centuries." The power of this collective pride in country explained why Basset de La Marelle's historical narrative did not highlight individual feats of patriotic sacrifice. "It is only in the body of the Nation [*le corps de la Nation*] that I want to admire this virtue, and compare it to [that of the English]."[80]

Basset de La Marelle's technique of equating the fidelity and glory of the likes of La Hire, Dunois, and Richemont with the selflessness of the bourgeois of Calais came to be a standard rhetorical feature of patriotic literature of the 1760s and after. The lawyer and royal propagandist Lefebvre de Beauvray offered a particularly illustrative example of this maneuver in his *Social and Patriotic Dictionary* (1770). Refuting the "vague discussions" of

77. Ibid., 31.
78. Ibid., 65–66.
79. Ibid., 39, 42.
80. Ibid., 74, 39.

Londoners who liked to flatter themselves by referring to the "imagined decadence of the French," Lefebvre asserted that the English remained somehow unaware of the "powerful principles that move this great monarchy. Honor, Courage, the love of the people for their kings, and the kings for their people, founded this monarchy and have sustained it for centuries." As his prime example of the mutual love binding king and people, Lefebvre recalled an anecdote related by the maréchal d'Harcourt in the time of Louis XIV. At a moment when French prospects had reached their nadir in the War for the Spanish Succession, the king announced to the maréchal that "in the event of a new emergency, he would convene the entire Nobility of his realm, that he himself would lead them to confront the enemy, even in spite of his advanced age of seventy-four years, and that he would perish by their side."[81] This episode, declared Lefebvre de Beauvray, demonstrated the king's abiding confidence in "the love of his people," and suggested a "unique union between the head and the members of a state." "There, without a doubt, one sees principles than can easily fill in for that Love of the *Patrie,* that great motive force of Republican Souls." Lefebvre declared that "these noble and generous sentiments have been engraved, for nearly eight hundred years, on the hearts of all Frenchmen."[82]

Simply disregarding the restricted context in which Louis XIV had evidently made his remark, Lefebvre co-opted the "Nobility" to have it stand in for all the "members" of the state. The feudal fidelity of the nobility toward its king became the "the love of [the king's] people," and the honor and courage for which the nobility had traditionally been known became sentiments engraved on the "hearts of all Frenchmen." Lefebvre's reconstruction of this well-known anecdote created certain incongruities in the text, but his ability to provide a proof of a patriotism comparable to that of virtuous republicans seemed worth the stylistic costs. "Honor! That is the word that must serve as a rallying point for all great hearts, and especially for French hearts."[83] Lefebvre's desire to link such sentiments to all French hearts helps to explain why the *Social and Patriotic Dictionary* contained entries for France, Patriotism, Virtues, Consideration, Liberty, the French, and even the Soldier, but allocated no space at all for a separate entry on Nobility. The nobility's defining characteristic now seemed to be everywhere at once, and little was to be gained in underlining the socially exclusionary function that the distribution of honors still played in French society.

81. Lefebvre de Beauvray, *Dictionnaire Social et Patriotique,* 166.
82. Ibid., 167.
83. Ibid., 337.

The moral identification of nobility and nation had actually received a more explicit theoretical elaboration in 1769 in one of the writings of Servan de Gerbey's brother, the accomplished lawyer and celebrated advocate of penal reform, Joseph-Michel-Antoine Servan.[84] Servan had a penchant for wordiness and turgid prose, as many of his reviewers remarked, but even one of the detractors of his style praised the "depth" of his thinking and predicted that his writings would remind readers of the "original touch" of "the immortal président of Bordeaux [Montesquieu]."[85] In any case, his reputation as a thoughtful moralist, reformer, and expert in law would later assure him a wide audience when he gained new fame as a prolific pre-Revolutionary pamphleteer in 1788–89.

Servan's text of 1769, a *Discourse on Morals* initially delivered as a speech before the parlement of Grenoble at its opening session in the autumn of that year, exemplifies the connection between the widespread perception of the moral nature of eighteenth-century problems, on the one hand, and the increased attention to moral examples associated with the history of the nobility, on the other hand. In an argument that owed a clear debt to a number of contemporary writers, including Rousseau, Montesquieu, Mirabeau, Mably, and Rollin, Servan called for renewed commitment to virtue and personal integrity on the part of all "honnêtes gens," that is, all those expected to be conscientious enough to care about "good morals," the "true foundation of the prosperity of empires."[86] Although the *Discourse on Morals* is actually an extended treatise on the necessity of moral education, Servan focused his remarks not on the need for pedagogical reform—an issue that occupied many minds in the years after the expulsion of the Jesuits in the early 1760s—but rather on the need for accessible models of virtuous behavior in the context of an increasingly corrupt cul-

84. Joseph-Michel-Antoine Servan had won recognition in enlightened circles with his *Discours sur la justice criminelle* (Grenoble, 1767) and the *Discours dans la cause d'une femme protestante* (Grenoble, 1767). His network of correspondents included Holbach, Helvétius, Grimm, and Voltaire. The two-volume study by Jacques François Lanier, *Michel Joseph Antoine Servan ou de Servan (1737–1807): Avocat-général de l'humanité* (Romans, 1995) and *Servan ou l'art de survivre* (Romans, 1997) is more an extended summary of Servan's writings than a genuine intellectual biography. For more on Servan, see the introduction to Xavier de Portets, ed., *Oeuvres choisies de Servan, avocat général au parlement de Grenoble*, 5 vols. (Paris, 1825).

85. See *AL*, 1772, vol. 6, 263–76. The *JE* also gave an appreciative review; see *JE*, 1773, vol. 1, 267–71, esp. 271. Only the reviewer for the *Correspondance Littéraire* was unable to overcome his dislike of Servan's rhetorical flourish and declared the text lacking in new ideas. See *Correspondance Littéraire*, 10: 216.

86. Servan, *Discours sur les moeurs* (Lyon, n.d.), 2. Servan's emphasis on the moral basis of politics owed a very clear debt to Mably's *Entretiens de Phocion*. Like Mably, Servan highlighted the correspondence between "domestic" and political virtues. See *Entretiens de Phocion*, 75. For discussion of Mably, see Wright, *A Classical Republican in Eighteenth-Century France*, 85–87.

ture. In good "classical republican" fashion, Servan believed that societies were shaped more by morals than by laws, and he assumed that the promotion of distinguished examples of good morals provided the surest technique of improving and preserving the moral health of a society.[87] Echoing both Rollin and Rousseau, Servan asserted that the citizen surrounded by models of virtuous behavior eventually finds that "his own heart is his legislator."[88]

History provided an almost inexhaustible stock of exemplary figures, and like so many eighteenth-century admirers of the classics, Servan turned first to the ancient world in his effort to find paragons of virtue capable of inspiring emulation. He celebrated the firmness of Brutus, the modesty of Cincinnatus, the chastity of Lucretius, and the patience of Fabius.[89] He declared that if he could be transported through time to visit Athens and Rome "in their days of glory," he would bypass the Lyceum, the Portico, and their abstract discourses and instead go straight to the homes of Aristides and Cato. There, ensconced in a true "sanctuary of morals" he could "contemplate these great and virtuous men," surrounded by their wives and children, and dream of cultivating "the immortal desire of imitating them."[90] But because ancient virtue, in both its form and its expression, was alien to the French character, Servan expressed doubts about ancient history's ability to reshape the imagination of the French citizen. "Nations are like men, in that the surest model that [a nation] can have is an image of itself making the right choices." Examples of a rectitude more compatible with the natural inclinations of the French would surely have a greater impact on French hearts. Servan therefore filled his discourse with examples gleaned from France's own past. "The French spirit speaks to us through our great men; it is that spirit that one must listen to and believe in."[91]

In what may well have been an indication of the widening influence of La Curne de Sainte-Palaye, Servan's search for the "great men" of France led him directly to the nobility of the later Middle Ages. Without having been constrained to do so by law, the nobility at its best had scrupulously observed an informal but all-encompassing code of honor. "In our history, if I were to choose the most glorious age for our morals . . . I would select

---

87. "Morals can accomplish anything, even without laws, but laws without morals can do nothing." Servan, *Discours sur les moeurs*, 2.
88. Ibid., 9. Cf. Rollin, *Traité des Etudes*, 4: 354–55.
89. Servan, *Discours sur les moeurs*, 11.
90. Ibid., 30–31.
91. Ibid., 83.

... the time from Charles the Wise [Charles V] to the brave Francis I. Those were the glory days of our valorous nobility, the days of that praiseworthy and brilliant chivalry, where an abundance of virtues overshadowed our faults."[92] The Romans' "ardent love of the *patrie*" had achieved great military victories because the Roman soldier had expressed his love through both a "strong body and an impassioned soul." Servan observed that, although it may have lacked virtue in the ancient style, the French nobility's combination of physical and moral resources had proven just as impressive as that of the Romans. "When our virile nobility preferred labor to leisure, when heavy armor served as its virile robe of manhood, what did honor achieve in those hardened bodies? It reconquered France from the gates of Orléans to the Ocean's edge, and it expelled from the continent those jealous islanders who returned to their proper element."[93] Honor, in other words, had done for the French during the Hundred Years' War what "love of the *patrie*" had done for the Roman republic, and spectacular proof of the moral equivalence of honor and virtue was offered in the annals of France's medieval, and largely aristocratic, history.

In the transitional period of the later Middle Ages, when art and civility had only just begun to make an impact on French culture, the nobility possessed a "singular mélange" of qualities.[94] At once rude and polished, violent and dutiful, religious and warlike, polite and natural, sensitive and impetuous, docile and impatient, nobles could not be regulated "except by honor." These morals were not "perfect," and they scarcely resembled the virtues of a Cato, but they were "well-suited to a people governed by a monarch." Precisely because it still lacked sophistication and was characterized by rough spontaneity, noble honor then had "a certain indefinable noble and virtuous quality which calls out for admiration." French citizens, Servan opined, could not help but be touched by the nobility's example. "What Frenchman is not enraptured by the sight of these brave and bygone knights leaping into the fray amid cries, dust, and arms, advancing on the strength of honor"?[95]

The fifteenth and early sixteenth centuries had produced an impressive honor roll of great men and families. "We then saw the Montmorency, the

---

92. Ibid., 33–34.
93. Ibid., 72–73. Servan refers to the ceremony in which young male citizens of Rome, typically aged fifteen, donned the *toga virilis*, symbolizing the passage to manhood. See Edmond Saglio, ed., *Dictionnaire des antiquités Grecques et Romaines d'après les textes et les monuments,* vol. 5 (Paris, 1919), 352–53. I wish to thank my colleague Richard Talbert for his assistance in interpreting this passage.
94. Servan, *Discours sur le moeurs,* 34.
95. Ibid., 34–38.

Chatillon, the Dunois, the La Trémoille, the Bayard, the Brissac, the Soubise; names cherished forever, true ancestors of the nation." But alas, the "virility," and the "proud and generous sentiments" for which the nobility had been known now lived on as little more than a dimly perceived cultural legacy. Servan's catalog of the moral evils afflicting eighteenth-century culture contained the familiar culprits of ambition, luxury, egoism, vanity, and "an uncontrollable love for money, [which] has rendered the soul insensitive to honors."[96] But Servan added to this standard portrait of corruption by constructing an allegorical image that showed the confusion of priorities and the structural imbalances that now threatened the French character. Like many critics, Servan complained that modern citizens valued money and possessions more than qualities of heart, and that they showed greater interest in indulging the pleasures of the mind than in preparing themselves physically and morally to defend the *patrie*. The seductive power of money and ambition had led to the confusion of moral and material motivations and the inevitable destabilization of the polity, and Servan looked for means to represent this disheartening development.

Ideally, wrote Servan, the female figure devised to represent "la politique moderne" would possess a "severe and noble beauty" reflected in her open but modest visage and a strong and confident gait that bestrode the heavens and the earth. Sadly, however, this was not the case. A faithful image of modern politics would necessarily show an enormous figure badly "out of proportion." An "excessive head" would be proudly perched on a "desiccated body." Marked by an "untrustworthy gaze," she would mask her words, and disguise her intentions, by concealing her mouth behind a veil. "In her right hand she carries a sword, and her left hand clasps both the pen of finance and the scales of commerce." Thrown into "convulsion" by the least agitation, the colossus would necessarily use its considerable force inefficiently and confusedly. "Coldly rational in her fury, and methodical in her violence, she calculates in the midst of combat, she evaluates men using specie, and she weighs blood against merchandise."[97] Though expressed in convoluted allegorical language that confounded at least one of his contemporaries, Servan's coded allusions would have been easily recognized by all readers of Mirabeau, Rousseau, or the debate over *noblesse commerçante*.[98] By citing the "coldly rational" calculations of modern politics, and the confusion of the forms of recompense that theoretically

96. Ibid., 35–38, 89.
97. Ibid., 59–60.
98. *Correspondance Littéraire*, vol. 10: 216.

bound the state and its servants—"a grand action cannot be appraised in terms of money, it requires public esteem," he wrote elsewhere—Servan lamented the enervating effects of money and profit-seeking. He suggested through his allegory that the distorted image of "la politique moderne" could be corrected only if all French "honnêtes gens" made the effort to recover the honorable inclinations that had characterized French heroes from the medieval past.[99]

Servan, it should be noted, did not champion the interests of the nobility as a social or political class. Although he himself came from a minor noble family, he criticized nobility's modern form and envisioned a social order in which nobility would be the reward for distinction in all of the esteemed civil and military professions.[100] In 1789 Servan even joined the most vocal critics of the second estate and penned several pamphlets in which he denounced the privileges and arrogance of the nobility and called for a constitution based on the equality of citizens. The *Discourse on Morals,* in fact, never mentions or alludes to the contemporary nobility, either as a subject of discussion or as a discrete segment of the expected reading audience. Servan's attention is fixed always on a historical and idealized nobility, one that represented for eighteenth-century students of history an authentically French, and therefore recoverable, model of moral integrity. In his eyes, the nobles of the later Middle Ages and early Renaissance stood as the "ancestors of the nation," and they had bequeathed to their common heir a legacy of honorable sentiments that now needed to be reclaimed for national uses. For Servan, the overriding imperative to seek moral improvement, and to establish solid foundations for the nation's moral recovery, encouraged him to look beyond existing and officially constituted boundaries between citizens. The patriotic effervescence of the postwar years allowed him to defer indefinitely lurking questions about the social reconfiguration demanded by the embrace of a universal political morality.

The common inclination to place the nobility's historical characteristics into a patriotic stew suitable for the nourishment of all French citizens, and to do so while avoiding mention of the official lines of stratification that separated nobles from *roturiers,* is perhaps most revealingly illustrated in a lengthy text written by a commoner. In a multivolume history titled *French Honor,* which exhibited some of the features of Servan's work and coincidentally happened to be published in the same year, Claude-Louis-Michel

99. Servan, *Discours sur les moeurs,* 89.
100. See chapter 5.

de Sacy found new patriotic reasons to put nobles and commoners on the same cultural plane.[101] In a review of the first two volumes of Sacy's work, the *Année Littéraire* noted the striking similarity of tone linking Sacy's history to Rossel's *History of French Patriotism*, the latter "attributing everything to the virtue of patriotism, this one attributing everything to Honor. The two collections are at base the same; only title and style differentiate their presentations of our history."[102] The reviewer found the later volumes of Sacy's history of honor so impressive, however, that he declared it "one of the most useful books to appear in a long time."[103]

As with many of the patriotic writers active since mid-century, Sacy's first concern was to refute the argument that monarchies, by definition, lacked political virtue and true citizens. "I call Citizen any man who cherishes his *patrie*, who prefers the common good to his own well-being, and who is prepared to sacrifice to the society in which he lives his tranquility, his liberty, his life. One need only glance at this history to see that France has been the cradle of many such souls." But Sacy did not stop at this rejection of the presumed inferiority of patriotic sentiment under monarchies; he also went on to assert the superiority of monarchical patriotism. "I will go further: this word *patrie*—this word that penetrates the soul and carries it to transcendent heights—has for the republican a less determinate meaning than for the man who lives under a monarchy." The republican's passion, directed toward "a thousand things at once," was inevitably diluted. The subject of a monarch, however, "never regards the *patrie* as a vague object, a figment of the imagination; he sees it, he hears it, he speaks to it. . . . This *patrie* is the king himself." As the literal embodiment of the general welfare, the king commanded a kind of respect, and inspired a form of emotional attachment, that the more abstract Republican *patrie* could not match. "When a French monarch advances to the head of his troops, this is the *patrie*, with laurels in hand, clearing the citizens' route to glory. . . . His presence creates heroes; and yet some would deny these heroes the title of citizen!"[104]

Sacy suggested that both Rousseau and Montesquieu had failed to recognize adequately the civic dimension of French honor. "Grant that virtue is the essence of a Republic, and that honor is [the essence] of a Monar-

---

101. Sacy's *Honneur François* appeared in seven volumes in 1769. The second edition of the work, published in Paris in 1783–84, expanded to an even more unwieldy twelve volumes.
102. *AL*, 1770, vol. 2, 189–94, esp. 194.
103. See both the reviews for volumes 5–6 and the review for volume 7. *AL*, 1771, vol. 6, 27–38, esp. 28; and 1772, vol. 4, 182–97, esp. 184.
104. Sacy, *L'Honneur François* 1: xxv, xxvii–viii, xxxii–xxxv.

chy. If the one and the other produce the same effects, then honor is virtue and virtue is honor."[105] Sacy was proud to proclaim that "honor is the idol of the French," but he intended to demonstrate that honor had too often been misrepresented, and misunderstood, by the philosophes and moralists who had spent so much time trying to correct and purify it.[106] The typical French citizen would be hard pressed to give a coherent account of honor's meaning, for "they feel it better than they know it." They inevitably disfigure honor by their words, Sacy reported, "but [they] embellish it through their actions."[107]

The true meaning of French honor could be discerned through any serious encounter with either a warrior (*guerrier*), who regularly puts himself at risk, or a merchant (*commerçant*), "who thinks only to love his king and enrich his *patrie*." If a foreigner were to ask a French soldier or merchant to render a definition of honor, he would undoubtedly receive an unsatisfactory response. The impromptu definition would incorporate vague and confused references to the "point of honor," "gallantry," and all the vices, charms, and horrors with which they were associated.

> But give this same soldier, this same merchant, the opportunity to display those male and sublime virtues which alone carry the imprint of true honor, and behold the metamorphosis that occurs! . . . He will see these generous hearts assist oppressed innocence with their wealth, their credit, and even at the cost of their blood; and when the poor unfortunate turns to them in gratitude, they will use the advantage gained by their generosity to thwart all praise; the only price they demand for their services is that those services should be forgotten.

The instinct of honor, in other words, carried the French—including merchants as well as warriors—toward the disinterested actions normally associated with the "male virtues" of the Romans. "It is in the name of honor that I bring to life for my French readers all the virtues that have made this monarchy strong and prosperous."[108]

By insinuating the imagery and argument of the abbé Coyer into the preliminary discourse of his work, Sacy provided subtle indication of the

---

105. Ibid., 1: xxxvii.
106. Ibid., 1: i. Philosophes, wrote Sacy, "search for the essence of honor by the light of some metaphysical morality, and they strain to purge the prejudices that have altered the idea; the people [naturally] follow the laws of honor in all their purity, and to their fullest extent" (iv).
107. Ibid., 1: ii.
108. Ibid., 1: ii–iii, xxiii.

social intentions behind *French Honor.* For Sacy, honor's status as a national mark of patriotism meant that all citizens had access to the sentiment, and that all deserved, or required, to have their honorable instincts encouraged and reinforced through steady exposure to proper moral examples, of which his multivolume history provided a particularly rich selection. "In general terms, I will call *honor* that sentiment of admiration which excites in us the whole range of civil virtues, and the desire—inseparable from [this sentiment]—to resemble the men we admire." Why is an observer invariably moved by the portrait of a great man? "It is because we feel that we, too, could have been great like him; it is because every man is capable of loving his country, of being just and beneficent, and because even the weakest souls have enough energy to strive after virtue." Echoing a point made by Servan, Sacy stressed that the cultivation of honorable inclinations depended above all on the availability of recognizable models that could be studied and emulated. "Man is only truly affected by those like himself. Virtue will astonish him without touching him if, set off at a great distance, it vanishes when he tries to approach it; [virtue] will strike him and move him . . . only if it appears always to be within his reach."[109] By recasting the noble and monarchical exploits of French history as expressions of the nation's natural honor, Sacy provided all "French readers" a stock of examples destined to inspire pride and imitation.

The cultivation of honor also required the promise of public recognition, since for all but the wisest of citizens "virtue is not . . . its own reward." But even as Sacy borrowed the nobility's traditional language of distinction and emulation to describe the psychological processes that underlay the craving for honor, he modified the language in significant ways. In a manner consistent with the writings of Arc or Mirabeau, for example, Sacy referred to honor as a "grand prejudice" and a "glorious chimera." In a prefatory "Essay on Ancient Chivalry," clearly indebted to La Curne de Sainte-Palaye, he cited the actions of "our ancient knights" as proof that honor "cedes nothing to republican virtue" in its positive effects. In other remarks, however, Sacy made clear that the French honor he wished to promote had less to do with rank and hereditary privileges than with the nation's collective veneration of its own past. Using an oblique language of cultural comparison, he condemned "certain peoples" who derive their virtue from "prejudices" regarding the passage of time and in whom "antiquity inspires a pride outrageous to their neighbors, even though it makes them no more formidable." After making this veiled but dismissive

109. Ibid., 1: vi, viii–ix.

allusion to the nobility's traditional genealogical pride, Sacy went on gladly to assert that "the French" did not assume that a reputation for generosity, justice, or bravery could ever rest on antiquity. The French took pleasure only in "speaking of the exploits of their ancestors, of their zeal for their Sovereigns, of their love for the *patrie,* and especially in resembling them." "I will praise Frenchmen [in this history] only for what they have done," assured Sacy, and "not according to what fortune has achieved for them."[110]

In setting out the broad patriotic function of honor over the course of French history, Sacy planned to "raise from their tombs" a panoply of national heroes, together with the memory of their virtuous deeds. He would put them "within reach" of all men inspired by the "chimera" of honor, thus ensuring that the living memory of past heroes would continue to "form men like themselves."[111] His national history would thereby encourage and reinforce "the most powerful prejudice in our hearts, that is . . . honor, such as it is conceived by all of the *people.*"[112] To underline the social as well as the moral implications of this national appropriation of honor, Sacy closed his preliminary discourse by emphasizing the diversity of honor's expression. "It is not only on the field of battle that the Frenchman will find this sublime phantom; he will find it at his own hearth, at the center of his own family; and honor has made heroes, citizens, fathers, magistrates, and ministers truly worthy of the name."[113]

Whereas Servan and Basset de La Marelle had attempted to seize elements of the nobility's past, and features of its reputed moral character, to reconstitute them as national possessions, Sacy had effectively gone one step further. He simply ignored the possibility that that past, and that character, were specifically noble at all. Slyly rejecting both genealogical pride and the "point of honor," Sacy declared that true honor lay within reach of every citizen of the nation who was "capable of loving his country," and capable of being moved by the portraits of great men. In some ways his text sounded echoes of earlier patriotic characterizations of the honor of the French nation, including those of Duclos, Mirabeau, and even the chevalier d'Arc. But in compiling his catalog of French historical examples, Sacy

110. Ibid., 1: xlii, xlix, xi, xiv.
111. Ibid., 1: x. "History grants a second existence to great men. They enjoyed the first, and their descendants enjoy [the second]. They are brought back to life for the benefit of [their descendants]. They are raised from their tombs to form men like themselves. Any other motive is unworthy of history."
112. Ibid., 1: xliii. "C'est l'honneur, tel qu'il est conçu par tout qui est *peuple.*"
113. Ibid., 1: xliv.

actually worked under assumptions much closer to those articulated by Rousseau in the *First Discourse*. Honor functioned in Sacy's moral universe in the same way that virtue and nobility had functioned in the historical consciousness of Rousseau. Equally available for the appropriation of all, Sacy's honor belonged not to a socially specific milieu but to the moral wills of all conscientious citizens who were determined to show the patriotic possibilities inherent in the French character.

With the benefit of hindsight, one might be tempted to attribute Sacy's seemingly democratic attitudes about honor to the frustrations supposedly inherent in his social position. An ambitious writer of modest talent, Sacy in his career and behavior revealed traces of envy. Like many commoners, he appropriated the noble particle (*de* Sacy) and thereby signaled his pretensions to more exalted status. Although he probably could not afford an ennobling venal office, he did purchase one of the dozens of offices of royal "censor," and thus gained a measure of official respectability. Despite contributing scores of articles to the supplement to the *Encyclopédie* in the 1770s, Sacy never approached the front ranks among men of letters.[114] In short, he remained suspended between the world of the established elites and the world of the scorned and dishonored, and one could argue that his effort to locate honor among "all of the *people*" channeled social resentments that would spill forth openly after 1789. An enthusiast of Revolution, Sacy eventually served the first republic as a "representative on mission" in 1793, and he still occupied a seat in the National Convention at the time of his death in October 1794.[115]

Sacy's perceptions of his own status and prospects were certainly not irrelevant to the content of *French Honor,* but those perceptions belonged to a complex of ideas that also included, for example, Sacy's attachments to existing institutions, his broad sense of justice, and his reactions to texts and arguments circulating through the world of letters with which he was so intimately familiar. Like all people in all times, Sacy found his bearings by combining and reflecting on the diverse ideas that shaped, and intruded upon, his consciousness. The interpretive environment through which he maneuvered in 1769 was strongly marked by a long postwar conversation about the meaning of French patriotism, a conversation fixated in the 1760s on patriotism's compatibility with French traditions of honor. In such a context, characterized by a new veneration of the French past

114. For Sacy's contributions to the supplement to the *Encyclopédie,* published in 1776–77, see John Lough, *The Contributors to the Encyclopédie* (London, 1973), 58, 67.
115. See Auguste Kuscinski, *Dictionnaire des conventionnels* (Paris, 1916), 199–200.

and of the presumed qualities of Frenchness whose traces the historical record was thought to contain, Sacy's moral arguments on behalf of the nation and its citizens were easily reconciled to an enthusiasm for monarchy and a genuine admiration for "ancient chivalry." Noble heroes and their oft-celebrated qualities—courage, generosity, honor—were simply assimilated to an image of the French people and thereby rendered representative of the glorious past and patriotic future of the nation at large.

Sacy's life and text thus exemplify the mediating function that ideas inevitably perform in the consciousness of the thinking human being. In the process of redefining honor's meaning and purpose, Sacy apprehended and synthesized a whole range of phenomena that weighed on his mind— relations between social groups, the nature of the French political order, the lessons of history, and concepts from moral philosophy. By working out his definition of French honor, Sacy not only communicated his own understanding of a particular idea but simultaneously grasped and articulated the relationships between a whole range of experiences that arrested his attention. *French Honor* expressed not the unadulterated experience of class-specific resentments, but an integrated vision of an imagined new world.

In making possible the vision of an alternative present, Sacy's readjusted notion of honor of course also mediated between his understanding of the past and his hope for the future, and it did so in ways that would have troubled some of his readers. The patriotic honor defined by Sacy, and many of his contemporaries, clearly presented new challenges to patriots whose hopes remained vested in the traditional society of orders. The widespread movement to recognize and affirm the honorable qualities of merchants, common soldiers, and others outside the nobility, combined with the patriotic resuscitation of the true honor of the Middle Ages, threatened to create what the chevalier d'Arc had alarmingly conjured in 1756 as a "people of nobles." The search for authentic honor, and the constitution of a genuinely national history after mid-century, had made it possible to imagine both the figurative ennoblement of the nation and the simultaneous displacement of the social institution of nobility from the moral center of French society. Evidently, what the marquis d'Argenson had innocently referred to as "efforts toward equality"—in his controversial essay predicting a "great change in the morals of the Nation"—could take place even under the auspices of honor itself.

National honor proved to be an indispensable mediating and unifying concept over the last decades of the old regime, as patriots of varying ideological dispositions and social backgrounds repeatedly articulated plans

of reform in its name. But lingering questions concerning the precise social implications of the nation's appropriation of honor—How equal were
the nation's honorable citizens? Did they possess one honor or many? In
a nation characterized by a noble honor, what role remained for a socially
distinct nobility?—divided the patriotic thinking of the age. Chapter 5 examines the continuing pressure toward equality that patriotic reform
brought to bear in the specific settings of the army and the school. The
subtle disagreements woven into the considerable literature devoted to
those institutions from the 1760s to the 1780s disclose the deepening of a
central fault line in the patriotic thought of the late old regime.

# Chapter Five

## NOBILITY IN A NATION OF CITIZENS
## (1760s–EARLY 1780s)

Patriotic thought and language saturated French culture so thoroughly in the years following the Seven Years' War that the editors of the *Mémoires Secrets* could proclaim, in a preface to their work in 1777, that the robust patriotism of recent years represented the culminating epoch in the rise of modern philosophy. After the groundbreaking efforts of Montesquieu and Voltáire, the editors noted, the Republic of Letters had been led first by the "Encyclopedists" and next by the "Economists." But "especially after the destruction of the Jesuits" in 1764, a new group of writers had emerged to dominate public discussion—"the Patriots." This new "crowd of philosophers" had investigated the historical legacy of the nation, explored "the origin of . . . the Constitution of Governments," and demonstrated the "reciprocal obligations of Subjects and Sovereigns." Just as significant, the patriots had now "placed themselves at the head of all the diverse parts of Literature." The profusion of patriotic programs had become an inescapable fact of literary life.[1]

Previous chapters of this book have shown that the editors of the *Mémoires Secrets* exaggerated the originality of writers who promoted patriotism in the 1760s and 1770s, and they were certainly wrong to identify patriots restrictively as a crowd of "philosophers." Nevertheless, the editors did detect an important turning point in the history of France's patriotic consciousness, for the texts of the 1760s—especially after the pivotal

1. *Mémoires Secrets*, 1: 3.

trauma of military defeat in 1763 and the expulsion of the Jesuits a year later—revealed a powerful new tendency to lend programmatic emphasis to the common moral traits uniting all French citizens. This tendency even touched reformers who respected and celebrated the distinct historical role of the French nobility. In the same decade that saw the moralizing histories of Sacy, Rossel, and Servan, for example, Saint-Lambert could blithely assert, in his essay on "honneur" for the *Encyclopédie,* that the quality belonged indistinctly to "all classes," like "the duties of the man and of the citizen."[2]

As an apprehensive Montesquieu might have predicted, the efflorescence of self-consciously patriotic commentary since the period of the Seven Years' War had led writers of various persuasions to insinuate into political discussion the assumption of an underlying moral equality between citizens. Even those who had sought to put a rehabilitated national "honor" in place of "virtue" as the abiding principle of French patriotism had emphasized the impressively wide social reach of that patriotic characteristic. Moreover, their portrayal of honor—which was made synonymous with love of the *patrie,* selflessness, instinctive bravery, and moral autonomy—brought honor startlingly close to the ancient virtue that Montesquieu had famously identified with the "love of equality." Whether it was understood to express honor or virtue or some hybrid of the two, then, writers seemed increasingly to agree that patriotism arose from a set of moral qualities that both preceded and transcended exterior markers of status. This moral egalitarianism emboldened some of the more radical writers of the age to portray the nobility as superfluous. To Montesquieu's venerable argument that nobility entered into the principle of monarchy and its laws, Rouillé d'Orfeuil simply retorted, "abolish nobility, and remake the laws," thus rendering them more "analogous to the present spirit of the nation."[3]

Few political observers advocated the outright abolition of nobility, however, and even Rouillé d'Orfeuil imagined the construction of a social order in which a newly reconstituted "high nobility" and "military nobility" would occupy the first ranks.[4] As a rule, the new impulse to recognize and augment the moral resources of all French "citizens" did not call into ques-

2. Saint-Lambert defined honor as a self-esteem that arises from one's commitment to the "principles of virtue," a sense of self that can be protected only by "fulfilling with care the duties of the man and of the citizen." *Encyclopédie, ou Dictionnaire raisonné des arts, des sciences, et des métiers,* vol. 8 (Neuchâtel, 1765; repr. Parma, 1970), H 62.
3. Rouillé d'Orfeuil, *Alambic des Loix,* 309, 408.
4. For Rouillé d'Orfeuil's ten classes of citizens, see ibid., 436–37.

tion the existence of nobility as such. Rather, the emphasis on the admirable patriotic traits of the French national character focused new attention on the criteria by which distinctions should be made and individual nobility of character rewarded. The boundary between noble and *roturier* inevitably attracted the attention of all self-consciously patriotic reformers, as they sought both to encourage the patriotic character of all Frenchmen and to define new standards of moral excellence in French civic life. Their efforts led them in many cases to blur, if not to efface, the boundaries between estates.

Two specific sites of reconceptualization—the school and the army—illustrate the degree to which the premise of the moral homogeneity of citizens informed reformers' thinking even in their approach to practical problems of organization and procedure. From the 1760s, reformist efforts in both institutions aimed increasingly to form future patriots, and those who took up that charge participated actively in the broad nationalization of honor that characterized the patriotic impulse after the Seven Years' War. In most cases, the self-consciously patriotic reformers who addressed educational and military problems sought to minimize, rather than to accentuate, the distinction between noble and common students and soldiers, and they cited the national and patriotic characteristic of honor, or honor/virtue, to explain their motives.

Other writings from the period reveal, however, that the moral egalitarianism that led some to ignore the boundary between noble and *roturier* in the 1760s and 1770s led others to contest vigorously the premise of homogeneity on which so many plans of reform rested. Many social conservatives reacted to the dilapidated state of the "modern" nobility not by decreeing its obsolescence but by insisting on the need to reform it and thus to restore its lost moral centrality. They drew strength from the postwar reinvigoration of the concept of honor, and, like Mirabeau or the chevalier d'Arc before them, they sought to protect noble distinctiveness precisely because of honor's importance to the moral life of the nation at large. The nationalization of honor served patriotic purposes for these writers, too, but their visions of the reformed patriotic polity consistently retained elements of the traditional system of social stratification, a system that others had come to see as an obstacle to the flourishing of French patriotism.

As many social and institutional historians have noted in recent years, the political events of the 1770s inspired a "patriotic" consensus on the need to oppose arbitrary government and the threat of ministerial "despotism."[5] Aroused by the Maupeou coup that brought controversial fiscal reforms and the abolition of the ancient parlements in 1770–71, a self-styled "patriot party" led by former parlementaires, lawyers, and discontented princes produced a steady stream of anti-ministerial propaganda whose aim was to defend the interests of the "nation" against evil usurpers of public authority. Resistance to Chancellor Maupeou opened a window of opportunity for the articulation of radical political ideas in the early 1770s, but few used the opportunity to launch explicit attacks against the nobility, either as an institution or as a concept.[6] The absence of inter-estate hostility can be explained both by the conspicuous involvement of a portion of the nobility in the opposition to Maupeou and by the existence of a galvanizing "despotic" enemy that focused patriotic energies and deflected attention from other sources of possible disagreement. The "patriot" lawyer Guy-Jean-Baptiste Target conceded, for example, that in the past the parlementaires had too often "behaved like the others." Occupied only with their own concerns, "they have fought fiercely for their distinctions and prerogatives, and only weakly for our rights." Target regretted the magistrates' past errors, but he instructed his readers that "it makes no difference at the moment, since it is our rights that are now at stake."[7]

Despite the unifying political consequences of events such as the Maupeou coup, however, the phenomenon of French patriotism harbored conflicting perspectives on the optimal social organization of the morally reinvigorated polity. These perspectives matured and hardened from the middle 1760s to the early 1780s, as the long postwar crisis of French self-confidence, the expulsion of the Jesuits, and the Maupeou coup reinforced both the broad French impulse toward patriotic revival and the need to determine the social ramifications of the moral renewal desired by all. By focusing on the objectives that guided reformers concerned

5. Durand Echeverria, *The Maupeou Revolution: A Study in the History of Libertarianism. France, 1770–1774* (Baton Rouge, 1985); Shanti Singham, "'A Conspiracy of Twenty Million Frenchmen': Public Opinion, Patriotism, and the Assault on Absolutism during the Maupeou Years, 1770–1775" (diss., Princeton University, 1991), esp. 77–161; Bell, *Lawyers and Citizens;* Dale K. Van Kley, *The Religious Origins of the French Revolution: From Calvin to the Civil Constitution* (New Haven, Conn., 1996), and "The Religious Origins of the Patriot and Ministerial Parties in Pre-Revolutionary France," in *Belief in History: Innovative Approaches to European and American Religion,* ed. Thomas Kselman (Notre Dame, Ind., 1991), 173–236.

6. On the radicalism of some of the opponents of Maupeou, see Echeverria, *The Maupeou Revolution,* 115–22; and Singham, "'A Conspiracy of Twenty Million Frenchmen,'" 110–41.

7. See *Lettres d'un Homme à un autre Homme, sur les affaires du temps,* in *Les Efforts de la Liberté & du Patriotisme contre le Despotisme du Sr de Maupeou, Chancelier de France, ou Recueil des écrits patriotiques publiés pour maintenir l'ancien Gouvernement Français* (London, 1775), 135.

specifically with the army and the school, this chapter helps to delineate two strains of patriotic thinking, and two interpretive dispositions, that gained new clarity in the 1760s and 1770s. The evidence suggests that the promise of moral equality between citizens, a possibility recognized and championed by many promoters of patriotism in this period, registered in other minds as a worrisome threat and as a misreading of the true nature of French patriotism. In the articulation of these two distinct reactions to the patriotic prospect of equality, one glimpses the foundations of moral and social arguments that would be marshaled systematically in 1789.

### ENVISIONING INSTITUTIONAL REFORM

The expulsion of the Jesuit order from France created an educational vacuum in the one hundred thirteen former Jesuit collèges that had played such a critical role in French secondary education since the seventeenth century.[8] In response to the crisis, magistrates of the parlements solicited plans of educational reform, and literally hundreds of jurists, educators, and interested bystanders went on to circulate and publish their proposals in the two decades following the ouster of the Jesuits. In addition, many authors, without devoting entire treatises to the subject, expounded on pedagogical issues in texts that addressed related concerns.[9] As one observer noted in 1768, "all of the literary weathervanes have now turned in the direction of education; even the most minor author has to say a few words about this important subject."[10] Systematic reform was never implemented before the Revolution, for lack of funds and political will, but in their efforts to inculcate a national spirit, and to develop a patriotic curriculum that could properly replace the perceived ultramontanist political loyalties and Latin-heavy instruction of the departed Jesuits, contributors to post-Jesuit educational debates anticipated many of the short-lived reforms of the Revolution. Their proposals also

8. Jean Morange and Jean-François Chassaing, *Le mouvement de réforme de l'enseignement en France, 1769–1798* (Paris, 1974), 12; see also R. R. Palmer, *The Improvement of Humanity: Education and the French Revolution* (Princeton, 1985), 12–16, 26–30, 48; C. R. Bailey, *French Secondary Education, 1763–1790: The Secularization of the French ex-Jesuit Colleges* (Philadelphia, 1978); and Roger Chartier, Madeleine Compère, and Dominique Julia, *L'éducation en France du 16e au 18e siècle* (Paris, 1976).
9. On the concern to inculcate national feeling, see the short and panoramic but still useful overview by James Leith, "The Idea of the Inculcation of National Patriotism in French Educational Thought, 1750–1789," in *Education in the Eighteenth Century*, ed. J. D. Browning (New York, 1979), 59–77.
10. [Reboul], *Essai sur les moeurs*, 85.

provided an early testing ground for the Revolutionary principle of fraternity between citizens.

In the prolonged debate about French "national education," which began in earnest in 1763, there were many disagreements about pedagogical technique and seemingly infinite variations in the detailed curricula that reformers proposed.[11] On two points, however, almost everyone seemed to agree. French students needed to have a greater knowledge of French history, and they needed to receive deliberate training in the moral duties of the citizen. Authors who focused on the importance of the French past, or who emphasized the necessarily patriotic content of the curriculum, worried not only about the intellectual lessons that students learned, but the moral lessons as well. To facilitate absorption of the right moral messages, they hoped to alter the whole learning environment of the typical classroom. Inevitably, then, their remarks often moved beyond the duties of the instructor to broach the important relationship of pupil to pupil. "The school," wrote the military reformer Servan de Gerbey, "must represent the *patrie* itself; there students should encounter citizens, magistrates, and laws."[12]

From the perspective of a great many educational theorists and would-be reformers, the imperative to populate schools with budding "citizens" meant that the educational "catechism" that replaced Jesuit principles must emphasize the common characteristics that united all Frenchmen. Rollin had stressed in the 1720s that public education had the advantage of creating the expectation of equality, and the instructional techniques of the Jesuits had often created an "atmosphere of equality" in the classroom by emphasizing competition, emulation, and rivalry among students.[13] Building on some of the useable examples of the Jesuits, and often recalling the specific pronouncements of Rollin, many educational writers saw the Jesuits' departure as an opportunity to rearticulate the importance of equality, not only as teaching practice but also as social principle.

Even educators who specialized in the training of the nobility often praised the salutary social effects of inter-estate fraternization in public schools. The educator Poncelet, for example, described the social environment of the best collèges in a way that makes it easy to understand why Robespierre would later praise the public schools of the old regime as

11. The debate over national education got its name from Caradeuc de La Chalotais's *Essai d'éducation nationale, ou plan d'études pour la jeunesse* (n.p., 1763), the first text to apply the adjective "national" to the system described therein.

12. Servan de Gerbey, *Le Soldat Citoyen*, 228.

13. The quote is from Palmer, *Improvement of Humanity*, 24; on equality in the Jesuit classroom see also Georges Snyders, *La pédagogie en France aux XVIIe et XVIIIe siècles* (Paris, 1965), 48–53.

"nurseries of republicanism."[14] There, wrote Poncelet, "one sees inspiring bonds of friendship form between persons of very different birth; one sees men of distinguished condition ally themselves, so to speak, with men of ordinary condition, only in consideration of their merit, their talents, [and] their virtues, and in this way [they] render a kind of homage to humanity."[15] This "homage to humanity," which seemed to affirm the underlying sameness between students of differing social conditions, could perhaps also be explained by the peculiarities of the French character. "Honor," Poncelet observed, "is a quality innate in the French Nation."[16]

To reinforce and improve upon the atmosphere of fellowship and equality that prevailed in the collèges, many authors aspired to provide vivid examples of social fraternity that could be integrated into classroom instruction. This was one of the purposes behind Jean-Jacques Fillassier's *Historical Dictionary of Education* (1771), a work that fully deserved to be placed "in the hands of young citizens," according to one reviewer.[17] Another commentator, noting the ubiquity of dictionaries in the published literature of the age, worried that children soon would be unable to read "except in alphabetical order," but he, too, applauded Fillassier's effort to deliver "moral lessons draped in the cloak of history," and he described the *Historical Dictionary* as a veritable "children's library."[18]

Fillassier cited ancient examples to underscore the importance of mutual respect between citizens. In one of the longest entries in his *Dictionary*, an extended essay on "love of the *patrie*," he used the broad subject of education as a pretext for exploring ancient laws and their relationship to social structure. Fillassier clearly believed that the model of the Roman republic remained relevant to modern French problems. He particularly emphasized the feeling of fellowship that arose from the public culture of Rome, which gave "each individual a part in government," and thus ensured that each citizen had "a personal interest in the prosperity of the state, on which his own happiness and security depended." Universal concern for the well-being of the *patrie* had been "cemented by this particular union of citizens to one another," and the need to maintain that closeness had mobilized the energies of "the first kings, [who] from the beginning devoted all of their care and their application to [it], convinced that the health of the state depended on it." The social mores of the Romans

14. Palmer, *Improvement of Humanity*, 26.
15. [Poncelet], *Principes Généraux pour servir à l'éducation des enfans*, 2: 223–24.
16. Ibid., 1: 52–53.
17. *AL*, 1771, vol. 7, 320–36, esp. 321.
18. *JE*, 1772, vol. 4, pt. 1, 3–16, esp. 3, 6.

supported both love of the *patrie* and the harmony of citizens that made that love possible. The "reciprocal obligations established . . . between the great and the small, tended toward this goal, and contributed greatly to the union of citizens, despite differences of profession, and inequality of conditions."[19]

Another reformer who acknowledged the reality of inequality of conditions even while working to instill feelings of mutual respect and equality among citizens was the now-retired lawyer from Grenoble, J.-M.-A. Servan. In a 1781 treatise devoted largely to the subject of public education, Servan, who had praised the honor of French knights in his *Discourse on Morals*, evinced a concern to promote civic virtue among all citizens. For Servan, though, the desire to promote virtue connected naturally to his earlier encomium to French honor, for he explained the deficit of virtue in French society by pointing to the unfairly limited distribution of honor throughout the social order. "If only all respectable men [*gens de bien*] could rely on a body of laws to provide recompense for virtue! But where are these laws?" Servan noted the existence of other bodies of law—civil, martial, religious—and he now called for the establishment of "remunerative law." "All across Europe we have signs and colors that prove that a man was born into the Nobility; we have others that prove that he served in the army; we have others," Servan acidly observed, "that prove nothing at all." But by what signs, he asked, "do we recognize the enlightened zeal of the ecclesiastic, the vigilance and integrity of the magistrate, the heroic valor of the [common] soldier, the good faith of the merchant, the industry of the artisan, the talent of the artist?" The merits of such men were either extinguished by neglect or forced to find their sustenance in their own innate excellence.[20]

Even "the most vulgar kings can rule over subjects," Servan noted provocatively, but if Louis XVI wished to have the "sweet and rare honor" of commanding "citizens," he would have to recognize that "the art of making men is also that of offering merit its just rewards."[21] Fortunately, Servan reported, he heard the human heart cry out from all directions, "*Look at me and I will do well; praise me, and I will do better.*"[22] The government alone "decides the recipients of its honors," which were "the magnetic needle di-

19. Jean-Jacques Fillassier, *Dictionnaire Historique d'Education*, 2 vols. (Paris, 1771), 1: 172–73.
20. J.-M.-A. Servan, *Discours sur le progrès des connaissances humaines en général, de la morale, et de la législation en particulier; lu dans une Assemblée publique de l'Académie de Lyon* (n.p., 1781), 107.
21. Ibid., 125, 109.
22. Ibid., 108.

recting merit," and the monarch could inspire in his subjects a "delirious enthusiasm" by taking advantage of the French sensitivity to marks of esteem and by distributing his honors widely, fairly, and conspicuously. He would thereby establish a much-needed "apprenticeship of the Citizen" through the agency of public education. By installing a new "remunerative law," the king would also demonstrate to all of France, and to his own "wayward Court," his own recognition that "good public education is the only plank left amid the universal shipwreck of morals" that French society now confronted.[23]

There would be no hope of rescue for the morally marooned, suggested the anonymous author of *A Project for Schools*, until educators made the formation of citizens their primary objective. Conceiving the debate about the future of French education as a contest between the social and political principles of Montesquieu and Rollin, this author came down squarely on the side of the latter-day Spartan. "Is it not humiliating that . . . a good son, a good father, a good brother, a patriot, is seen as an exception among Citizens?" The humiliation would continue unless the state reached the "breeding ground of the nation" through a sound plan of public education.[24] In the reformed schools, the subject of history should take pride of place, just as Rollin, whose memory lived in every "patriotic heart," had always intended.[25] "The history of our own Nation should receive particular attention," the author wrote, because its examples showed how wrong Montesquieu had been in declaring that monarchies can subsist "independently of love of the *patrie*, of the love of real glory, of renunciation of the self."[26]

Challenging the alternate scheme of political morals that Montesquieu had attempted to apply to France, this author attacked the "false" honor said to characterize monarchies, and insisted that virtue remained the true mark of the citizen. "Study our history, read the memoirs. . . . We will find that those who have served the state, its cities, and its citizens out of duty and sentiment have served them without making them fear for their well-being, without making them tremble; [we will find] that those who have pursued only so-called honor through their services have frequently been harmful or dangerous; we will find that it is the men of virtue who honor, sustain, and elevate States." Alluding to the ubiquitous "three notable bourgeois of Calais" whose example had been celebrated by Rollin and

23. Ibid., 110–11, 124–25.
24. *Projet d'Ecoles Publiques*, 88.
25. Ibid., 129.
26. Ibid., 135.

others, the author asked, "did those tender Citizens sacrifice themselves on the principles of this honor that some say suffices in a Monarchical state?" Honor would have been an "unfaithful guardian" of the "precious liberties" that the men of Calais had sought to protect. The lessons of the French past taught the superiority of civic virtue, whose sentiments are "independent of the prejudice of persons and conditions," and can never be subjected to the laws of "a *bizarre honor*."[27]

Servan, Fillassier, and the anonymous author of *A Project for Schools* all assumed that the "apprenticeship of the citizen" would necessarily break down the social barriers erected by "false" honor, and would put in their place unifying feelings of patriotic fellowship and a virtuous commitment to duty and country. One of the most aggressive statements of that common view happened to come from the pen of the abbé Coyer, who in 1770 reentered public debates about social order and institutional reform with the publication of his *Plan of Public Education*. Coyer's plan could hardly be called a democratic one. He advised that the peasantry be given no education at all, and artisans and common laborers would have to settle for a scaled-back version of a form of instruction designed specifically for the "leaders" (*conducteurs*) of society.[28] But among his mixed class of leaders— including future military officers, magistrates, clerics, men of commerce, and members of the learned professions, all of whom were identified in his Preliminary Discourse as the different "orders of citizens"—Coyer sought to establish a perfect equality between individuals, an equality that would naturally give rise to uniformly sound morals and differing vocational inclinations.[29]

As he had done in *La noblesse commerçante*, Coyer built his arguments on a refutation of Montesquieu, who had declared that only republican governments, with their dependence on citizens' reflexive and selfless love of the *patrie*, truly relied on "the power of education." Montesquieu had written that "today we receive three different, even contradictory, educations: that of our fathers, that of our teachers, and that of the world [*le monde*]. What is learned in the last [of these educations] overturns all the ideas received in the other two." Elsewhere he noted that, in monarchies, the young received their "principal education" in *le monde*, since that was "the school of what is called *honor*, that universal master that leads us in all situations."[30]

27. Ibid., 136, 141, 143.
28. Coyer, *Plan d'éducation publique*, 106, 334–36.
29. Ibid., iv, 106–7.
30. Montesquieu, *De l'Esprit des Lois*, 1: 131, 137–38.

Coyer responded to Montesquieu's observations about the contrary effects of education by declaring that his plan would avoid altogether "the first of the contradictory influences, the education of the parents." Evoking Rollin's restatement of the Spartan principle that the young "belong more to the Republic than to their parents," Coyer claimed that he would simply get around the problem of parental influences by enrolling students at the tender age of four years. He promised that "whatever [the education of the parents] has achieved before the age of four will be completely nullified."[31] Unable to do much about the distorting lessons of *le monde,* Coyer focused his energies on the lessons imparted in school. In addition to inventing a curriculum heavy on "useful" knowledge and the elements of a genuine social conscience, he stressed the importance of establishing an environment of equality.[32]

The proper tone would be set by the students' dress. "It is now common practice [in the schools] for this one to wear handsome clothes, for that one to be modestly attired; some are made conscious of the poverty of their families. What do all these colorful patterns produce? A disdainful air, a tone of superiority, at the very least, a taste for finery in him who dresses well; and in the others, a useless emulation." Coyer would remove all occasion for jealousy or haughtiness by having all students wear the simple clothes of the common sailor. "Uniformity . . . favors equality," and equality would be the bedrock of Coyer's system. "In vain has so much been written and said about Genealogy, Titles, Coats of Arms, Birth; all men are born equal, of the same father. Nature has engraved that truth in ineffaceable letters on every cradle."[33]

Coyer himself egregiously ignored the cradles of peasants and common laborers, but his commitment to the principle of equality—among all men of adequate means—prepared him to go to extreme lengths to prevent manifestations of pride, social superiority, and distinction. Students of distinguished birth or fortune frequently had private rooms at their collèges, and they also had the benefit of private instructors or "governors." They brought with them their titles of nobility, their valets and lackeys, and their distinctive dress. Many even lived outside the school, returning to the comforts of home at the day's end. At Coyer's reformed institutions, however, there would be "no little knights, no little counts, no little marquis, no little princes, be they princes of the blood," because the title of "Monsieur" would be common to all. All students would have "the same rooms, the

31. Rollin, *Traité des Etudes,,* 4: 418; Coyer, *Plan d'éducation,* 331.
32. Coyer, *Plan d'éducation,* 107–10, 237–41.
33. Ibid., 277–79.

same clothing, the same instructors, the same servants." Students would bow to the rule of "equality in all things."[34]

Coyer made one apparent concession to the educational traditions of the nobility when he incorporated horsemanship and fencing into his reformed curriculum. Nevertheless, his insistence that all students, "without distinction," should receive such training only accentuated the social leveling that his proposed schools both reflected and encouraged. Swords, he noted, were used almost exclusively to settle "affairs of honor." But since honor, "originally reserved for the nobility," had now come to be shared by "clerks, tax officials, and household valets," the proper handling of a sword had become a skill equally useful to all. Paradoxically, then, instruction in swordplay in the new collèges would serve as a resounding sign of equality, not an expression of noble superiority. Until the last two years of instruction, when vocational training would be introduced and differing professional inclinations would be encouraged, students would work to absorb the knowledge necessary for success in all the professions, and they would develop the social habits characteristic of the properly patriotic citizen.[35]

The writings of many of the promoters of public education in France show that the articulation of a "national" civic project exerted powerful leveling pressures on the social imagination of self-described patriots. Between the imagined poles of "false aristocracy" and "democracy"—those stark alternatives articulated in the 1730s by the marquis d'Argenson and envisioned by a multitude of others ever since—the conceptual negotiations over the social characteristics of virtue and honor led many educational reformers to favor what d'Argenson had characterized as "efforts toward equality." Coyer's mocking references to honor, or the attack on "bizarre honor" in the *Project for Schools*, might lead one to believe that this craving for equality directed only the thinking of unabashed admirers of the ancients, or those for whom "true" French honor could manifest itself only as equalizing virtue. The nature of reformist agitation in the army, however, shows clearly enough that the patriotic attraction of equality exerted its pull even in contexts where the pursuit of a differentiating honor remained the unquestioned, and celebrated, motor of human action.

As a career soldier who dedicated his life to the military in 1756 at the tender age of thirteen, Jacques-Antoine-Hippolyte de Guibert (Figure 10) became an exceptionally well connected and renowned figure in the world

34. Ibid., 280–81.
35. Ibid., 86–87, 283–84.

FIGURE 10. The comte de Guibert. Guibert was named to lead the ill-starred Conseil de la Guerre in 1787. This reforming council alienated many because, although it tried to ensure that meritorious soldiers and officers received speedy promotion, it also retained privileged paths of advancement for the high nobility. In 1789, Guibert failed to win election to the Estates-General, in part because of his association with the Conseil, though the rhetoric of an address he prepared for delivery to the electoral assembly of the nobility of Berry—in which he renounced "honor" as a "phantom impostor" of virtue—may have helped to clinch his fate. See *Projet de Discours d'un Citoyen, aux trois ordres de l'Assemblée de Berry* (n.p., 1789). Bibliothèque Nationale de France

of letters. Dramatist and poet, lover of the salonnière Mademoiselle de Lespinasse, and one of the immortals of the Académie Française after 1785, Guibert developed friendships with Buffon, Diderot, and Rousseau, whose *Considerations on the Government of Poland* (1772) treated many of the same themes discussed in the essay that launched Guibert's literary career. The *Essay on Tactics,* which had circulated in manuscript for at least two years before its publication in 1772, caused such a sensation that Voltaire declared it a work of "genius," and women of polite society began debating whether it would be more glorious to be the mother, the wife, or the mistress of Guibert.[36] Dedicated "to my *patrie,*" Guibert's *Essay* called for a regeneration of morals that would enable the French to recapture that "sentiment of patriotism and virtue" that had characterized ancient Rome.[37] Such a regeneration, he enthused, would boost the reputation and desirability of the military profession, make all citizens soldiers and all soldiers citizens, and ensure that "the name *patrie* is no longer a word devoid of meaning."[38]

Guibert placed the responsibility for this hoped-for work of regeneration at the feet of the agency that had made it necessary in the first place, "the government." For Guibert, it was "the fault of the government" that corruption had overwhelmed the French people, because "government must look after morals, opinions, prejudices, and courage." Instead of having exercised benevolent oversight, however, the monarchy had neglected and even worked actively to undermine the health of French morals. Guibert charged that "the morals of the nation changed" under the ministry of Richelieu, who had degraded the French nobility and thereby enslaved the people. Paid off with privileges, the nobility, who had once supported the people, became a staggering burden to them. "Soon there was no more national spirit, no energy, no virtues." By the end of the seventeenth century, everyone had come to mistake luxury for real wealth and "brilliance for glory."[39]

Guibert's proposed cure for this epidemic may have been inspired by Montesquieu's observation that kings could alter a nation's morals only by the example of alternative morals.[40] If the king was to have any hope of

36. See Emile G. Léonard, *L'armée et ses problèmes au XVIIIe siècle* (Paris, 1958), 259.
37. Jacques-Antoine-Hippolyte (also called François-Apolline) de Guibert, "Essai général de tactique," in *Ecrits Militaires, 1772–1790* (Paris, 1977), 57.
38. Ibid., 82, 213.
39. Ibid., 82, 60–61.
40. Montesquieu had written that "one must not change [morals and manners] through laws." "When a king wishes to make great changes in the nation, he should reform by laws that which is established by laws, and he should change through manners that which is es-

leading his courtiers back toward an "active and military life," wrote Guibert, then "let that be his own life, let him raise his children by those principles, let him attend their [military] exercises, let him condemn by his indifference all lazy, voluptuous, and ignorant men, let him offer distinctions to the others." Eventually, after the king's own intentions had been made plain, all the vices that "degrade the great lords" would disappear into thin air.[41]

> From the court and capital, the spirit of honor and courage will flow outward
> into the astonished provinces. The nobility, giving up the petty enjoyments
> of luxury and leisure, will abandon the cities to return to its chateaus. . . . It
> will regain the morals of its ancestors. While retaining its enlightened out-
> look, it will once again become warlike and gallant. The taste for arms and
> military exercises, rekindled in the nobility, will soon make its mark on the
> people.[42]

Then the French would once again display the physical and moral vigor befitting "a free people . . . that possesses morals, virtues, courage, and patriotism," a people ready to take up arms "for the common defense." The king and nobility would set the pace, but real renewal required the unified effort of all citizens. Only a "confederation of all hearts and all forces" could make France "as happy as I desire to see it." All citizens must regard their compatriots with a fondness "like that of a brother toward brothers." "Love of the *patrie*," Guibert exclaimed, "it is in this way that you shape the feelings in my heart!"[43]

Guibert's celebrity made him unusual, of course, but the broad moral themes broached in the *Essay on Tactics*—resistance to the enervating effects of corruption, the emulation of Roman patriots, the formation of citizen soldiers, the unifying demands of patriotism—saturated the reformist literature devoted to military problems in the decades after the Seven Years' War.[44] The drive to enact a general moral reform of the army began

---

tablished by manners. It is very bad politics to change by law what must be changed through manners." See *De l'Esprit des Lois,* 1: 577.

41. Guibert, "Essai," 106.

42. Ibid., 107.

43. Ibid., 213, 51–52.

44. On the military see Albert Latreille, *L'armée et la nation à la fin de l'ancien régime: Les derniers ministres de la guerre de la monarchie* (Paris, 1914); Rafe Blaufarb, "Noble Privilege and Absolutist State Building: French Military Administration after the Seven Years' War," *French Historical Studies* 24 (2001): 223–46, and *The French Army,* 12–45; and Smith, *The Culture of Merit,* 191–261.

even in the midst of the war, and the movement gained new momentum after the dismissal in 1771 of the minister Choiseul, whose controversial administrative reforms in the early 1760s had raised concerns about the state of morale among both common soldiers and lower officers. Choiseul himself declared that "one of the objects of my administrative system is to reestablish love of the *patrie* and of its interest in French hearts." His detractors claimed, however, that those reforms—especially his decision to transfer all responsibility for recruitment to the central administration, thus severing the link between captains and the soldiers whom they had formerly recruited personally—had had precisely the opposite effect.[45] The war minister Saint-Germain's implementation of new penal procedures in 1776, which included humiliating beatings by the "flat of the sword" for common soldiers, only exacerbated critics' concerns about the moral direction of change in the French military.[46]

All of these concerns elicited from officers and former officers a wide variety of manuscripts and published commentaries that addressed the organization of regiments, policies of recruitment, training, the duration of the soldier's term of service, the treatment of veterans, and more. But given the wider cultural context in which these reform projects were composed—the assertion of French patriotism, the critique of "false" honor, the simultaneous appropriation of true honor by the nation at large—the theme that commands special attention is that of the relationship between soldiers and their mostly noble officers. In a manner consistent with Guibert, for whom the need to achieve "a confederation of all hearts" equaled if it did not surpass in importance the expected moral leadership of the nobility, many reformers saw both patriotism and the "national" characteristic of honor as social solvents that required the renegotiation or, in some cases, the effective abolition of the barrier that separated the second and third estates.

In a representative essay titled "The Military Patriot," the vicomte de Flavigny, who called himself an "unfortunate victim of the system that will scarcely survive its illustrious author [Choiseul]," described to the government "the enormous abuses of its military administration."[47] The com-

45. As quoted in Guy Chaussinand-Nogaret, *Choiseul: Naissance de la gauche* (Paris, 1998), 91. On reaction to Choiseul's reforms, see Blaufarb, "Noble Privilege and Absolutist State Building." Blaufarb points out that even before Choiseul, many captains had come to rely on professional recruiters to fill their companies, and that their defense of "private" administration idealized "feudal" recruitment procedures that had long been in decline.
46. On Saint-Germain's reforms, see Latreille, *L'armée et la nation,* 54–134; and Blaufarb, *The French Army,* 27–30.
47. AN, M 650, no. 3, Vicomte de Flavigny, "Le Militaire Patriote" [1771], 3, 5.

panies were now filled with "young men without morals, libertines, rebels against parental authority . . . the corrupt, the cowardly," none of whom served "for the love of their prince and their *patrie*."[48] Recruits of higher quality could not be hoped for, Flavigny charged, unless the government transformed its methods of attracting soldiers and invented new means of rewarding and encouraging their good performance. The administration failed utterly to appeal "to the vanity and self-regard of a Nation more avid for honor and glory than for money," and it shamefully neglected the "French prejudices" that presented "an inexhaustible source of recompenses" that could cause to be reborn "the glorious days of the Monarchy." By appealing to the self-regard (*amour-propre*) and the sense of emulation in the common soldier, Flavigny assured, "we will be able to expect everything of his fidelity and his courage."[49]

Another military observer, writing in the late 1760s or early 1770s, proposed measures designed to take advantage of the "French prejudices" hailed by Flavigny. He argued, for example, that veterans should earn a distinctive mark that would bring them the "Veneration of Citizens," a mark of respect that would be affirmed in annual public spectacles where veterans would pass in review before the "eye of the Nation."[50] But this anonymous author of "Project of a Military Man" confronted more directly than had Flavigny the discrepancy between the inequalities of social status in the army and the common qualities and motivations that necessarily characterized every successful soldier. Frustrated by the humiliating differences between the honored status of the noble officer and the degraded status of the soldier, the author aimed to give "more honor and dignity to the function" of soldier, and thereby to "inspire in my fellow Patriots a taste for arms, and to render them soldiers."[51]

To accomplish this task, he proposed establishing a new military class, labeled simply "officers of war," that would be composed of common soldiers of outstanding merit. Entry into this unofficial corps would facilitate soldiers' passage toward the higher ranks monopolized by the nobility.

> I do not mean to belittle the merit of the officer whose birth attaches him to the profession of arms; the Nobility is naturally warrior-like. But I regard the soldier who has reached the grade of officer as a man ennobled by his own advancement, and when I see him in a position superior to his birth I see this

48. Ibid., 20.
49. Ibid., 30–32.
50. SHAT, MR 1709, no. 54, "Projet d'un militaire" [after 1763], 9, 23.
51. Ibid., 1.

only as proof of fortune's error in deciding the cradle from which he was raised. He is truly noble, and his Nobility is all the more capable of rendering service to the *Patrie* which enabled him to obtain it through his faithful service and impressive valor.[52]

"Let us give men the means to rise above their birth and to bring down the barriers that fix them in the class of common men," the author continued, for in doing so, "we will multiply great and glorious actions" and provide "every imaginable encouragement to emulation."[53]

The marquis de Beaupoil St. Aulaire likewise made "French prejudices" the central theme of his reform project of 1776, a lengthy *mémoire* on discipline and desertion.[54] "The shameful delirium of our Anglomaniacs, and the declamations of our admirers of things German, would have caused an epidemic as harmful as it is detestable if they had weakened our own self-respect and destroyed the belief that there exists in all the classes of our fellow citizens a national character filled with nobility and heroism." The only ambition of the French soldier, wrote Beaupoil, was "to be accepted among his comrades . . . as a brave man beyond reproach." The government's failure to recognize and respond to the soldier's innate honor explained the army's alarmingly high rate of desertion. "When the French soldier senses that [the state] esteems him enough to govern him by the laws of honor, he will submit to them with pride; he will love and respect them; he will make a cult of them."

Structural and procedural flaws in the operation of the army prevented the government from taking full advantage of the soldier's "nobility and heroism." Beaupoil expressed special contempt for the recent introduction of punishment through beating with the flat of the sword, a punishment to which soldiers alone could be subjected. "The soldier sees that those above him cannot be subjected to [this punishment], for the simple reason that such a chastisement is incompatible with the honor of a *gentilhomme* and an officer." Anyone, though, could detect the lapse in logic that allowed for such differentiation in the army. "Are there, then, . . . two different honors in the same career? If these are the consequences of such an idea, all is lost." One must speak to French soldiers not through the "voice of terror," but through "a language made for their hearts." Only a

52. Ibid., 16.
53. Ibid., 16–17.
54. AN M 640, no. 6, "Mémoire sur la Discipline et les moiens propres à détruire l'esprit de désertion dans les Troupes Françaises, par M. le Marquis de Beaupoil St. Aulaire, Capitaine reformé au Regiment Provincial de Soissons" [1776?], unpaginated.

"dangerous sophist" would maintain that "the same vehicle" does not have "similar effects" on men of "different conditions." And in any case, in a "spiritual and sensitive nation" such as France, "estates and men are less distant from one another. Their prejudices and their sentiments are more uniform. This truth has been confirmed by experience."

Military treatises that stressed the army's "uniform" sentiments and called attention to the common nobility of officers and soldiers could be cited endlessly.[55] But of all the military treatises that emerged out of the long period of political ferment that followed the Seven Years' War, perhaps the most influential was Joseph Servan de Gerbey's *Citizen Soldier* (1780). The book caused an immediate stir, and it brought Servan de Gerbey significant rewards. Soon after publication of *The Citizen Soldier,* its author—who until this time had been a relatively obscure major in a regiment of grenadiers—was elevated to a prestigious position as sub-governor of the royal pages at Versailles. In 1783 Servan de Gerbey was awarded the Cross of Saint-Louis, at least in part on the basis of literary merit, and the publisher Panckoucke soon invited him to oversee the composition of the volumes devoted to the military art in the *Encyclopédie Méthodique,* the successor to Diderot and d'Alembert's encyclopedic project. Because of the reputation he had earned through *The Citizen Soldier,* at the time of the Revolution Servan de Gerbey exerted great influence on the direction of military reform, and he even served two brief but eventful stints as Minister of War in the summer of 1792.[56] Contemporary reviewers observed that *The Citizen Soldier* was "difficult to summarize" because of its length and theoretical density.[57] Wrote this appreciative but

55. In 1771, Duchesne de Bettencourt referred to military veterans as "nobles without birth." SHAT, MR 1711, no. 101, "Observations intéressantes sur les troupes, relativement aux Vétérans" [1771], p. 3. An infantry captain declared that "it is only honor and consideration that can reward the disinterested courage that has characterized us for so long." AN, M 640, no. 4, "Observations pour servir à un plan de Constitution militaire, selon le génie des français, par Laureau, Capitaine d'Infanterie" [1772], "Récompenses." Another noted that "the métier of war" is the métier "of honor and equality." See M. d'Ey, *L'Esprit du Militaire, ou Entretiens avec Moi-même* (Paris, 1771), 72–73. Captain Louis de Boussanelle declared that the French soldier naturally breathed in "the love of his king and his Nation, honor, nobility . . . and the most respectable sensibilities." See *Le Bon Militaire* (Paris, 1770), 20–21, 49–50. His assumption that "the soldier is a citizen . . . whose actions stand in for his pedigree" explains why Boussanelle later reminded French officers that common soldiers were their "equals." See his *Aux Soldats* (Paris, 1786), 73.

56. Jacques-François Lanier, *Le Général Joseph Servan de Gerbey (Romans 1741–Paris 1808): Pour une armée au service de l'homme* (Valence, 2001), 18, 90. On the influence of *Le Soldat Citoyen* in military circles, see Alan Forrest, *Soldiers of the French Revolution* (Durham, N.C., 1990), 40–42.

57. *MF,* 20 January 1781, 123.

overwhelmed contemporary reviewer, "One can only judge it well by read-ing it carefully from cover to cover." But despite its complexity, Servan de Gerbey's text shows better than any other single work the connection be-tween the eighteenth century's determined revival of patriotic ideas and the pressures toward equality that attended the application of those ideas to specific social and institutional contexts.

Like Guibert, whose work he had clearly read, Servan de Gerbey launched his discussion by lamenting the decrepit state of French civic culture, and by throwing in the face of his readers the superior morals of the ancients. The Romans, he wrote, had made valor and constancy "necessary virtues" by linking humans' natural love of oneself to love of "their families, of their *patrie*, and of all that is most dear to man. They had rendered sacred these various duties by subsuming them all under their love of the *patrie*." Sounding the pessimistic echoes of *The Spirit of the Laws*, Servan de Ger-bey observed that "this love had produced among them great and prodi-gious virtues, immortal actions whose brilliance blinds our weakened eyes, and many great men whose antique virtues we can scarcely perceive." Mod-ern France resembled ancient Rome only in its age of decadence. "In our days, commerce and luxury have produced mercenary soldiers, as well as the debasement of a profession that is not sufficiently lucrative at a time when everything is measured against weight in gold."[58]

In a passage in which he plagiarized freely from Mirabeau's *Ami des Hommes*, and where he signaled his departure from Montesquieu's mod-ernist resignation, Servan de Gerbey nevertheless went on to express op-timism about French prospects for recovery. What had characterized the Romans' love of the *patrie*? "A superstitious mélange of religion, respect, and esteem for the different orders of the republic, tenderness for one's relations and one's fellow citizens, a pride mixed up with the glory of the *patrie*. Why are we not susceptible to those same sentiments? Can they not emerge from the heart of our own families, and extend over the territory of the state? Can all of France not become the homeland of the French-man?"[59] Servan de Gerbey found the answer to his questions in the pres-ence of the moral resource that had been dear both to Mirabeau and to all of those who had tried to nationalize its reach since the early 1760s. "Honor, that divinity of our ancient knights, which can still serve as a mo-tive force in our own time, is merely another name for the ancients' love of the *patrie*." And in what context was love of the *patrie* likely to be revived

58. [Servan de Gerbey], *Soldat Citoyen*, 49–50.
59. Ibid., 50. Cf. Mirabeau, *L'Ami des Hommes*, 1: pt. 2, 73–74.

sooner or more easily, he asked, than in the army, "that profession whose very basis must be honor?"[60]

The imperative "to render the profession of soldier honorable" had become a vital national concern. "It is more essential than one might think for the nation to contribute, by its esteem for the soldier, to maintaining his sensitivity toward honor." Echoing the words of the chevalier d'Arc, Servan de Gerbey claimed that the professional soldier's self-esteem "is very delicate, like everything having to do with honor." For that very reason, he advised against admitting into the military "vagabonds," or others "who have nothing to attach them to the *patrie.*" Such rootless men could not be expected to respond to the enticements of honor and respect, and the "military spirit" would have no hold over their consciences.[61] Despite these prejudicial remarks about the social origins of soldiers, Servan de Gerbey's proposed method of boosting and maintaining the honor of the soldier and his profession actually differed markedly from that of the chevalier d'Arc. Whereas Arc had stressed the identity between the military profession and the noble estate, and had argued that honor in the army could best be maintained by reserving the officer corps, and even whole companies, for example-setting *gentilshommes,* Servan de Gerbey focused on the issues of training, promotion, and reward. Ignoring the boundaries of estate, he focused on the need to appeal generally to the soldier's innate desire for honor and glory, and he connected the honor of the military vocation to the soldier's ability to satisfy his reasonable expectations of recognition.

In order to preserve the honorable demeanor of the "free and happy citizen," and to avoid producing a mere "slave, always disposed to sacrifice his duties to his interests," the army and the state had to clear the soldier's path to glory. Only merit's unfettered access to grades and distinctions could preserve the honor of each rank and the honor of each occupant. "Establish, then, this invariable rule, that only through voting [*par les suffrages]* can anyone have means of advancing to a higher grade: protection, birth, length of service, all must disappear in the face of unanimously recognized merit." Servan de Gerbey went on to cite several examples of court favoritism and the routine practice of offering premature promotion to young officers from well-connected families.

> The prejudice of birth is no less dangerous, and it is one that . . . becomes more harmful to the people in whose minds it comes to be rooted. In monarchical governments, a man without illustrious blood cannot serve his *patrie,*

60. Servan de Gerbey, *Soldat Citoyen,* 51.
61. Ibid., 54, 55, 423.

except through infinite labors. Please tell us how the privilege of descending from this or that man provides a title to merit.

Occupied with "the minutiae of etiquette" and the pursuit of pleasure, the young seigneur of the court "has never learned to command men," but he secured high appointments just the same.[62]

Servan de Gerbey's critique of the privileges of birth and favor, and his disdain for luxury and cupidity, carried him toward the elaboration of a hybrid administrative regime. Like Montesquieu and his disciples, he wished to place the state on the firm foundation of the principle of honor, which he represented as the driving force of "monarchical government."[63] But like the most fervent admirers of the classical republics, he also insisted on eliciting both the contributions and the consensus of all the "citizens" of the nation. Even as he promoted honor, Servan de Gerbey effectively effaced the presence of the legal nobility from the milieu of the citizen soldier. In his new regime of honor, the nobility's role as moral exemplar was given over to the military profession itself, whose heterogeneous social makeup Servan de Gerbey pointedly emphasized.

"Let us continue to regard our military," wrote Servan de Gerbey, "as the first order of the state." Let it stand as "a corps apart," and let "the love of honor and glory [grow] continually among men who will have been chosen to be defenders and models." Servan de Gerbey's substitution of the "military" for the "nobility" as the leading order of the state, far from representing a mere rhetorical slip, carried real social significance. For he went on to explain that the officer corps should be open "to citizens of all classes," and that all titles, distinctions, and preferences, including nobility itself, should be a sign and consequence of public acclamation. The ancients had provided the relevant model, with their laurel wreaths and civic crowns, and their long success in inspiring emulation and pride in *patrie* meant that the French, too, should accord titles and honorific marks to deserving individuals. "Distribute praise, ribbons, and crosses. May they all be distributed in public, with great fanfare; may the nation applaud, and all collaborate to create the most lasting impression." But in granting these distinctions, the government must be "guided by the voice of the public; allow no intrigue, no cabals. And let officers and soldiers enjoy the right of designating those among them whom they believe merit distinction."[64]

62. Ibid., 426, 429.
63. Ibid., 435–36. "All must depend on the love of glory and honor," he wrote. "Read your history, and see that everywhere pecuniary recompenses have been granted for bravery, it has necessarily [weakened] a monarchical government."
64. Ibid., 433–34, 437, 444–45.

Servan de Gerbey had no plans to abolish the existing nobility outright, as Rouillé d'Orfeuil had recommended in 1773, but he would force nobles to regard themselves as citizens similar in all essentials to citizens of humbler backgrounds. In newly established military schools, for example—schools which, unlike the Ecole Royale Militaire established for the poor nobility, would be open to "all the young men who should form the future corps of officers"—instructors would need to "bind [noble students] to all the orders of the state. Let them believe themselves to be the first [among men], but they must esteem others." In their study of history, "make them value certain heroic actions performed by the magistracy, and by men of the church. Let them see that heroism is found wherever duty is confronted courageously, and with risk." In any case, through their daily interactions with other students, and in their competition for academic honors, they would learn the true nature of fraternity between citizens, because "the choice of recompenses must be in conformity with the general interest," and "the students themselves, in the presence of the nation, [will be] the unique dispensers of recompenses." Soon all students, like all prospective officers in the military, would exhibit the same level of emulation, secure in the knowledge that "public recognition can be accorded only to actions that promote virtue."[65]

As someone who had benefited from his own noble status, Servan de Gerbey did not oppose the concept of nobility. His willingness to allow established nobles to "believe themselves" to be natural leaders shows that the idea of a standard-setting elite remained attractive to him. Nevertheless, for Servan de Gerbey the assimilation of French honor to the value of "patriotism" meant that Montesquieu's ambivalent description of the classical republics—where distinctions arose from "equality" itself—had become relevant, and desirable, in modern France.[66] The existence of honors that could be arrogated exclusively to some, and awarded without common consent, seemed incompatible with the "love of the *patrie*" to which all legitimate "passions" had to be subordinated, and on which the unity of the citizenry depended.[67] Like the historian Rossel, who desired a system that would stimulate "noble emulation" in "all French hearts," and like his brother Servan, who called for a "remunerative law" that would

---

65. Ibid., 277, 219, 230.
66. Montesquieu had written that, in republics, "distinctions are born from the principle of equality, even when [the principle] seems undone by glorious services, or by superior talents." See *De l'Esprit*, 1: 149.
67. He wrote that, unlike the "vicious passions," the "useful" and "virtuous passions" should be encouraged by "all that strikes the senses and the imagination." Servan de Gerbey, *Soldat Citoyen*, 225.

quench a common thirst for honor, Servan de Gerbey believed that nobility should devolve naturally on the zealous citizen.

Although a significant cross-section of France's broad political and literary elite could agree on the desirability of cultivating what Holbach had called "the heart and spirit of a citizen Nobility, for whom honor—always inseparable from virtue—would be the prime mover," the social parameters of that citizen nobility remained open to dispute. Servan de Gerbey and others argued, in effect, that citizens should make nobles, and that the citizen's natural craving for honor, and instinct for virtuous self-sacrifice, should be the gateway to the highest honor of nobility. Others believed, conversely, that nobles made the best citizens, and they argued that the creation of a genuinely patriotic culture that sustained and rewarded the honor of the French people required social delineation and the existence of a corps of nobility that could preserve moral standards. The articulation of this other vision of "citizen nobility" from the 1770s showed a very different side of the process by which honor became nationalized in the second half of the eighteenth century. Analysis of this conservative patriotic vision offers the prospect of interpreting anew the long disdained concept of the pre-Revolutionary "aristocratic reaction."

## CONTENDING WITH EQUALITY IN A CONTEXT OF REFORM

In the late 1770s, an infantry captain named Blangermont evoked the medieval past, and its contrast with a corrupt modern age, for purposes similar in many respects to those of C.-L.-M. de Sacy and the other exponents of French national honor after the Seven Years' War. The ancient knights of the Middle Ages, he wrote admiringly, educated the young nobles who surrounded them "as much in morals as in the handling of arms; while forming their bodies, they also formed their spirit and their heart." In losing the prejudices that had characterized that age, Blangermont asked, "did the nation gain anything? I doubt it. The nobility in those days was not what it has since become, a chimera founded on parchments that register the actions of others," parchments that rarely inspire "the desire to imitate their valor and especially their loyalty." Blangermont lamented the "good spirit that, in centuries past, characterized the French, and which, little by little, has been extinguished." Like the comte de Guibert, he believed that "it is up to the prince to halt the slide. The remedy is in his hands, and that remedy is education."[68]

68. SHAT, MR 1781, no. 70, "Mémoire sur l'éducation des jeunes militaires et sur la com-

Blangermont, "pushed by my love for my *patrie* and my profession," took the liberty of offering the king his own suggestions about the shape that the new educational reform should take. The king and the leaders of his military must "speak to your young officers in the language of honor; show them the route to glory; teach them the means of following that road; excite their emulation; you will soon see a military worthy of that age when honor and love of the *patrie* were its guide." The properly formed and naturally grateful young officer would develop a bond to his king rooted in "duty and patriotism. That virtue, almost extinct, will be reborn. The word [patriotism] will no longer be devoid of meaning. It is in the integrity of the warrior that we can still revive patriotic enthusiasm!"[69]

There is very little in Blangermont's rhetoric of patriotism, and his nostalgia for ancient chivalry, that separates him from La Curne de Sainte-Palaye, Servan de Gerbey, the marquis de Beaupoil, or Guibert, whose *Essay on Tactics* clearly helped to inspire Blangermont's treatise. His remarks on the primitive "French" character, on the meaninglessness of legal nobility, and on the need for a simultaneous revival of emulation, honor, and patriotism were consonant with those of many advocates of national moral renewal in the second half of the eighteenth century. What distinguishes Blangermont's plan of reform are its rigid prescriptions regarding the social origins of the officers who would benefit from the new instruction. Blangermont reacted to the "chimera" that nobility had become by seeking to reconstitute an authentic nobility untainted by the shameful pursuit of "interest" and undiluted by the infiltration of "opulent financier[s]," whom Blangermont regarded as the true culprits behind the debasement of French morals.[70] Anticipating the controversial Ségur règlement of 1781, which restricted the officer corps to nobles of at least four generations, Blangermont called for the establishment of an "administrative council" to "examine rigorously and without partiality" the proofs of nobility of all who wished to present themselves as candidates for the officer corps.[71]

Blangermont explained in two ways the need to pay ever more careful attention to the "parchments" whose empty symbolism he elsewhere criti-

---

position des officiers des Regts d'Infanterie française, par Blangermont, capne au regt. D'Austrasie" [1777–80], 12, 22.

69. Ibid., 2, 11–12.

70. Ibid., 10. "All the orders of the state have their place," he wrote. "To grant one the liberty to leave [its place] is to crush the other, to cause its disappearance. It is to put the opulent financier in the place of the nobility."

71. Ibid., 11, 17.

cized. First, he asserted that "the commoner is the born enemy of the noble," who attracted nothing but the "jealousy and hatred" of the common man. Because they were motivated by different principles—honor for the nobility, interest for the people—the mixture of nobles and commoners in the same corps inevitably created insubordination, disorder, and "anarchy." Second, a "mercenary" spirit had already invaded the army, thus rendering increasingly difficult the cultivation of that taste for glory and selflessness that every army required. Commoners, as the bearers of the threatening virus, had to be kept at bay.

> Already in the regiments . . . there are few military conversations, but many financial ones. They discuss salary, retirement, supplements from the court; if they speak of an expedition, it's only to ask if the pay will be augmented. There is no question here of glory; that is a calculation in which most of them see nothing but smoke. Is this the spirit of a good soldier, or of the ancient knights? A large part of the corps having become common, their spirit necessarily derogates [from nobility].

To correct the problem, the king needed to establish a new school in each regiment, where carefully screened "gentlemen cadets" would be instructed in the moral and technical details of their profession before assuming their own positions of command.[72] By taking steps to reconstitute the honorable moral milieu that had characterized ancient chivalry, the king could ensure the "patriotic enthusiasm" of his officers and the survival of his beleaguered nobility.

Blangermont's description of nobles and commoners as "born enemies" would have appealed to few of his fellow defenders of nobility in the last decades of the old regime, but his highly class-conscious views were situated on the far end of a spectrum that encompassed the ideas of many other like-minded reformers. Showing the same fear of money and moneyed interests, the baron de Bohan declared in 1781 that it is "wealth that corrupts all, and that erases all the separations that honor and glory have set up between citizens." Riches provided "sufficient title to claim all positions," and it was that development, Bohan candidly explained, "that has already produced these efforts by the nobility to uphold the distinction that must eternally separate [the nobility] from the commoner."[73]

Admiration for the morals of the Middle Ages fueled national pride,

72. Ibid., 10–12.
73. François-Philippe Loubat, baron de Bohan, *Examen critique du militaire français*, 2 vols. (Geneva, 1781), 1: 58.

and inspired the national appropriation of honor, in the years following the Seven Years' War. But Blangermont's treatise helpfully reveals the socially conservative purposes that the reinvigoration of honor, and the celebration of France's historic heroism, could also serve. In 1784, another critic of the military followed Blangermont in evoking the distant French past as a model for the future. In a treatise titled "Ideas on Several Military Subjects," he waxed lyrical about the moral instruction typically received by the noble youth of the French past. When great seigneurs educated the children of their vassals, he wrote, the young had developed more than "robust bodies." "In hearing incessant talk of the point of honor, [and] of glorious actions, their souls were opened at an early age to those noble sentiments that make the sacrifice of one's life seem unimportant next to the good of the state and [the conservation] of our reputation."[74]

Like La Curne de Sainte-Palaye, it is important to note, the author professed to admire many features of modern culture. The "passing of the prejudices that enchained our ancestors" meant that "social virtues" and "sweet urbanity" had replaced the "crudity" and "impulsive violence" that characterized an earlier age. He also praised what he clearly regarded as a recent moral turn in philosophical thought. The earliest works of the philosophes, "in showing all men and all countries as perfectly equal, suppressed this taste for the *patrie* [which is] the first passion of sensitive hearts." In making interest the sole source of human action, they had "destroyed all sentiments of love and friendship" and turned human beings into "unfortunate creatures." Fortunately, "that illusion was short lived," and philosophes now taught that "happiness is found only by fulfilling with zeal the duties imposed by nature and society."[75]

For this author, the resuscitation of "taste for the *patrie*," and the renewed appreciation for the moral dimension of social life, now particularly demanded the conscious reinforcement of "the characteristic marks of the French nobility," including "love for its king," a "passion for service," and, especially, "honor." The chivalric tradition of household education obviously could not be recovered, but the unconscious abandonment of all of its ideals had been a regrettable mistake. "We separate ourselves from our children [when they are] at a most tender age, and we begin by rendering foreign everything in the world that they should cherish. We enclose them in collèges where, delivered to men who are often guided by interest alone, they lose the good qualities to which they had been susceptible. In these

74. BNF, manuscrits français 9174, ff. 16–52, "Idées sur quelques objets militaires, adressé aux jeunes officiers," fol. 19r.
75. Ibid., fol. 18r–v.

large establishments, *which are still so imperfect*, . . . is there a single instructor whose role is to teach the civil virtues?" The typical *gentilhomme*, "mixed up in the crowd," gains little in the collège other than a "slight imprint of knowledge" that soon fades. This neglect of proper moral instruction was only to be expected. "Love of the *patrie*? He knows it not. . . . Honor? How can instructors *who are not subjected to the severity of its laws* transmit those sentiments in all their purity?"[76]

In direct contrast to the abbé Coyer, who had proposed that children be taken from their parents at the age of four to be given a thorough education in equality and useful citizenship, this anonymous author championed "domestic" education. Probably encouraged by Rousseau's *Emile*, he urged the fathers of noble children to work to impart the distinctive moral lessons present in their own homes and implicit in their own traditions. "I exhort fathers . . . not to separate themselves from their children. Their good examples, their simple words, conveyed with tenderness, would be more useful than the lessons of the most able instructors." Childhood provided parents a valuable opportunity to instill the right moral assumptions in their progeny, for "whatever efforts we may take to rise above the prejudices with which we were imbued in childhood, they always maintain a power over our soul."[77]

Blangermont, Bohan, and the author of "Ideas on Several Military Subjects" formed part of a large group of writers, particularly well represented in the military but active outside the army as well, for whom the imperative to inspire a patriotic and national spirit demanded not the effacement but the reinforcement of the distinction between nobility and commoners. These writers were not unaware of recent efforts to nationalize the sentiment of honor and to encourage what the merchant Bedos had called "unanimity of patriotic sentiments in all the orders of the state." In fact, many built on the theme. Barthès de Marmorières, in a treatise of 1781 devoted to establishing once and for all the Frankish and Gaulish precedents for the distinction between noble and commoner, conspicuously praised the "courage and sensitivity to honor" of the "simple bourgeoisie" of modern France.[78]

Nevertheless, political writings linking the moral health of the nation to the distinctiveness of the nobility became quite common after about 1770.

76. Ibid., fol. 19v.
77. Ibid., fols. 20v, 39r, note m.
78. M. Barthès de Marmorières, *Nouveaux Essais sur la Noblesse, où, après avoir recherché l'origine & l'état civil de l'homme noble chez les peuples connus, on se propose de le guider dans les différens âges & emplois de la vie* (Neuchâtel, 1781), 33.

In his *Historical, moral, and political précis on the French nobility* (1777), the vicomte Toustain de Richebourg openly declared, in a prefatory epistle dedicated "To Citizen Nobles," that "because your illustrious corps is especially
devoted and consecrated to the public good, it seems to me just and natural to reserve for it the most glorious positions, the most brilliant functions, the most important offices of a society in which it occupies the
first rank."[79] In a work that showed considerable erudition—the author
demonstrated his familiarity with and appreciation for the mainstream of
Enlightenment thought as well as the precepts of the "civic humanist" tradition—Toustain de Richebourg confidently declared that "the distinction
between Noble and Commoner, whose antiquity, generality, and utility we
have already established, is not vain and barbarous, or odious and humiliating," as some had unjustly maintained.[80] Expressing a sentiment that
would have raised the hackles of the abbé Coyer, he simply noted that "Nobles were established to look after the splendor and the conservation of
the country, whose abundance and cultivation are secured by the Commoners."[81] Those who criticized the distinction of orders, and who sought
to undermine the legitimacy of feudal rights, worked unwittingly to ensure
that the state became fatally "infected by luxury."[82] Toustain de Richebourg hoped that his readers would accept the good will of his intentions.
"Those who will do me the honor of reading my ideas will recognize, I
hope, the views of humanity, honor, and patriotism that have inspired
them."[83]

A national regeneration rooted in the benefits of noble distinctiveness
also formed the subject of Pierre Augustin de Varennes's *Moral Reflections
Relative to the French Soldier* (1779), the first edition of which had been
praised for its "great utility" by the *Journal Encyclopédique*.[84] The object of

79. Charles Gaspard, vicomte Toustain de Richebourg, *Précis historique, moral et politique sur
la noblesse françoise* (Amsterdam, 1777), iv.
80. Ibid., 8. Among the authors whose work is discussed in the *Historical Précis:* Mirabeau
(p. 2), Beccaria (p. 3), Mably (p. 4), Montesquieu (pp. 4–5), Boulainvilliers (p. 4), Gourcy
(p. 5), Linguet (p. 12), d'Alembert (p. 39), Duclos (p. 60), Rousseau (p. 68), d'Argenson
(p. 100), Pufendorf (p. 165), and Machiavelli (219–21). Study of both the *Discourses* and *The
Prince,* wrote Toustain, could prove useful to a "people who possess and cherish liberty (221)."
81. Ibid., 9.
82. Ibid., 149. Toustain de Richebourg insisted on the essential unity of the second estate.
"However fresh the Nobility that has been granted, it must be united to the [second] Order
and form part of the corps along with it, because once again, there are not two nobilities in
France" (29).
83. Ibid., iv.
84. *JE,* 1772, vol. 1, pt. 1, 21–29, esp. 23. The *Réflexions* were Varennes's augmented version
of an *Essai d'une morale relative au militaire françois* (Paris, 1771).

the book, as described in approving tones by the *Année Littéraire,* was "to awaken and maintain in the soul of French soldiers that national honor" that had supported the monarchy since its inception.[85] Showing the influence of Montesquieu and an awareness of the threat posed by the recent Maupeou coup, Varennes affirmed that "each people has its primitive and unique character. It is a mistake, which has often caused harm in France, to imagine that the Administration has the ability to change it." Varennes thought it important now to "state the constitutive principles of the morality of the state, to render them pure, and therefore to elevate them above arbitrary and vicious interpretation." With those principles clearly stated, "we must then see to their circulation in all hearts by way of a national education."[86]

In view of his status as a former officer, Varennes's focus on the military aspects of the "morality of the state" was not surprising, but he made the military nobility peculiarly central to his vaguely defined project of "national" education. Genuine reform evidently depended on a social cleansing of the army's officer ranks. Varennes proposed to revive the national character in "all hearts" by strictly excluding all non-nobles from the officer corps. "Luxury having been banished from the troops," he wrote, "only the Nobility will be able to enter the [corps]." Strict social screening would allow the nobility to wrest control of the army back from "a crowd of newborns who, raised on their piles of gold . . . by abusing their fortunes[, have] usurped the places to which the nobility is called by right of birth." The recently purchased ("new-born") nobility of the interlopers did not change the "vicious" environment from which they had emerged, and it did nothing to prevent the degradation of the morals which only the true nobility could be entrusted to uphold.[87]

With the nobility back firmly in place, and with procedures for promotion and reward having been regularized for each grade, the officer would be able to mold the soldier, through his own words and examples, into "a generous citizen who devotes himself to the glory and happiness of the *patrie.*" The officer had this ability, Varennes explained, because the hierarchy of honor made officers the object, rather than the beneficiaries, of *emulation.* The military, he wrote, divided into three classes. In the first belonged "those who, guided by the general point of honor, join to this purified sentiment a vast and luminous mind that lifts them from the crowd for the

85. *AL,* 1772, vol 7, 57–70, esp. 57.
86. Pierre Augustin de Varennes, *Réflexions Morales, Relatives au Militaire François* (Paris, 1779), 12–13.
87. Ibid., 17–18, 155.

achievement of glory and grand enterprises." "Emulation," he continued, "is not made for creatures so privileged . . . their existence is too pure and sublime for them to have need of the means necessary to the multitude."[88]

Emulation needed to work its magic only in the second and third "classes" of the military, whose profiles corresponded roughly to the conventional social division between the respectable urban class and the mass of laboring humanity placed beneath them. "I place in the second class those who, with the same foundation in honor, lack the same resources of mind; those with ideas less clear; those who, less [sic] timid, do not dare to deviate from what the vulgar call wisdom." Varennes placed in the third and least distinguished class those who, though they also possessed honor, nevertheless followed instinct, "and never distance themselves from the dangerous habits of routine where they crowd in with the multitude; [they] vegetate while murmuring about their fate."[89] Varennes explained that "in changing the object of emulation" for the second class of men, the army would persuade them to abandon "a frivolous and tumultuous life" and to commit themselves to "the true goal of the Military Art." Even in the third class, Varennes assured, "every individual . . . will be susceptible to a certain kind of emulation," and by offering recompenses "analogous and proportionate to the kind of service [he is] in position to render," the administration would increase his "exactitude" and his commitment to duty. In France, "consideration and honor are the first riches of the Nation," and because all soldiers shared the same "foundation in honor," all could be expected to strive for the forms of excellence modeled by their officers.[90] The circulation of the sentiment of honor would therefore be central to the project of national and patriotic education, just as Duclos had imagined a generation earlier, but in Varennes's understanding this education depended on the examples set by those who possessed honor in its "purified" form, the authentic military nobility.

This idea of reinvigorating, and shaping, national mores through the re-creation of a standard-setting nobility received perhaps its most extended theoretical treatment in a text written two years after publication of the first edition of Varennes's *Moral Reflections*, Louis-Gabriel Du Buat-Nançay's six-volume *Elements of Politics, or Search for the True Principles of Social Economy* (1773).[91] The twentieth century's preeminent historian of French constitutional thought under the old regime characterized Buat-Nançay, with

88. Ibid., 128, 32, 24.
89. Ibid., 33.
90. Ibid., 34–35, 128.
91. Louis-Gabriel Du Buat-Nançay, *Eléments de la Politique, ou Recherche des Vrais Principes de l'Economie Sociale,* 6 vols. (London, 1773).

some justification, as a cranky and confused disciple of Montesquieu with far too high an opinion of his own originality.[92] Grimm properly described Buat-Nançay's writing style as "diffuse," "obscure," and "undisciplined."[93] One contemporary reader nevertheless heard echoes of "the immortal *Spirit of the Laws*," and he predicted that the wide-ranging *Elements of Politics* would "cause a sensation."[94] The prediction proved to be extravagant—few readers seem to have had the patience to distill Buat-Nançay's "undisciplined" prose, and he was cited only infrequently in later years—but the work deserves attention nonetheless. Few other books illustrate so clearly the conceptual challenges presented to the society of orders by the egalitarian premises pressed so insistently in postwar patriotic thought.

Like Guillame-Joseph Saige, the fierce "republican" opponent of the Maupeou parlements, Buat-Nançay cited the need for a new French "catechism of the citizen," and he called for "the spread of patriotism" through the medium of print. But in opposition to the "detestable works" he had seen bearing the catechistic title, Buat-Nançay proposed a plan of national regeneration that reinforced inequalities between citizens.[95] His "patriotic reflections" focused on the moral differences that separated the various estates of the realm, and he argued that the nobility simply had a superior capacity to feel and express patriotism.[96]

When estimating human worth, Buat-Nançay asserted, all that is purely physical about man "should count for nothing," since one never owes respect, esteem, or consideration to another man simply because "he is a man, because he lives, drinks, eats, and works." Only "moral goods and needs" establish "the distancing of which we speak. The more a man has [moral] needs to a high degree, and the more he possesses [moral] goods in abundance, the more he enjoys superiority over those who have neither, or who have them only in small amounts."[97]

92. Carcassonne, *Montesquieu et le problème*, 244–55.

93. Grimm's comments were made in 1757, after the publication of Buat-Nançay's *Les Origines ou l'Ancien Gouvernement de la France, de l'Allemagne et d'Italie, ouvrage historique*, 4 vols. (The Hague, 1757). See *Correspondance Littéraire*, 3: 419. Buat-Nançay was only forty-one years old in 1773, but he had already lived a full life as a knight in the Order of Malta, as a French envoy in Dresden and Ratisbon, and as a prolific historian of the European Middle Ages. Among his earlier publications were the *Tableau du gouvernement actuel de l'empire d'Allemagne* (Paris, 1755) and *Histoire ancienne des peuples de l'Europe* (Paris, 1772).

94. The *JE* devoted a total of 69 pages to its review of *The Elements of Politics*. In particular see 1774, vol. 3, pt. 3, 394, and 1774, vol. 4, pt. 2, 204–19, esp. 218–19.

95. Buat-Nançay, *Eléments*, 2: 263. For more on Saige's *Catéchisme du citoyen* (which circulated in manuscript before its 1775 publication date), see Baker, *Inventing the French Revolution*, 128–52, esp. 148.

96. Buat-Nançay, *Eléments*, 2: 57.

97. Ibid., 3: 59.

Buat-Nançay derived from this general principle an explanation for the French nobility's relatively greater patriotic attachment to king and country.

> Among the inhabitants of a large state, some must be attached inalterably [to the land] for the purposes of cultivation; some must be ready to leave in order to protect the common *patrie*. One cannot ascribe to each class the same sort of attachment to its native region [*pays natal*], nor to the *patrie* in general. [Attachment to the *patrie*] is necessarily weak among common laborers who, on the other hand, have a vivid attachment to the region in which they were born, the only place they truly know. These citizens are precisely those who rely more on their physical powers than on their moral powers.[98]

Given the context in which he was writing—after more than a decade of literary efforts to publicize the patriotism inherent in the French character—Buat-Nançay's emphasis on the patriotic deficiencies of the rustic French citizen seems to support Elie Carcassonne's contention that he lived in denial and sought refuge in the past.[99] But his willingness to assert such claims can just as easily be read as a sign of his close engagement with contemporary currents of thought, for he clearly had a keen desire to counter the opposing views of his imagined interlocutors, some of whom "wish to destroy inequality of conditions."[100]

Buat-Nançay insisted that "love of the common *patrie* will necessarily be stronger among those . . . having greater moral force, . . . [and] whose connection to [the common *patrie*] is as direct as the bond that links laborers to the land that nourishes them." The strength of the nobles' attachment to the "common *patrie*" was exemplified by their passion for the king. None could imagine "the head of the society being loved equally, and in the same way, by all citizens. Moral and physical distances must produce differences in that love," and those differences should be welcomed. "What would become of society if . . . all of the inhabitants of a great realm loved their king like a man who is particularly attached to him, and who would pay any price to be seen by him and to attract his attention, [what if all] were sorely afflicted by each misfortune that befalls him? The majority could not possibly be content." The manifestations of patriotism distinc-

---

98. Ibid., 2: 21.
99. Carcassonne suggested that Buat-Nançay "gradually lost in the course of his studies the capacity to adapt to his times." See *Montesquieu et le problème*, 244.
100. Buat-Nançay, *Eléments*, 2: 281.

tive of a monarchy, where the affective bonds between king and nobility are essential to the constitution, show that it is the noble citizen "who is, so to speak, a moral man."[101]

National education naturally formed part of Buat-Nançay's plan of moral reform, and its details filled one of the six volumes of his work. For Buat-Nançay as for Varennes, however, a "truly national education" concerned only "moral persons and true citizens," and he therefore found the model for his reform in "the old education that the Nobility received, a very good education with regard to the morals of our fathers and the constitution of the government under which they lived, an education worthy of Sparta and Crete." In the age of chivalry, young nobles had received training in the military art from an experienced and honorable mentor, one who inevitably instilled in his charge, through his own examples and careful guidance, a selfless "desire for glory." Although that ancient education "would be insufficient today" because of the technical transformation of the military art, it still provided a model on which to build, and Buat-Nançay proposed a three-tiered system of education designed to cultivate the moral dispositions central to the success of every patriot.[102] After having absorbed moral lessons in the paternal household and some specialized training in regional academies, at eighteen years of age students would choose to enter one of a dozen honorable vocations. After a solemn initiation ceremony, they would then return home for a sojourn of from one to three years, during which they would "meditate" on the knowledge they had acquired in the academy before embarking on their new professional lives. The period of meditation in the noble moral environment of family and community would reinforce lessons learned in youth, thus ensuring the exemplary conduct of those who occupied society's highest ranks.[103]

Having recaptured "the spirit of chivalry," having arranged to raise its children in suitable educational environments, and having gained the support of a state newly determined to eliminate unjust upward mobility, the nobility would be in position to supplant city and court and perform once again its essential role as "an intermediary corps in the realm of morals." This corps would communicate the moral bearing of the king himself "to all classes, even those most distant from the throne." It would exercise its special powers, however, "without jurisdiction, and without any power of constraint over the rest of the nation, which [for its part] would not be re-

101. Ibid., 2: 21–22, 275.
102. Ibid., 4: 1, 10.
103. The length of stay varied by profession. Ibid., 4: 135, 146–62.

quired to imitate [the corps], but must desire to do so. . . . There must be an analogy between the values of this corps, in all their various manifestations, and the values of all the different classes, so that the examples set by the corps would seem applicable in every context, and the bonds linking it [to the other classes] would make its examples seem always within reach." Inspiring even "the last citizen" to emulate its examples, the nobility would become "the arbiter of honor, without issuing any declarations, the conserver of morals, without prescribing laws to anyone, the creator of courage, where none existed, . . . [it would be] the protector of national mores."[104] As a pure "moral man," the noble in Buat-Nançay's reformed France would shape the behavior of other classes through the grandeur of his sentiments and the power of his example.

Buat-Nançay did not simply dismiss all arguments for equality between citizens. The first chapter to book one of the *Elements* even bore the striking title "That Men are equal, whether they share common origins or not."[105] As a concession to the principle of equality, Buat-Nançay even made provisions for the gradual assimilation into the nobility of members of the third estate who were willing to abandon their former careers and who aspired to live a noble life.[106] But although he conceded that human beings were born as equals, Buat-Nançay contended that "the difference between conditions has nothing to do with the essential equality of man." The greater good of society required that "intrinsic equality" hide itself behind "an inequality of orders or conditions, without ever disappearing," for only by reconciling these different principles could a society foster the moral sentiments needed to sustain it.[107] True honor could not be detached from sentiments arising from the knowledge of one's "legal superiority" and the exalted social standing that accompanied it, and those who would claim that the same honor united all Frenchmen, even including merchants, merely engaged in a "childish game of words" that took advantage of honor's different meanings.[108] Only by upholding formal inequalities and accentuating their positive effects could society secure itself the leadership of individuals whose disinterested sentiments made them the very manifestation of "moral man."

104. Ibid., 3: 180, 183, 174–75, 180.
105. Ibid., 1: 1.
106. For the details of this elaborate and intergenerational process, see ibid., 3: 132–40.
107. Ibid., 1: 8, 283.
108. Ibid., 2: 62.

## RETHINKING THE "ARISTOCRATIC REACTION"

The abundant evidence attesting the desire of social conservatives to rees-tablish the line "that must eternally separate the nobility from the com-moner," as the baron de Bohan put it in 1781, recalls to memory the long-moribund historiographical concept of the eighteenth-century aris-tocratic "reaction," a concept that was once used to help explain the com-ing of the French Revolution. Clearly, reformers in a variety of contexts worked to reinvigorate France's fragmented corporate nobility in the years before the Revolution. In 1777 Toustain de Richebourg called for the re-vival of a noble "esprit de corps," and at roughly the same time the army captain Blangermont characterized nobles and commoners unabashedly as "born enemies."[109]

The relatively benign professionalizing intentions that lay behind the famously provocative Ségur regulation of 1781, which restricted the army's officer corps to nobles of at least four generations, were brought to light years ago in a set of powerful articles that helped put to rest the Marxist conception of an aristocratic reaction driven by class interests. David Bien showed that the formulators of the rule mostly had in mind the need to in-crease professional dedication and to exclude irresponsible dilettantes; the idea of selecting new officers only from noble families with long and illustrious military backgrounds seemed consistent with that goal.[110] But in light of the broad literary clash of ideas that had preceded the Ségur regulation—with Servan de Gerbey's liberalizing vision of army reform in *The Citizen Soldier* (1780) doing battle with the socially rigid prescriptions expressed in Varennes's *Moral Reflections* (1779), and with different visions of French national honor competing for primacy after the Seven Years' War—one can easily see why the Ségur reform would have been construed as part of a program aimed first at hardening the distinction between no-bles and commoners. Toustain de Richebourg, who had insisted on the utility of the distinction between noble and commoner in 1777, defended the Ségur regulation in a journalistic essay of 1782, and many others clearly desired new efforts to delineate the social estates and to establish firmer boundaries between them.[111]

109. Toustain de Richebourg, *Précis historique*, 29–31.
110. Bien, "La réaction aristocratique avant 1789," and "The Army in the French Enlight-enment: Reform, Reaction, and Revolution," *P&P* 85 (1979): 68–98.
111. Toustain de Richebourg, "Observations sur la noblesse, communiqués aux memes, par M. le comte de Toustain, major de cavalerie, au service de France, ancien commissaire des états de Bretagne," in *JE*, 1782, vol. 2, 486–92; see esp. 491, n. 4.

Among those who sought firmer boundaries was one of the royal genealogists, Antoine Maugard. In 1787–88, on the eve of the Revolution,
Maugard proposed to the deputies of the crown's newly established provincial assemblies a rigorous new *recherche de la noblesse* (investigation of the
nobility) designed to weed out the unworthy. "Today no one would disagree that all ranks are confused, and that titles of honor . . . have been
usurped, in the most scandalous manner, by people whose nobility, if not
highly equivocal, is at least very recent."[112]  True nobles now found themselves "mixed up in the crowd." By instituting a "heraldic tribunal" consisting of dozens of *gentilshommes,* and by empowering the tribunal to
conduct a "general investigation of all the nobles of the realm," the nation
could finally pay proper respect to the descendants of the French knights,
"who were the glory of the nation, and the model of all the patriotic
virtues."[113]  Maugard's call for a new *recherche de la noblesse* was soon to be
seconded by the chief genealogist Chérin.[114]

Maugard's rhetoric, reflecting his attention to the "glory of the nation"
and the need to promote "patriotic virtues," underscores the considerable
thematic overlap between the conservative projects of a Varennes or a
Buat-Nançay, on the one hand, and the programmatically inclusive proposals of men such as Servan de Gerbey and Beaupoil, on the other hand.
Recognizably social "interests" were certainly caught up in the articulation
of these projects. Buat-Nançay, for example, envisioned the redistribution
of land and wealth to the poor rural nobility, and he deliberately promoted
the economic, as well as the political, well-being of a noble elite. But the
noble elite that Buat-Nançay envisioned differed significantly from the existing second estate, and he promoted a moral program that would have
led not only to the nobility's purification but also to its transformation.
Like Blangermont, he regarded the modern incarnation of nobility as a
"chimera." "The title of noble," he wrote, "granted without sufficient cause
and separated from the idea it carries, is nothing more than a word and
not a reality." Indeed, in light of its recent corruption, the elimination of
the word "noble" would amount to a salutary "reform [of] the language,
and nothing more; that can never be an injustice."[115] Whether designated

---

112. Antoine Maugard, *Remarques sur la noblesse* (2nd ed., Paris, 1788), 3. Maugard sent
copies of the first edition to the provincial assemblies established by the finance minister
Calonne. The edition of 1788 included grateful letters from individual deputies who pledged
to take Maugard's plan under consideration.
113. Ibid., 43, 61.
114. See *La Noblesse considérée sous ses divers rapports, Dans les Assemblées Générales & Particulières
de la Nation, ou Représentations des Etats-Généraux et Assemblées de Notables, pour et contre les Nobles*
(Paris, 1788), 42–43.
115. Buat-Nançay, *Eléments,* 3: 368.

as "noble" or not, the reconstituted class of "moral" men that he saw
perched atop the reformed polity would incorporate a steady stream of
properly assimilated common families, and it would be defined above all
by its moral qualities, which would be carefully reinforced by educational
institutions and the structure of society.

The aristocratic reaction elaborated by the likes of Buat-Nançay after
mid-century promoted not *the* nobility—at least not in its contemporary
social state—but rather *a* nobility. Fighting against modern corruption
and the various moral threats associated with it, "reactionaries" stressed the
distinction between nobles and *roturiers* both to stigmatize illegitimate nobles and to discourage commoners deemed unworthy of aspiring to noble
status. Their ideas had been inspired by opposition to many of the same
enemies identified by the authors of aggressively liberalizing plans of reform—selfishness, egoism, the unjust distribution of honors, neglect of
civic duty—and in the end, the ultimate objectives of the two groups of reformers were not so dissimilar. Toustain de Richebourg's appeal to his restricted audience of "Citizen nobles" in 1777 recalled Holbach's call for a
broad-based "citizen nobility" in 1776, and whether one emphasized the
moral uniformity of citizens or the particular morals traditionally associated with the different social estates, all foresaw the creation of moral exemplars fit to lead the nation by patriotic example.

Still, even if the specific proposals of Buat-Nançay and Coyer, or Servan
de Gerbey and Varennes, can be seen as resulting from the same process
of patriotic awakening in the second half of the eighteenth century, their
plans diverged because of irreducible differences arising from perceptions
of the promise, and perils, of patriotic equality. These differences of perspective were so elemental that even the most creative efforts to finesse the
meanings of honor and virtue could not overcome them. Varennes acknowledged that all soldiers had the same "foundation in honor" even
though they possessed it in different degrees; Barthez de Marmorières
praised the honor and courage of the "simple bourgeoisie"; Buat-Nançay
recognized the "intrinsic equality" of citizens, and asserted that the values
of the nobility were linked by "analogy" to "the values of all the different
classes." All of these rhetorical gestures bespoke an effort to accommodate
the principle of patriotic equality—and perhaps even to gain rhetorical advantage from the nationalization of honor—without allowing the spirit of
equality to undermine the hierarchical distinctions considered essential to
the salvaging of modern morality.

Evidence of contemporaries' awareness of this mental tug of war over
the principle of equality is found in the review of Buat-Nançay's *Elements of
Politics* published by the *Journal Encyclopédique* in 1774. In one of the few

critical passages of the review, the author balked at Buat-Nançay's assertion that formal inequalities merely masked, without ever obliterating, the natural equality of man. If this were the case, wrote the reviewer, "politics" must emulate nature by "compensating" for existing inequalities and thus undoing injustice, for the principle of natural equality always took precedence over mere positive law. The reviewer exploited Buat-Nançay's own emphasis on the formative effects of education to raise doubts about his argument for the moral superiority of the noble class. Buat-Nançay had observed, in his first volume, that a "man of the people" could not absorb the "sentiments of superiority and elevation suited to a noble child." Yet in remarks that had stressed the power of education, Buat-Nançay had also observed that one could recreate the Athenians at Marathon if one simply took ten thousand sons of artisans or farmers and raised them in the manner of the ancient Athenians. "If one can make ten thousand heroes out of artisans and farmers, then on the basis of education alone one can teach farmers to embrace the sentiments that characterize the nobility. Many readers will no doubt conclude that there is a contradiction here." The reviewer accordingly challenged Buat-Nançay to "reconcile these two passages."[116]

In the 1770s, it may still have been possible to imagine a reconciliation of the two emergent strains of patriotic thought outlined in this chapter. Few would have objected to the sentiments of "humanity, honor, and patriotism" invoked by Toustain de Richebourg. Buat-Nançay and Varennes both imagined projects of national education that would use the moral example of the nobility to expand and strengthen the honorable instincts of all French citizens. Moreover, none of the reformers who promoted the common soldier's honor, or who sought patriotic education in the schools, associated equality with radical social leveling. Coyer explicitly excluded peasants and common laborers from his thought experiment, and his attitude was representative of all who wished to "break down the barriers" that fixed men "in the class of common men." In almost every case, the intended beneficiaries of such reforms were dedicated professionals, merchants, and the respectable strata of the third estate. Those who insisted on the moral equality of patriots railed against legal barriers not because they detested nobility as such, but because they wished to widen the circle of those acknowledged to possess "the sentiments that characterize the nobility," in the words of the *Journal Encyclopédique*.

The reconciliation of reformist perspectives became less rather than

116. *JE* 1774, vol. 3, pt. 1, 19; 1774, vol. 3, pt. 3, 401–2.

more likely over the course of the 1780s. The constitutional relationship between the nobility and the third estate would emerge as the central issue of public discussion in 1788–89, when the convocation of the Estates-General forced the clarification of assumptions formulated and expressed only fitfully in the preceding decades. By then, though, the proponents of an inclusive and ennobling patriotism were inclined to distinguish between the moral nobility that they claimed for themselves and the institution of nobility, which they increasingly defined as unpatriotic to the core. A series of developments in the 1780s, including the promulgation of the Ségur regulation, the popularization of a patriotic rhetoric derived from the realm of fiscal debate, and the repeated exposure of courtly excess and scandal, encouraged critics of the social order to assimilate all components of the existing nobility to a single, unappealing, unpatriotic mass.

Consequently, liberalizing patriots were disposed to regard the argument that patriotic reform required sharper delineation between estates as a disingenuous rhetorical ploy that masked an unseemly selfishness. Unfortunately for the cause of civil harmony, in the eyes of many conservative nobles the convocation of the Estates-General, with the imminent threat of egalitarianism that it represented, seemed precisely the time to articulate boldly the staunchly hierarchical vision of French patriotism that they and their predecessors had elaborated over the course of decades. The constitutional debates of 1788–89 focused on the respective rights of the king, the nation, and the citizens who comprised the French nation, but, as the next chapter reveals, those debates were also fueled by irreconcilable understandings of honor, virtue, and the patriotic polity.

---

# Chapter Six

# DEFINING NOBILITY AND NATION
## IN 1788–1789

For historians, one of the most curious aspects of the period known as the
French pre-Revolution—that pivotal two years of turmoil that preceded
the dramatic events of June–July 1789—was the sudden and dramatic deterioration of the nobility's public image that began in the fall of 1788. Until that time, the politically attuned public seems to have given the nobility,
or at least certain segments of the nobility, much credit for having resisted
the ministerial "despotism" of the finance minister Calonne, and of his successor Brienne. Supported by Louis XVI, Calonne and Brienne had attempted to address the crown's latest fiscal crisis by restructuring the tax
system and by eroding or demolishing longstanding privileges. Calonne's
reform program had been rejected in the spring of 1787 by an Assembly
of Notables that claimed to lack the authority to approve new taxes, and
the assembly's positions had been reaffirmed by the parlement of Paris in
November of that year, when Louis XVI tried to force the court to approve
new loans to the crown. Both the Notables and the parlement called on
the king to convene a meeting of the Estates-General—a national representative assembly last convened in 1614—and the parlement's contentious struggles with the king from the fall of 1787 through the summer
of 1788 had resurrected the rhetoric, and some of the personnel, of the
former "patriot party" that had resisted the reforms of Maupeou.[1] The

---

1. On the continuities between the vocabularies, and the personnel, involved in the conflicts
of the early 1770s and the later 1780s, see especially Van Kley, *The Religious Origins of the French
Revolution*, 251–53, 309–15.

many opponents of ministerial despotism applauded the defiance of the parlements and even rushed to defend them when the crown tried to bypass them in May 1788, in a kind of replay of the Maupeou coup.[2]

The phase of inter-estate solidarity in the struggle against despotism ended late in the summer of 1788, after the crown fixed the public's attention on a new issue: the form to be taken by the coming Estates-General. In August, the utter collapse of the monarchy's credit, following the attempted coup against the parlements, had forced Brienne to clarify the crown's vague promises for a future Estate-General, and he announced that the meeting would be held in May 1789. Having already solicited opinions from the public on how such an assembly might be constituted, Brienne failed to specify forms and procedures before his own resignation from office on August 25, and a wide-ranging discussion over the shape and authority of the assembly soon began. A power struggle between estates was hardly a foregone conclusion. In that same summer of 1788, after all, the province of Dauphiné had set an inspiring example of collaboration between estates in its ongoing struggle with the crown over rights of representation within the province. There an ad hoc committee of nobles, magistrates, and professionals from the third estate had succeeded in reviving the provincial Estates-General, and they had agreed on a form of representation for the estates that preserved the reality of orders while granting new powers to commoners, including double representation and vote by head rather than by estate.[3]

Despite the Dauphinois example, on 25 September 1788 the parlement of Paris intervened in public discussion by declaring that the Estates-General should meet according to the forms of 1614. According to the parlement, those forms gave each of the three estates the same number of representatives, called for the orders to deliberate separately, and allowed any of the three orders to veto proposals agreed upon by the others. The parlement's decree created the impression that the Estates-General would protect the clergy and nobility from the consequences of fiscal reform, and soon the "privileged orders" came under attack from all sides for their lack of patriotism and their presumed opposition to fundamental change. By January 1789 the Swiss journalist Jacques Mallet du Pan could report that

2. On 7 June 1788, the famed "day of tiles," a wide cross-section of the population of Grenoble pelted royal troops from the rooftops of the city with tiles and other debris, resisting the army's attempt to enforce the exile of the parlement. See Jean Nicolas, *La Révolution française dans les Alpes: Dauphiné et Savoie* (Toulouse, 1989), 47–51.

3. Ibid., 45–55; Tackett, *Becoming a Revolutionary*, 82–83; P. M. Jones, *Reform and Revolution in France: The Politics of Transition, 1774–1791* (Cambridge, 1995), 149–54.

"public debate has assumed a different character. King, despotism, and constitution have become only secondary questions. Now it is war between the Third Estate and the other two orders."[4] Regarded as the natural leader in the fight against arbitrary government in 1787 and much of 1788, the nobility became the chief target of criticism for so-called patriot writers in late 1788 and early 1789.

Historians have long been challenged to offer a compelling explanation for this turn of events.[5] For the proponents of the old "social" interpretation of the French Revolution, the decree of the parlement of Paris, and the political struggle to which it gave rise, represented the inherent power of class conflict in the dynamic of historical change. The parlement had simply "showed its true colors" in September by finally moving to defend the interests of the aristocratic class to which it belonged, and the furor it elicited signaled the bourgeoisie's long-delayed assumption of historical agency.[6]

The "social" historians' reliance on the teleological device of class conflict failed to convince revisionist historians of the 1970s and 1980s, however. Seeing little evidence of conflict between a unified aristocracy and a self-conscious bourgeoisie in the years before the Revolution, revisionists instead attributed the apparent change in public opinion after September 1788 to a variety of political factors and the conspiratorial work of a handful of individuals. In a powerful account that synthesized revisionist findings, William Doyle represented the decree of 25 September as a political miscalculation, or accident, that was then exploited for rhetorical effect by the shadowy Society of Thirty, a group of liberal reformers dominated by free-thinking nobles.[7] Still fearful of the despotic schemes of the crown's ministers, wrote Doyle, the parlement merely intended that its decree in favor of the forms of 1614 should "resolve the uncertainty and deprive the government of a free hand to gerrymander the forthcoming assembly."[8]

According to Doyle's account, the tumult that arose over the parlement's decision surprised nearly everyone, since it had been "carefully orchestrated" by a small band of propagandists working with the Society of

4. See Georges Lefebvre, *The French Revolution,* trans. Elizabeth Moss Evanson, 2 vols. (New York, 1962), 1: 102.
5. For discussion of the interpretive problems, and an explanation that highlights previously undetected influences from earlier debates over religious authority, see Dale K. Van Kley, "The Estates General as Ecumenical Council: The Constitutionalism of Corporate Consensus and the *Parlement's* Ruling of September 25, 1788," *JHM* 61 (1989): 1–52.
6. Lefebvre, *French Revolution,* 1: 102.
7. Doyle, *Origins of the French Revolution,* 131–38.
8. Ibid., 132.

Thirty. The pamphleteers' "calculated assault" on public opinion, whose purpose was to rally support for a doubling of the third estate's representatives at the Estates-General, partially backfired by making readers conscious of social divisions that they had overlooked in happier times of political unity. The clamor for the doubling of the third "scared" the nobility, many of whose members became "intransigent" in their defense of constitutional traditions. When a second Assembly of Notables convened in late November 1788, they held firm to the sprit of the parlement's decree, defeating by a vote of 114 to 33 a motion to double the third estate's deputies. In early December, five Princes of the Blood who had attended the assembly issued an even more explicit denunciation of the third estate's claims, and from that point social tensions between the estates, which had been set off by short-sighted political calculations, spiraled out of control. Passions were quelled temporarily when the finance minister Necker announced in late December that the third estate would indeed have double representation at the Estates-General, but his failure to specify procedures of deliberation left room for wrangling that would extend beyond the convocation of the assembly.[9]

Other revisionist accounts of the pre-Revolutionary period differ in their points of emphasis. Some point to the effect of Louis XVI's well-intentioned but incompetent management of the political debate in the summer of 1788, or to the existence of internecine disputes within the nobility, which allowed an anti-noble rhetoric designed for limited purposes to become generalized to the detriment of the nobility as a whole.[10] Others stress the unintended political consequences of royalist and ministerial efforts to whip up anti-aristocratic feeling during the crown's clash with the parlements in 1787–88, or the collapse of state power after 1786, which invited a political free-for-all among those who rushed to fill the void.[11] In all analyses marked by the spirit of revisionism, however, one theme remains constant. Before the summer of 1788, the story goes, the attention of the politically engaged classes had been fixed on the dispute between ministers suspected of despotism, on the one hand, and the various self-appointed spokesmen for the interests of the "nation," on the

9. Ibid., 135–37.

10. On Louis XVI, see, for example, Bosher, *The French Revolution*, 116–17. Daniel Wick shows that court agitation against courtiers—carried out in the context of the Society of Thirty—ultimately boomeranged on the entire nobility. See Wick, *A Conspiracy of Well-Intentioned Men*.

11. François Furet and Ran Halévi, *La monarchie républicaine: La constitution de 1791* (Paris, 1996), 10–11; Bell, *The Cult of the Nation*, 71, 75, 199.

other hand. Animosity between estates, which would eventually come to fuel the Revolutionary dynamic, was created and perpetuated by developments specific to the circumstances of 1788: the parlement's invocation of "anachronistic" social and political categories in its September decree, the miscalculations and hypersensitivity of pamphleteers who responded to the decree, the astonishment of a public that had not expected to hear assertions of noble corporate pride. Even Timothy Tackett, whose nuanced analysis of the deputies to the Estates-General illustrates the profound differences in status, wealth, and perspective that separated nobles and commoners, confirms the decisive role played by unpredicted "events" in the formation of inter-estate hostility.[12]

Rare is the historian who would deny that events influence thought and behavior. Revisionists performed a valuable service by rejecting the teleological tendencies of the old social interpretation and by insisting on the multiple outcomes implicit in the pre-Revolutionary crisis that began in 1787. But emphasis on the determining power of the "event" is not a viable substitute for analysis of the ideational context that makes any event meaningful, both for individuals and for groups. Events sharpen perception, they throw into relief the working assumptions that guide thought and action, and they sometimes lead to a rearrangement of the hierarchy of beliefs through which agents apprehend the world. Events make a difference in processes of historical change, but they do so only by interacting with existing interpretive dispositions and by inviting the refinement or reformulation of the networks of ideas that prepare individuals to see the world in certain ways. Indeed, the occurrences of daily life become "events" only if they arrest the attention of individuals already disposed to react interestedly and passionately to the incidents in question—only if they engage individuals previously disposed, in other words, to define such incidents as "events."

The September decree of the parlement of Paris may have served a short-term political strategy, but its invocation of supposedly "anachronistic" categories also expressed the court's "profound attachment to the social hierarchy and inequality characteristic of the old regime," an attachment the parlement had also made clear in its response to Turgot's assault on privilege in 1776.[13] The parlement's decree on the forms of 1614, and the third

---

12. Tackett, *Becoming a Revolutionary*, see esp. 119–75.

13. Bailey Stone, *The French Parlements and the Crisis of the Old Regime* (Chapel Hill, N.C., 1986), 94. In a remonstrance protesting Turgot's abolition of *corvée* labor and his imposition of a universal land tax, the parlement complained that "any system" that had for an object the destruction of social distinctions would lead to disorder, "the inevitable result of absolute equal-

estate's denunciation of privilege in the fall of 1788, may be interpreted as mutually reinforcing developments that polarized public opinion in the months before the Revolution, but the public's existing disagreements over the constitutional role of the nobility merely awaited new opportunities for restatement and clarification in 1788. Why would calculating pamphleteers, or extremists, in pursuit of precise political objectives "orchestrate" an assault on noble privilege unless those objectives entailed the critical re-examination of corporate privilege? Why would they succeed in eliciting a loud public outcry unless their arguments struck a resonant chord with an audience long attuned to the dissonant harmonies of modern French patriotism? The assertion of the nobility's corporate prerogatives could not have provoked outrage among commoners if members of the third estate had not already begun formulating a rationale to support a claim to greater political power. Similarly, the Notables and other "intransigent" nobles would not have evinced a sense of alarm over the pretensions of the third estate if they had lacked a robust commitment to a particular view of the world, one that reserved a privileged space for nobility.

"Events" undoubtedly concentrated differences and accelerated the pace of confrontation, but the rapidly deteriorating image of the nobility from the fall of 1788 cannot be explained without taking into account the varieties of patriotism that had been articulated in the years and decades preceding the pre-Revolutionary crisis. Disagreements over patriotism's social and constitutional ramifications could not be contained indefinitely, especially in the context of a political conflict carried out in the name of national interests, a conflict in which all parties claimed patriotic intent. The tone of political discourse changed in the fall of 1788, and the evidently placid relations between spokesmen for the nobility and commoners in the months prior to the September decree certainly call out for explanation, as the revisionists wisely recognized. But the language in which the conflict worked itself out in 1788–89 shows that both phenomena—that is, both the widespread disposition toward conciliation and the passionate choosing of sides when procedural disagreements finally arose—were consistent with the inexorable expansion of French patriotism over the entire second half of the eighteenth century.

Evidence from the abundant pamphlet literature of 1788–89 reveals that politically motivated writers of the pre-Revolutionary period obsessed

---

ity." The "rights of birth and estate" could be traced to "the origin of the Nation." See *Remontrances du Parlement de Paris au XVIIIe Siècle (1715–1788)*, ed. Jules Flammermont, 3 vols. (Paris, 1888–98), 3: 278–79.

over the meaning of the same concepts that had preoccupied civic-minded authors dating to the 1740s and earlier. The evidence further reveals that the varying definitions of patriotism and nobility that writers employed in the debate over the Estates-General in 1788–89 incorporated different understandings, and different arrangements, of the key moral vocabulary that had saturated patriotic thought for decades. The opinions of earlier "patriots" of course should not be seen as having exerted a direct influence over the combatants of 1788–89. As Jack Censer has remarked in his study of journalistic commentary in the age of Enlightenment, "virtually every contemporary idea found some resonance" in the periodical literature of the time, and one would be foolish to try to connect the dots between the appearance of a given text and the ideas and assumptions later expressed by its presumed readers.[14] The broad rhetorical continuities between patriotic writing of the later old regime and the pamphlet literature of the pre-Revolution nevertheless underscore one of the inescapable cognitive effects of the efflorescence of French patriotism in the eighteenth century: the need to adjust or refine one's vision of privilege and social distinction in light of the supposed requirements of a patriotic morality. That process of cognitive adjustment, involving the correlation of patriotic "honor" or "virtue" with a particular vision of social and political order, continued through 1789. Political arguments from the period throw light on the conceptual prioritizing that marked the transition to Revolutionary culture.

## THE ELUSIVE GOAL OF UNITY

As Kenneth Margerison has observed in his study of pre-Revolutionary pamphlets, "unity and patriotism were indissolubly linked in the public mind," and for the period between September 1788 and May 1789 an impressive proportion of the 857 pamphlets sampled for his study—between 15–20 percent—called insistently for a "union" of the orders in the Estates-General.[15] The authors of these pamphlets aimed to secure both social tranquility and political cooperation between estates in the pressing struggle to establish a constitution, to lay claim to the rights of the nation, and to eliminate royal despotism. Thanks to the spirit of patriotism, wrote abbé Gabriel Brizard hopefully in late 1788, "all political distinctions, all indi-

14. Jack Censer, *The French Press in the Age of Enlightenment* (London, 1994), 87.
15. Kenneth Margerison, *Pamphlets and Public Opinion: The Campaign for a Union of Orders in the Early French Revolution* (West Lafayette, Ind., 1998), 46, 49.

vidual pretensions, and the petty interests of corps" would soon dissolve within the "grand title of Citizen."[16]

The writers who envisioned union and cooperation between the social orders at the Estates-General elaborated a powerful late eighteenth-century impulse to define a French patriotism that reconciled the principle of civil equality with the concepts of honor and nobility. Perhaps the most representative example in this diverse group was the Parisian lawyer and impassioned social reformer Guy-Jean-Baptiste Target. A future "radical patriot" who helped to craft the pivotal Tennis Court Oath (20 June 1789), served on the National Assembly's important constitutional committee, and became president of the Assembly in January 1790, Target in the months immediately following the parlement's September decree wrote a series of influential pamphlets that combined advocacy for the third estate with a residual respect for hierarchy and fear of a "too perfect equality" that would only engender "confusion."[17]

For Target, the need for a national show of unity against despotism did not imply that "our most ancient institutions must disappear." Honor had played an important role in the political history of the French, and it would inevitably continue to do so, given the special moral character of the emerging French patriotism. "Here I must say what I think of privileges: I distinguish them from honors and precedence. Honor and precedence are just, whether they are attached to one of the powerful functions delegated by the Monarch, or whether national sentiment has assigned them to the classes habitually occupied with the services most essential to . . . the Empire." Unlike privileges, which are harmful to a "national constitution" because they "break all bonds, [and] discourage the people who are the true strength" of the state, honors should be seen as an expression of the people's desire to reward the virtuous. "In vain would someone try to compromise this sentiment. As free as our soul, it will defy even the laws; as just as public opinion, it renders unto each what each deserves; analogous to that principle of honor that, I believe with Montesquieu, is natural to monarchies, it fills with intermediary ranks the immense interval separating the throne from the mass of subjects." Distinctions of honor were both

16. [Abbé Brizard], *Modestes observations sur le Mémoire des Princes, Faites au nom de 23 millions de Citoyens Français* (n.p., 22 December 1788), 45.

17. On Target as "radical," see Tackett, *Becoming a Revolutionary*, 263. For Target's background as a reforming lawyer see Maza, *Private Lives*, 98–99; and Paul Boulloche, *Un avocat du XVIIIe siècle* (Paris, 1893), 11–33. The "too perfect equality" is in *Les Etats-Généraux Convoqués par Louis XVI* (n.p., n.d.), 17. For the expression of similar sentiments in later pamphlets, see *Suite de l'Ecrit intitulé Les Etats-Généraux convoqués par Louis XVI* (n.p., n.d.), 6–8; *IIe suite de l'écrit intitulé: Les Etats-Généraux convoqués par Louis XVI* (n.p., n.d.), 56–58.

natural and desirable. Only when they hardened into separate rights, such as "pecuniary exemptions," did they become harmful to the state. "Granting power to certain classes . . . not only debases them—a truth that, in certain times, is difficult to perceive—but also violates justice, in whose eyes everyone is equal."[18]

As Target saw it, France had reached a stage in its historical development where privilege could finally be eliminated and equality and honor could happily coexist. Until recently, he explained, privilege had necessarily taken the place of patriotism, and it had produced some good effects. "When morals are corrupted, . . . personal interest must provide the services that a healthier society expects to derive from the patriotism of its members."[19] But after invoking Montesquieu's familiar account of the compensatory function of honor in virtue-deprived modern monarchies, Target simply went on to assert that the evolution of French morals had now rendered obsolete the privileges of the intermediary bodies. France had arrived at "a moment of regeneration" made possible by the general improvement of morals and "the character of the Nation." Only those who vainly wished to prevent "enlightenment from making any progress, and morals from perfecting themselves," would allow their misguided respect for unnecessary traditions to stand in the way of common deliberations and the expression of a "universal morality." Without making any "essential" change to "the form of our ancient convocations," the representatives of the nation would now bring together the political features of "*liberty, equality, universality,* and *unity,* without which real representation would not be possible."[20]

The anonymous author of an *Essay on Patriotism* echoed Target's stated respect for "our most ancient institutions," insisting in particular that the institution of nobility had an important role to play in a reformed France. "What is nobility?" he asked. "It is a recompense demanded by the Nation, and accorded by the king. . . . In all times [nobility] has been coveted, esteemed, and respected. What better excites emulation to do well and animates patriotism?"[21] He disagreed with these "indiscreet, turbulent, audacious men," these "anti-patriots," who now argued that "the People constitute the entire Nation." The existence of nobility was essential "in an Empire, in a Monarchy, and in any political society," because in all polities "the savior of the *Patrie* and the virtuous man of merit" must not be permitted to become "mixed up in the crowd."[22]

18. Target, *Les Etats-Généraux.*, 16–17, 19, 22.
19. Ibid., 18–19.
20. Ibid., 19, 22, 31.
21. *Essai du Patriotisme* (n.p., 1789), 56.
22. Ibid., 67, 57.

Tellingly, though, the author of the *Essay* actually envisioned the creation of a nonexclusive noble status that would encourage and excite by virtue of its accessibility. "The hour has come to unite all the orders of the state . . . to make our morals healthier, and our virtues more sweet, to convince ourselves that nothing is great beyond the public good, that that noble object is superior to all." This uniting of the orders of the state had implications not only for the procedures followed in the Estates-General— there should be no distinction between the orders, and they should deliberate together, since "patriotism does not like to hide"—but also for the very shape of the second and third estates.[23] "The nobility," he wrote, "must be the limit of what all French citizens, full of love for their king and zeal for the *Patrie,* can rightfully expect to attain." Never bought or sold, never acquired through office, but awarded only for "our actions," nobility would become "what it must be for the sake of its own glory, and for the happiness of the Nation." Members of the third estate could be considered nobles-in-waiting. "The Third Estate are no longer serfs, they are citizens; they may belong to the nobility if they wish. All the routes are open." Competing with one another for a prize that clearly lay within their reach, commoners would make virtue general and take turns achieving distinguished rank.[24]

Building on the assumption to which Target had given voice—that the "character of the Nation" now made possible the expression of a "universal morality"—the reformer Raup de Baptestin called for the more systematic exploitation of the honorable sentiments common to the French.

Honor, this precious sentiment of self-esteem . . . honor, this great principle of Monarchies; honor, which has always been so dear to the French nation, and has always moved good citizens to acts of virtue, patriotism, and valor worthy of admiration down through the centuries; honor, in sum, this sublime and powerful sentiment equally present in all French hearts, needs only to be awakened in order to produce generous actions and the kind of devotion for which the *Patrie* has a pressing need. It is in the hearts of the French people that this vast Empire will always find immense resources, [it is] there that Monarchs can search without fear of ever being disappointed.[25]

23. Ibid., 24, 254.
24. Ibid., 183–84.
25. [Raup de Baptestin], *Mémoire sur un moyen facile et infaillible de faire renaître le Patriotisme en France, dans toutes les classes des Citoyens, comme dans les deux sexes; et d'assurer le remboursement des dettes de l'Etat, sans nouveaux impôts, sans emprunt, et sans faire éprouver aucune réduction* (Amsterdam, 1789), 12–13.

Even "opulent" citizens could be expected to respond to appeals to their honor, and Raup de Baptestin saw in the universality of this French sentiment a means of escape from fiscal crisis.

His plan involved the creation of a new form of distinction analogous to nobility itself. He called for the institution of an Order of Patriotic Merit, an order open to all rich citizens who contributed a minimum of 25,000 livres toward the deficit in the royal budget. The order would be purely honorific—members would be awarded crosses, ribbons, and titles whose level of distinction varied according to the sums contributed—but those decorated by the Order of Patriotic Merit would have the opportunity to pass their status on to their children, provided only that the heir pay three-quarters of the admission price fixed for the level he wished to enter. The nobility, with its Order of Saint Louis created by Louis XIV to recognize valor, would undoubtedly take satisfaction "in seeing Louis XVI create a *similar recompense for Patriotism,* in favor of all citizens indistinctly." The existence of such an order would offer to "rich Patriots" a "new means of satisfying the ambition for honors inherent in the national character," and it would create "a sort of patriotic equality between the three Orders of the State, [which] would be useful for morals."[26]

Philippe-Antoine Grouvelle clearly spoke for many when he announced that his own advocacy for greater rights for the third estate was "not about destroying all vestiges of the distinctions between Orders, but [about] . . . regulating them, and modifying their political influence."[27] This effort to regulate and modify the structure of the French social order grew out of immediate political circumstances, to be sure, but it also reflected and elaborated much earlier patriotic efforts to define honor as a "national" characteristic, to emphasize the moral homogeneity uniting the patriotic French citizenry, and to argue for the ennobling power of patriotic sentiment. The liberal vicomte d'Aubusson, for example, revived ideas expressed earlier by the abbé Jaubert and the historian Rossel when he stated that he dreamed of becoming king, "only to have the pleasure of granting an edict by which I would ennoble all the citizens and inhabitants of my realm."[28] "In France," wrote a similarly inspired pamphleteer, "all conditions, and all men, are guided by honor."[29] The usurpations of the nobility in the Middle Ages, he asserted, had only obscured but not extinguished

26. Ibid., 16–19, 63, 39–40.

27. Philippe-Antoine Grouvelle, *De l'autorité de Montesquieu dans la révolution présente* (n.p., 1789), 126–27.

28. P.A., vicomte d'Aubusson, *Adresse à Messieurs de l'Ordre de la Noblesse* (Paris, 1789), 7.

29. *Réponse à la Question Quels sont les moyens, conciliables avec la Législation Française, d'animer & d'étendre le Patriotisme dans le Tiers Etat? Proposée pour sujet du Concours en 1790, par la Société Royale des Sciences & Arts de Metz* (n.p., n.d.), 15.

the "natural nobility attached to the state of liberty," and in their moral capacities "the French who compose the third Estate cede nothing to the other Orders of the realm."[30]

Hostility toward the formal privileges of the second estate did not necessarily imply lack of respect for the institution of nobility, then, but the quest for a union of orders rooted in patriotic fellowship clearly *did* imply the need for taxonomic revision. Raup de Baptestin's "Order of Patriotic Merit" represented one creative effort to satisfy the honorable cravings of commoners while simultaneously mollifying the defenders of hierarchy, but there were many others. Charles-Philippe-Toussaint Guiraudet, for example, referred to the orders of society as a mere "system of nomenclature" that should never enter into the "Procrustean bed" of law. He advocated suppressing once and for all the words "commoner, third estate, etc." so that "brilliant distinctions can and will forever belong to what we call today the first orders, but without there being any humiliating distinction" to mark those who lacked such honors.[31] Another writer, aroused particularly by the exclusionary Ségur ruling, appealed for new means to recognize those "born of *honnêtes* parents," the "most dignified and well-to-do class of the Third Estate, which has received the same education and has the same sentiments as the nobility."[32]

Perhaps the most revealing example of taxonomic experimentation in the pamphlets of the pre-Revolution—combining a version of what Raup de Baptestin had called "a sort of patriotic equality" with a recognizably traditional social and moral order—was the anonymously authored *Discourse on the Rights, Duties, and Functions of the Seven Classes of Citizens That Compose the Political Body*. The author spoke the language of national liberation in calling for the repudiation of "our laws, our customs, our usages, our prejudices, our habits," and in inviting his readers to "swear never to institute a law that can harm the rights of man." Nevertheless, despite his commitment to "liberty" and "equality," the author of the *Discourse* had no intention of abandoning the hierarchical vision of society inherited from the past. The author devised a new political, social, and moral hierarchy for a "regenerated" nation, a hierarchy that, though evidently free of "prejudices" and irrational "customs," reabsorbed the skeletal remains of the society of orders into its structure and its very rationale.[33]

30. Ibid., 12, 16.
31. [Charles-Philippe-Toussaint Guiraudet], *Qu'est-ce que la nation? et qu'est-ce que la France?* (n.p., 1789), 13, 62, 56–57.
32. *Réclamation du Tiers Etat aux Etats-Généraux* (n.p., n.d.), 4–7.
33. *Discours sur les droits, les devoirs & les fonctions des sept Classes de Citoyens, qui composent le Corps politique* (n.p., n.d.), 2–3.

The bottom four "classes" of the new society corresponded to particular professions or types of work. In descending order, those classes consisted of the "sciences and arts," the commercial professions, artisans, and day laborers. The three eminent classes were also associated with particular kinds of work, but their work deserved higher status not because of its utility or productivity, but because of its moral worth. The first class, fittingly labeled the "Moral" class, roughly corresponded to the first estate in the traditional society of orders, though the author altered its defining characteristics in revealing ways. Made up of the "apostles of morality," the first class would be exempt from any form of military or administrative service, and its members would need to abstain from any lucrative profession, since such selfish pursuits might distract them from their spiritual duties. Those duties, however, were not specified as purely Christian duties, and the civic value of the apostles' guidance meant that the state had to take measures to keep alive their examples. "The more you excel in virtues, the more the *Patrie* wishes to see perpetuated a race of men descended from your stock, imbued with your lessons, [and] formed on your example; it will therefore provide for your honorable subsistence, . . . and also ensure the establishment of your children." The proposed organization of the first "class" was intended not so much to challenge the principle of clerical celibacy—or at least not only so—as to purify and recombine certain aspects of the prevailing definition of the French elite.

The second estate, in the traditional society of orders, would now be redefined and reorganized as the Political and Administrative "classes" in the new regime. The political, or second, class would consist of "the heads of state and their auxiliaries, that is, the troops of land and sea, true ramparts of the [polity]." Equivalent to "the Government itself," the political class had the duty of protecting the state against all external enemies. Its rights "must be circumscribed by the constitution," and all of its honorable functions "shared among the elite citizenry." The administrative, or third, class would consist of the "members of the councils of justice and finance" and their dependent officers. The "text of the law and its precise application" form "the circle of their powers and the limits of their functions." The members of this third class would serve as elected "representatives" of the citizenry, bound by a mandate and prohibited from exceeding that mandate under any pretext.[34]

The organization of the new "classes of citizens" managed to combine the egalitarian and participatory claims of would-be constitutional re-

34. Ibid., 6, 8.

formers with the key moral and structural aspects of the traditional society of orders. The functions controlled by the "political" class—particularly in the army and at court—would be "shared" among a wide elite, and the individuals who occupied them would evidently have no hereditary claims to preference. Meanwhile, the "administrative" class—that other segment of the nobility, largely constituted through venality under the old system— would be rendered elective, its offices made accessible to all who could win the confidence of the citizenry. Still, the ranking of occupations according to their moral worth was a hallmark of the society of orders, and the strict separation of the first class from all "lucrative" professions, as well as the author's disdainful remarks about both commerce and finance, attest to a continuing prejudice against profit-seeking and the vices of self-interest.[35] The first three classes in the new system thus retained many of the key features of the first two orders in the old system, with two important adjustments having been made: hereditary eminence would now finally be reserved for those enjoying a unique and demonstrable moral superiority, and recruitment for all offices beneath the circle of this austere and rarefied company would now be open to all respected citizens.

As these various efforts at conciliation and compromise indicate, many of the writers who promoted the fiscal and political rights of the third estate in 1788–89 still felt a residual respect and admiration for the nobility and for the standards of moral excellence that nobility was held to represent. The signs of this enduring respect for nobility among the politically engaged writers of the early Revolution, which other historians of 1789 have also emphasized, are consistent with evidence of social attitudes derived from the *cahiers de doléances,* or grievance lists, drawn up by the three estates during the spring of 1789 in anticipation of the Estates-General.[36] As George V. Taylor demonstrated long ago, virtually none of the *cahiers* of the third estate called for the abolition of nobility. Overwhelming majorities in the local *bailliage* assemblies that drew up the *cahiers* favored the opening of all state offices to meritorious men without regard to birth, and practically every *cahier* called for equality of taxation, but the elimination of nobility was not forecast in the grievance lists compiled before the Revolution.[37]

---

35. The text referred, for example, to "this Hydra that devours us, this frightening and insatiable Finance." Ibid., 18.

36. The lingering respect for nobility has been noted by Patrice Higonnet, *Class, Ideology, and the Rights of Nobles during the French Revolution* (Oxford, 1981), 48–55.

37. George V. Taylor, "Revolutionary and Non-Revolutionary Content in the Cahiers of 1789: An Interim Report," *FHS* 7 (1972): 479–502.

The absence in the *cahiers* of explicit opposition toward the institution of nobility should not necessarily be seen, however, as a reflection of essentially conservative, or "non-Revolutionary," social attitudes in France on the eve of the Revolution. Sophisticated content analyses of the *cahiers* recently carried out by John Markoff and Gilbert Shapiro have drawn attention to evidence of "strong conflict" between noble and commoner *cahiers* over the issue of social and professional mobility. In the drawing up of their respective *cahiers,* the assemblies of the nobility and the third estate were more likely to disagree over the criteria regulating mobility—and particularly the question whether birth should provide access to certain offices—than over the details of the seigneurial system or even the organization of the Estates-General.[38] Fully half of the noble *cahiers* composed at the parish level specified the nobles' desire to retain the symbols of their honor and their right to the deference of their inferiors, and Markoff notes the curious gap between the reality of the phenomenon of social mobility, which remained a viable possibility for most commoners, and "the *idea* of mobility restrictions," which focused the critical attention of the third estate's *bailliage* assemblies in surprising ways. He suggests that the divergence in perception between the estates points to the existence of a contemporary "ideological process" involving "something beyond a mere reflection of experience."[39]

The *cahiers,* of course, do not represent a pure distillation of popular opinion on the eve of the Revolution. The wording and some of the basic content of the *cahiers* were shaped by the local legal elite charged with drafting the documents, and grievances were articulated within the horizons imposed by the politically plausible. Even if one allows for the possibility that circumstances constrained or muffled the expression of the deepest sentiments of the people, however, an important question leaps out from one of the apparent contradictions of the *cahiers.* How could the rhetoric of the *cahiers* signal wide acceptance of the institution of nobility while it also expressed increased sensitivity to, and resentment toward, the privileges of noble status?

If one accepts Markoff's invitation to move beyond the immediate context of pre-Revolutionary politics, and to consider the broader conceptual context through which the claims and expectations of estates and citizens were conceived in the late 1780s, the ambiguity of the *cahiers* on the issue

38. John Markoff and Gilbert Shapiro, eds., *Revolutionary Demands: A Content Analysis of the Cahiers de Doléances of 1789* (Stanford, 1998), 292.
39. Ibid., 312. For the noble attention to honor, see Markoff, *The Abolition of Feudalism,* 47–48.

of nobility comes to look much less puzzling. In all likelihood, the *cahiers* contained the seeds of both quiescence and conflict for the same reason that spokesmen for the third estate initially acquiesced in the nobility's leadership in the fight against despotism before becoming highly critical of the nobility in the fall of 1788. The multivalent image of nobility that had grown out of the patriotic imagination of the later eighteenth century prepared the civic-minded to accommodate, and even eagerly to incorporate, a role for nobility in their visions of the reformed polity. The conflicting resonances of the noble image also prepared them, however, to exclude from the patriotic compact a nobility too firmly attached to its privileges.

Earlier attempts to nationalize and render "French" an honor formerly associated specifically with the second estate, to celebrate the ideal of a "citizen nobility," and to represent patriotism as a form of moral nobility had left a powerful imprint on the French understanding of patriotism by the 1780s; in the minds of the politically engaged, the concepts of nobility and honor had been largely assimilated to the ideals of patriotism and citizenship over the course of the preceding decades. Thus, all who looked forward to a post-despotic politics in 1787–88 had reasons to imagine the eventual negotiation of a new definition of nobility that would preserve the idea of an exemplary moral status but also encourage and facilitate the patriotic moral achievements of all citizens. Few doubted that nobility would occupy a position of moral and cultural importance in a reformed French state, but many had also been conditioned to expect the natural emergence of a newly "patriotic" form of nobility that would accommodate the principle of civil equality. The new nobility might serve as a subtle sign of moral differentiation, distinguishing patriotic exemplars from all of their hopeful emulators, but many self-styled patriots agreed that in the future nobility should not function as a mark of rigid social differentiation, distinguishing beneficiaries of privilege from a mass of excluded citizens.

The seemingly selfless behavior of noble agitators against despotism in the earliest phase of the pre-Revolutionary crisis only heightened expectations for an eventual negotiated solution to the meaning of noble status. As one pamphleteer wrote in 1787, in an essay that addressed the meaning of patriotism in a monarchy, even the royal princes who had attended the first Assembly of Notables in February of that year had magnanimously shown that "they forget their rank, in order to associate with us all, and to identify with all Frenchmen." For this writer, the broad recognition that "there is, properly speaking, only one Order in France," meant that "the nobility of the national character" could be depended upon "to close the gap" in the royal budget.[40] The writings of Target, Raup de Baptestin, the vicomte d'Aubusson, and others show the continuing power, in 1788–89, of this ideal of a nobility that somehow united "all Frenchmen."

Those who embraced the ideal of a national, or even universal, nobility simultaneously disdained what social observers of the 1750s had derisively termed "noblesse moderne." Like the many conservative and noble critics of nobility, they lamented the effects of venality of office, expressed contempt for the noble beneficiaries of court favoritism, and mocked the honor that supposedly belonged to parvenus and hopelessly corrupt fops. Unfortunately for sincere noble patriots, who also looked forward to a redefinition of nobility along distinctly "patriotic" lines, a series of developments in the 1780s helped implant in many minds a sharp dichotomy between patriotism and privilege, and this development threatened to break down the mental boundary separating the good nobles from the bad. When the parlement of Paris and the second Assembly of Notables gave expression to an ideal of corporate solidarity in the fall of 1788, their actions confirmed the widely held suspicion—aroused if not invented by recent developments—that the current constituents of the institution of nobility could never overcome selfish interests, were incapable of virtuous sentiments, and therefore lacked the capacity to be truly patriotic.

## PATRIOTISM AND THE NOBILITY, THE 1780S

As a social group, the nobility came to be stigmatized as selfish and corrupt for a number of reasons. In light of the financial character of the debates that precipitated the Revolutionary crisis, and given Jacques Necker's own involvement in the constitutional uncertainties of late 1788 and 1789, the origins of the phenomenon might be traced, however, to the appearance of Necker's two spectacularly successful publications of the early 1780s, the *Statement of Accounts for the King* (1781) and *On the Administration of Finances in France* (1784). Necker, a Genevan banker who had become Louis XVI's controller-general in 1777, had already made waves in 1778–79 by establishing several provincial assemblies to supervise the local assessment of taxes.[41] In these assemblies of landowners, voting took place by head

40. *Réflexions Politiques sur la Question Proposée par l'Académie de Châlons: Quels sont les moyens de faire naître & d'encourager la Patriotisme dans une Monarchie, sans altérer ni gêner le pouvoir exécutif propre à ce genre de Gouvernement* (n.p., n.d.), 5, 9, 16.
41. Necker had entered the royal service as director of the treasury in October 1776; by June 1777 he had also supplanted Taboureau des Réaux as controller-general. Jean Egret, *Necker: Ministre de Louis XVI* (Paris, 1975), 51–52.

rather than by order, and their procedures gently challenged the principle of noble preeminence in representative assemblies.[42]

In his fabulously popular *Statement of Accounts,* which sold as many as ten
thousand copies per week according to one contemporary witness, the
seemingly disinterested finance minister subtly laid the foundations for a
new political dynamic that played on the opposition between the health of
the state budget and the interests of the beneficiaries of royal largess.[43]
Necker's purpose in the *Statement of Accounts,* he would later explain, was
to "summon the Nation . . . to an examination of the public administration, and to make the affairs of state, for the first time, a matter of common knowledge."[44] He aimed to assure readers that the crown had
managed, by cutting expenses and restructuring its debt, to balance its
budget and even to secure a small surplus for future use. But in addition
to issuing a general bill of health for the treasury, the *Statement of Accounts*
specified publicly for the first time the costs associated with each regular
item in the royal budget. By prominently displaying the expenses of the
*Maison du roi* at the top of his list, Necker drew readers' attention to what
he called the "excessive" sum—at more than 28 million livres, the figure
certainly looked disproportionate in comparison to the other listed expenses—devoted to royal pensions.[45]

After being dismissed from his post, amid controversies generated in
part by his innovative use of the tactics of "publicity," Necker went on to
write a lengthy treatise on finance that created an even greater sensation
among readers than had the best-selling *Statement of Accounts. On the Administration of Finances in France* went through 20 editions between 1784
and 1789, and it sold some 80,000 copies, making it one of the great best-
sellers of the century.[46] In *On the Administration,* Necker complained of the
"impure winds" that dominated royal courts and frustrated the designs of
those motivated by "virtue" and "occupied only with public objects." Un-

42. On Necker's assemblies in Berry and the Haute-Guienne, see Peter M. Jones, "Reforming Absolutism and the Ending of the Old Regime in France," *Australian Journal of French
Studies* 29 (1992): 220–28, esp. 223–24; Jones, "The Provincial Assemblies, 1778–1790: Old
or New?," *The Consortium on Revolutionary Europe, 1750–1850: Proceedings, 1993* (Tallahassee,
1994), 379–86; and Kwass, *Privilege and the Politics of Taxation,* 263–64.
43. The councilor of state Vidaud de la Tour claimed that the text sold at a rate of 10,000
per week in the initial weeks after its release date of 19 February. See Egret, *Necker,* 171. See
also Robert Harris, *Necker: Reform Statesman of the Ancien Régime* (Berkeley, 1979), 217–18.
44. As cited in Egret, *Necker,* 170.
45. Jacques Necker, *De l'Administration des Finances de la France,* 2 vols. (2nd ed., n.p., 1785),
2: 378. (The 1785 edition of *De l'Administration* included in its second volume a reprint of the
*Compte rendu.*)
46. Perrot, "Nouveautés: L'économie politique et ses livres," 254–55.

fortunately, "all is ambition" at court. "[Ambition] is the fruit of the region, so to speak, and for too long [courtiers] have regarded love of order and of the public good as a wild and foreign plant."[47]

Necker not only castigated courtiers—that easy target whose selfishness had already been exposed in the *Statement of Accounts*—but also utilized the concept of honor in a new way that redirected its searing moral power toward all who benefited from the veil of secrecy. He located honor not in a specific social milieu, or even in the heroic French past venerated by so many soldiers, historians, and magistrates, but in the vast and anonymous realm of public opinion. "The spirit of society, and the love of praise and consideration, have constructed in France a tribunal where all men who attract the attention of others are obliged to present themselves. There, public opinion, as from the heights of a throne, distributes prizes and crowns, it makes and unmakes reputations." In France, a famously "sensitive nation," the passion for praise, honor, and esteem easily surpassed the passion for money or fortune. If some people felt compelled to pursue "luxury and vain splendor" in the hope of making a proper impression on observers, why should one be astonished at the strength of that "more noble and reasonable empire of public opinion, this opinion which reigns over men in order to inspire in them the love of true glory, in order to elicit great things through honor and praise, and to repel all base and cowardly sentiments through the specter of scorn and shame?"[48]

Necker advised the king that his own power and the authority of his ministers must ultimately rest on the force of "confidence," a product of "this union of opinions, this spirit of society, this continual communication between men," that made everyone value "consideration, recognition, esteem, and renown" above all else. "Yes," Necker asserted, "only [public] opinion, and the esteem accorded it, grants the nation a sort of influence, by giving it the power to reward or punish by praise or by scorn." With public opinion exercising its influence properly, the king's ministers would find their course of action dictated by "sentiments of honor, love of reputation, politics itself." Policies and decisions elaborated in secrecy, on the other hand, violated essential bonds of trust and encouraged citizens to follow inclinations inimical to patriotism and civic unity. Under secretive policies, "all of their self-interested sentiments will reappear, they will no longer tie their own interests to political projects, and they will isolate themselves all the more." Citizens "will abandon themselves entirely to

47. Necker, *De l'Administration*, 1: 3, 60–61.
48. Ibid., 28, 30–31.

those passions that run contrary to public order," and they will be forced to regard themselves as "foreigners in their own *patrie*." Happily, Necker saw the custom of publishing explanatory preambles to new royal edicts as a vital sign that, in France, state power "continues to recognize the national character," for it showed that the state's ministers "feel at each moment the need to win public approbation."[49]

Because of his well-known personal rivalries with various courtiers, and because of his own craving for attention, Necker became a galvanizing figure in the 1780s, and his works proved to be widely influential.[50] An edited collection of writings "for and against" Necker became a bestseller in its own right, and thanks to his reputation as a patriotic reformer, Neckerian concepts and arguments would come to saturate the pamphlet literature of 1787–88.[51] A representative example is Mathon de La Cour's prize-winning essay on monarchical patriotism written in 1787. The author, who in 1788 imitated Necker by publishing a "Collection of Statements of Account" devoted to royal budgets since the 1750s, echoed the Genevan in 1787 by associating courtiers with wastefulness, by linking openness and publicity to the wide cultivation of "patriotic virtues," and by suggesting that the king should cede to the people the right to bestow honors on citizens who distinguished themselves by their patriotism.[52] This last idea recalled the military reforms proposed by Servan de Gerbey, who had likewise insisted that the government should be "guided by the voice of the public" in its distribution of distinctions.[53] Prizes of honor, Mathon de La Cour averred, should always be distributed on the recommendation of deputations of municipal officers in each town, for then the prince and his ministers, who were "so often mistaken" in their choices, "would be guided and enlightened by the esteem of all [*l'estime générale*], which never errs."[54]

The moral language that had infused Necker's treatises opposed an enlightened, critical, and patriotic public to the hidden machinations of the corrupt, and his working definition of patriotism incorporated a national

---

49. Ibid., 6–7, 30–31, 33–34, 36.
50. On Necker's wide impact on public opinion, see Kwass, *Privilege and the Politics of Taxation*, 243–48. For discussion of pamphlets critical of Necker, see Jeremy Popkin, "Pamphlet Journalism at the End of the Old Regime," *Eighteenth Century Studies* 22 (1989): 351–67, esp. 357–61.
51. *Collection complètte de tous les ouvrages pour et contre m. Necker* (Utrecht, 1782).
52. Charles-Joseph Mathon de La Cour, *Collection de comptes rendus, pièces authentiques, états et tableaux concernant les finances de France* (Lausanne, 1788), and *Discours sur les Meilleurs Moyens de Faire Naître et d'Encourager le Patriotisme dans une Monarchie, qui a remporté le prix dans l'académie de Châlons-sur-Marne, le 25 août 1787* (Paris, 1787), 44–45.
53. Servan de Gerbey, *Le Soldat Citoyen*, 444.
54. Mathon de La Cour, *Discours*, 46.

"honor" whose operation depended on publicity and whose legitimacy came from the collective will of the people. The army's Ségur regulation, which was announced, ironically, just three days after Louis XVI's dismissal of Necker on 19 May 1781, held up a far more restrictive definition of honor than that made popular by Necker and his admirers. By decreeing that only nobles with lineages stretching four generations or more could rise to the rank of superior officer, the army offended precisely that sense of honor and dignity to which many commoners had recently come to feel entitled by virtue of their status as active and patriotic members of the nation. Even though very few commoners were directly affected by the decree—there are reasons to believe that the new rule especially took aim at the newly ennobled—the broad principle of exclusion that it seemed to announce aroused animosity that lingered until 1789, as evinced by the large proportion of *cahiers* of the third estate that attacked the ruling in explicit terms.[55] The measure not only barred potentially worthy candidates from honorable offices, but also suggested, in the eyes of its critics, a connection between corporate insularity and the distinctly unfraternal qualities of selfishness and arrogance.

A prime example of the kind of embittered backlash to which the Ségur regulation and other exclusionary measures by the nobility eventually gave rise was Pierre Ambroise Choderlos de Laclos's salacious novel *Dangerous Liaisons* (1782). The book satirized the supposed sexual libertinage of the aristocracy of court and city, and it went to new lengths of irony to dramatize the degradation, and perversion, of noble "honor." A third-generation noble whose grandfather had acquired nobility in 1725 by purchasing the expensive but derided office of *secrétaire du roi*, Laclos himself had been forced by his deficient lineage to pursue his military career in the artillery, where looser requirements often permitted *anoblis* and even some commoners to become superior officers.[56] In May 1781, having failed to move beyond the captaincy he had obtained nine years earlier, and frustrated that a lack of financial resources and useful connections had prevented him from joining the American war, the forty-year old Laclos heard news of the Ségur ruling, a measure designed specifically to exclude men like himself from all superior ranks, even within the artillery.

It seems not entirely coincidental that Laclos put the finishing touches on his novel, and requested permission to have it published, in the months immediately following the Ségur announcement.[57] Unlike Charles-Pinot

---

55. On the army's suspicions toward the newly ennobled, see Bien, "The Army in the French Enlightenment."
56. Georges Poisson, *Choderlos de Laclos, ou l'obstination* (Paris, 1985), 10, 19.
57. Laclos drafted part of the novel in 1778–79, while stationed in Besançon. The rest was

Duclos's *Comte de \*\*\**, discussed in chapter 1, Laclos's corrupt protagonists, the vicomte de Valmont and the marquise de Merteuil, evinced no
pangs of conscience and experienced no mid-life moral awakening. Find-
ing their "honor" in sexual conquest and frivolous competition, mocking
the sincerity and constancy of others, and boasting brazenly of the falsity
of their own sentiments, they pursued their deformed image of glory to
the point of disgrace and, in the case of Valmont, an only partially re-
deeming death.[58] Evidence of the connection between the propagation of
this unflattering image of nobility in the 1780s and the future radicalism
of Revolutionary politics can be found in the political career of Laclos himself. He went on to become a propagandist for the Society of Thirty
in 1788, formed a close relationship to Servan de Gerbey in 1792, and
achieved success as a military officer under the first French Republic.

Laclos's novel contributed to the identification of the ideas of corruption and aristocracy in the minds of critical readers of the 1780s, but the
inclination to identify the defense of privilege with irredeemably selfish
motives received reinforcement from many quarters during the decade. In
the literary realm, Beaumarchais's play *The Marriage of Figaro* (1784) fea-
tured the corrupt Count Almaviva, whose moral failings were linked directly to his sense of entitlement and his possession of an ancient, and
probably fictitious, feudal right. The so-called *droit de seigneur* allegedly permitted him to sleep with the bride of a personal dependent—in this case,
his servant Figaro—on her wedding night. The play shows Figaro and
Suzanne outwitting and ultimately escaping the clutches of the vain and
arrogant Almaviva, but not before Figaro delivers a scathing soliloquy in
which he denounces the privilege of birth and underlines the insensitivi-
ties and cruelties sanctioned by the possession of noble status. "Nobility,
fortune, rank, and position have made you so proud!" Figaro complains.
"What have you done to deserve such things? You've gone to the trouble
of being born, nothing more. Otherwise, you're a rather ordinary man!"[59]

Beaumarchais, one can safely assume, had no intention of discrediting
the nobility as a whole, for like Laclos's grandfather, he himself had pur-

---

finished in 1780–81, after he completed a miserable assignment at the remote isle of Aix.
See Poisson, *Laclos,* 97–98, 117–25.

58. In recounting the details of some of her victories and explaining the "principles" that
guide her, the marquise de Merteuil openly mocks both *"men of principle"* and *"women of feeling."* In one of the novel's final ironies, Valmont's death at the hands of the wronged chevalier d'Anceny is hidden from public officials, for fear that his involvement in an illegal duel
"would inevitably reflect upon his honor." See *Les Liaisons Dangereuses,* ed. Yves Le Hir (Paris,
1961), 170–81, 188–97, 376–77.

59. Pierre Auguste Caron de Beaumarchais, *Le Mariage de Figaro,* ed. E. J. Arnould (Oxford,
1952). 129.

chased entry into the nobility by acquiring the office of *secrétaire du roi*.[60] He aimed his barbs especially at the great nobles, the high and mighty, whose libertine manners and obliviousness to their social inferiors had aroused his indignation in the past.[61] Nevertheless, the play's indictment of count Almaviva did not spare the broad concepts of nobility, birth, and rank, and, as noted in the *Correspondance Littéraire*, Beaumarchais addressed the defects of the *grands* "with a boldness we have not heard before."[62] The frenzied excitement that surrounded his play attests to the heightened stakes suddenly involved in the creation and reception of critical images of the nobility and other traditional institutions of French society. The performance of *Figaro* had been repeatedly delayed but widely anticipated ever since Beaumarchais completed it in 1778. The salons of Paris had been abuzz with gossip about the author and his play for years, and parties of supporters and detractors of the play included the most exalted nobles in the land. When the Comédie Française finally performed the play in 1784, three would-be spectators died in the rush for tickets, and the audience reacted so warmly that the play attracted attention from all over Europe.[63]

The whole Figaro phenomenon—from the royal censoring, to the grand spectacle of the initial performance in April 1784, to its dissemination to the provinces and its unprecedented one-hundredth showing in Paris in 1787—happened to coincide with a series of scandals involving highly placed nobles at court. In October 1782, the ancient noble family of Rohan-Guéménée declared bankruptcy after accumulating debts unheard of in their size and scope, and the court cronyism that had allowed such profligate spending and borrowing came in for wide public discussion, not least because so many small creditors felt the unfortunate ripple effects of this devastating bankruptcy.[64] Then, the riveting Diamond Necklace Affair of 1785–86 compounded the injury done to the image of court nobles in the Rohan-Guéménée case, for a member of the clan, the cardinal de Rohan, happened to play a central role in the escapade.[65] The car-

---

60. On Beaumarchais, and the sensation caused by Figaro, see the colorful account of Jones, *The Great Nation*, 322–26.

61. Maza, *Private Lives*, 131–40.

62. As discussed in Claude Petitfrère, *Le scandale du Mariage de Figaro: Prélude à la Révolution française?* (Paris, 1989), 24.

63. Jones, *The Great Nation*, 323–4; Petitfrère, *Le scandale*, 10–12.

64. See Thomas Kaiser, "Nobles into Aristocrats, or How an Order Became a Conspiracy" (unpublished essay), cited by permission of the author.

65. Rory Browne, "The Diamond Necklace Affair Revisited: The Rohan Family and Court Politics," *Renaissance and Modern Studies* 33 (1989): 21–39.

dinal's ardent desire to regain the good graces of the queen had left him vulnerable to the resourceful conniver Jeanne de La Motte, whose scheming lay behind the entire Affair. By lying about the queen's motives, and by hiring an impersonator of the queen, La Motte tricked Rohan into arranging the purchase—on credit—of a beautiful gem-studded necklace, which was transferred to the valet of the ersatz queen in February 1785. Soon after the jewels had been sold off on the black market, the scheme came to light, and news of the event ignited a firestorm of controversy and led quickly to the arrest of all the players involved.

As Sarah Maza has shown, the main casualty in the Diamond Necklace Affair was the reputation of Marie-Antoinette, but the charges of greed, duplicity, and underhandedness that were unfairly leveled at the queen in the popular press branded the entire royal court as an alarmingly corrupt and "effeminate" institution.[66] The impression was reinforced in 1786 when another noble family closely allied to Marie-Antoinette, the Polignacs, became involved in another public relations disaster, this one involving the prospect of unsavory profit-taking following the crown's attempted expropriation of land belonging to proprietors in and around Bordeaux.[67] In the end the landowners successfully resisted the crown's maneuver, thanks to the dogged opposition of the parlement of Bordeaux, but not before the royal court had once again been made to appear as a den of iniquity where select noble families parlayed their privileges and connections into unimaginable profits and power.

The narrow-mindedness, fraudulence, and corruption of nobles at court had been decried for years, of course, and noble detractors of "noblesse moderne" had been among the most vociferous critics of the court and of the sordid moral examples that it set for French society. As early as 1782, Toustain de Richebourg could be heard complaining about the unjust ranting of "those who judge the nobility in general on the basis of that of the court in particular."[68] In 1789 the marquis d'Av*** bristled at the suggestion that the crimes of courtiers and fops proved the corruption and obsolescence of the whole institution of nobility. The "true *gentilhomme*" had always been distinguished by "honor, scrupulousness, and generous bravery," and those who raised the objection that "some nobles fall short of this portrait" only missed the real point. "Where do you draw your ex-

66. Maza, *Private Lives*, 167–211.
67. For the details of the scheme, see William Doyle, *The Parlement of Bordeaux and the End of the Old Regime, 1771–1790* (London, 1974), 249–63.
68. Toustain de Richebourg, "Observations sur la noblesse, communiquées aux memes, par M. le comte de Toustain," *JE* 1782, vol. 2, 489.

amples? At the heart of corruption, in the capital and at court . . . [where] the spirit of the Nobility has been most altered."[69] "There exists among the [nobles of the provinces]," insisted one noble soldier in 1789, "more virtues, energy, and patriotism than among the *grands.*"[70] Needless to say, courtiers did not represent the entirety of the nobility, and nobles anxious to end "abuses" in all their forms were able to laugh heartily at satirical images of courtiers.

Nevertheless, the Ségur reform and the attention-getting scandals and satires of the 1780s were filtered through patriotic categories of thought that produced increasingly refined perceptions of privilege, secrecy, rank, and favoritism. In light of the Neckerian emphasis on patriotism's link to publicity, and the minister's compelling definition of the patriot as one "occupied only with public objects," the nobility's most conspicuous forays onto the public stage in the 1780s served mainly to focus new attention on the function of privilege—both as a barrier between citizens who might otherwise be construed as equals and as a lever determining the distribution of the nation's collective material and moral resources. The events of the 1780s also reinforced what had already been a growing preoccupation, at least among self-consciously patriotic writers and readers, with the need to determine the place of noble birth in a nation of fraternally united and morally homogeneous "citizens."

Processes of cognitive adjustment do not announce themselves to consciousness in fully coherent terms, and they therefore leave only scattered traces in the documentary record. But one can reasonably surmise that contemporaries who accepted the utility of distinctions, and who admired nobility as a signifier of moral excellence, reacted to controversial events of the 1780s by reprocessing the constellation of ideas and assumptions that informed their understanding of French patriotism. Conservative noble writers had reacted to leveling expressions of patriotic fellowship in the 1760s and 1770s by rearticulating the connection between nobility and hierarchy. In the 1780s, I suggest, conspicuous manifestations of noble privilege raised new doubts in the minds of patriots from the third estate, and some liberal nobles, about whether *the* nobility—as distinct from *nobility*—could be reconciled with the imperatives of political fellowship built into the patriotic ideal. The decree of the parlement in September 1788 confirmed mounting suspicions to the contrary and, for many, brought an end to false hopes raised earlier by the vigorous aristocratic defense of the na-

69. M. le Marquis d'Av***, *Réflexions en faveur de la Noblesse* (n.p., n.d.), 12–13.
70. *L'Armée Française au Conseil de la Guerre* (n.p., 1789), 31.

tion's rights. Participants in political debate were moved to readjust that amorphous and tension-ridden conceptual compound that had made up the meaning of French patriotism under the old regime: honor, virtue, nobility, the nation, equality, love for the *patrie* and its laws. Despite their residual attachment to ideas of nobility, they gave new priority to the principle of civil equality, and thus gave expression to an egalitarian vision of the patriotic polity that had been gestating for years. That vision would find itself in open confrontation with a noble and conservative vision of patriotism that boasted an equally impressive conceptual lineage. The connections between past and present thinking were revealed in arguments about the properly patriotic relationship between nobility and equality.

## ANTI-NOBLE HOSTILITY IN A PATRIOTIC KEY

The process of conceptual refinement accelerated by the parlement's decree in favor of the forms of 1614 is perhaps best expressed in the writings of a political activist encountered earlier in this study, the lawyer J.-M.-A. Servan. After spending years in retirement as a minor philosophe of sorts, in 1788 Servan joined Mounier, Barnave, and other Dauphinois patriots in speaking in favor of constitutional reform. His early contribution to the debate about the Estates-General focused especially on the need to eliminate "abuses" and the existence of fiscal privileges. He asked rhetorically "whether the nobility will show that it has *nobility*" by renouncing its "doubtful rights." In return for its demonstrating a "noble heart," he wrote, the nation would gladly leave intact the nobility's "arms, liveries, titles, dignities, honors," and everything that "distinguishes it from others."[71] To reclaim its place of honor, Servan suggested, the nobility had only to give up privileges that defied "reason" and "justice," privileges that "their fathers would have been embarrassed to claim."[72]

Servan's attitudes about the nobility's marks of distinction became progressively more radical in his later writings, as the nobility's determination to preserve the separation of estates at the Estates-General moved him to rethink the balance between hierarchy and equality in his own conception of nobility. The announcement of the second Assembly of Notables, and the memorandum of the Princes in December, had convinced Servan by

71. Servan, *Petit Colloque Elémentaire entre Mr. A. et Mr. B, sur les abus, le droit, la raison, les états-généraux, les parlemens, & tout ce qui s'ensuit. Par un vieux jurisconsulte allobroge* (n.p., 1788), 46–48.
72. Ibid., 15–16, 48.

early 1789 that although "nobles are common, nobility is quite rare."[73] If
the Notables had only devoted themselves to securing the happiness and
prosperity of the state, instead of attempting "to fix in the constitution of
the state the very abuses that have brought it to ruin," the nobility might
have found itself liberated from wicked ministers and financiers, and the
people would finally be free to enjoy "the sacred rights of man and citizen."
By refusing to live up to the inspiring examples of their ancient forebears
and to reclaim the true nobility that their "fathers" had demonstrated so
effortlessly, Servan implied, the second estate had become guilty of dero-
gation of status. In a rhetorical gesture that betrayed his own recent mental efforts to reconcile the principles of honor and virtue and to recuperate
for modern uses past examples of noble patriotism, Servan chided nobles
for diverging from their own ancient ideals. "If the great lords of the
clergy, of the sword, and of the robe cling obstinately to their demand for
an Estates-General according to the ancient forms, the Third Estate, for
its part, may very well demand Bishops, Magistrates, and *Gentilshommes*
consistent with ancient forms. From the nobility, they will expect men
such as Duguesclin, Dunois, and Bayard; from the Parlements, they will
expect Cuquières, d'Orgemont, Lavaquerie, l'Hôpital . . . all of whom,"
he remarked sarcastically, "observed ancient forms."[74] Their predecessors'
"ancient forms," however, had concerned the "eternal forms of integrity
and public virtue" that applied to all who possessed nobility in a pre-corrupt
age, not the accretions of privilege that their heirs were now content to enjoy without having merited them.

The juxtaposition of the ancient ideal with the modern particularistic
reality of the nobility ultimately led to the rearrangement of Servan's own
moral categories as he thought his way through a provisional reversal of
previous assumptions. Whereas he had once suggested, in his *Discourse on
Morals,* that the path to virtuous citizenship lay in the emulation of the
honor of the historical nobility, Servan now determined that noble status
necessarily rested on the anterior virtues of the citizen. It is "only the Order of the Citizen that forms the state and sustains it."[75] When confronted
with the nobility's arrogance and claims to privilege, he advised his readers among the third estate, "do not hesitate to ask the nobility if [noble sta-
tus] can have any legitimate origin other than the civil virtues; ask next
what privileges derive from the civil virtues, and if one of these privileges

73. Servan, *Commentaire roturier, sur le noble Discours adressé, par Monseigneur le prince de Conti,
à Monsieur, frère du Roi, dans l'Assemblée des Notables de 1788* (Paris, 1789), 38.
74. Ibid., 32–35.
75. Ibid., 34–35.

consists of the right to harm the state."[76] In Servan's eyes, the nobles' evident willingness to harm the general good disqualified them for the status of citizen, which perforce denied them the "nobility" on which they based their claims to privilege and distinction.

Angered by the legal nobility's abdication of moral responsibility, Servan turned viciously on the very category of nobility, and he drew from a wide repertoire of existing criticism to discredit its claims to superiority. In one pamphlet, for example, he represented luxury, which he had previously understood as a broad social problem affecting all classes, as a particular sign of the nobility's self-indulgence and declining vigor.[77] In another essay, he used the language of neoclassical stoicism to accentuate the moral disparities separating nobles from non-nobles. "Take a hard look at these men who dare to scorn you," he advised his readers.

> Compare the strength and resourcefulness of your organs with the weakness and ineptitude of theirs; the patience and moderation of your character with the impetuosity of their souls and the enormity of their desires; the justice of your well-measured reason with their flights of imagination, which exceed all limits. Then you will recognize . . . this great and eternal truth: on the basis of an original equality, nature alone elevates [men] and establishes differences according to the faculties of the mind, and the dispositions of the body.[78]

Nobles now needed to hear common citizens utter "that sweet and powerful word, equality, the cry of reason and justice. . . . [Tell them] that without equality, all morality is a chimera, and justice is nothing but an insoluble problem."[79]

In giving moral priority to the category of "citizen" over that of "noble," Servan not only challenged the basis of the superior status claimed by the second estate but also sought to empower and embolden those officially excluded from the circle of nobility. In 1781 he had written of the monarchy's need to establish a kind of "apprenticeship of the citizen" through

---

76. Servan, *Avis salutaire au Tiers Etat. Sur ce qu'il fut, ce qu'il est, & ce qu'il peut être* (n.p., 1789), 30.

77. Servan, *Glose et Remarques sur l'Arrêt du Parlement de Paris, du 5 décembre 1788* (London, 1789), 10. Magistrates, he wrote, had been compromised by venality and hereditary power, the clergy by their resistance to *lumières,* and the nobility by "the growth of its luxury" which made it "ever more dissipated." On the association of luxury with nobility in the years before the Revolution, see Shovlin, "The Cultural Politics of Luxury, 577–606.

78. Servan, *Avis salutaire,* 27.

79. Ibid., 29.

promotion of a national education that would surround the young with edifying examples of patriotic sacrifice and images of French heroes of the past. Just eight years later, he effectively declared that apprenticeship to be complete, as the imperative of "equality" made it necessary for the third estate to assume the full responsibilities, and to enjoy the dignity, of the citizen.

Nobility had worn many faces in the political and moral discourse of the old regime, but the constitutional crisis that began in the fall of 1788 reduced the range of its representations. For Servan, who had used an idealized and historical image of the nobility for edifying and patriotic purposes in 1769, the recent actions of noble assemblies had filtered out all images of the nobility except two: that of the emasculated courtier, "weakened" and laden with "luxury," and that of the unruly feudal baron, whose brutal and egoistic desires lived on among the legion of nobles who unfortunately lacked true "nobility."[80] Just as the "forms" of 1614 evacuated the middle ground and forced all citizens into one of two groups with incommensurable status, writers like Servan reacted to noble conservatism by finally deciding which of two familiar arguments—the argument to accentuate civil equality or the argument to perfect and strengthen existing hierarchies—had greater moral authority on its side. Elaborating a theme present in his earlier writings, where equality had implicitly united all conscientious citizens, and where public honors had been available to all men of merit, Servan announced that civil equality had now to become a central feature of a reformed France. Symbolic of this resettling of his own moral priorities was his new language of self-identification. Referring to himself as a "mere bourgeois," the noble Servan struck an indignant pose as he drew ever starker contrasts between a nobility blindly inured to its privileges and a third estate unjustly deprived of its rights.[81]

The exaggerated rhetoric of Servan's later pamphlets temporarily superseded his prior mental efforts to constitute a new kind of spiritual nobility, one open to all "honnêtes gens" who exhibited patriotic honor and sound morals, but traces of that earlier ideal are still detectable in the interstices of his radical project of 1789. He had become convinced that "without equality, all morality is a chimera," but he still assumed that an education in virtue required careful mentoring and heroic leadership. "The reform of morals must always precede, or at least accompany, the reform of laws," wrote the author of the *Discourse on Morals* in 1789. "To provide a

---

80. Ibid., 11, 27, for examples of anti-feudal rhetoric worthy of Mably's *Observations sur l'Histoire de France*.
81. Servan refers to himself as a "mere bourgeois" in *Glose et Remarques*, 5.

liberating constitution to a corrupt people is like lowering anchor far from shore and into a bottomless sea."[82] As his later interventions in public debate would show, Servan never doubted that the valuable moral guidance required in a corrupted society must come from a class of leaders distinguished by their wisdom and demonstrated patriotism.[83] In 1789 he had still retained the hope that the overhaul of the old regime's system of legal stratification would lead not in the direction of full democracy but rather toward the rearrangement of society's legal categories and the constitution of a superior "condition," a spiritual nobility, whose moral authority would be beyond dispute.

The doctor to Louis XVI's brother, the comte de Provence—or someone brazen enough to assume the doctor's identity—echoed Servan's critique of noble selfishness by simultaneously chiding the second estate for its attachment to its pretensions and reminding the nobles of their supposed ideals. He questioned the wisdom of a system that granted nobility to those who held themselves above the rest of humanity but left in obscurity those "who conserved the sentiments of [their] ancestors" and "never altered their purity with conduct unworthy of French magnanimity." Seeking explanations for the current state of affairs, the doctor found his answers in the glorious national history of the French Middle Ages. "When [the fifth-century Frankish king] Pharamond was proclaimed king by his soldiers and by the Nation . . . hereditary nobility did not exist at all. The Nation resided in the people—free, brave, faithful, robust, generous, and noble only by their qualities of soul." The "male heroism that the national interest inspires" then took no comfort in "shameful exceptions."[84] Clovis first introduced "the ways of honor" to the French, and his examples helped "to develop with brilliance the warlike character of the nation," but even Clovis's own chiefs had known nobility only as a "glorious attribute of their valor." Not until fiefs became inheritable—thanks to "the indefatigable activity of courtiers" and the weak will of Charles the Bald—

82. Servan, *Avis Salutaire*, 32.

83. In 1790, Servan took up the pen against Rabaut de St. Etienne and others who had begun to label constitutional moderates as "aristocrats." In *Seconde Lettre à M. Rabaud de St.-Etienne, sur la raison et la logique. Par un aristocrate sans le savoir* (n.p., n.d.), he complained that the developing constitution provided no intermediary bodies and that it violated the principles of monarchy (39). In the *Troisième Lettre à M. Rabaud de St.-Etienne sur l'humanité. Par un aristocrate sans le savoir* (n.p., n.d.), he argued that Rousseau, Mably, and Voltaire had never sanctioned democracy, and he expressed dismay that those on the left would resort to name-calling in their effort to impose a fanatical agenda (16).

84. *Le Patriotisme, ou Très-Humble et Très Respectueuse Représentations du Tiers Etat, par M\*\*\* Médecin de Son Altesse Royale* (n.p., 1789), 5.

did nobility become a legal status and, therefore, a fiction. "Real nobility was destroyed, and fictive nobility reared its ugly head. [They] preferred names to sentiments, they substituted phantoms for realities." Worse, nobility soon became a purchasable commodity, thus compounding the injustice of separating the naturally magnanimous "people" from the all too self-interested "nobles." Nobility should be retained in the new polity, the "doctor" asserted, but only as a purely personal sign of moral distinction. Then "the French will become once again a People of happy Citizens," and the king will find that he once again commanded "a People of Heroes." If nobles resisted this change, "let us deploy against them the consuming patriotic fires that have been stifled for too long."[85]

Not unlike the marquis d'Argenson in the 1730s, the writers who promoted the interests of the third estate in 1788–89 found that their patriotic ideas carried them ever more swiftly in the direction of equality. The imperative to equality grew progressively clearer as the writers focused on the moral homogeneity that theoretically bound all politically virtuous citizens, and as they emphasized anew the socially indiscriminate character of French national honor. "I salute you holy equality, primitive equality," wrote Jean-Baptiste Cordier. So often treated as a "chimera," he observed, this equality "will open up the door to honors, [and] enable us to share in ranks and dignities." Without rendering equal "all degrees of wealth and power," it will "close the extreme gaps that separate the nobility from citizens."[86] In elaborating this theme, Cordier's compatriots drew on earlier arguments about the patriotic equality of citizens.

In one of many pamphlets that reprised themes first explored by the abbé Coyer, for example, M. Anquetil Du Perron refuted the idea that "the essential sentiments of nobility" must never come into contact with professions that have material gain as one of their objects. "Base motives" were indeed incompatible with nobility, he wrote, "but one must take account of the man, not the profession."[87] "True nobles," he asserted, would refuse

85. Ibid., 7, 42, 44, 49–51.

86. [Jean-Baptiste Cordier], *L'Ave du Tiers Etat, Suivi de la Profession de Foi de cet Ordre; pour servir de suite au Pater, par M. C . . . R, roturier angevin* (n.p., n.d.), 4.

87. Anquetil Du Perron, voyageur, *Dignité du Commerce, et de l'Etat de Commerçant* (n.p., 1789), 13, 15. Anquetil Du Perron acknowledged his debt to Coyer explicitly (see 37, n. 1). Among the other pamphleteers who drew from or otherwise engaged Coyer or his arguments, see *Véritable Patriotisme* (n.p., 1788), 25; Grouvelle, *De l'autorité de Montesquieu dans la révolution présente*, 69, 86–88, 129–32; *Essais Critiques sur l'Etat Actuel de l'Esprit Public; ou Elemens de Patriotisme, à l'usage des Français* (Brussels, 1789), 8–9, 42; *Ouvrage d'un Citoyen, Gentilhomme et Militaire, ou Lettres sur la Noblesse, qui présentent le tableau de son origine, de ses droits, dénoncent les abus en indiquant les moyens d'y remédier, & d'opérer des changemens importants pour ce corps & la patrie* (London, 1787), 77; and Sieyès, *Essai sur les privilèges*, in *Qu'est-ce que le tiers état, par Em-*

the command that they remain idle in order to prove their nobility, and a "truly patriotic" law would render eligible for noble status merchants of every type, including even the small retail merchants disdained by earlier royal ordinances.[88] Anquetil Du Perron declared that "every Frenchman is noble by stock and by sentiment, simply because he is a Frenchman." Elimination of the distinction between the people and the hereditary nobility would ensure that "honor, which constitutes the national character, will soar to new heights."[89]

The national character of honor and the natural nobility of the French people figured prominently in pamphlets written on behalf of the third estate. The power of the national character, "so sensitive to honor," needed only to be liberated from the prejudices that had held it back for so long. "If the sentiment of honor alone has often propelled [the people] to merit [positions] without having any hope of obtaining them, what would it accomplish if it had this hope?" By treating "all of its children equally" and with the strictest "impartiality," the *patrie* would "warm in all hearts the most noble sentiments; it would awaken every type of talent; it would ennoble all professions."[90] The same idea found expression in an essay by "M. Alitèphe, French Citizen." End venality, abolish tax exemptions for nobles, and multiply "fivefold" the personal honors accorded to those who merit nobility through their civic virtues, the author urged. Then France would finally see flourish that "nobility of nobilities, meaning [the nobility] of sentiments."[91] The author of *Noblemania* concurred. "O virtuous citizens, members of the third estate, whether you are bourgeois, professionals, merchants, landowners, artisans, even farmers, you are Frenchmen. . . . You have talents and virtues; see yourselves as noble, and more noble than all these new nobles of whom we speak."[92]

The shape of the criticism unleashed by the furor over the "forms of 1614" showed the effects of literate society's sustained contemplation of honor, nobility, and the meaning of social status in the years and decades that preceded the debate over the composition of the Estates-General. Even the abbé Sieyès, whose *What Is the Third Estate?* is typically represented

manuel Sieyès, précédé de l'Essai sur les Privilèges, ed. Edme Champion (Paris, 1982), 1–26. Cf. also Sieyès, Qu'est-ce que le tiers état?, ed. Zapperi, 119, 123, 125. (All references to Qu'est-ce que le tiers état? are to the Zapperi edition.)
88. Du Perron, Dignité, 30, 119.
89. Ibid., 152, 156.
90. Observations sur le préjugé de la Noblesse Héréditaire (London, 1789), 54–55.
91. Le Vrai Patriote. Dissertation Philosophique et Politique, par M. Alitèphe, Citoyen Français (n.p., 1789), 230, 245.
92. La Noblimanie (n.p., 1789), 51.

as a sudden expression of an elemental and theretofore dimly perceived resentment against nobility, had been indelibly marked by earlier debates about the nobility and its values. In his *Essay on Privileges* of 1788, Sieyès resumed and elaborated arguments used by Coyer in 1756, and his commentary on the sources and effects of public esteem suggested a familiarity with writers such as Servan de Gerbey, Necker, and the Rousseau of the *Considerations on the Government of Poland*.[93] By challenging the conventional opposition between honor and money, and by contrasting the self-absorbed arrogance of the noble with the honest industry of the "bourgeois" and "the people of the city," Sieyès, like Coyer before him, held up for derision the ethos of honor that underlay the existing social order.[94]

Together, he claimed, honor and money worked as "the two great motors of society," and Sieyès insisted that each profession had its own claim on public esteem. The survival and health of a society required the pursuit of both honor and money, since "the desire to merit public esteem . . . provides a check on the passion for riches."[95] Unfortunately, the "privileged" had come to believe that honor resided in the "portraits of their ancestors," their "old chateaus," and their ancient genealogies. They failed to recognize that "the honor of descending from men who lived in the thirteenth and fourteenth centuries" is an advantage "common to all families."[96] Having nourished the myth of their own superiority, they no longer desired to be distinguished *by* their fellow citizens, but only *from* them. "The idea of the *patrie* narrows for the [privileged man]; it encompasses only the caste that has absorbed him," and he finds contentment and security only in the

93. Sieyès's connection to Coyer may have been mediated by the physiocrats, and evidence for the connection is only circumstantial, but the affinities between their texts are striking. Coyer had placed nobles in the class of citizens "created only to consume" (*Développement et défense*, 1: 38). Sieyes wrote that "an entire class of citizens finds glory in remaining immobile amid general movement," and he labeled the nobility "foreign to the nation by its *idleness*." See *Qu'est-ce que le tiers état?*, 125. Coyer called idleness a "continual crime committed against the Nation" (*La noblesse commerçante*, 46). Sieyès declared noble idleness "treason against the public good" (*Qu'est-ce que le tiers état?*, 123). Coyer complained that the merchant had to abandon his career "*to be something*," even though the noble was free to "live as *nothing*" (*La noblesse commerçante*, 192). Sieyès later asked, "What has [the third estate] been until now in the political order? NOTHING. What does it demand? TO BE SOMETHING" (*Qu'est-ce que le tiers état?*, 119).

94. "The privileged has his eyes fixed incessantly on the noble *past*. . . . The bourgeois, on the contrary, with eyes fixed on the ignoble *present* and the uncertain *future*, prepares for the one and sustains the other through the resources of his own industry." See Sieyès/Champion, 11, n. 3.

95. Ibid., 18.

96. Ibid., 10, n. 3.

"false hierarchy" that separated the citizens of the nation from one another.[97]

The *Essay on Privileges* certainly bore the imprint of recent debates about taxes, privileges, and the royal budget, but the tone and structure of the *Essay* also show that Sieyès saw himself as a participant in an ongoing debate about the moral condition of the polity. Sieyès attacked privilege not only because of its irrationality, inefficiency, or cost. He attacked privilege especially because it transferred the adjudication of honor from the people to the court and thereby robbed the *patrie* of its natural moral mechanism of service and recompense. "Let the public freely dispense the tokens of its esteem," he wrote. Public recognition was a "moral money" that had powerful and beneficial effects on behavior. But the prince must not arrogate to himself the power to distribute such tokens. That power should be considered "public property," and nature had arranged that the sentiment of consideration could arise only from "the opinion of the people," which was where "the *patrie* resides." "True distinction" consists in the services one renders to the *patrie,* and "public consideration will never fail to attach itself to this form of merit. . . . Never disrupt this sublime commerce between the services rendered to the people by great men and the tribute of esteem offered to great men by the people. It is pure, it is true, and it generates happiness and virtues so long as it arises from these free and natural relations."[98]

The interference of the court in these "natural relations" had led tragically to the perversion of honor, and to the separation of the signs of distinction from the services and the esteem that they were meant to signify. Thanks to intrigue, favor, and criminal complicity, Sieyès observed, "virtue and talent lack recompense, [while] a collection of signs of many colors imperiously command respect for mediocrity, baseness, and vice; in a word, honors have extinguished honor, and souls are debased." Consequently, honors and distinctions were now borne by men whose most fitting title might be "enemy of the *patrie.*" Only the "free competition of all energetic souls, engaged in all useful activities," Sieyès declared, could enable "the great motor of public esteem" to work its salutary effects on the common project of "social advancement."[99]

As William Sewell has shown, Sieyès deserves credit as an important political innovator. His *What Is the Third Estate?* creatively combined Rous-

97. Ibid., 8, 9, 17, n. 1.
98. Ibid., 5–6.
99. Ibid., 7–8.

seau's ideas about natural sovereignty and the general will with the political economists' concept of the division of labor to form an ingenious new theory of representation, one that helped to guide the early work of the National Assembly.[100] Sieyès's efforts as a political theorist nevertheless grew out of his preoccupation with the need to re-theorize the French social order, and the *Essay on Privileges* provides clear evidence that in 1788 Sieyès was busy manipulating the same conceptual building blocks—honor, virtue, and equality—that had been used by commentators on nobility and patriotism since Montesquieu. His concern about the replacement of honor by "honors," and the "debasement" of souls brought about by the power of the court evoked the rhetoric of Montesquieu, and it could easily have derived from Mirabeau's damning analysis of courtiers.[101] His decision, in *What Is the Third Estate?*, to identify the third estate with patriotic "virtue" and the nobility with an "honor" that had become hopelessly egoistic reflected his engagement with earlier admirers of the classical republics.[102] Finally, Sieyès's attitudes toward the institution of nobility—he mixed glib condescension (he dismissed nobility as "just a word") with palpable resentment toward undeserved privilege (he accused the nobles of *aristocracisme*)—owed a debt to Coyer and the many sardonic critics of "noblesse moderne" who had imitated him.[103] Showing the same talent for synthesis that marked his efforts as a political theorist, Sieyès combined disparate strands of existing social criticism to form a powerful stigma with which to brand, and ultimately exclude from the nation, the entire institution of nobility.

Of course, while Sieyès was developing his virulent form of anti-noble criticism, beginning in the fall of 1788, defenders of noble prerogatives also elaborated their own vision of social and political reform. Their rhetoric reflected a similar indebtedness to earlier commentary on nobility and patriotism, and the key difference that they emphasized in their opposition to arguments such as that of Sieyès showed the effect of lengthy meditations over the "problem" of equality. Conservative nobles, too,

100. See Sewell, *A Rhetoric of Bourgeois Revolution*, 88–94.

101. Mirabeau, *L'Ami des Hommes*, 1: pt. 2, 80–81.

102. Expressing contempt for the authority of "the aristocrat Montesquieu," Sieyès declared that France's historical nobility had been replaced by a "caste of aristocrats" that spoke of "honor" out of habit but nevertheless pursued its own "interest." The third estate, fortunately, was now in position to develop "virtue, because if corporate interest lies in egoism, the national interest lies in virtue" (*Qu'est-ce que le tiers état?*, 195, 194, n. 1).

103. Nobility is labeled "just a word" in *Qu'est-ce que le tiers état?*, 196. The charge of *aristocracisme* is from *Essai sur les privilèges*, 12. For more on the parallels between the rhetorics of Coyer and Sieyès, see n. 93.

spoke the language of unity and fellowship, but they insisted on the importance of maintaining the reality of corporate distinction.

## VISIONS OF A NOBLE REVOLUTION

Some of the conservative members of the nobility reacted to the claims of the third estate with stubborn pride and defensiveness. The Norman Achard de Bonvouloir, for example, rejected out of hand all of the third estate's "boundless" pretensions, even including the call for equalization of the tax burden.[104] And others, such as Chaillon de Jonville and the self-proclaimed *Disciple of Montesquieu*, reflexively cited *The Spirit of the Laws* and the principle of the separation of orders in an effort to protect the nobility's traditional constitutional prerogatives at all costs.[105] Most of the pamphlets written on behalf of the nobility, or in defense of the separation of orders, nevertheless reflected and reinforced the fraternal tone of the published literature about nobility that had appeared in the decades before the revolutionary ferment of 1787–89. The authors advocated various conciliatory gestures toward the third estate, they invoked the common bonds of patriotism and honor that united all French citizens, and in some cases they promoted renegotiation of the boundary separating nobles from commoners.

The abbé Lubersac de Livron, for example, entered into "the arena of patriotism" in the guise of "citizen conciliator," and his comments suggested his close familiarity with the egalitarian strain in patriotic thought.[106] "Every Frenchman, of whatever profession or estate," he wrote, "becomes a citizen by birth." Lubersac then described the moral outlook of the citizen, an outlook he deemed universal among the French. "No prerogative other than equality, no sentiment other than respect and love for the prince, no will other than that of the general and public good; in a word, no virtue other than patriotism; that is the political morality with which every minister at the altar, every noble warrior, every magistrate, in a word, every French citizen, must be imbued."[107] Wide belief in the existence of

104. See the discussion of Achard de Bonvouloir, in the context of a broader discussion of "noble opinion" on the eve of the Estates-General, in Tackett, *Becoming a Revolutionary,* 115.
105. For discussion of Chaillon de Jonville, the anonymously authored *Disciple de Montesquieu, à MM. les Députés aux Etats Généraux* (Paris, 1789), and others indebted to Montesquieu in 1789, see Carcassonne, *Montesquieu et le problème,* 597–608.
106. Charles-François Lubersac de Livron, *Le Citoyen Conciliateur, contenant des idées sommaires politiques et morales sur le gouvernement monarchique de la France* (Paris, 1788), Lettre à Monsieur.
107. Ibid., pt. I, 75.

CAR:GASP: Vice-comes de T**
natus an: 1746. pictus 1788.

Hic filius, conjux, pater, hic frater, civis, amicus:
Moribus, ingenio, doctrinâ prædat et armis .
fecit J.V.N.D.**

FIGURE 11. Vicomte Toustain de Richebourg (1788). A committed man of letters and enthusiast of patriotism, Toustain de Richebourg sought to reconcile the principle of noble preeminence with the principle of social fraternity. Bibliothèque Nationale de France

a unifying political morality explains why other noble writers metaphori-
cally sought a fraternal embrace with their compatriots.

Toustain de Richebourg—who referred to the members of the three orders as "fellow citizens and brothers"—struggled to retain and revive the
feelings of patriotic unity that, he knew from experience, had long characterized reformers of both noble and non-noble status (Figure 11). "Admir-

ing [and] sharing this enthusiasm for the *patrie*, avoiding or rejecting the fanaticism of party, . . . I believe that I have warmly and genuinely pleaded the cause of the third order as well as that of the first two [orders]," he wrote in a text that sought common ground between nobility and third estate.[108] He suggested that many of the details involving the organization of the Estates-General, and the procedural relations between and among the different chambers, could be settled after the convening of the assembly. In March 1789, he even concocted a hopelessly elaborate set of deliberating procedures in an effort to reconcile the just claims of the third estate with the corporate privileges of the nobility.[109] The aged chevalier d'Arc attempted a similar feat in his *On the Convocation of the Estates-General*. He suggested that the king create a fourth estate of merchants. The move would "flatter" merchants always desirous of honors, and it would help to balance the powers of the orders in the upcoming assembly, thus allaying the fears of commoners that the Estates-General would only reaffirm and ratify existing abuses.[110]

Even as Toustain de Richebourg sought unifying middle ground between the estates, however, he also argued for the need to seek "clarification" of the orders, and the dual rhetorical purposes of his pre-Revolutionary pamphlets are representative of the most refined expressions of noble patriotism in 1789.[111] "No great people of ancient or modern times, I believe, has ever subsisted without this hereditary institution, born, so to speak, with society itself." Waking the echoes of the late Buat-Nançay, who had defined the noble as "moral man," Toustain affirmed that the *gentilhomme* should be considered "the man of the Nation par excellence."[112]

A pamphlet written in 1787, when pre-Revolutionary agitation had only just begun, laid out in only slightly exaggerated form the core assumptions behind the distinctively conservative patriotism that had shaped the thinking of many noble reformers since the 1750s and that now motivated Tou-

108. [Toustain de Richebourg], *Eclaircissement à l'Amiable Entre la Noblesse & le Tiers Etat* (n.p., 1788), 9.
109. Ibid., 10; Toustain proposed forming three chambers at the Estates assembly, each consisting of equal parts clergy, commoners, and *gentilshommes*. Each chamber would deliberate separately and vote by head, with a majority of two chambers able to overrule the opposition of the third. Nobles, clerics, and commoners would take turns presiding over each of the chambers, and the chambers would be ranked by lot every fortnight. See *Conservation des trois ordres, et destruction de leur rivalité, ou lettre du vicomte de Toustain, à M. l'abbé Brizard, de la Société patriotique bretonne, sur une nouvelle histoire* (n.p., n.d.), 9–10.
110. [Arc], *De la convocation des Etats-Généraux, et de la Nécessité de Former un Quatrième Ordre de l'Etat* (n.p., 1789), 33–34.
111. Toustain, *Conservation des trois ordres*, 11. He praised the parlement's opinion on the "forms of 1614" because the traditional arrangement combined "the equality of the orders with their clarification."
112. Toustain, *Eclaircissement*, 8, 15–16.

stain de Richebourg and other defenders of the nobles' constitutional privileges. After noting the nobility's uniquely felt devotion to the well-being
of the *patrie,* the anonymous author observed that "other citizens cannot
have the same interests, the same spirit. . . . Pressed by his needs, occupied
with his petty affairs, the humble citizen can neither contemplate nor be
filled with the sublime ideas that lead to virtues and patriotic talents." In
fact, the people's connection to the *patrie* was necessarily mediated
through the nobility. Seeing and appreciating the nobility's "wisdom, support, and protection" in all "extraordinary" occasions, the people eventually received "certain impressions" about the *patrie* and its needs. "[Nobles]
alone communicate to the people a few parcels of [their] patriotic ideas,
which are too foreign" to the people to be perceived naturally.[113] These
ideas included the sentiments of "generosity, integrity, [and] honor" which
formed the nobility's special esprit de corps.

The author of these "letters on nobility" acknowledged that on some occasions individuals in the other estates provided evidence of a "pure
honor" that even a Bayard or a DuGuesclin would have admired. But even
the extraordinary qualities of commoners had to be credited, in the end,
to the nobility, since only the nobility could provide the moral examples
necessary to inspire the pursuit of honor in milieus where "patriotic talents" and "patriotic ideas" were normally unknown. "Where did they learn
these qualities that are not a part of their profession? In what *temple* did
they conserve *this sacred fire?*" Commoners of proven moral excellence
should certainly be permitted to enter the *temple* of the nobility, but the
French must never be persuaded that "this natural and vaunted equality"
should bring the elimination of "all differences of condition." Such an
equality would only deprive future French kings of the "people of Heroes"
on whom they had always counted in confrontations with their enemies.[114]

Many nobles, such as the Languedocian magistrate Barthez, claimed to
look forward to "compet[ing] equally with other Citizens for all the honorable offices in which one can serve the state."[115] Addressing a fellow *gentilhomme* from Brittany, the vicomte de Chastenay Saint Georges cajoled his
friend, "let us find in the Third Estate rivals; let us compete with them for
the prize in bravery; . . . let us praise their merit; let us recognize them as
brothers in arms; let us expel a base jealousy that would deny them a Nobility that our fathers acquired by distinguishing themselves from their

113. *Ouvrage d'un Citoyen,* 16–17.
114. Ibid., 20, 9, 14, 77.
115. M. de Barthez, *Libre Discours sur la Prérogative que doit avoir la Noblesse dans la Constitution et dans les Etats Généraux* (Paris, 1789), 33.

equals."[116] But a commitment to the principle of natural equality, and recognition of the benefits of free competition for offices and honors, remained compatible with a fierce attachment to the principle of corporate distinction. Lubersac de Livron, whom we have earlier seen extolling the prerogative of "equality" and the common obligations of patriotism, insisted that the first two orders should never again be "mixed up with the multitude." He complained of the "confusion of ranks," of "prerogatives usurped and debased," and his assessment of the nobility led him to call for the "repair of this immense fortress that, for twelve centuries, was the strength of the French empire . . . but which a false and revolting ministerial policy has tried unsuccessfully to overturn."[117] Lubersac even proposed limiting membership in elected noble assemblies to those whose noble origins predated the fifteenth century.[118]

Barthez and Chastenay Saint Georges showed greater flexibility than Lubersac, but their assumption that the nobility had to remain separate and distinct remained unshaken. For Barthez, honor, "if not the sole principle of Monarchies, . . . has at the very least a great influence on the durability of their constitution," and he defended both "inequality of conditions" and nobles' right to "transmit honorific privileges to their posterity."[119] A purely personal understanding of honor threatened to concentrate "ambitious passions" in the mind of the individual, after all, thus tainting glory with a vile egoism "always harmful by nature."[120] Chastenay Saint Georges, who announced to his noble interlocutor that he was ready to open the gates of the nobility to all meritorious commoners, trusted the Nation to determine the "privileges that distinguish us." Still, he expressed hope that "it will perhaps see that it is essential, even necessary, that our Order conserve those [privileges] that are not harmful to the Nation." Indeed, he advised the nobles to make clear to their fellow citizens its reluctance to "make any sacrifice of our privileges."[121]

Let us return, then, to the questions that opened this chapter. Why did the nobility suffer an apparent reversal of fortune in its broad relationship to public opinion in late 1788? Why, after managing to work together in

116. Vicomte de Chastenay Saint Georges, *Lettre d'un gentilhomme bourguignon à un gentilhomme breton, sur l'attaque du tiers-état, la division de la noblesse et l'intérêt des cultivateurs* (n.p., 1789), 16.
117. Lubersac, *Citoyen Conciliateur,* pt. III, 8–9.
118. Ibid., pt. III, 56.
119. Barthez, *Libre Discours,* 18–19, 43.
120. Ibid., 9–10.
121. Chastenay Saint Georges, *Lettre,* 16, 20, 25.

the fight against "despotism" in 1787, did spokesmen for the second and third estates begin to express mutual hostility after the controversial decree of the parlement in September 1788? Why did a galvanizing political movement conceived out of concern for the rights of the "nation" lead ultimately to a Revolution that redefined both nation and nobility, a Revolution carried out on the premise that corporate privileges were antipatriotic, anti-national, and therefore inconsistent with the moral regeneration of the French people?

The evidence surveyed in this chapter suggests that political activists from the second and third estates occupied much common ground in the period of pre-Revolutionary turmoil that preceded the pivotal events of June–July 1789. Not only was there a consensus on the need to restrain the despotic tendencies of the king's ministers; writers on all sides also expressed a desire for patriotic union, optimistically evoked the honorable character of the nation, and promoted the dignity of the citizen. Nobles expressed in overwhelming numbers a commitment to fiscal equality.[122] Self-styled patriots of all kinds contemplated a substantial revision of the existing relationship between the nobility, on the one hand, and citizens on the other side of the legal barrier of nobility, on the other hand.

Beneath the surface harmony inspired by anti-despotic feeling in 1787, however, lay important disagreements over the meanings of the terms that comprised the multifaceted language of French civic consciousness. The proliferation of such titles as *True Patriotism, Patriotism, An Essay on Patriotism,* and *The True Patriot* in 1788–89 attests to the semantic divergence that underlay the emerging dispute between estates.[123] Since at least the middle of the eighteenth century, magistrates, soldiers, lawyers, historians, and publicists of various kinds had been struggling to define the relationship between honor and virtue, to determine the shape of the social reform that would necessarily accompany French moral reform, and to balance the hierarchical traditions of French society against the fraternal impulses that grew out of the century's patriotic awakening. Under the pressure of the patriotic imperative, the conceptual experimentation of successive generations of civic-minded writers had yielded by the late 1770s two different visions of the connection between nobility and the French nation, visions that—despite their common patriotic pedigree—

---

122. Nearly 90 percent of noble *cahiers* expressed a willingness to abandon the nobility's fiscal privileges. See Doyle, *Origins of the French Revolution,* 144.

123. *Véritable Patriotisme; Le Patriotisme, ou Très-Humble et Très-Respectueuse Représentations du Tiers-Etat, au Roi. Par M*** Médecin de Son Altesse Royale Monsieur; Essai du Patriotisme; Le Vrai Patriote. Dissertation Philosophique et Politique, par M. Alitèphe, Citoyen Français.*

divided ever more sharply over the meaning and function of equality in civic life.

The assertions of noble corporate solidarity that marked French political discussion from the fall of 1788 were not "anachronistic" invocations of long-moribund social categories, ill-considered reactions of alarm on the part of politically naive nobles, or a convenient pretext for political radicalization carried out by "extremist" proponents of the third estate. They were expressions of a long-developing disagreement over the definition and role of the "citizen-noble" in the patriotic polity. For some—as represented by men such as Target, Servan, and Sieyès—recognition of the rights of the nation entailed recognition of the equal potential for honor, and of the natural nobility, enjoyed by every French citizen. The moral unity that bound citizens, a unity rooted in national traditions of honor and in a virtuous commitment to the well-being of the nation, implied an equality that required the elimination, or mitigation, of legal barriers between citizens. For others—such as Toustain de Richebourg and Lubersac de Livron—the moral reform necessary to protect the nation's interests required not only the general promotion of generosity and selflessness but also the specific designation of a noble class whose examples could inspire the patriotic emulation of other citizens.

The parlement's decree of September 1788, and the repeated affirmations of that decree by nobles in Paris and elsewhere in subsequent months, amounted to a definitive declaration of the social agenda built into the distinctly noble program of moral reform that had taken shape since mid-century. In rendering clear and explicit what had formerly been implicit and contested, these affirmations of noble distinctiveness shattered an illusion of inter-estate unity that had been created by reliance on a common patriotic language. Differences of emphasis within that language now hardened into antithetical visions of patriotism and nobility that would prove impossible to reconcile. Divided over the issue of equality, spokesmen for the second and third estates increasingly spoke past one another in articulating their own visions of reform. Lubersac de Livron praised the nobility in 1788 for having become "enflamed with the most patriotic zeal," but in that same year a critic of the nobility could denounce the "ridiculous" idea that one could "expect patriotism of those who have no interest in the existence of the *patrie*."[124]

The chief criterion separating the competing patriotisms that emerged

---

124. Lubersac de Livron, *Citoyen Conciliateur*, Lettre à Monsieur; *Le Gouvernement Senato-Clerico-Aristocratique* (n.p., 1788), 26.

fully into view in the course of 1788 is perhaps best illustrated in the rival conceptions of that "people of heroes" whose existence the chevalier d'Arc had first invoked in his marvelously ambiguous exposition of the French national character in 1756. The authors of two of the pamphlets whose conflicting renditions of patriotism were just cited used an identical rhetoric of exhortation whose profoundly different meanings can be understood only in light of the divergent trajectories of patriotic thought since mid-century. Having interpreted the recent revival of French national honor in different ways, the two authors drew upon the innate heroism of the French for diametrically opposed political purposes.

For the author who represented the nobility as the source of all "patriotic ideas," the creation of the desired "people of heroes" depended precisely on those "differences of condition" that the proponents of this "vaunted equality" now wished to destroy. France's "heroes," who were reminiscent of the "proud and brave knights" who served Charles VII, necessarily emerged from a restricted social circle organized around a culture expressly devoted to "generosity, integrity, [and] honor."[125] For the putative "doctor" to the royal prince, by contrast, the "male heroism" and nobility intrinsic to the French meant that "shameful exceptions" could no longer be tolerated. The "ways of honor" were grasped intuitively by all citizens, who possessed "a grand, energetic, and truly noble soul." The French would become both a "people of happy Citizens" and a "People of Heroes" once possession of the "real nobility" of sentiment became the only legitimate claim to public esteem.

The differing constitutional prescriptions embedded in these formulations of honor, nation, and nobility forecast, of course, the evidently unavoidable impasse that would propel the nation toward violent Revolution in July 1789. They also encapsulate a century's worth of debate over the social and moral meanings of French patriotism.

125. *Ouvrage d'un Gentilhomme*, 77, 19.

*Conclusion*

## PATRIOTIC REVOLUTION

One [need not] believe in the perfectibility of the social order, but this is a useful goal for legislators to propose for themselves. Thus, in this work . . . it is necessary to put aside all that
arises from the spirit of party or from present circumstances:
the superstition of royalty, the horror that the crimes we have
witnessed properly inspires, even enthusiasm for the republic, this sentiment which, in all its purity, is the highest that
man can conceive. It is time to examine the very essence of
institutions, and recognize that one great question still divides thinkers: to wit, if in all the permutations of mixed government, heredity should or should not be admitted.

MME DE STAËL
*On the Influence of the Passions on the Happiness*
*of Individuals and Nations* (1796)

The growth of French patriotism in the eighteenth century, and the rethinking of the society of orders that the phenomenon inspired and required, did not make the French Revolution inevitable. The monarchy's
multiple foreign policy failures, the subsistence crises of 1788–89, the
credit crunch of the 1780s, and the institutional paralysis that undermined
all royal efforts at reform would also need to be integrated into any comprehensive analysis of the causes of the old regime's collapse in 1789. The
passions of the Revolution cannot be traced directly to Fénelon's patriotic
virtue of "pure love," Coyer's paean to merchant glory, Montesquieu's
honor-bound intermediary bodies, or to the many writers who mediated

and reformulated the seminal ideas of these authors over the course of the eighteenth century.

As Michael Kwass's analysis of debates over royal taxation policies indicates, however, the various political and fiscal crises that preceded the old regime's final convulsions cannot be neatly separated from the patriotic sensibilities of those whose restlessness and resistance dictated events in the long lead-up to the Revolution.[1] I argue that the nature of the disagreements that launched the Revolution cannot be understood if they are extracted and isolated from the long-term process of conceptual reordering—the collective reimagining of nobility and nation—that the revival of patriotic feeling had initiated at the dawn of the eighteenth century. The sequence of events that precipitated the old regime's collapse, including the reconstitution of a "patriot party" in 1787–88, the debate over the respective powers of the estates in the upcoming Estates-General, the decision by deputies of the third estate in June 1789 to constitute a "National Assembly," the fast-developing fears of monarchical and aristocratic reaction that fueled the popular violence of July 1789, and the drafting of the Declaration of the Rights of Man and of the Citizen later in the same month, all emerged from that long public discussion about honor, virtue, and nobility that had attended the rise of French patriotic sensibilities over the course of the eighteenth century. The Revolution was not the inevitable product of that discussion, but contemporary perception of the stakes involved in pre-Revolutionary debates had been decisively shaped by its divergent themes.

Much evidence, some of it direct and some of it circumstantial, connects those themes to the ideas of important participants in the constitutional debates of 1788–89. Some of the individuals who had contributed to the French patriotic efflorescence after mid-century, such as the lawyers Servan and Target, the former officer and *homme de lettres* Toustain de Richebourg, the wizened chevalier d'Arc, and the public-spirited administrator Necker, happened to participate actively in pre-Revolutionary debates. As shown in chapter 6, many other pamphleteers who addressed the controversy over voting procedures invoked the concepts of honor, virtue, and nobility in ways that revealed their connectedness to earlier trains of patriotic thought.[2] On the basis of their educated, overwhelmingly urban,

---

1. Kwass, *Privilege and the Politics of Taxation,* 213–52 and 292–303.
2. I sampled an admittedly small set of pamphlets—about 200 of the roughly 3,000 published between the summer of 1788 and June 1789. But to keep my project manageable, I read only those titles that contained the words "patriotism," "nobility," "commoner," or "nation," or that obviously addressed the constitutional relationship between estates. The

and surprisingly Parisian backgrounds, one can also assume that the deputies to the Estates-General would have been aware of the decades-long discussion about patriotism and nobility that had filled the world of print since the middle of the century.[3] John Markoff, in his analysis of the *cahiers,* has noted that urban assemblies produced the most aggressively demanding grievance lists compiled by the second and third estates, and that the nobility of towns and cities actually tended to be more conservative than their rural counterparts.[4] The elected representatives of the nobility and the third estate at the Estates-General, three-quarters of whom came from urban centers where the presence of published literature devoted to moral and political issues can be taken for granted, may also have been disproportionately likely to have firm opinions about the proper relationship between the estates.

In any case, the lawyers, magistrates, and civic officials who made up two-thirds of the delegation of the third estate would certainly have been familiar with or receptive to the ideas of a Servan or a Target, even if they had not studied their earlier texts. Similarly, the distinguished and well-to-do families, the career army officers, and the Parisian elite who dominated the delegation of the second estate would have recognized, even if they could not always recite, the precepts of Montesquieu, Rousseau, Mirabeau, and perhaps even Buat-Nançay.[5] Even if Timothy Tackett is right that the deputies of the two estates came to Versailles with open minds and unattached to any particular brand of *philosophie,* they likely responded knowingly to moral and social arguments about patriotism whose basic contours their chief spokesmen and natural leaders would have known well.[6]

The role played by self-styled "patriots" of the 1760s and 1770s in the rhetorical battles of the pre-Revolution is certainly telling, and the social and intellectual profiles of the deputies to the Estates-General support intriguing hypotheses about the circulation and reception of patriotic lan-

rhetoric of those pamphlets—if not the precise arguments—was undoubtedly replicated in countless others. On the figures see Jeremy Popkin, *Revolutionary News: The Press in France, 1789–1799* (Durham, N.C., 1990), 25–26.

3. This profile especially fits the membership of the second and third estates at the Estates-General. Timothy Tackett notes that "if one excludes the deputy parish priests [of the first estate, who came overwhelmingly from rural parishes], the proportion of urban deputies rises to almost 75 percent—compared to only 18 percent for the overall French population" (*Becoming a Revolutionary,* 22). On the clerical membership see 24–25.

4. Markoff and Shapiro, *Revolutionary Demands,* 321.

5. Tackett writes that the delegation of the second estate was dominated by "sword nobles of ancient lineage residing in Paris or the major provincial towns" (*Becoming a Revolutionary,* 35). For the profiles of the deputies, see 22–23, 28–47.

6. Ibid., 14, 63–64.

guage in 1789. I do not argue, however, that a "discourse" of patriotism somehow enveloped the unsuspecting minds of early revolutionaries, determining their actions in ways they could not understand. "Discourses" are not historical agents. In fact, discourses do not exist at all—except in the inventive minds of outside observers who, for analytical convenience, abstract words from individual and intersubjective processes of moral and conceptual negotiation and bind them together in a putatively meaningful whole. Language is shaped and utilized in response to the endlessly complex motives, desires, beliefs, commitments, and objectives of people who are moved for their own reasons to engage in self-expression. When shared ideas coalesce around a set of words, or idiom, this merely signifies that those words have captured some of the dominant motives, attitudes, and dispositions of many individuals in a given community.

The common recourse to a language of patriotism in the political pamphlets of the pre-Revolutionary period attests to the widespread commitment to establish a basis for political fellowship and national solidarity in eighteenth-century France. This patriotic commitment had arisen from several sources dating to the early decades of the century, including dissatisfaction with the despotic tendencies of the absolutist monarchy, renewed appreciation for the political morality of the classical republics, and recognition of the need to redefine the qualities of the citizen in light of the nobility's structural deterioration, on the one hand, and its ambition to speak for a "nation," on the other hand. But the use of a common vocabulary can easily mask the diversity of ideas with which any word is associated, and evidence from the pre-Revolutionary pamphlets reveals the special, and inevitably divisive, challenge that confronted French expositors of the patriotic ideal under the old regime.

Living still in a society of orders, where the categories of the estates provided the inescapable mental framework for navigating social, legal, and political life, all who craved patriotic morals and sought to kindle feelings of patriotic fraternity had to contend with or explain the nobility's traditional claims to legal and moral distinction. As chapters 1–5 have shown, in the course of the eighteenth century the effort to reconcile patriotism and corporatism led to the assimilation of potentially conflicting and divergent ideas even in the same mind. Some promoted the honor of the nation while simultaneously recognizing the honor of the nobility, for example. Others called for a return to virtue while supporting honorific scales of distinction. Still others denounced the institution of nobility while calling for the validation of a new nobility to be based on virtuous sentiments. The commitment to patriotic morals and national solidarity required mental engagement with inherited legal and moral hierarchies, in other words, but it required no particular form of resolution to the tensions between existing schemes of social differentiation and the homogenizing impulses of patriotic citizenship.

The rhetoric of the pamphlets of 1788–89 expressed the sorting and winnowing of ideas that had long been permitted to exist side by side, and for that reason it exemplifies and encapsulates a process of conceptual refinement and prioritizing that had proceeded slowly over the course of the century. Because of the broader conceptual context in which the patriotic ideal made its appeal, one can assume that this process was traversed, with differing degrees of self-consciousness and at a pace that would have varied by circumstance, by *every* French citizen who embraced Revolutionary or reactionary ideas out of patriotic motives. The constitutional crisis that began in September 1788 had been precipitated by a confident patriotic resistance to despotism, but the crisis also served, in turn, as a crucible for condensing and clarifying assumptions about the unavoidable relationship between moral reform and social order. By requiring this process of clarification—this resettling of interpretive dispositions—the crisis inaugurated neither a distinctly "political" nor a distinctly "social" revolution, but rather a *patriotic* revolution. Drawing on conceptual resources long familiar to them, reformers reassessed the moral priorities inherent in their vision of the world and thereby sought to establish new grounds for a patriotic polity. The thoughts elicited by the constitutional crisis inevitably encompassed "social" phenomena (the validity of the society of orders, the relationship between nobility and other citizens), "political" phenomena (the definition of the citizen, the constitutional distribution of powers), "cultural" phenomena (the meaning of honor and virtue), and all else that impinges on the mind of the thinking human agent, for, as Michael Oakeshott has remarked, "there is no experience that is not a world."[7] There is no "experience," in other words, that does not present itself as part of a unified system of understanding, one that strives incessantly toward coherence.

As even the most casual student of the French Revolution knows, political debate never reached definitive conclusions after July 1789, and the ultimately irresolvable incoherence of the patriotic project impeded all efforts to achieve consensus. The patriotic revolution of 1788–89 had in fact produced several compelling but increasingly incompatible visions of the reformed polity. The vicomte d'Escherny, looking back on events from the

7. Oakeshott, *Experience and Its Modes*, 90.

vantage point of the relative calm that followed the reign of Terror (1793–94), expressed frustration over the plasticity of the term "patriotism" and represented the course of Revolutionary events as a sequential, and usually cynical, appropriation of patriotic legitimacy. From the taking of the Bastille to the pivotal massacre of radical activists by National Guardsmen in 1791 to the Jacobin purge of the Girondins in 1793 and the fall of Robespierre a year later, Escherny saw allegedly "patriotic" motives at work.

> It was *patriotism* that brought down the Bastille in '89, that set fire to chateaux, marched to Versailles, and made the king a captive at the Tuileries. These were *patriots*, with Lafayette and Bailly at their head, who fired on citizens whose *patriotism* had inspired them to assemble at the Champs de Mars around the altar of the *patrie*. These were *patriots* . . . who gathered around the constitution and the Tuileries palace on 10 August [1792] to protect both from any insult. . . . What was 31 May [1793], except a struggle between two parties both of whom claimed the mantle of *patriotism*? . . . On 9 Thermidor [27 July 1794], patriots, practicing an absolute equality, were happily vanquished by inconsequential patriots who desired equality only in theory.[8]

According to the vicomte, the future held out little prospect for change. "The idea of patriotism," he wrote, "becomes more and more impenetrable." The word had become a thick "veil" that only obscured the true intentions of those who invoked it.[9] In Escherny's eyes, *patriotism* functioned as exhibit A in the Revolution's "abuse of words," the phenomenon that so many critics of Jacobinism held responsible for the progressive radicalization of politics after the summer of 1789.[10]

Despite Escherny's assertion that the word "patriotism" had come to serve any purpose devised by its appropriators, however, the very title of the vicomte's book—*On Equality*—pointed to the key difference in perspective that had divided self-described patriots since the civic awakening of the early eighteenth century. As suggested in Madame de Staël's epigraph at the head of this chapter, the tension between equality and hereditary distinction lay behind the "one great question" that continued to afflict French politics through the 1790s and beyond. Disagreement over

8. François-Louis d'Escherny, *De l'Egalité, ou principes généraux sur les institutions civiles, politiques, et religieuses; précédé de l'Eloge de J. J. Rousseau, en forme d'introduction*, 2 vols. (Basel, 1796), 2: 454–55. All italics in the original.
9. Ibid., 477.
10. On debates over the "abus des mots," see Sophia Rosenfeld, *A Revolution in Language: The Problem of Signs in Late Eighteenth-Century France* (Stanford, 2001), esp. 181–226.

the form and degree of equality most appropriate to the French social and political order had already emerged as a widening fault line in patriotic thinking by late 1788, and the progressive articulation of the principle of equality in the course of the Revolution proved decisive in settling the priorities and loyalties of those who had had unclear or conflicting objectives in early 1789. Escherny himself had become "drunk" on revolution and had supported the initial reforms of the National Assembly. But he explained that his eventual estrangement from the movement came precisely from the revolutionaries' unrestrained enthusiasm for equality.[11]

Escherny had favored what he called a "philosophical equality," one that would pave the way for the creation of a new aristocracy "composed of all the proprietors of land and industry, of all nobles and those, such as the upper bourgeoisie, wealthy merchants, and great artists, who aspire to become [noble]; in a word, of every part of the nation that has been raised, through a liberal and painstaking education, to the dignified status of thinking being."[12] Instead, the passion for "absolute equality" and "chimerical homogeneities" had led, on 19 June 1790, to the abolition of nobility itself. This reform had violated every principle of wise government, in which "moral forces," "inequalities," and "different measures of consideration" were essential to the execution of the laws. Escherny freely admitted that the nobility of the old regime had been in need of serious reform, but why had the third estate not sought to "repair the errors of the nobility through its wisdom and moderation[?] Was it not possible to bring the nobility lower without annihilating it?"[13] Was the "pride of a republican" really so incompatible with the distinction of ranks, and was a Frenchman not capable of "casting his eyes on a superior without feeling dishonored?" Under a system in which citizens acquired nobility for the right reasons, "the Frenchman [would] see in the classes raised above him only equal citizens. . . . The great man would exist in his eyes only as a symbol of what he himself can become."[14]

The impact of the abolition of nobility on noble attitudes toward the Revolution has long been recognized. Between June 1790 and the dissolution of the National Assembly in September 1791, about one-fifth of the remaining noble deputies repudiated the Assembly's work and left France to join the gathering counter-Revolutionary armies. At the end of 1792, Rabaut Saint-Etienne—who had been among the first to wield the pejora-

---

11. Escherny, De l'Egalité, "Eloge de J. J. Rouseau, en forme d'introduction," 1: vii.
12. Ibid., 1: 69–70. For the phrase "philosophical equality" see 2: 124.
13. Ibid., 1: 199, 61.
14. Ibid., 2: 123.

tive term "aristocrat" as a stigmatizing weapon—looked regretfully back on 19 June 1790 as the moment when "the majority of the nobles of the kingdom became the irreconcilable enemies of the Constitution."[15] Much anecdotal evidence supports his claim. The comte de Sanois, who applauded the abolition of feudalism on 4 August 1789, nevertheless pronounced the Assembly's action of 19 June 1790 "inconceivable."[16] Even the noble lawyer Servan, who had railed effectively against privileges and was hailed by the firebrand Desmoulins in 1789 as "the first to call the French to liberty," was soon persuaded to disavow "democratic" principles, and he eventually emigrated to Switzerland, despite his having "passionately desired" the Revolution "that now chases me from my home."[17] Toustain de Richebourg, who actually remained in France and who pointed proudly to his longstanding reputation as a "warm partisan" of "equal and social" liberty, also criticized the Assembly for "rigorously forbidding all forms of distinction." In a public letter of October 1792 in which he identified himself as "Charles Gaspard Toustain, Citizen of the Section of the Temple," he vowed every effort to conserve the sentiments of his ancestors, those "hereditary principles which won the acclaim and consideration of their superiors, their peers, and their inferiors, [those] sentiments and principles that constitute this imperishable *nobility* whose titles are those of virtue."[18]

The abolition of nobility clearly made a difference in the lives of individuals and in the course of the Revolution, but if the event surprised contemporaries at all, this was only because of the underhanded legislative strategy by which the radical egalitarians carried out their designs—under cover of night, with few nobles present to express their opposition—and by the utter finality of the measure they passed (Figure 12). Rumors of the nobility's abolition had been circulating since late 1789, after all, and one of the noble deputies who expressed his indignation over the decree of 19

15. Tackett, *Becoming a Revolutionary*, 295. On Rabaud's early use of "aristocrat," see J.-M.-A. Servan's pamphlets of March and April 1790, *Seconde Lettre à M. Rabaud de St.-Etienne*, and *Troisième Lettre à M. Rabaud de St-Etienne*.

16. Michael P. Fitzsimmons, *The Night the Old Regime Ended: August 4, 1789, and the French Revolution* (University Park, Pa., 2003), 130.

17. For the remarks by Desmoulins, see *Les Révolutions de France et de Brabant*, no. 1, 28 November 1789, as cited in Robert Chagny, "Mounier et Barnave," in *Les débuts de la Révolution française en Dauphiné, 1788–1791*, ed. Vital Chomel (Grenoble, 1988), 231–58, esp. 249. On Servan's disavowal of democratic principles, see *Troisième Lettre à M. Rabaud de St-Etienne*, 4. On his emigration in 1792, see his manuscript journal cited in *Oeuvres choisies*, ed. Portets, 1: xcviii. For more on Servan's life after 1792, see *Oeuvres choisies*, 1: xcv–cxxv; and *Dictionnaire historique et biographique de la Révolution et de l'Empire, 1789–1815*, ed. Jean-François-Eugène Robinet, 2 vols. (Paris, 1899): 2: 749.

18. *JE*, 1792, vol. 8, 517–18, 522.

*de Tlack*

DÉDIÉ À LA NOBLESSE SAVONNÉE

LA MARQUE DES SOTS.

*Aussi-tôt maint esprit fécond en reveries
Invente le blason avec les armories*

*L'Homme de mérite va sans marque ni sur-nom
Et de ces ayeux n'emprunte jamais le nom*

FIGURE 12. "The mark of the fool." This anonymous engraving commemorates the abolition of titles of nobility on 19 June 1790. Its "dedication" to the former nobility makes an ironic allusion to the "savonette à vilain," the so-called cleansing of common status that the acquisition of noble titles supposedly effected under the old regime. Here all signs of nobility—genealogies, coats of arms, titles—are being "cleansed" by the feces of demons. Bibliothèque Nationale de France

June admitted that he had expected nothing better from this "illegal and monstrous" assembly.[19] "Divided since its origin," he wrote, the assembly's "birth" had been the harbinger of "trouble."[20]

The Estates-General had especially been "divided," of course, over the respective rights of nobility and third estate in a patriotic polity, and the abolition of nobility, with the outrage it provoked, continued and culminated the moral arguments about honor and equality that had infused the differing reformist visions articulated in 1788–89. One indignant defender of the nobility named La Croix, who claimed to have provided past "proofs of the patriotism that animates every true Frenchman," attacked the increas-

19. On the rumors, see Fitzsimmons, *The Night the Old Regime Ended,* 118; and Tackett, *Becoming a Revolutionary,* 292.
20. Comte de Reuilly, *Protestation du comte de Reuilly, Député de la noblesse du bailliage de Châlons en Bourgogne, contre toutes les opérations de l'assemblée se disant nationale* (n.p., n.d.).

ingly common perception that the ancients had promoted patriotism by establishing a perfect equality between citizens.[21] Sparta had lacked an order of nobility, he wrote, but only because citizenship itself functioned there as a distinction reserved for the few. The practitioners of "lucrative" and "mercenary" professions had been expressly forbidden to enter the army, which opened the only path to citizenship in Sparta. "Thus, far from citing Greek usage as proof that a people can do without nobles, it is truer to say that the republics of Greece were composed only of nobles."[22] Those offended by the title of nobility might justifiably substitute the word "citizen" for "noble," but distinction itself—and the moral excellence represented by distinctions—must be maintained. Instead of abolishing nobility, the National Assembly should consider recreating the orders of chivalry, restoring the point of honor, and reviving the tournament and the joust. Commoners could even be systematically "aggregated" to the new orders of chivalry through the reservation of certain positions of command from which hereditary nobles would be excluded. In recovering the old ways, La Croix asserted, the Assembly would not only promote "the most energetic courage," which could be employed "at all times when the *patrie* is in danger," but would also renew nobility by making it "the consecration of virtue."[23]

Others critical of the abolition of nobility also invoked the traditions of honor with which the second estate had long been identified. The marquis de Ferrières, for example, lamented the nobility's loss of its titles and honorific distinctions precisely because those symbols "most recall the feudal system and the spirit of chivalry."[24] An anonymous pamphleteer of 1790 even insisted that the "descendants of these heroes" from "the centuries of chivalry"—the author predictably mentioned DuGuesclin, Bayard, la Hire, and other luminaries—should be called on to revive "the noble ambition of their ancestors" and to expand the dominion of the French, perhaps by conquering Egypt![25] But such defenses of the principle of noble distinctiveness generally failed to acknowledge the diametrically opposed, and essentially egalitarian, definitions of honor that lay behind the opposition to legal hierarchies.

Jacques-Antoine Dulaure, for example, authored a *Critical History of the Nobility* (1790) that repudiated nobility and the whole historical apparatus that went along with it. His anger derived precisely from the nobility's

21. M. de La Croix, *Hommage à ma Patrie. Considérations sur la Noblesse de France* (France, 1790), 1.

22. Ibid., 12.

23. Ibid., 6, 39, 41, 44.

24. Tackett, *Becoming a Revolutionary,* 295.

25. *Les Intérêts de la Nation, conciliés avec ceux de la Noblesse* (Paris, 1790), 7–8.

misappropriation of the term "honor," which he defined through an un-compromisingly egalitarian lens. Dulaure claimed that the eighteenth cen-tury's idealization of the age of chivalry, which had been done in part to boost the self-image of all French citizens, had been misguided from the start. "I am not like these moralists, dramatic historians, or publicists who, by ignorance, routine, interest, or fear, accept and reproduce the self-serv-ing lies about the so-called historic period of our past, so as to soothe or excite national pride."[26] Such texts always celebrated the honor of me-dieval seigneurs, but "their kind of honor," Dulaure charged, had merely presented a fraudulent disguise behind which they practiced "the shame-ful métier of brigand."[27] The honor boasted by *gentilshommes,* he insisted, "was immoral, destructive, opposed to laws and common sense, and com-pletely different from true honor."[28] Any sound government found its "strength and honor" in "equality of rights." The continued existence of hereditary nobility, an institution that had perpetuated and been sup-ported by a false notion of honor, would only represent "a crime against the rights of that part of the nation deprived of it."[29] Resuming a theme touched on by many writers over the decades, Dulaure here suggested that "nobility" could be considered legitimate only if it included all citizens.

In a pamphlet written before the formal abolition of nobility, but di-rected against the point of honor and the noble custom of dueling, Philippe-Antoine Grouvelle likewise rejected the conventional association between the morality of the nobility and the historical essence of the French character. Before the nation had assembled to draft a constitution, asserted Grouvelle, the Frenchman was "without a character, without his own prejudices, just as he was without liberty."[30] Responding in particular to Montesquieu's venerable argument that honor had been the principle of the French character, Grouvelle flatly declared that "there is no national character, or national prejudices, except among a free People." As for the "opinion" upon which honor had supposedly rested in the past—and whose assumed power still motivated duelists in 1790—Grouvelle ex-plained that opinion, too, had been perversely defined in the "times of an-archy" and "anti-social barbarism."[31] Those who lived with the "false" perceptions of the past believed that honor could be adjudicated by "a mul-

26. J.-A. Dulaure, *Histoire Critique de la Noblesse* (Paris, 1790), 259.

27. Ibid., 259, 47.

28. Ibid., 314.

29. Ibid., iii–iv.

30. Philippe-Antoine Grouvelle, *Adresse des Habitans du ci-devant bailliage de . . . A M. de\*\*\*, leur Député à l'Assemblée Nationale; Sur son Duel & sur le préjugé du Point d'Honneur* (Paris, 1790), 39.

31. Ibid., 11.

titude of brigands, or debased men." But "what is OPINION? Opinion . . . is the sentiment and judgment of the greater number, whether about men or things. Opinion is therefore a moral power that resides, like all powers, in the People." This word *people* "is no longer equivocal. It encompasses the entirety of active Citizens."[32]

As Grouvelle explained it, the meaning of honor, as well as its distribution and its affirmation, now depended on the collective judgment of a "free" people, and all citizens must be regarded as having the right to participate equally in its regulation. "Of all the social superstitions," he charged, "that of false honor, the one most opposed to a civic regime, should be the first to suffer a withering indictment before the emergent Civic Tribunal."[33] Indeed, persuaded that the continuing manifestations of "false" honor posed anti-patriotic dangers to their work, and moved by the imperative to recognize the moral equality of all citizens, a majority of the deputies present at the National Assembly on 19 June 1790 confronted the nobility, along with all its honorific distinctions, and simply legislated them out of existence. The Assembly's measure neatly symbolized the collective migration of the third estate, and of some nobles, toward a position summarized in 1789 by the disillusioned Servan: "without equality, all morality is a chimera."[34]

Even though the event occurred just one year after the third estate had fatefully decided that representatives of the nobility were not needed for the constitution of a "National Assembly," and though it came at a time when many nobles still conceived a distinct moral identity and a special patriotic role for themselves, the Assembly's measure effectively ended—for a time—the long process of reimagining nobility, a process that had been central to the French civic consciousness for nearly a century. By erasing the external signs that had formerly separated nobles from commoners, the Assembly finalized the nation's appropriation of moral qualities once identified with the nobility, and it removed a telling ambiguity from a patriotic project that had confusingly impelled the celebration of both "citizens" and "nobles"—for similar reasons and through a nearly identical language. The suppression of hereditary nobility announced the emergence of a patriotic culture in which French "nobility" of character would be taken for granted, even though its relationship to "the nobility" would not be discussed (Figure 13).

32. Ibid., 31–32.
33. Ibid., 40.
34. Servan, *Avis salutaire*, 30.

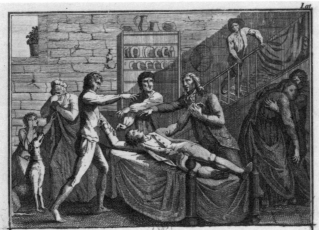

FIGURE 13. "Stoicism of a Republican of Givet" (1795). After the death of a brave young civilian who had confronted three enemy "hussards" caught pillaging "the land of his father," his two brothers swear to avenge his loss while the stoical father exclaims, "O, my patrie! My children are worthy of their country, as they are [worthy] of their father." The classical and gendered imagery of the composition recalls David's *Oath of the Horatii* (1785), but the melodramatic poses assumed by the four central characters also suggest the emotional states of the soldiers shown earlier surrounding the heroes Bayard and Toiras. The scene captures the Revolutionary and republican ideal of a nobility of character that transcended social status. Bibliothèque Nationale de France

Within the successive regimes that ruled France after 1790, however, the tensions between hierarchy and equality that had been inherited from the patriotic thinking of the old regime never receded fully from consciousness. In the quarter-century after 1789, the devotees of the cult of the citizen continued to balance their various intellectual and moral commitments in ways that betrayed lingering respect for rank and distinction and recalled the pre-Revolutionary nobility's patriotic quest for glory. Following Robespierre's austere reign of "virtue," for example, reformers in the republican army sought a variety of ways to reintroduce a system of rewards based on honorific distinctions and conspicuous enhancements of the soldier's moral status.[35] A thirst for distinction characterized civil servants, journalists, soldiers, and all who rejected the label of "bourgeois" throughout much of the nineteenth century, and the social habits observed under the Restoration and the July Monarchy suggested a taste for exclusiveness that recalled the salons and provincial academies of the old regime.[36] Napoleon's creation of a Legion of Honor in 1802 and the reappearance of nobility in 1808—albeit in a new, imperial guise—likewise revived the hardy ideal of a nobility of merit, an ideal that predated the Revolution and would have looked strangely familiar to writers as diverse as Servan, Holbach, Toustain de Richebourg, Servan de Gerbey, and Target.[37]

The Napoleonic ideal aimed at the formation of an elite that combined rank and distinction, on the one hand, with the principles of equality of opportunity and passionate civic commitment, on the other hand. Under the old regime, the simultaneous and increasingly vigorous promotion of two loosely conceived "programs" of patriotic reform prevented that broadly appealing ideal from ever generating consensus. One of the two programs, whose main outlines reappeared from the time of Fénelon through the mid-century heyday of Mirabeau to the prescriptions of Buat-Nançay, Varennes, and others in the 1770s and 1780s, had aimed at the restoration of a traditionally honor-bound nobility, a nobility that would seek to emulate the virtues of the ancients while fraternally embracing common citizens and serving as an honored object of emulation for all

35. John Lynn, "Toward an Army of Honor: The Moral Evolution of the French Army, 1789–1815," *FHS* 16 (1989): 152–82.

36. See Anne Martin-Fugier, *La vie élégante, ou la formation du tout-Paris, 1815–1848* (Paris, 1990); William Reddy, *The Invisible Code: Honor and Sentiment in Postrevolutionary France, 1814–1848* (Berkeley, 1997); and Maza, *Myth of the French Bourgeoisie*, 120–30, 180–90.

37. For discussion of Napoleon's "improbable synthesis," see Blaufarb, *The French Army*, 164–93.

conscientious Frenchmen. The other program, discernible in the peda-
gogy of Rollin, promoted aggressively in the polemics of Coyer and his admirers, and given new impetus by the "nationalization" of honor in the
1760s and 1770s, aimed at the dismantling of desiccated legal barriers between citizens and the inculcation of a civic morality that subordinated all
marks of status to the greater imperative of fraternal union. Although various hybrid positions emerged along the margins of these two developing
patriotisms of the old regime, the mutually repellent images of unrestrained equality and undeserved hereditary privilege rendered impossible a meeting of the minds in the years before 1789.

Mona Ozouf notes that literature provides historians an "incomparable
observatory" for studying what she calls the nineteenth century's "hundred years war between the Old Regime and the Revolution." Central to
this war of memory was a search for a "solution to the contradiction" between the democratic legacy of the Revolution and the "aristocratic values"
that the French could not bring themselves to abandon. Novelists and po-
ets waged their campaign, Ozouf explains, by carrying out a project of "hy-
bridization" (*métissage*). They obsessively imagined the creation of "new
elites, issued from the depths of democratic society, but still aristocratic in
their morals and style."[38] The proponents of honor and virtue had attempted much the same thing in the century before the Revolution, but
the patriotic imagination of the old regime had been so haunted by the
twin specters of equality and heredity that their efforts ultimately fell short.
Perhaps the ground for compromise could be located, at least in the imagination, only after extreme visions of egalitarian and hierarchical polities
had both been repudiated. The French resumed the process of rethinking
the nature of elite status in a patriotic nation only after they had absorbed
images of tyranny and social dissolution more terrifying than any of the
threats conjured by Arc, Coyer, or their collaborators.

38. Mona Ozouf, *Les Aveux du Roman: Le dix-neuvième siècle entre ancien régime et Révolution*
(Paris, 2001), 10, 20–21.

# Bibliography

**Primary Sources**

*Manuscripts*

Bibliothèque Nationale de France
Manuscrits Français 9174, ff. 16–52, "Idées sur quelques objets militaires, adressé aux jeunes officiers." 1784.

Archives Nationales
M 640, no. 6. "Mémoire sur la Discipline et les moiens propres à détruire l'esprit de désertion dans les Troupes Françaises, par M. le Marquis de Beaupoil St. Aulaire, Capitaine reformé au Regiment Provincial de Soissons." [1776?].
M 640, no. 4. "Observations pour servir à un plan de Constitution militaire, selon le génie des français, par Laureau, Capitaine d'Infanterie." [1772].
M 650, no. 3. Vicomte de Flavigny. "Le Militaire Patriote." [1771].

Service Historique de l'Armée de Terre
MR 1709, no. 54. "Projet d'un militaire." [after 1763].
MR 1709, no. 15. "Réflections sur la Constitution Militaire." [1762–63].
MR 1711, no. 101. Duchesne de Bettencourt. "Observations intéressantes sur les troupes, relativement aux Vétérans." 1771.
MR 1781, no. 70. "Mémoire sur l'éducation des jeunes militaires et sur la composition des officiers des Regts d'Infanterie française, par Blangermont, capne au regt. D'Austrasie." [1777–1780].

### Contemporary Journals/Newspapers

*Année Littéraire*
*Journal Encyclopédique*
*Journal de Trévoux*
*Mercure de France*

### Printed Primary Sources

Aguesseau, Henri-François d'. *Oeuvres*, 13 vols. Paris, 1759.

Alès de Corbet, Pierre-Alexandre, vicomte d'. *Nouvelles Observations sur les Deux Systèmes de la Noblesse Commerçante ou Militaire*. Amsterdam, 1758.

——. *Origine de la Noblesse Françoise, depuis l'Etablissement de la Monarchie, contre le système des Lettres imprimées à Lyon en 1763. Dédiée A La Noblesse Françoise*. Paris, 1766.

Arc, Philippe Auguste de Sainte-Foy, chevalier d'. *De la convocation des Etats-Généraux, et de la Nécessité de Former un Quatrième Ordre de l'Etat*. N.p., 1789.

——. *La noblesse militaire, opposée à La noblesse commerçante: Ou le patriote français*. Amsterdam, 1756.

Argenson, R. L. de Voyer de Paulmy, marquis d'. *Considérations sur le gouvernement ancien et présent de la France*. Amsterdam, 1765.

*L'Armée Française au Conseil de la Guerre*. N.p., 1789.

Aubusson, P. A., vicomte d'. *Adresse à Messieurs de l'Ordre de la Noblesse*. Paris, 1789.

Av***, M. le marquis d'. *Réflexions en faveur de la Noblesse*. N.p., n.d.

Bachaumont, Louis Petit de. *Mémoires Secrets pour Servir à l'Histoire de la République des Lettres en France, depuis 1762 jusqu'à nos jours*. 36 vols. London, 1777–89.

[Baptestin, Raup de]. *Mémoire sur un moyen facile et infaillible de faire renaître le Patriotisme en France, dans toutes les classes des Citoyens, comme dans les deux sexes; et d'assurer le remboursement des dettes de l'Etat, sans nouveaux impôts, sans emprunt, et sans faire éprouver aucune reduction*. Amsterdam, 1789.

Barthès de Marmorières. *Nouveaux Essais sur la Noblesse, où, après avoir recherché l'origine & l'état civil de l'homme noble chez les peuples connus, on se propose de le guider dans les différens âges & emplois de la vie*. Neuchâtel, 1781.

Barthez, M. de. *Libre Discours sur la Prérogative que doit avoir la Noblesse dans la Constitution et dans les Etats Généraux*. Paris, 1789.

Basset de La Marelle, Louis. *La Différence du Patriotisme National chez les François et chez les Anglois*. Paris, 1766.

Beaumarchais, Pierre Auguste Caron de. *Le Mariage de Figaro*. Edited by E. J. Arnould. Oxford, 1952.

Beaumont, Elie de. *Discours sur le Patriotisme dans la Monarchie*. Bordeaux, 1777.

[Bedos]. *Le négociant patriote*. Brussels and Paris, 1779.

Belot, Octavie Guichot, dame. *Observations sur la noblesse et le tiers-état*. Amsterdam, 1758.

——. *Réflexions d'une provinciale, sur le discours de m. Rousseau, touchant l'origine de l'inégalité des conditions parmi les hommes*. London, 1756.

Bohan, François-Philippe Loubat, baron de. *Examen critique du militaire français.* 2 vols. Geneva, 1781.

Bolingbroke, Henry St. John, Viscount. *Bolingbroke's Political Writings: The Conservative Enlightenment.* Edited by Bernard Cottret. Houndmills, 1997.

Bonneval. *Les Elémens et Progrès de l'Education, par M. de Bonneval.* Paris, 1743.

Boulainvilliers, Henry de. *Essais sur la Noblesse de France, contenans une dissertation sur son origine & abaissement.* Amsterdam, 1732.

———. *Histoire de l'ancien gouvernement de la France: avec XIV lettres historiques sur les parlements ou états généraux.* 3 vols. Amsterdam, 1727.

Boussanelle, Louis de. *Aux Soldats.* Paris, 1786.

———. *Le Bon Militaire.* Paris, 1770.

Brizard, Gabriel. *Modestes observations sur le Mémoire des Princes, Faites au nom de 23 millions de Citoyens Français.* N.p., 1788.

Brucourt, chevalier de. *Essai sur l'éducation de la noblesse,* 2 vols. Paris, 1748.

Buat-Nançay, Louis-Gabriel Du. *Eléments de la Politique, ou Recherche des Vrais Principes de l'Economie Sociale.* 6 vols. London, 1773.

———. *Histoire ancienne des peuples de l'Europe.* Paris, 1772.

———. *Les Origines, ou l'ancien Gouvernement de la France, de l'Italie, de l'Allemagne.* 4 vols. The Hague, 1757.

———. *Tableau du gouvernement actuel de l'empire d'Allemagne.* Paris, 1755.

Bury, M. de. *Essai Historique et Moral sur l'Education Françoise.* Paris, 1777.

Champdevaux. *L'Honneur considéré en lui-même, et relativement au duel.* Paris, 1752.

[Chansierges, M. de.] *L'Idée d'un Roy Parfait. Dans laquelle on découvre la véritable Grandeur, avec les moyens de l'acquérir.* Paris, 1723.

Chastenay Saint Georges, vicomte de. *Lettre d'un gentilhomme bourguignon à un gentilhomme breton, sur l'attaque du tiers-état, la division de la noblesse et l'intérêt des cultivateurs.* N.p., 1789.

Chérin, Louis-Nicolas-Hyacinthe. *La Noblesse considérée sous ses divers rapports, Dans les Assemblées Générales & Particulières de la Nation, ou Représentations des Etats-Généraux et Assemblées de Notables, pour et contre les Nobles.* Paris, 1788.

*Le Citoyen philosophe, ou examen critique de La Noblesse Militaire. Dédié à M. l'Abbé Coyer.* N.p., 1756.

*Collection complètte de tous les ouvrages pour et contre m. Necker.* Utrecht, 1782.

[Cordier, Jean-Baptiste]. *L'Ave du Tiers Etat, Suivi de la Profession de Foi de cet Ordre; pour servir de suite au Pater, par M. C . . . R, roturier angevin.* N.p., n.d.

*Correspondance Littéraire, Philosophique et Critique, par Grimm, Diderot, Raynal, Meister, etc.* 16 vols. Paris, 1877–82.

Coyer, Gabriel-François. *Développement et défense du système de la noblesse commerçante,* 2 vols. Amsterdam & Paris, 1757.

———. *La noblesse commerçante.* London, 1756.

———. *Plan d'Education Publique.* Paris, 1770.

———. *Gabriel-François Coyer, Jacob-Nicolas Moreau: Ecrits sur le patriotisme, l'esprit public, & la propagande au milieu du XVIIIe siècle.* Edited by Edmond Dziembowski. La Rochelle, 1997.

Crevier, Jean-Baptiste. *Observations sur le Livre de l'Esprit des Lois.* Paris, 1764.

*De l'éducation d'un jeune seigneur.* Paris, 1728.

Denesle. *Les Préjugés du Public sur l'Honneur, avec des Observations Critiques, Morales, & Historiques.* 3 vols. Paris, 1766.

*Dictionnaire de l'Académie Française,* eds. of 1694, 1718, 1740, 1762, 1798.

*Dictionnaire universel françois et latin.* Paris, 1704.

*Discours sur les droits, les devoirs & les fonctions des sept Classes de Citoyens, qui composent le Corps politique.* N.p., n.d.

Duclos, Charles-Pinot. *Les Confessions du Comte de ***.* Edited by Laurent Versini. Paris, 1969.

———. *Considérations sur les moeurs de ce siècle.* Edited by F. C. Green. Cambridge, 1939.

Dudevant, L. *L'Apologie du commerce, essai philosophique et politique, avec des notes instructives: suivi de diverses réflexions sur le commerce en général, sur celui de la France en particulier, & sur les moyens propres à l'accroître & le perfectionner. Par un jeune négociant.* Geneva, 1777.

———. *Stabilité et garantie de la république française, une et indivisible. Moeurs républicaines. Adressé à la convention nationale.* Agen, Year III.

Dulaure, Jacques-Antoine. *Histoire Critique de la Noblesse.* Paris, 1790.

Du Perron, Anquetil. *Dignité du Commerce, et de l'Etat de Commerçant.* N.p., 1789.

Du Pradel, Jean. *Traité Contre le Luxe des Hommes et des Femmes, et contre le luxe avec lequel on élève les enfans de l'un & de l'autre sexe.* Paris, 1705.

[Dutot, Charles.] *Réflexions politiques sur les finances et le commerce,* 2 vols. The Hague, 1738.

*Encyclopédie, ou Dictionnaire Raisonné des Sciences, des Arts et des Métiers, par une Société de Gens de Lettres.* Neuchâtel, 1765; repr. Parma, 1970.

Escherny, François-Louis d'. *De l'Egalité, ou principes généraux sur les institutions civiles, politiques, et religieuses; précédé de l'Eloge de J. J. Rousseau, en forme d'introduction.* 2 vols. Basel, 1796.

*Essai du Patriotisme.* N.p., 1789.

*Essais Critiques sur l'Etat Actuel de l'Esprit Public; ou Elemens de Patriotisme, à l'usage des Français.* Brussels, 1789.

Ey, M. d'. *L'Esprit du Militaire, ou Entretiens avec Moi-même.* Paris, 1771.

Fénelon, François de La Mothe-. *Ecrits et Lettres Politiques.* Edited by Charles Urbain. Paris, 1920.

———. *Telemachus, Son of Ulysses.* Edited by Patrick Riley. Cambridge, 1994.

Fillassier, Jean-Jacques. *Dictionnaire Historique d'Education.* 2 vols. Paris, 1771.

Flammermont, Jules, ed. *Remontrances du Parlement de Paris au XVIIIe Siècle (1715–1788).* 3 vols. Paris, 1888–98.

Forbonnais, François Véron Duverger de. *Lettre à M.F., ou examen politique des prétendus inconvéniens de la faculté de commercer en gros, sans déroger à la noblesse.* N.p., 1756.

[Forges, comte de.] *Des véritables intérêts de la patrie.* Rotterdam, 1764.

Fresnais de Beaumont, M. *La Noblesse Cultivatrice, ou Moyens d'élever en France la Culture de toutes les Denrées que son Sol comporte, au plus haut degré de production, & de l'y fixer irrévocablement, sans que l'Etat soit assujetti à aucunes dépenses nouvelles; ces Moyens portant sur le mobile de l'amour-propre.* Paris, 1778.

[Garnier, Jean-Jacques.] *Le Commerce Remis à sa Place: Réponse d'un Pédant de Collège aux Novateurs Politiques, adressé à l'auteur de la Lettre à M.F.* N.p., 1756.

Godard d'Aucourt, Claude. *L'Académie Militaire, ou Les Héros Subalternes.* 2 vols. N.p., 1745–46.

*Le Gouvernement Senato-Clerico-Aristocratique.* N.p., 1788.

Grouvelle, Philippe-Antoine. *Adresse des Habitans du ci-devant bailliage de . . . A M. de\*\*\*, leur Député à l'Assemblée Nationale; Sur son Duel & sur le préjugé du Point d' Honneur.* Paris, 1790.

——. *De l'autorité de Montesquieu dans la révolution présente.* N.p., 1789.

Guibert, Jacques-Antoine-Hippolyte de. *Ecrits Militaires, 1772–1790.* Paris, 1977.

——. *Projet de Discours d'un Citoyen, aux trois ordres de l'Assemblée de Berry.* N.p., 1789.

[Guiraudet, Charles-Philippe-Toussaint]. *Qu'est-ce que la nation? et qu'est-ce que la France?* N.p., 1789.

Hénault, Charles-Jean-François. *Nouvel abrégé chronologique de l'histoire de France, contenant les Evénemens de notre histoire, depuis Clovis jusqu'à Louis XIV, les Guerres, les Batailles, les Sièges, etc. Nos loix, nos moeurs, nos usages, etc.* 2 vols. Paris, 1756.

[Holbach, Paul Henri Thiry, baron d'.] *Ethocratie, ou le Gouvernement fondé sur la morale.* Amsterdam, 1776.

*Les Intérêts de la Nation, conciliés avec ceux de la Noblesse.* Paris, 1790.

Jaubert, Pierre. *Eloge de la Roture, dédié aux Roturiers.* London, 1766.

La Bruyère, Jean de. *Les caractères de Théophraste, traduits du Grec, avec Les caractères, ou les moeurs de ce siècle.* Edited by Robert Pignarre. Paris, 1965.

La Chalotais, Caradeuc de. *Essai d'éducation nationale, ou plan d'études pour la jeunesse.* N.p., 1763.

Laclos, Pierre Ambroise Choderlos de. *Les Liaisons Dangereuses.* Edited by Yves Le Hir. Paris, 1961.

La Croix, M. de. *Hommage à ma Patrie. Considérations sur la Noblesse de France.* France, 1790.

La Curne de Sainte-Palaye, Jean Baptiste de. *Memoirs of Ancient Chivalry. To which are added, the anecdotes of the times, from the romance writers and historians of those ages.* London, 1784.

Lambert, Madame de. *Oeuvres.* Edited by Robert Granderoute. Paris, 1990.

Lefebvre de Beauvray, Pierre-Claude-Rigobert. *Dictionnaire Social et Patriotique, ou Précis Raisonné de Connaissances relatives à l'Economie Morale, Civile & Politique.* Amsterdam, 1770.

*Lettres d'un Homme à un autre Homme, sur les affaires du temps,* in *Les Efforts de la Liberté & du Patriotisme contre le Despotisme du Sr de Maupeou, Chancelier de France, ou Recueil des écrits patriotiques publiés pour maintenir l'ancien Gouvernement Français.* London, 1775.

Lubersac de Livron, Charles-François. *Le Citoyen Conciliateur, contenant des idées sommaires politiques et morales sur le gouvernement monarchique de la France.* Paris, 1788.

Lucet, [Jean-Claude]. *Pensées recueillies de l'Histoire Ancienne et du Traité des Etudes de M. Rollin.* Paris, 1780.

Mably, Gabriel Bonnot de. *Entretiens de Phocion, sur le rapport de la morale avec la politique.* Amsterdam, 1763.

[M.C.C.A]. *Le Négociant Citoyen, ou Essai dans la Recherche des Moyens d'augmenter les lumières de la Nation sur le Commerce & l'Agriculture.* Amsterdam, 1764.

Mandeville, Bernard. *The Fable of the bees; or, Private vices, public benefits.* Edited by Douglas Gorman. London, 1974.

Marchand, J. H. *La Noblesse Commerçable ou Ubiquiste.* Amsterdam, 1756.

Mathon de La Cour, Charles-Joseph. *Collection de comptes rendus, pièces authentiques, états et tableaux concernant les finances de France.* Lausanne, 1788.

———. *Discours sur les Meilleurs Moyens de Faire Naître et d'Encourager le Patriotisme dans une Monarchie, qui a remporté le prix dans l'académie de Châlons-sur-Marne, le 25 août 1787.* Paris, 1787.

Maugard, Antoine. *Remarques sur la noblesse.* Paris, 1788.

Mignot de Bussy. *Lettres sur l'origine de la noblesse françoise, et sur la manière dont elle s'est conservée jusqu'à nos jours.* Lyon, 1763.

Mirabeau, Victor de Riqueti, marquis de. *L'Ami des Hommes, ou Traité de la Population.* 2 vols. Avignon, 1756; reprint, Darmstadt, 1970.

Montesquieu, Charles-Louis de Secondat, baron de. *Considérations sur les causes de la grandeur des Romains et de leur décadence.* Paris, 1987.

———. *De l'Esprit des Lois.* Edited by Laurent Versini. 2 vols. Paris, 1995.

———. *Lettres Persanes.* Edited by Laurent Versini. Paris, 1986.

Moreau Le Jeune. *Figures de l'Histoire de France, dessinées par M. Moreau Le Jeune, et gravées sous sa direction; avec le discours de Monsieur l'Abbé Garnier.* Paris, 1785.

Necker, Jacques. *De l'Administration des Finances de la France.* 2 vols. N.p., 1785.

*La Noblimanie.* N.p., 1789.

*Observations sur le préjugé de la Noblesse Héréditaire.* London, 1789.

*Ouvrage d'un Citoyen, Gentilhomme et Militaire, ou Lettres sur la Noblesse, qui présentent le tableau de son origine, de ses droits, dénoncent les abus en indiquant les moyens d'y remédier, & d'opérer des changemens importants pour ce corps & la patrie.* London, 1787.

*Le Patriotisme, ou Très-Humble et Très Respectueuse Représentations du Tiers Etat, par M*** Médecin de Son Altesse Royale.* N.p., 1789.

Plumard de Dangeul, Louis-Joseph. *Remarques sur les Avantages et les Desavantages de la France et de la Grande Bretagne, par rapport au commerce.* Leyden, 1754.

[Poncelet.] *Principes Généraux pour servir à l'éducation des enfans, particulièrement de la Noblesse Françoise.* 3 vols. Paris, 1763.

Prezel, Honoré Lacombe de. *Dictionnaire du citoyen, ou Abrégé historique, théorique, et pratique du commerce.* 2 vols. Paris, 1761.

Prévost, Abbé Antoine François. *Manon Lescaut.* Translated by Leonard Tancock. New York, 1991.

*Projet d'Ecoles Publiques, qui répondront aux voeux de la nation, & dont l'exercice n'exige que quatre professeurs.* Bordeaux, n.d.

Ramsay, Andrew Michael. *Histoire de la vie de M. François de Salignac de la Motte-Fénelon.* Paris, 1723.

[Reboul]. *Essai sur les moeurs du temps.* London, 1768.

*Réclamation du Tiers Etat aux Etats-Généraux.* N.p., n.d.

*Réflexions Politiques sur la Question Proposée par l'Académie de Châlons: Quels sont les moyens de faire naître & d'encourager la Patriotisme dans une Monarchie, sans altérer ni gêner le pouvoir exécutif propre à ce genre de Gouvernement.* N.p., n.d.

*Réponse à la Question Quels sont les moyens, conciliables avec la Législation Française, d'animer & d'étendre le Patriotisme dans le Tiers Etat? Proposée pour sujet du Concours en 1790, par la Société Royale des Sciences & Arts de Metz.* N.p., n.d.

Reuilly, comte de. *Protestation du comte de Reuilly, Député de la noblesse du bailliage de Châlons en Bourgogne, contre toutes les opérations de l'assemblée se disant nationale.* N.p., n.d.

Richelieu, Armand-Jean du Plessis, cardinal de. *Testament Politique de Richelieu.* Edited by Françoise Hildesheimer. Paris, 1995.

Rollin, Charles. *Traité des Etudes. De la manière d'Enseigner et d'Etudier les Belles Lettres, par rapport à l'esprit et au Coeur.* 4 vols. Paris, 1805.

Rossel, M. *Histoire du patriotisme François, ou Nouvelle Histoire de France, Dans laquelle on s'est principalement attaché à décrire les traits de Patriotisme qui ont illustré nos Rois, la Noblesse, & le Peuple François, depuis l'origine de la Monarchie jusqu'à nos jours.* 6 vols. Paris, 1769.

Rouillé d'Orfeuil, Augustin. *L'Alambic des Loix, ou Observations de l'Ami des François sur l'Homme et sur les Loix.* Hispaan, 1773.

Rousseau, Jean-Jacques. *Discours sur les Sciences et les Arts.* Edited by George R. Havens. New York, 1946.

——. *Du Contrat Social.* Paris, 1966.

——. *Emile, ou de l'éducation.* Paris, 1966.

——. *The First and Second Discourses.* Edited by Roger D. Masters. New York, 1964.

——. *Julie, ou La Nouvelle Heloise.* Paris, 1988.

Sacy, Claude-Louis-Michel de. *L'Honneur François, ou Histoire des Vertus et des Exploits de Notre Nation, depuis l'établissement de la Monarchie jusqu'à nos jours.* 12 vols. Paris, 1783–84.

Saint-Evremond, Charles de. *Oeuvres meslées.* Paris, 1684.

——. *Réflexions sur les divers génies du peuple romain dans les divers temps de la République.* Edited by Bertrand Hemmerdinger. Paris, 1795; repr. Naples, 1982.

Saint-Hiappy. *Discours contre le luxe: il corrompt les moeurs, & détruit les empires.* Paris, 1783.

Saint-Pierre, Charles Irénée Castel de. *Projet pour rendre la paix perpétuelle en Europe.* Edited by Simone Goyard-Fabre. Paris, 1981.

Saurin, Bernard-Joseph. *Les Moeurs du Temps.* Vienna, 1761.

Sedaine, Michel. *Le Philosophe sans le savoir.* Edited by Robert Garapon. Paris, 1990.

Servan, Joseph-Michel-Antoine. *Avis salutaire au Tiers Etat. Sur ce qu'il fut, ce qu'il est, & ce qu'il peut être.* N.p., 1789.

——. *Commentaire roturier, sur le noble Discours adressé, par Monseigneur le prince de Conti, à Monsieur, frère du Roi, dans l'Assemblée des Notables de 1788.* Paris, 1789.

——. *Discours dans la cause d'une femme protestante.* Grenoble, 1767.

——. *Discours sur la justice criminelle.* Grenoble, 1767.

——. *Discours sur les moeurs*. Lyon, n.d.

——. *Discours sur le progrès des connaissances humaines en général, de la morale, et de la législation en particulier; lu dans une Assemblée publique de l'Académie de Lyon.* N.p., 1781.

——. *Glose et Remarques sur l'Arrêt du Parlement de Paris, du 5 décembre 1788.* London, 1789.

——. *Oeuvres choisies de Servan, avocat général au parlement de Grenoble.* 5 vols. Edited by Xavier de Portets. Paris, 1825.

——. *Petit Colloque Elémentaire entre Mr. A. et Mr. B, sur les abus, le droit, la raison, les états-généraux, les parlemens, & tout ce qui s'ensuit. Par un vieux jurisconsulte allobroge.* N.p., 1788.

——. *Seconde Lettre à M. Rabaud de St.-Etienne, sur la raison et la logique. Par un aristocrate sans le savoir.* N.p., n.d.

——. *Troisième Lettre à M. Rabaud de St.-Etienne sur l'humanité. Par un aristocrate sans le savoir.* N.p., n.d.

[Servan de Gerbey, Joseph.]. *Le Soldat Citoyen, ou Vues Patriotiques sur la manière la plus avantageuse de pourvoir à la Défense du Royaume.* Dans le Pays de la Liberté, 1780.

Sieyès, Emmanuel Joseph. *Essai sur les privileges.* In *Qu'est-ce que le tiers état, par Emmanuel Sieyès, précédé de l'Essai sur les Privilèges.* Edited by Edme Champion. Paris, 1982.

——. *Qu'est-ce que le tiers état?* Edited by Roberto Zapperi. Geneva, 1970.

Soret, Jean. *Essai sur les moeurs.* Brussels, 1756.

*Les Soupirs de la France Esclave, qui aspire après la liberté.* Amsterdam, 1689.

Staël, Germaine de. *Essai sur les Fictions, suivi de De l'influence des passions sur le bonheur des individus et des nations.* Edited by Michel Tournier. Paris, 1979.

Target, Guy-Jean-Baptiste. *IIe suite de l'écrit intitulé: Les Etats-Généraux convoqués par Louis XVI.* N.p., n.d.

——. *Les Etats-Généraux Convoqués par Louis XVI.* N.p., n.d.

——. *Suite de l'Ecrit intitulé Les Etats-Généraux convoqués par Louis XVI.* N.p., n.d.

Toustain de Richebourg, Charles Gaspard, vicomte. *Conservation des trois ordres, et destruction de leur rivalité, ou lettre du vicomte de Toustain, à M. l'abbé Brizard, de la Société patriotique bretonne, sur une nouvelle histoire.* N.p., n.d.

——. *Précis historique, moral et politique sur la noblesse françoise.* Amsterdam, 1777.

——. *Eclaircissement à l'Amiable Entre la Noblesse & le Tiers Etat.* N.p., 1788.

Varennes, Pierre Augustin de. *Réflexions Morales, Relatives au Militaire François.* Paris, 1779.

Vauvenargues, Luc de Clapiers, marquis de. *Oeuvres Complètes de Vauvenargues.* 2 vols. Edited by Henry Bonnier. Paris, 1968.

*Véritable Patriotisme.* N.p., 1788.

Voltaire, François-Marie Arouet, called. *Candide.* Edited by Daniel Gordon. Boston, 1999.

*Le Vrai Patriote. Dissertation Philosophique et Politique, par M. Alitèphe, Citoyen Français.* N.p., 1789.

**Secondary Sources**

Adams, Leonard. *Coyer and the Enlightenment*. Banbury, U.K., 1974.

Amelang, James. *Honored Citizens of Barcelona: Patrician Culture and Class Relations, 1490–1714*. Princeton, 1986.

Andrivet, Patrick. *Saint-Evremond et l'histoire romaine*. Orléans, 1998.

Annandale, Eric. "Patriotism in de Belloy's Theatre: The Hidden Message." *SVEC* 304 (1992): 1225–28.

Bailey, C. R. *French Secondary Education, 1763–1790: The Secularization of the French Ex-Jesuit Colleges*. Philadelphia, 1978.

Baker, Keith Michael. *Inventing the French Revolution: Essays on French Political Culture in the Eighteenth Century*. Cambridge, 1990.

Barny, Roger. "Les aristocrates et Jean-Jacques Rousseau dans la Révolution." *Annales Historiques de la Révolution Française* 50 (1978): 534–68.

———. *Prélude idéologique à la Révolution française: Le Rousseauisme avant 1789*. Paris, 1985.

Bell, David A. *The Cult of the Nation in France: Inventing Nationalism, 1680–1800* Cambridge, Mass., 2001.

———. *Lawyers and Citizens: The Making of a Political Elite in Old Regime France*. Oxford, 1994.

———. "The Unbearable Lightness of Being French: Law, Republicanism, and National Identity at the End of the Old Regime." *AHR* 106 (2001): 1215–35.

Bevir, Mark. *The Logic of the History of Ideas*. Cambridge, 1999.

Bien, David D. "The Army in the French Enlightenment: Reform, Reaction, and Revolution." *P&P* 85 (1979): 68–98.

———. "Manufacturing Nobles: The Chancelleries in France to 1789." *JMH* 61 (1989): 445–86.

———. "La réaction aristocratique avant 1789: L'exemple de l'armée." *AESC* 29 (1974): 23–48, 505–34.

Biernacki, Richard. "Language and the Shift from Signs to Practice in Cultural History." *H&T* 39 (2000): 289–310.

Biou, Jean. "Le Rousseauisme, idéologie de substitution," *Roman et Lumières au 18e Siècle*, 115–28. Paris, 1970.

Bitton, Davis. *The French Nobility in Crisis, 1560–1640*. Stanford, 1969.

Blaufarb, Rafe. *The French Army, 1750–1820: Careers, Talent, Merit*. Manchester, 2002.

———. "Noble Privilege and Absolutist State Building: French Military Administration after the Seven Years' War." *FHS* 24 (2001): 223–46.

———. "Nobles, Aristocrats, and the Origins of the French Revolution." In *Tocqueville and Beyond: Essays on the Old Regime in Honor of David D. Bien*, 86–110. Edited by Robert A. Schneider and Robert M. Schwartz. Newark, Del., 2003.

———. "Noble Tax Exemption and the Origins of the French Revolution: The *Procès des Tailles* of Provence, 1530s–1789." Manuscript.

Bluche, François. *Les honneurs de la cour*. Paris, 1957.

——. *La vie quotidienne de la noblesse française au XVIIIe siècle*. Paris, 1973.

Bock, Gisela, Quentin Skinner, and Maurizio Viroli, eds. *Machiavelli and Republicanism*. Cambridge, 1990.

Bonnell, Victoria E., and Lynn Hunt, eds. *Beyond the Cultural Turn: New Directions in the Study of Society and Culture*. Berkeley, 1999.

Bosher, J. F. *The French Revolution*. New York, 1988.

Boulloche, Paul. *Un avocat du XVIIIe siècle*. Paris, 1893.

Brancourt, Jean-Pierre. "Un théoricien de la société au XVIIIe siècle: Le chevalier d'Arc." *Revue Historique* 250 (1973): 337–62.

Brengues, Jacques. *Charles Duclos (1704–1772), ou l'obsession de la vertu*. Saint-Brieuc, 1971.

Brennan, Thomas. *Public Drinking and Popular Culture in Eighteenth-Century Paris*. Princeton, 1988.

Browne, Rory. "The Diamond Necklace Affair Revisited: The Rohan Family and Court Politics." *Renaissance and Modern Studies* 33 (1989): 21–39.

Bryson, Scott. *The Chastized Stage: Bourgeois Drama and the Exercise of Power*. Stanford, 1991.

Cabrera, Miguel. *Postsocial History: An Introduction*. Lanham, Md., 2004.

Carcassonne, Elie. *Fénelon: L'homme et l'oeuvre*. Paris, 1946.

——. *Montesquieu et le problème de la constitution française au XVIIIe siècle*. Paris, 1927; repr. Geneva, 1978.

Carré, Henri. "Querelles entre gentilshommes campagnards, petits bourgeois et paysans du Poitou, au XVIIIe siècle." *Revue du Dix-huitième Siècle* 2 (1914): 24–39.

Castan, Yves. *Honnêteté et relations sociales en Languedoc, 1715–1780*. Paris, 1974.

Censer, Jack. *The French Press in the Age of Enlightenment*. London, 1994.

——. "Social Twists and Linguistic Turns: Revolutionary Historiography a Decade after the Bicentennial." *FHS* 22 (1999): 139–67.

Cerutti, Simona. "La construction des catégories sociales." In *Passés recomposés: Champs et chantiers de l'histoire*, 224–34. Edited by Jean Boutier and Dominique Julia. Paris, 1995.

Chagny, Robert. "Mounier et Barnave." In *Les débuts de la Révolution française en Dauphiné, 1788–1791*, 231–58. Edited by Vital Chomel. Grenoble, 1988.

Chaponnière, Paul. "Les premières années d'exil de Saint-Evremond." *Revue d'Histoire Littéraire de la France* 29 (1922): 385–408.

Charles, Loïc, and Philippe Steiner. "Entre Montesquieu et Rousseau. La Physiocratie parmi les origines intellectuelles de la Révolution française." *Etudes Jean-Jacques Rousseau* 11 (1999): 83–159.

Charlton, David. *Grétry and the Growth of Opéra-Comique*. Cambridge, 1986.

Chartier, Roger. *The Cultural Origins of the French Revolution*. Translated by Lydia Cochrane. Durham, N.C., 1991.

Chartier, Roger, Madeleine Compère, and Dominique Julia. *L'éducation en France du 16e au 18e siècle*. Paris, 1976.

Chaussinand-Nogaret, Guy. *Choiseul: Naissance de la gauche*. Paris, 1998.

——. *The French Nobility in the Eighteenth Century: From Feudalism to Enlightenment*. Translated by William Doyle. Cambridge, 1985.

Chérel, Albert. *Fénelon au XVIIIe siècle en France (1715–1820): Son prestige, son Influence.* Paris, 1917.

Chevallier, Jean-Jacques. "Montesquieu ou le libéralisme aristocratique." *Revue Internationale de Philosophie* 9 (1955): 330–45.

Childs, Nick. *A Political Academy in Paris, 1724–1731: The Entresol and Its Members* Oxford, 2000.

Cognet, Louis. *Crépuscule des mystiques: Le conflit Fénelon-Bossuet.* Tournai, 1958.

Colley, Linda. *Britons: Forging the Nation, 1707–1837.* New Haven, Conn., 1992.

Corvisier, André. "Les 'héros subalternes' dans la littérature du milieu du XVIIIe siècle et la réhabilitation du militaire." *Revue du Nord* 66 (1984): 827–38.

Darnton, Robert. *The Great Cat Massacre and Other Episodes in French Cultural History.* New York, 1984.

Delorme, Suzanne. "Le salon de la marquise de Lambert, berceau de l'Encyclopédie." In *L'"Encyclopédie" et le progrès des sciences et des techniques,* 20–24. Edited by Suzanne Delorme and René Taton. Paris, 1952.

Depitre, Edgard. "Le système et la querelle de La noblesse commerçante (1756–1759)." *Revue d'Histoire Economique et Sociale* 6 (1913): 137–76.

Desan, Suzanne. "What's after Political Culture? Recent French Revolutionary Historiography." *FHS* 23 (2000): 163–96.

Descimon, Robert. "The Birth of the Nobility of the Robe: Dignity versus Privilege in the Parlement of Paris, 1500–1700." In *Changing Identities in Early Modern France,* 95–123. Edited by Michael Wolfe. Durham, N.C., 1997.

Devyver, André. *Le sang épuré: Les préjugés de race chez les gentilshommes français de l'ancien régime, 1560–1720.* Brussels, 1973.

Dewald, Jonathan. *Aristocratic Experience and the Origins of Modern Culture: France, 1570–1715.* Berkeley, 1993.

Doyle, William. *Origins of the French Revolution.* New York, 1999.

———. *The Oxford History of the French Revolution.* Oxford, 2002.

———. *The Parlement of Bordeaux and the End of the Old Regime, 1771–1790.* London, 1974.

———. *Venality: The Sale of Offices in Eighteenth-Century France.* Oxford, 1996.

Dupuy, Hélène. "Genèse de la patrie moderne: La naissance de l'idée moderne de la patrie en France avant et pendant la Révolution." Mémoire de Doctorat, University of Paris I, 1995.

Dziembowski, Edmond. *Un nouveau patriotisme français, 1750–1770: La France face à la puissance anglaise à l'époque de la guerre de Sept Ans.* Oxford, 1998.

Echeverria, Durand. *The Maupeou Revolution: A Study in the History of Libertarianism. France, 1770–1774.* Baton Rouge, 1985.

Egret, Jean. *Louis XV et l'opposition parlementaire, 1715–1774.* Paris, 1970.

———. *Necker: Ministre de Louis XVI.* Paris, 1975.

Eisenstein, Elizabeth. "Who Intervened in 1788? A Commentary on The Coming of the French Revolution." *AHR* 70 (1965): 77–103.

Ellis, Harold A. *Boulainvilliers and the French Monarchy: Aristocratic Politics in Early Eighteenth-Century France.* Ithaca, N.Y., 1988.

———. "Montesquieu's Modern Politics: The Spirit of the Laws and the Problem of

Modern Monarchy in Old Regime France." *History of Political Thought* 10 (1989): 665–700.

Fabre, Jean. "Jean-Jacques Rousseau et le prince de Conti." *Annales de la Société Jean-Jacques Rousseau* 36 (1963–65): 7–48.

Fairchilds, Cissie. "The Production and Marketing of Populuxe Goods in Eighteenth-Century Paris." In *Consumption and the Worlds of Goods*, 228–48. Edited by John Brewer and Roy Porter. London, 1993.

Farr, James R. *Hands of Honor: Artisans and Their World in Dijon, 1550–1650*. Ithaca, N.Y., 1988.

Ferté, Louis Henri. *Rollin: Sa vie, ses oeuvres, et l'université de son temps*. Paris, 1902.

Fink, Z. S. *The Classical Republicans: An Essay in the Recovery of a Pattern of Thought in Seventeenth-Century England*. Evanston, Ill., 1945.

Fitzsimmons, Michael P. *The Night the Old Regime Ended: August 4, 1789, and the French Revolution*. University Park, Pa., 2003.

Fizet, Marianne. "'Je n'ai aucun droit à votre confiance.' Réflexivité et stratégies de légitimation dans la correspondance de Madame Belot (1719–1804) avec la marquise de Lénoncourt." In *Dans les miroirs de l'écriture: La réflexité chez les femmes écrivains d'ancien régime*, 145–55. Edited by Jean-Philippe Beaulieu and Diane Desrosiers-Bonin. Montreal, 1998.

Fletcher, D. J. "Montesquieu's Conception of Patriotism." *SVEC* 56 (1967): 541–55.

Ford, Franklin. *Robe and Sword: The Regrouping of the French Aristocracy after Louis XIV*. Cambridge, Mass., 1953.

Forrest, Alan. *Soldiers of the French Revolution*. Durham, N.C., 1990.

Fox-Genovese, Elizabeth. *The Origins of Physiocracy: Economic Revolution and Social Order in Eighteenth-Century France*. Ithaca, N.Y., 1976.

Furet, François. *Interpreting the French Revolution*. Translated by Elborg Forster. Cambridge, 1981.

Furet, François, and Ran Halévi. *La monarchie républicaine: La constitution de 1791*. Paris, 1996.

Furet, François, and Mona Ozouf. "Deux légitimations historiques de la société française au XVIIIe siècle: Mably et Boulainvilliers." *AESC* 34 (1979): 438–50.

Galliani, Renato. *Rousseau, le luxe, et l'idéologie nobiliaire: Etude socio-historique*. Oxford, 1989.

Gembicki, Dieter. *Histoire et politique à la fin de l'ancien régime: Jacob-Nicolas Moreau, 1713–1803*. Paris, 1979.

Gidel, Gilbert. *La politique de Fénelon*. Paris, 1906; repr. Geneva, 1971.

Gondal, Marie-Louise. *Madame Guyon (1648–1717): Un nouveau visage*. Paris, 1989.

Goodman, Dena. *The Republic of Letters: A Cultural History of the French Enlightenment*. Ithaca, N.Y, 1994.

Gordon, Daniel. *Citizens without Sovereignty: Equality and Sociability in French Thought, 1670–1789*. Princeton, 1994.

Gossman, Lionel. *Medievalism and the Ideologies of the Enlightenment: The World and Work of La Curne de Sainte-Palaye*. Baltimore, 1968.

Grell, Chantal. *Le dix-huitième siècle et l'antiquité en France*. Oxford, 1995.

———. *L'histoire entre érudition et philosophie: Etude sur la connaissance historique à l'âge des lumières*. Paris, 1993.

Gribbin, William. "Rollin's Histories and American Republicanism." *William and Mary Quarterly* 29 (1972): 611–22.

Gruder, Vivian. "Whither Revisionism? Political Perspectives on the Ancien Régime." *FHS* 20 (1997): 245–85.

Halévi, Ran. "The Illusion of Honor: Nobility and Monarchical Construction in the Eighteenth Century." In *Tocqueville and Beyond: Essays on the Old Regime in Honor of David D. Bien*, 71–85. Edited by Robert A. Schneider and Robert M. Schwartz. Newark, Del., 2003.

Hampson, Norman. "The French Revolution and the Nationalisation of Honour." In *War and Society: Historical Essays in Honor and Memory of J. R. Western, 1928–1971*, 199–212. Edited by M. R. D. Foot. London, 1973.

Harris, Robert. *Necker: Reform Statesman of the Ancien Régime*. Berkeley, 1979.

Higonnet, Patrice. *Class, Ideology, and the Rights of Nobles during the French Revolution*. Oxford, 1981.

Hirschman, Albert O. *The Passions and the Interests: Political Arguments for Capitalism before Its Triumph*. Princeton, 1977.

Hulliung, Mark. *The Autocritique of Enlightenment: Rousseau and the Philosophes*. Cambridge, Mass., 1994.

———. *Montesquieu and the Old Regime*. Berkeley, 1976.

Hundert, E. G. *The Enlightenment's Fable: Bernard Mandeville and the Discovery of Society*. Cambridge, 1994.

Hunt, Lynn. *Politics, Culture, and Class in the French Revolution*. Berkeley, 1984.

Israel, Jonathan. *Radical Enlightenment: Philosophy and the Making of Modernity, 1650–1750*. Oxford, 2001.

Jacob, Margaret. *Living the Enlightenment: Freemasonry and Politics in Eighteenth-Century Europe*. Oxford, 1991.

Johnson, Neal. "L'idéologie politique du marquis d'Argenson, d'après ses oeuvres inédites." In *Etudes sur le XVIIIe siècle*, 21–28. Edited by Roland Mortier and Hervé Hasquin. Brussels, 1984.

Jones, Colin. "Bourgeois Revolution Revivified: 1789 and Social Change." In *Rewriting the French Revolution*, 69–118. Edited by Colin Lucas. Oxford, 1991.

———. "The Great Chain of Buying: Medical Advertisement, the Bourgeois Public Sphere, and the Origins of the French Revolution." *AHR* 101 (1996): 13–40.

———. *The Great Nation: France from Louis XV to Napoleon*. Oxford, 2002.

Jones, Gareth Stedman. "Une autre histoire sociale?" *AHSS* 53 (1998): 383–92.

———. "The Determinist Fix: Some Obstacles to the Further Development of the Linguistic Approach to History in the 1990s." *History Workshop Journal* 42 (1996): 19–35.

———. *Languages of Class: Studies in English Working Class History, 1832–1982*. Cambridge, 1983.

Jones, Peter M. "The Provincial Assemblies, 1778–1790: Old or New?" *The Consortium on Revolutionary Europe, 1750–1850: Proceedings, 1993*, 379–86. Tallahassee, 1994.

———. *Reform and Revolution in France: The Politics of Transition, 1774–1791.* Cambridge, 1995.

———. "Reforming Absolutism and the Ending of the Old Regime in France." *Australian Journal of French Studies* 29 (1992): 220–28.

Jouanna, Arlette. "Les gentilshommes français et leur rôle politique dans la seconde moitié du XVIe et au début du XVIIe siècle." *Il Pensiero Politico* 10 (1977): 22–40.

———. *L'idée de race en France au XVIe et au début du XVIIe siècle (1498–1614).* 3 vols. Paris, 1976.

Kaiser, Thomas E. "The Abbé Dubos and the Historical Defence of Monarchy in Early Eighteenth-Century France." *SVEC* 267 (1989): 77–102.

———. "Louis le Bien-Aimé and the Rhetoric of the Royal Body." In *From the Royal to the Republican Body: Incorporating the Political in Seventeenth- and Eighteenth-Century France,* 131–61. Edited by Sara E. Melzer and Kathryn Norberg. Berkeley, 1998.

———. "Madame de Pompadour and the Theaters of Power." *FHS* 19 (1996): 1025–44.

———. "Nobles into Aristocrats, or How an Order Became a Conspiracy." Manuscript.

Kaplan, Nira I. "A Changing Culture of Merit: French Competitive Examinations and the Politics of Selection, 1750–1820." Ph.D. diss., Columbia University, 1999.

Kaplan, Steven Laurence. "Social Classification and Representation in the Corporate World of Eighteenth-Century France: Turgot's 'Carnival'." In *Work in France: Representation, Meaning, Organization, and Practice,* 176–228. Edited by Steven Laurence Kaplan and Cynthia Koepp. Ithaca, N.Y., 1986.

Kelly, George Armstrong. "Duelling in Eighteenth-Century France: Archaeology, Rationale, Implications." *Eighteenth Century: Theory and Interpretation* 21 (1980): 236–54.

Kennett, Lee. *The French Armies in the Seven Years' War.* Durham, N.C., 1967.

Keohane, Nannerl. *Philosophy and the State in France: The Renaissance to the Enlightenment.* Princeton, 1980.

———. "Virtuous Republics and Glorious Monarchies: Two Models in Montesquieu's Political Thought." *Political Studies* 20 (1972): 383–96.

Kingston, Rebecca. *Montesquieu and the Parlement of Bordeaux.* Geneva, 1996.

Klaits, Joseph. "Men of Letters and Political Reform in France at the End of the Reign of Louis XIV: The Founding of the Académie Politique." *JMH* 43 (1971): 577–97.

———. *Printed Propaganda under Louis XIV: Absolute Monarchy and Public Opinion.* Princeton, 1976.

Koebner, R. "Despot and Despotism: Vicissitudes of a Political Term." *Journal of the Warburg and Courtauld Institutes* 14 (1951): 275–302.

Kramnick, Isaac. *Bolingbroke and His Circle: The Politics of Nostalgia in the Age of Walpole.* Cambridge, Mass., 1968.

Kuscinski, Auguste. *Dictionnaire des conventionnels.* Paris, 1916.

Kwass, Michael. "A Kingdom of Taxpayers: State Formation, Privilege, and Political Culture in Eighteenth-Century France." *JMH* 70 (1998): 295–339.

———. "Consumption and the World of Ideas: Consumer Revolution and the Moral Economy of the Marquis de Mirabeau." *Eighteenth-Century Studies* 37 (2004): 187–213.

———. *Privilege and the Politics of Taxation in Eighteenth-Century France: Liberté, Egalité, Fiscalité.* Cambridge, 2001.

Labatut, Jean-Pierre. "Patriotisme et noblesse sous le règne de Louis XIV." *RHMC* 29 (1982): 622–34.

Labriolle-Rutherford, M. R. de. "L'évolution de la notion du luxe depuis Mandeville jusqu'à la Révolution." *SVEC* 26 (1963): 1025–36.

Lanier, Jacques François. *Le Général Joseph Servan de Gerbey (Romans 1741–Paris 1808): Pour une armée au service de l'homme.* Valence, 2001.

———. *Michel Joseph Antoine Servan ou de Servan (1737–1807): Avocat-général de l'humanité.* Romans, 1995.

———. *Servan ou l'art de survivre.* Romans, 1997.

Lanson, René. *Le goût du moyen âge en France au XVIIIe siècle.* Paris, 1926.

Latreille, Albert. *L'armée et la nation à la fin de l'ancien régime: Les derniers ministres de la guerre de la monarchie.* Paris, 1914.

La Vopa, Anthony J. "Doing Fichte: Reflections of a Sobered (but Unrepentant) Contextual Biographer." In *Biographie schreiben,* 107–71. Edited by Hans Erich Bödeker. Göttingen, 2003.

Leclercq, Henri. *Histoire de la Régence.* 3 vols. Paris, 1922.

Lefebvre, Georges. *The French Revolution,* 2 vols. Translated by Elizabeth Moss Evanson. New York, 1962.

Legagneux, Michel. "Rollin et le 'Mirage Spartiate' de l'éducation publique." In *Recherches nouvelles sur quelques écrivains des lumières,* 111–63. Edited by Jacques Proust. Geneva, 1972.

Leith, James. "The Idea of the Inculcation of National Patriotism in French Educational Thought, 1750–1789." In *Education in the Eighteenth Century,* 59–77. Edited by J. D. Browning. New York, 1979.

Léonard, Emile G. *L'armée et ses problèmes au XVIIIe siècle.* Paris, 1958.

Levine, Joseph M. *Between the Ancients and the Moderns: Baroque Culture in Restoration England.* New Haven, Conn., 1999.

Lévy-Bruhl, Henry. "La noblesse de France et le commerce à la fin de l'ancien régime." *Revue d'Histoire Moderne* 8 (1933): 209–35.

Lewis, Gwynne. "Rethinking the Debate." In *The French Revolution in Social and Political Perspective,* 118–25. Edited by Peter Jones. London, 1996.

Linton, Marisa. *The Politics of Virtue in Enlightenment France.* Houndmills, 2001.

Lombard, Alfred. *Fénelon et le retour à l'antique au XVIIIe siècle.* Neuchâtel, 1954.

Longino, Michèle. *Orientalism and French Classical Drama.* Cambridge, 2002.

Lougee, Carolyn. *Le Paradis des Femmes: Salons and Social Stratification in Seventeenth-Century France.* Princeton, 1976.

Lough, John. *The Contributors to the Encyclopédie.* London, 1973.

Lowenthal, David. "Montesquieu and the Classics: Republican Government in *The*

*Spirit of the Laws*." In *Ancients and Moderns*, 258–84. Edited by Joseph Cropsey. New York, 1964.

Lucas, Colin. "Nobles, Bourgeois, and the Origins of the French Revolution." *P&P* 60 (1973): 84–126.

Lynn, John. *Giant of the Grand Siècle: The French Army, 1610–1715*. Cambridge, 1997.

———. "Toward an Army of Honor: The Moral Evolution of the French Army, 1789–1815." *FHS* 16 (1989): 152–82.

Mackrell, J. Q. C. *The Attack on "Feudalism" in Eighteenth-Century France*. London, 1973.

Manin, Bernard. "Montesquieu et la politique moderne," *Cahiers de Philosophie Politique* 2–3 (1984–85): 157–229.

Margerison, Kenneth. *Pamphlets and Public Opinion: The Campaign for a Union of Orders in the Early French Revolution*. West Lafayette, Ind., 1998.

Marion, Marcel. *Dictionnaire des institutions de la France aux XVIIe et XVIIIe siècles*. Paris, 1923; repr. Paris, 1984.

Markoff, John. *The Abolition of Feudalism: Peasants, Lords, and Legislators in the French Revolution*. University Park, Pa., 1996.

Markoff, John, and Gilbert Shapiro, eds. *Revolutionary Demands: A Content Analysis of the Cahiers de Doléances of 1789*. Stanford, 1998.

Martin, John. "Inventing Sincerity, Refashioning Prudence: The Discovery of the Individual in Renaissance Europe." *AHR* 102 (1997): 1309–42.

Martin-Fugier, Anne. *La vie élégante, ou la formation du tout-Paris, 1815–1848*. Paris, 1990.

Maza, Sarah. *The Myth of the French Bourgeoisie: An Essay on the Social Imaginary, 1750–1850*. Cambridge, Mass., 2003.

———. *Private Lives and Public Affairs: The Causes Célèbres of Prerevolutionary France*. Berkeley, 1993.

Morange, Jean, and Jean-François Chassaing. *Le mouvement de réforme de l'enseignement en France, 1769–1798*. Paris, 1974.

Mornet, Daniel. "Les enseignements des bibliothèques privées." *Revue d'Histoire Littéraire de la France* 17 (1910): 449–96.

Mosher, Michael. "Monarchy's Paradox: Honor in the Face of Sovereign Power." In *Montesquieu's Science of Politics: Essays on the Spirit of Laws*, 159–229. Edited by David W. Carrithers, Michael A. Mosher, and Paul A. Rahe. Lanham, Md., 2001.

Muir, Edward. *Civic Ritual in Renaissance Venice*. Princeton, 1981.

Murphy, Antoin E. "Le développement des idées économiques en France (1750–1756)." *RHMC* (1986): 521–41.

Nicolas, Jean. *La Révolution française dans les Alpes: Dauphiné et Savoie*. Toulouse, 1989.

Nye, Robert. *Masculinity and Male Codes of Honor in France*. Oxford, 1993.

Oakeshott, Michael. *Experience and Its Modes*. Cambridge, 1966.

Ozouf, Mona. *Les Aveux du Roman: Le dix-neuvième siècle entre l'ancien régime et la Révolution*. Paris, 2001.

——. *Festivals and the French Revolution.* Translated by Alan Sheridan. Cambridge, Mass., 1988.

Pagden, Anthony, ed. *The Languages of Political Theory in Early-Modern Europe.* Cambridge, 1987.

Palmer, R. R. *The Improvement of Humanity: Education and the French Revolution.* Princeton, 1985.

Pangle, Thomas. *Montesquieu's Philosophy of Liberalism: A Commentary on "The Spirit of the Laws."* Chicago, 1973.

Pappas, John. "La campagne des philosophes contre l'honneur." *SVEC* 205 (1982): 31–44.

Patrick, Alison. "The Second Estate in the Constituent Assembly." *JMH* 62 (1990): 223–52.

Perrot, Jean-Claude. "Nouveautés: L'économie politique et ses livres." In *Histoire de l'édition française,* vol. 2, *Le livre triomphant, 1660–1830,* 240–57. Edited by Henri-Jean Martin and Roger Chartier. Paris, 1984.

Petitfrère, Claude. *Le scandale du Mariage de Figaro: Prélude à la Révolution française?* Paris, 1989.

Pocock, J. G. A. *The Machiavellian Moment: Florentine Political Thought and the Atlantic Republican Tradition.* Princeton, 1975.

——. *Virtue, Commerce, History: Essays on Political Thought and History, Chiefly in the Eighteenth Century.* Cambridge, 1985.

Poisson, Georges. *Choderlos de Laclos, ou l'obstination.* Paris, 1985.

Popkin, Jeremy. "Pamphlet Journalism at the End of the Old Regime." *Eighteenth Century Studies* 22 (1989): 351–67.

——. *Revolutionary News: The Press in France, 1789–1799.* Durham, N.C., 1990.

Price, Munro. *Preserving the Monarchy: The Comte de Vergennes, 1774–1787.* New York, 1995.

Quine, W. V., and J. S. Ullian. *The Web of Belief.* New York, 1978.

Reddy, William. *The Invisible Code: Honor and Sentiment in Postrevolutionary France, 1814–1848.* Berkeley, 1997.

——. "The Logic of Action: Indeterminacy, Emotion, and Historical Narrative." *H&T* Theme Issue 40 (2001): 10–33.

——. *The Navigation of Feeling: A Framework for the History of Emotions.* Cambridge, 2001.

——. *The Rise of Market Culture: The Textile Trade and French Society, 1750–1900.* Cambridge, 1984.

Rétat, Pierre. "De Mandeville à Montesquieu: Honneur, luxe et dépense noble dans l' 'Esprit des Lois.'" *Studi Francesi* 50 (1973): 238–49.

Richter, Melvin. "Despotism." In *Dictionary of the History of Ideas: Studies of Selected Pivotal Ideas,* vol. 2: 1–18. Edited by Philip Wiener. New York, 1973.

Riley, Philip F. *A Lust for Virtue: Louis XIV's Attack on Sin in Seventeenth-Century France.* Westport, Conn., 2001.

Robinet, Jean-François-Eugène. *Dictionnaire historique et biographique de la Révolution et de l'Empire, 1789–1815.* 2 vols. Paris, 1899.

Roche, Daniel. *France in the Enlightenment.* Translated by Arthur Goldhammer. Cambridge, Mass., 1998.

Rosenfeld, Sophia. *A Revolution in Language: The Problem of Signs in Late Eighteenth-Century France.* Stanford, 2001.

Ross, Ellen. "Mandeville, Melon, Voltaire: The Origins of the Luxury Controversy in France." *SVEC* 155 (1976): 1897–1912.

Rothkrug, Lionel. *Opposition to Louis XIV: The Political and Social Origins of the French Enlightenment.* Princeton, 1965.

Ruff, Julius. *Crime, Justice, and Public Order in Old Regime France: The Sénéchaussées of Libourne and Bazas, 1696–1789.* London, 1984.

Saglio, Edmond, ed. *Dictionnaire des antiquités grecques et romaines d'après les textes et les monuments.* Paris, 1919.

Schalk, Ellery. *From Valor to Pedigree: Ideas of Nobility in France in the Sixteenth and Seventeenth Centuries.* Princeton, 1986.

Schama, Simon. *Citizens: A Chronicle of the French Revolution.* New York, 1989.

Schelle, Gustave. *Vincent de Gournay.* Paris, 1897; repr. Geneva, 1984.

Scott, Joan. "The Evidence of Experience." *Critical Inquiry* 17 (1991): 773–97.

Serna, Pierre. "Le noble." In *L'homme des lumières,* 39–93. Edited by Michel Vovelle. Paris, 1996.

Sewell, William H., Jr. *A Rhetoric of Bourgeois Revolution: The Abbé Sieyès and What Is the Third Estate?* Durham, N.C., 1994.

———. "Whatever Happened to the 'Social' in Social History?" In *Schools of Thought: Twenty-Five Years of Interpretive Social Science,* 209–16. Edited by Joan W. Scott and Debra Keates. Princeton, 2001.

———. *Work and Revolution: The Language of Labor from the Old Regime to 1848.* Cambridge, 1980.

Shackleton, Robert. *Montesquieu: A Critical Biography.* Oxford, 1961.

Shklar, Judith. "Montesquieu and the New Republicanism." In *Machiavelli and Republicanism,* 265–79. Edited by Gisela Bock, Quentin Skinner, and Maurizio Viroli. Cambridge, 1990.

Shovlin, John. "The Cultural Politics of Luxury in Eighteenth-Century France." *FHS* 23 (2000): 577–606.

———. "Luxury, Political Economy, and the Rise of Commercial Society in Eighteenth-Century France." Ph.D. diss., University of Chicago, 1998.

———. "Toward a Reinterpretation of Revolutionary Antinobilism: The Political Economy of Honor in the Old Regime." *JMH* 72 (2000): 35–66.

Singham, Shanti. "'A Conspiracy of Twenty Million Frenchmen': Public Opinion, Patriotism, and the Assault on Absolutism during the Maupeou Years, 1770–1775." Ph.D. diss., Princeton University, 1991.

Smith, Jay M. "Between Discourse and Experience: Agency and Ideas in the French Pre-Revolution." *H&T* Theme Issue 40 (2001): 116–42.

———. *The Culture of Merit: Nobility, Royal Service, and the Making of Absolute Monarchy in France, 1600–1789.* Ann Arbor, Mich., 1996.

———. "No More Language Games: Words, Beliefs, and the Political Culture of Early-Modern France." *AHR* 102 (1997): 1413–40.

———. "Recovering Tocqueville's Social Interpretation of the French Revolution: Eighteenth-Century France Rethinks Nobility." In *Tocqueville and Beyond: Essays* on the Old Regime in Honor of David D. Bien, 52–70. Edited by Robert A. Schneider and Robert M. Schwartz. Newark, Del., 2003.

——. "Social Categories, the Language of Patriotism, and the Origins of the French Revolution: The Debate over Noblesse Commerçante." JMH 72 (2000): 339–74.

Snyders, Georges. La pédagogie en France aux XVIIe et XVIIIe siècles. Paris, 1965.

Sonenscher, Michael. Work and Wages: Natural Law, Politics, and the Eighteenth-Century French Trades. Cambridge, 1989.

Souchon, Paul. Vauvenargues: Philosophe de la gloire. Paris, 1947.

Spang, Rebecca L. "Paradigms and Paranoia: How Modern Is the French Revolution?" AHR 108 (2003): 119–47.

Speier, Hans. "Honor and Social Structure." In The Truth in Hell and Other Essays on Politics and Culture, 1935–1987, 50–69. Oxford, 1989.

Spitz, Jean-Fabien. L'amour de l'égalité: Essai sur la critique de l'égalitarisme républicain en France, 1770–1830. Paris, 2000.

Starobinski, Jean. Jean-Jacques Rousseau: Transparency and Obstruction. Translated by Arthur Goldhammer. Chicago, 1988.

Stone, Bailey. The French Parlements and the Crisis of the Old Regime. Chapel Hill, N.C., 1986.

Storez, Isabelle. Le chancelier Henri-François d'Aguesseau (1668–1751): Monarchiste et libéral. Paris, 1996.

Stuurman, Siep. "On Intellectual Innovation and the Methodology of the History of Ideas." RH 4 (2000): 311–19.

Sutherland, Donald. The French Revolution and Empire: The Quest for a Civic Order. Oxford, 2003.

Swann, Julian. Politics and the Parlement of Paris under Louis XV, 1754–1774. Cambridge, 1995.

Tackett, Timothy. Becoming a Revolutionary: The Deputies of the French National Assembly and the Emergence of a Revolutionary Culture, 1789–1790. Princeton, 1996.

——. "Nobles and Third Estate in the Revolutionary Dynamic of the National Assembly, 1789–90." AHR 94 (1989): 271–301.

Taylor, Charles. Sources of the Self: The Making of the Modern Identity. Cambridge, Mass., 1989.

Taylor, George V. "Revolutionary and Non-Revolutionary Content in the Cahiers of 1789: An Interim Report." FHS 7 (1972): 479–502.

Tholozan, Olivier. Henri de Boulainvilliers: L'anti-absolutisme aristocratique légitimé par l'histoire. Aix-en-Provence, 1999.

Tocqueville, Alexis de. The Old Regime and the French Revolution. Translated by Stuart Gilbert. New York, 1955.

Van Kley, Dale K. The Damiens Affair and the Unraveling of the Ancien Régime, 1750–1770. Princeton, 1984.

——. "The Estates General as Ecumenical Council: The Constitutionalism of Corporate Consensus and the Parlement's Ruling of September 25, 1788." JMH 61 (1989): 1–52.

——. The Jansenists and the Expulsion of the Jesuits from France, 1757–1765. New Haven, Conn., 1975.

———. "Pure Politics in Absolute Space: The English Angle on the Political History of Pre-Revolutionary France." *JMH* 69 (1997): 754–84.

———. *The Religious Origins of the French Revolution: From Calvin to the Civil Constitution.* New Haven, Conn., 1996.

———. "The Religious Origins of the Patriot and Ministerial Parties in Pre-Revolutionary France." In *Belief in History: Innovative Approaches to European and American Religion,* 173–236. Edited by Thomas Kselman. Notre Dame, Ind., 1991.

Vial, Fernand. *Une philosophie et une morale du sentiment. Luc de Clapiers, marquis de Vauvenargues.* Paris, 1938.

Viroli, Maurizio. *Jean-Jacques Rousseau and the "Well Ordered Society."* Cambridge, 1988.

Wahrman, Dror. *Imagining the Middle Class: The Political Representation of Class in Britain, c. 1780–1840.* Cambridge, 1995.

Wick, Daniel. *A Conspiracy of Well-Intentioned Men: The Society of Thirty and the French Revolution.* New York, 1987.

———. "The Court Nobility and the French Revolution: The Example of the Society of Thirty," In *The French Revolution in Social and Political Perspective,* 214–30. Edited by Peter Jones. London, 1996.

Wickberg, Daniel. "Intellectual History vs. the Social History of Intellectuals." *RH* 5 (2001): 383–95.

Wright, Johnson Kent. *A Classical Republican in Eighteenth-Century France: The Political Thought of Mably.* Stanford, 1997.

# *Index*